Beyond the IT
Productivity Paradox

Wiley Series in Information Systems

Beyond the IT Productivity Paradox

Edited by

LESLIE P. WILLCOCKS

Templeton College, University of Oxford, UK

and

STEPHANIE LESTER

Lucidus Management Technologies, UK

JOHN WILEY & SONS

Chichester · New York · Weinheim · Brisbane · Singapore · Toronto

Copyright © 1999 by John Wiley & Sons Ltd,
Baffins Lane, Chichester,
West Sussex PO19 1UD, England
National   01243 779777
International (+44) 1243 779777
e-mail (for orders and customer service enquiries):
cs-books@wiley.co.uk
Visit our Home Page on http://www.wiley.co.uk
or http://www.wiley.com

Other Wiley Editorial Offices

John Wiley & Sons, Inc., 605 Third Avenue,
New York, NY 10158–0012, USA

WILEY-VCH Verlag GmbH, Pappelallee 3,
D-69469 Weinheim, Germany

Jacaranda Wiley Ltd, 33 Park Road, Milton,
Queensland 4064, Australia

John Wiley & Sons (Asia) Pte Ltd, 2 Clementi Loop #02–01,
Jin Xing Distripark, Singapore 129809

John Wiley & Sons (Canada) Ltd, 22 Worcester Road,
Rexdale, Ontario M9W 1L1, Canada

Library of Congress Cataloging-in-Publication Data
Beyond the IT productivity paradox: assessment issues / edited by
    Leslie P. Willcocks and Stephanie Lester.
        p.   cm. — (Wiley series in inormation systems)
    Includes bibliographical references and index.
    ISBN 0-471-98692-5 (cloth)
    1. Information technology—Management.   2. Industrial
productivity.   I. Willcocks, Leslie.   II. Lester, Stephanie.
III. Series: John Wiley series in information systems.
HC79.I55B496   1999
658.4'038—dc21
                                                98–36047
                                                CIP

British Library Cataloguing in Publication Data
A catalogue record for this book is available from the British Library

ISBN   0-471-98692-5

Typeset in 10/12pt Palatino by Vision Typesetting, Manchester
Printed and bound in Great Britain by Biddles Ltd, Guildford and King's Lynn.
This book is printed on acid-free paper responsibly manufactured from
sustainable forestation, for which at least two trees are planted for each one
used for paper production.

Contents

Contributors

JOAN BALLANTINE   Previously a financial systems consultant and later a Lecturer in Computer Applications in Accounting and Finance, Queen's University, Belfast. She is presently Lecturer in Accounting and Finance at Warwick Business School, UK.

DR MARIANNE BROADBENT   Previously Professor in the Melbourne Business School, University of Melbourne. In 1998 she took up her present position as Director, IT Executive Program, for the Gartner Group in Australia and New Zealand.

ERIK BRYNJOLFSSON   Associate Professor of Management at MIT Sloan School of Management, USA, where he holds the Douglas Crane Chair. He received his PhD from Sloan and in 1997 was Visiting Professor at Stanford Business School, USA.

BARBARA FARBEY   Currently at University College, London. Previously a Research Officer at the London School of Economics. Prior to this she was a Research Fellow at the School of Management, Bath University, and has also worked in industry and consultancy.

GUY FITZGERALD   Professor at Brunel University, London. Previously Cable and Wireless Professor of Business Information Systems at Birkbeck College, University of London, and Research Associate at Templeton College, Oxford. He is also Joint Editor of the *Information Systems Journal.*

ROBERT GALLIERS   Holds the Lucas Chair in Business Systems Engineering and was previously Foundation Professor of Information Systems at Curtin University, Curtin, Western Australia. He is Editor in Chief of the *Journal of Strategic Information Systems.*

Valerie Graeser   Research Associate in the Oxford Institute of Information Management, Templeton College, Oxford. Formerly she was project manager with American Management Systems and Exxon.

Rudy Hirschheim   Professor in the School of Business Administration, University of Houston, USA. His PhD is from the London School of Economics and he holds visiting chairs at several universities.

Lorin Hitt   Assistant Professor of Operations and Information Management at the University of Pennsylvania, Wharton School. His PhD is from MIT Sloan School of Management. His work has appeared in *Management Science, MIS Quarterly* and the *Economics of Innovation and Technology.*

Mary Lacity   Associate Professor of MIS at University of Missouri, St Louis, and Associate Research Fellow of the Oxford Institute of Information Management, Templeton College, Oxford. Her research work has focused on information systems outsourcing.

Frank Land   Emeritus Professor at the LSE, London, and Visiting Professor in Information Systems at the University of Bath. His early career was in programming and systems analysis in industry. He was then Professor at the London School of Economics and at London Business School. His current research is into corporate evaluation of IS.

Stephanie Lester   Principal Consultant with Lucidus Management Technologies and a Research Affiliate of the Oxford Institute of Information Management, Templeton College, Oxford. Previously she worked as Technology Change Director for Lloyds Register, London, and Change Manager for Information Technology and Engineering at Cellnet, UK.

M.C. Augustus van Nievelt   35 years of management experience in manufacturing, in R&D and as a Chief Information Executive. He is a former General Manager and Director of Nestlé (USA), where his responsibilities included product development, process technology and corporate management services. He is presently CEO of research organization VN International.

Dr Philip Powell   Professor at Goldsmiths College, London, and Associate Editor of the *Information Systems Journal*. Previously he was at Warwick Business School and University of Southampton.

Janne Ropponen   Currently on leave from his post at Nokia Telecommunications Ltd where he was responsible for improving requirement and risk management practices. He holds a Finnish licentiate degree in business administration and information systems from the University of Jyväskylä. He is also a pilot with Mission Aviation Fellowship.

STEVE SMITHSON   Senior Lecturer in Information Systems at the London School of Economics, UK and Co-Editor-in-Chief of the *European Journal of Information Systems.*

STEPHANIE STRAY   Lecturer in the Operational Research and Systems Group within Warwick Business School, UK. She formerly held posts at Aston Business School and Bradford Management Centre.

DAVID TARGETT   Professor at Imperial College, London. Previously ICL Professor of Information Systems in the School of Management at the University of Bath, UK. He was previously at London Business School and British Leyland. He has been particularly concerned with the impact of IT on general management and evaluation issues.

N. (VENKAT) VENKATRAMAN   Professor of Management and a Research Principal at the Systems Research Center, Boston University School of Management. His research on the interface between strategic management and IT has appeared in many leading journals. His doctoral thesis received the 1986 AT Kearney Award for Outstanding Research in General Management.

GEOFF WALSHAM   Research Professor at the the Judge Institute of Management Studies, Cambridge University, UK, where he has also been Director of the MBA. He was previously Professor in Information Systems at Lancaster University, UK.

DR PETER WEILL   Holds the Foundation Chair of Management (Information Systems) at the Melbourne Business School, University of Melbourne, and is Director of the School's Centre for Management of Information Technology.

LESLIE WILLCOCKS   Fellow and University Lecturer in Management Studies at the Oxford Institute of Information Management, Templeton College, University of Oxford. He received his doctorate from University of Cambridge, is Visiting Professor at Erasmus Universiteit, Rotterdam and is also Editor-in-Chief of the *Journal of Information Technology.*

Wiley Series in Information Systems

Series Preface

The information systems community has grown considerably since 1984, when we began publishing the Wiley Series in Information Systems. We are pleased to be a part of the growth of the field, and believe that this series of books is playing an important role in the intellectual development of the discipline. The primary objective of the series is to publish scholarly works which reflect the best of research in the information systems community.

THE PRESENT VOLUME

As the information systems field matures, there is an increased need to carry the results of its growing body of research into practice. The series desires to publish research results that speak to important needs in the development and management of information systems, and our editorial mission recognizes explicitly the need for research to inform the practice and management of information systems. Leslie Willcocks and Stephanie Lester's book *Beyond the IT Productivity Paradox* serves such a purpose. It brings together a number of papers from authors whose intent it is to explore the broad issue of IT and its productive use in organizations. This is not an easy task. In weaving together the many themes and issues that surround the organizational use and misuse of IT, Willcocks and Lester delve deeply into one of the most perplexing issues of the day: *viz*, does IT *really* help or hinder organizational performance. The papers in this volume explore the linkage between IT use, productivity and organizational performance. The unit of analysis is the organization and the book focuses on the disparate and conflicting results that appear in the literature. Are these conflicting results the product of measurement error, differing practices, or simple confusion? What are the problems associated with understanding the impact of IT on organizational performance? Clearly, these are important questions the answers to which can have major repercussions on the way we approach and understand the organizational design, implementation and use of IT. The contributors to this volume do an excellent job of exploring such salient issues, and in particular, blending theory with practice. The book should be of great interest to anyone who wishes to get behind the façade of the IT imperative.

Acknowledgements

Versions of several of the chapters in this book have also been published in journals. Chapter 1 was originally published as Brynjolfsson, E. and Hitt, L. "Paradox Lost? Firm-Level Evidence on the Returns to Information Systems Spending," *Management Science*, 42, 4, April (1996). Sections of Chapter 2 appeared in the *Journal of the Operational Research Society*, 48 (1997), 1082–94. Chapter 4 has been developed from research originally reported by the authors in *Journal of Information Technology*, 11, 2 (1996), 129–42. An earlier version of Chapter 7 appeared as "Beyond Outsourcing: Managing IT Resources as a Value Center" in *Sloan Management Review*, Spring (1997), 51–64. An earlier, shorter version of chapter 10 appeared in *European Journal of Information Systems*, 5, 3 (1996), 143–60. Portions of Chapter 11 originally appeared in Weill, P., Broadbent, M. and St Clair, D. "IT Value and the Role of IT Infrastructure Investments" in Luftman, J. (ed.) (1996) *Competing in the Information Age: Strategic Alignment in Practice*, Oxford University Press, New York.

Sources of figures and tables are indicated in the text. We gratefully acknowledge the permissions granted to reproduce the materials listed above. Every effort has been made to trace copyright and gain permissions, but please contact the authors if there are any omissions or oversights.

We would like to thank all at the Wiley Information Systems series for their unfailing professionalism, speed and support throughout the production of this book. We would also like to offer immense thanks to Pam Reeder at Templeton College for all the work she put into different aspects of this book while it was being developed. Yes, Pam, you did yet another book.

In memory of Leonard, beloved father.

Introduction
Information Technology: Transformer or Sink Hole?

LESLIE P. WILLCOCKS AND STEPHANIE LESTER
Oxford Institute of Information Management

INTRODUCTION

The proposition is simultaneously shocking and attractive—that despite the massive accumulated and rising investments in information technology (IT), on the whole these have not contributed to significant rises in productivity. The shock of this so-called IT productivity paradox comes from the sheer size of IT expenditure, together with its pervasiveness in so much of everyday organizational and domestic life in the developed economies. On research company IDC's estimates, in 1995 the worldwide IT market was $530 billion. This covered packaged software, data communications equipment, services, and single and multi-user systems. Moschella (1997) suggests that on a wider definition of IT—to include voice telecommunications, special-purpose computer equipment, (e.g. automatic teller machines, mail sorting systems) and customer expenditure on their own information systems personnel—a market size of $1 trillion could easily be defended. IDC expected the overall IT market to grow at 10 per cent annually in the 1996–2000 period, an estimate that (to early 1998) proved on the cautious side given the rising cost of fixing the Year 2000 problem, estimated by some to be as high as $300 billion for corporate America alone (Strassmann, 1997a).

There seems to be little let-up in the onward march of IT costs.

Beyond the IT Productivity Paradox.
Edited by L. P. Willcocks and S. Lester © 1999 John Wiley & Sons Ltd.

According to a 1998 Compass report, IT in the developed economies has rocketed from a typical 2–3 per cent of total costs in the 1980s to 7–10 per cent in 1998, with some leading financial service firms in 1998 devoting more than 20 per cent of their expenditure to IT. Taking just one country as a further example, UK IT spend in 1998 was estimated at £44.4 billion, up 5 per cent from 1997. Of this aggregate expenditure, £3.9 billion was for Year 2000 work, £1.47 billion for Economic and Monetary Union conversion and £1.58 billion was spent on the Internet—each registering between 45 and 70 per cent increases over 1997 (Graeser, Willcocks and Pisanias, 1998).

The IT productivity paradox was a child of the 1980s. But even for the 1990s, according to Roach (1997), "there's not a shred of evidence to show that people are putting out more because of investments in technology". As evidence, he cites manufacturing being responsible for one-fifth and services four-fifths of North American (US) IT spend. If IT boosted productivity, according to Roach, US services should show higher output-per-worker advances than manufacturing. Throughout the 1990s, however, US manufacturing productivity rose more than 3 per cent a year on average, while in US services average annual gains were less than 1 per cent. Can it really, shockingly, be the case that so many corporations, governments and even individuals have chosen, or been induced, to spend so much on a so-called IT revolution in order, in practice, to achieve so little productivity improvement?

Because it *is* shocking, the notion of IT as a financial sink hole has also proven perennially attractive. For over 25 years the mass media has followed two main routes for information technology stories—focusing predominantly on either its transformative capacity or on IT disasters. When the IT productivity paradox was coined by economists in the 1980s, it fitted comfortably into the second category. Not only did it seem to have a quantified, "factual" basis provided by economists, the scientific soothsayers of modern capitalism, the proposition also had deeper resonances. People's own experiences, and their fears, could be read into how the technology was increasingly being utilized and what it meant—opportunity, but also the unknown, an uprooting, a threatening future for which many (we have been told) would not be skilled or mentally prepared. Since its inception there has always been a mythic quality and an element of technological demonization inherent in the notion of the IT productivity paradox. Looked at from this perspective, it has played well for over 10 years because, like Eskimos having over 50 words for snow and the existence of Father Christmas, it has become a story too good to be false.

As ever, there is a more informed debate to be had and an altogether more complex set of issues and analyses struggling to leave this old skin behind. Much of the debate in the 1980s and 1990s has been addressed at the aggregate, national level, in particular focusing on US figures. The collected chapters of this book report on research in developed economies and significantly expand our understanding of IT contribution and how it can be assessed at the more meaningful organizational level. In this introduction we will focus on three tasks. The first is to provide an update on the IT productivity paradox debate as it has been conducted in the 1990s. This is designed to complement, and act as a lead into, the first three chapters. Secondly, we consider whether, organizationally, we are shifting from a mainframe and PC-dominated to a network-centric technological landscape. If, as we shall argue, this is indeed the case, then there are a range of implications for the economics and payoffs from IT and how these can be assessed. These matters are discussed in some later chapters. Finally, we describe the structure and argument of the book and the positioning of each chapter in addressing assessment issues and practices designed to take the debate beyond the IT productivity paradox. As a first step, we will now review and critique the existing debate as it has been pursued over the last five years.

THE IT PRODUCTIVITY PARADOX IN THE 1990s—AN UPDATE

In retrospect, there have been two core issues in the IT productivity debate: how can and should the net IT contribution be assessed; and what is the reliability, usefulness and relevance of the data employed in that assessment. The reason that the debate has been able to take place for so long, and indeed that it remains largely unresolved as far as different participants are concerned, is precisely because of disagreements on the former and fundamental questions about the latter. These points need to be borne in mind throughout what follows.

Paradox Lost

The whole debate is considered in detail in Section 1 of this book, and especially in Chapter 2. Here we focus only on selected aspects in the 1993–8 period. In the 1990s there have been several high-profile attempts to declare the IT productivity paradox, if it ever existed, at an end. By way of example, in June 1993 *Business Week* produced a special report entitled "The Technology Payoff". Focusing mainly on the USA, it reported that a $1 trillion business investment in IT in the 1980s saw only a 1 per cent annual rise in the national US productivity rate.

However, following the bottom of the recession in 1991, productivity outpaced growth and rose nearly 3 per cent in 1992, with the service sector matching manufacturing gains. The explanations, illustrated by case studies, lay with the time lag needed for the 1980s IT investments to pay off, and new corporate structures, downsizing and reengineering combining in powerful ways with increasingly cheaper, pervasive technology and more accessible and useful software. At the same time, the report suggests that it was simply too early in the process to see concrete evidence that the USA was on the verge of a productivity explosion.

In September 1994, *Computerworld* produced a lengthy report entitled "The Productivity Payoff" (Gillin, 1994). Focusing on the 100 most productive US users of IT, it argued that some organizations were much better at utilizing IT than others; that IT was probably finally making contributions to productivity; and that previous IT impacts were probably disguised by measurement problems. Even a proponent of the existence of the IT productivity paradox is moved to state: "Courtesy of restructuring, America is beginning to move to the other side of its technology quandary ... the saga comes full circle ... let memories of the paradox endure, however, as a warning of how easy it is to stray from the path" (Roach, 1994).

By 1996, in a survey of the world economy, *The Economist* felt able to head a section: "Paradox Lost". What followed was in fact a carefully reasoned review of the evidence for and against the existence of a productivity paradox, finally siding with the case against. David (1990) is cited, showing how the introduction of the electric dynamo in the 1880s took 40 years to yield significant productivity gains. The computer revolution only began in earnest with the microprocessor in 1971 and by 1996 about half of American workers were using computers. Since David's research showed that productivity benefits started to be reaped once the diffusion rate of a technology passed 50 per cent, "the productivity gains [from IT] may be just around the corner". The work by Brynjolfsson and Hitt (see Chapter 1) is cited as evidence of computers boosting productivity at the firm level.

The survey also suggests that the productivity returns were being lost "in a statistical black hole". First, computers account for only 2 per cent of the USA's total capital stock—too small to make much much difference to overall productivity growth. (However, the report notes that when telecommunications and software are added in, this approaches 12 percent, the same as for railways at the peak of the railway age in the late nineteenth century). Secondly and, according to the report, most persuasively, "the benefits are already coming through, but standard economic statistics are failing to capture them". Griliches

(1994) is quoted arguing that economies are shifting towards services, which have always been tricky to measure; and that the nature of the gains from IT often makes them hard to quantify (see also Chapters 2, 5 and 6). Nakamura (1995) is also used to show that the US inflation rate has been overstated by two to three percentage points since 1974, mainly because new products or product improvements had been neglected: "If this is correct then productivity growth in the rich industrial economies has been much higher than the official figures suggest." Worse still, the mismeasurement problem has increased as product cycles have shortened: "The greater understatement of growth that this implies would be almost enough to explain all of the apparent slowdown in America's productivity growth in the last two decades."

Further attacks on the IT productivity paradox appeared in 1997. Faced with strong US economic growth, little unemployment and low inflation a special report in *Business Week* asked: "How long can this last?" (Mandel *et al.*, 1997). Evidently a new growth formula had been found. This time around the gains from downsizing, outsourcing and reengineering were sticking. Furthermore, companies had finally learned to make good use of IT by buying into computer networks, speeding communications internally and forging electronic links with their customers. According to the report, there was compelling evidence that the productivity improvements would continue: "the answer lies largely with the now-pervasive use of IT throughout the economy ... that so-called productivity paradox now seems to be over. Starting around 1994—when the Internet suddenly became big business—companies began diverting bigger chunks of their capital budgets into computers, software and communications equipment. That's also when productivity growth started climbing." The implication here that Internet investments in the 1995–7 period have contributed immediately and significantly to US productivity growth needs to be treated with some caution, however. One would expect a time lag for the payoffs to come through, not least because there is evidence that few companies have learned to focus and use the investments effectively (see below).

The report points to business spending on computers growing more slowly than spending on other types of goods in the 1986–95 period. However, from 1995 US businesses reversed the trend, increasing spending on IT at twice the rate of other capital goods. Two Federal Reserve economists, Sichel and Oliner, are quoted as suggesting that this growing spending on IT provided evidence in itself for businesses getting payback from their investments. Of course, this argument tends to stand the IT productivity paradox on its head. While refreshing, the contention would be more convincing if more evidence of productivity correlating with the IT investment could be found. In a more cautious *Financial Times* review entitled "Anatomy of a Miracle", Baker (1997) points to there being little statistical evidence to back up the notion of an IT-driven US productivity miracle from 1995—a position confirmed by US Federal Reserve chairman Alan Greenspan (1997). Once again, the curious disparity arises of heavy IT investment in both manufacturing and services, coupled with rising manufacturing and stagnating services productivity. In particular, while US manufacturing productivity gained 3.4 per cent in 1995 and 3.8 per cent in 1996, productivity in the whole of the non-agricultural business sector grew by only 0.7 percent in 1996. Once again, however, both sources point to most economists being deeply suspicious of the ability of the official figures to pick up improvements in service-sector, as opposed to manufacturing-sector, productivity.

The Search for Evidence

Nevertheless, scepticism about the withering away of the IT productivity paradox has also been rife. We have seen Roach (1986, 1994; interview with Griffith, 1997) move between strong and weak versions of the paradox thesis depending on the vagaries of the economic indicators over time. A limitation of Roach's analyses over the years is that they fundamentally relate to the macroeconomic level. As we shall see in Section 1 of this book, for several reasons the more relevant and meaningful focus is undoubtedly on the microeconomic and organizational levels of investment and activity. Landauer (1995) focuses on both macroeconomic and intra-organizational levels, but finds little evidence for IT investments raising productivity. Countering well-known difficulties in obtaining reliable published data, Hu and Plant (1998) constructed three overlapping US-company-based data sets covering four-year periods in the 1990s. Many previous studies suffer from a potential flaw in comparing IT investments and performance impacts for the same time period. The researchers therefore investigated whether, allowing for time lags, IT spending had a positive impact on firm productivity. In fact, they found no statistical evidence for this. Moreover, IT spending had little, if any, effect on three important measures of firm performance: sales per employee, return on equity and return on assets.

More recently, Strassmann (1997b) provided a detailed examination of the topic. Generally, he—quite rightly—rejects US government macroeconomic productivity data, on the grounds that it fails to account properly for the output of the service and public sectors (see also below). One of the progenitors of the productivity paradox, Loveman

(1988), is criticised for choosing to concentrate on the productivity of computers as capital assets. Quite simply, firms in his 1980s sample reported installed asset valuations of computers with little consistency. Also, treating computers as if they were machine tools rather than organic elements of information management led to the misapplication of theories useful mainly for studying investments in industrial capital. Moreover, Loveman showed that, on average, any marginal capital investment in computers would be the worst investment choice, missing the point that it is not average performance, but the differences in the profit performance between superior and inferior firms, that matters.

Strassmann (1997b) then purports to examine the paradox by using published data on 138 giant US corporations and data from his own clients in the 1988–94 period. Strangely, his analysis proceeds to ignore his own (good) advice and uses aggregated data and averages across the selected sample. He also argues that if the growth of profitability of corporations were greater than the growth in spending for IT, then the computer paradox would vanish. In fact, he found total IT budgets (67.4 per cent) growing faster than profits (39.7 per cent). Moreover, sales, general and administrative (SGA) expenses, in which, according to Strassmann, the costs of information handling, management and coordination are concentrated, also grew at 41.9 per cent in the period. If IT expenditure had a productivity effect, this SGA figure would be much lower. The assumption here is that a growth in IT expenditure should result in at least a comparable percentage growth in profits, and a comparable percentage decrease in SGA expenses. However, comparing *percentage* growth, as opposed to actual dollar growth in figures of considerably different sizes, hardly provides a meaningful analysis of the effects of IT spending.

In his various analyses Strassmann also spends most of his time looking at correlations between two factors. Indeed, Strassmann (1990, 1997b) is replete with diagrams usually showing that there is little or no correlation between two factors, one of his most reiterated (and sustainable) findings being that research shows no systematic direct correlation between IT expenditure and corporate profitability. In this type of analysis he is not alone. In fact, at the macro economic level, the IT productivity paradox itself is founded on the assumption that two factors—IT expenditure and labour productivity—should correlate positively but do not. But as van Nievelt shows in Chapter 3, restricting the search to linear relationships between IT expenditure and one single other factor is almost definitely misplaced. His research found that many statistically significant two-factor interaction effects on organizational performance were stronger than the component single-factor effects: "a key characteristic of organizational performance on which the academic literature remains virtually silent".

There have been many attempts to marshal evidence and arguments to explain or even resolve the IT productivity paradox. One important reminder is that much of the discussion has been about US performance. By comparison, Kraemer and Dedrick (1996) looked at the factors influencing investment in IT and the payoffs they achieved between 1984 and 1990 in 12 newly industrialising, developing and developed countries in the Asia-Pacific region. Conducted at the macroeconomic level, the research found compelling evidence that both GDP growth and productivity increases were highly correlated with growth in IT investment: "More importantly, we discovered that productivity and GDP growth are also correlated with rises in IT as a percentage of total investment ... countries which increase their investments in IT relative to other investments experience higher growth rates in productivity and GDP." At the very least, this must throw into some question the US national statistics, on which the IT productivity paradox was largely founded.

In 1991, the US National Research Council was sufficiently worried by the seeming lack of productive IT spend as to set up a three year study of "IT Productivity in Services". It found that national accounts data were extremely misleading and contained major gaps. Thus industry productivity statistics covered only about 42 per cent of service-sector employment. For some major service industries output is measured solely on the basis of input: "By definition, output divided by input is constant for these industries. This assumption affects about 25–30 per cent of the services sector" (Quinn and Baily, 1994). Moreover, existing productivity data did not capture important elements of service quality. Willcocks (1996a) also made this point in debate with Landauer, Roach and Strassmann. Quality features—such as timeliness, speed, response times, flexibility, reliability—are the ones most often influenced by IT and only hit the "bottom line" indirectly.

Quinn and Baily, who chaired the study, also point out that macro-productivity measures ignore many important performance dimensions critical to customers, and fail to pick up incremental performance improvements passed along to customers and suppliers. Nor do they reflect the "alternative cost" of what would have happened without the IT investments. In some cases, entire enterprises and industries could not exist at their present scale and complexity without IT. They conclude that IT had improved the performance of the services sector significantly, and that measurement difficulties from 1973–90 had led macroeconomic productivity statistics to understate absolute levels of service productivity by a substantial margin. However, Landauer

(1995) and Strassmann (1997b) are sceptical of the microeconomic evidence of positive IT effects provided to the study by 46 US companies. For Strassmann, not only was the evidence "anecdotal"; it was hardly surprising to find that companies with public reputations as IT innovators gave glowing reports of IT impacts.

Meanwhile, company-level evidence for and against the IT productivity paradox which has been arrived at more rigorously has hardly been free of disputation and problems. In work using data sets derived from the Management Productivity and Information Technology (MPIT) programme in the 1980s, Strassmann (1990) and Barua, Kriebel and Mukhopadhyay (1991) found little evidence of IT spending correlating positively with productivity improvements. However, the MPIT data were coded so that they could only be used as dimensionless ratios. Coding involved occasional moving of decimal points and also removal of currency denominations. If these researchers interpreted the coded MPIT data as absolute figures and dollar denominated, then their findings may be of limited statistical value. During the 1990s, the statistical work at firm level for the 1988–92 period by Brynjolfsson and Hitt (1993, 1994, 1996) has been much quoted as evidence for believing that, if the IT productivity paradox had ever existed in the USA, it had disappeared by 1991. Part of their findings appear in Chapter 1 and will not be described in detail here. However, Strassmann (1997b) does question the reliability and accuracy of their data and measures. Even more pertinently, he does question their—and by inference other econometricians'—dependence on outdated Cobb-Douglas production function equations, pointing out that "information and knowledge are a significant component in the costs of goods and services, but they do not fit Cobb-Douglas".

As Strassmann attests, Brynjolfsson and Hitt's later work does introduce revisions and improvements. Taking these on board, their 1996 study is particularly interesting for positing three logically separate measures of IT contribution. Their subsequent analysis finds that IT has led to higher productivity and created substantial value for customers. However, these benefits failed to result in measurable improvements in business performance. For van Nievelt this would not be surprising. For the data set used in Chapter 3 he too finds that applying a linear regression reveals no direct relationship between IT and business profitability. But if, like him, other researchers were to fit a quadratic equation to the same data, they would probably obtain much more significant explanatory power. This prediction is reinforced by Brynjolfsson and Hitt's finding that IT stock in fact created significant value for consumers (van Nievelt, 1997).

Strassman (1997b) does not make this extension. Instead, he argues that Brynjolfsson and Hitt, in exploring the relationship between IT and profitability, found that the effect of IT on performance was consistently negative, therefore the paradox persists. This is a peculiar argument to make and ignores the manifest purpose of the paper. After all, the paradox was essentially about productivity, not profitability, and Brynjolfsson and Hitt clearly argue in the paper that computers *have* led to higher productivity, at least at the firm level.

It becomes clear that there are fundamental disagreements about the nature of the evidence, and what it tells us, for IT impacts not only on national aggregate productivity figures but also at the firm level. A consideration of Allen's (1997) carefully detailed review provides us with several final insights on these issues. Allen agrees with the vast majority of commentators that: "a cursory look at the aggregate statistics suggests there has been no phenomenal productivity growth from the rapid growth in IT". Allen's caution is appropriate because, as this sentence highlights, the IT productivity paradox essentially assumes that there should be a direct correlation, indeed a causal effect, between IT spend and productivity. Even if the issue of unreliable aggregated national data is set aside, there has been a surprising lack of attention given to the crudity of these assumptions, given the complexity of macroeconomic activity and the range of intervening variables.

While Allen (1997) is silent on this point, he does review three explanations for aggregated national figures not showing rapid growths in productivity. By now these are familiar, but the detail is new. The first explanation points to measurement error. As early as 1988, Baily and Gordon were providing many examples of IT already offering valuable customer services and improved working conditions that were not being picked up in the official output data. Moreover, such improvements at the firm level may lead to some firms being more successful than others, resulting in a redistribution effect that would not show up in the aggregate data. More technically, Baily and Gordon (1988) questioned the index-number methodology and price deflators used to assess the price of computers and producer durable equipment. These resulted in significant, unfavourable distortions in aggregate measured real output. Finally, taking the case study of the US finance, insurance and real-estate sectors, Baily and Gordon (1988) showed how the methods of estimating output were steeped in distorting assumptions tying ouput to labour input and to performance in the sectors they serve. When different measures of output were used, much better productivity growth was observed. As one example, in the stock brokerage industry, total trades per employee rose from 48 000 to 124 000 in the 1979–87 period. In banking, cheques processed per worker hour rose from 265 to 825 in the 1971–86 period. Their estimates suggest that from 1973 onwards growth in the whole sector was underestimated by 2.3 per cent per year.

The second explanation reviewed is the familiar one of Oliner and Sichel (1994), that computers still represent only a small fraction of total capital stock and cannot make a large impact on aggregate productivity, therefore there is no missing productivity. Allen (1997) comments, correctly, that this can still be consistent with Brynjolfsson and Hitt's (1996) findings of positive productivity impacts at firm level. But Oliner and Sichel's assessment of returns from IT as simply returns to a specific investment in equipment still seem to ignore the wider, potentially transformational effect on work methods. As Allen comments: "the externalities are precisely what is interesting about IT—the potential for synergism from the increasing networks formed by computers and other information technology ... the impact of a paradigm shift is likely to extend beyond the direct productivity improvement of the individual piece of equipment."

This statement in fact implies the third explanation reviewed by Allen—that IT has not yet been exploited fully. Here Allen (1997) has considerable sympathy with the position of David (1990) and Mokyr (1990)—that several factors must be in place to achieve innovations, then enhance their diffusion over time through an economy. A time lag of years can be expected before the significant benefits from investment can be reaped. In this IT is no different from previous technical innovations. Allen (1997) points to evidence of some US sectors with a head start in building IT capital experiencing productivity gains that would not have been possible without IT. The point is underlined by an analysis of eight US manufacturing and service sectors demonstrating variations in the time lags, use and payoffs from IT in the 1970–94 period.

Allen's example of the US electricity utility industry—a service industry with, unusually, a highly measurable commodity—is particularly pertinent to our purpose here. Annual total utility investment in IT increased substantially from $216 million in 1970 to $4792 million in 1987. If we can assume a direct relationship between IT investment and productivity (see above), the investment would appear to have paid off. Certainly, electricity utilities' productivity growth exceeded average manufacturing productivity growth between 1971 and 1994. As one example, the 1993–4 productivity growth rate was 6.4 per cent for utilities, compared to 4.3 per cent for total manufacturing. In the 1990s, rising labour productivity growth coincided with sizeable reductions in the number of employees. However, significant IT investment and acceleration preceded these employee reductions by about five years, with the first signs of labour force reductions at the peak of IT investment in 1986. Subsequent reductions in labour input might not have been possible if the utilities had not increased their ability to exploit the potential of previously acquired technology. Allen therefore suggests that a five-year time lag occurred between IT investment and productivity. Plausibly, he suggests that, while this may not be valid for all industries, the sequence of events and the notion of a multi-year time lag are likely to be a reasonable starting point for explanations.

Variations in Organizational Performance with IT: Assessment Issues

In all the above disputation, one of the few agreed points about the evidence is that, if not economies or sectors, then at least organizations vary greatly in their ability to harness IT to enhance productivity and performance (Banker, Kaufman and Mahmood, 1993; Strassmann, 1997b; Willcocks and Lester, 1996). This book contributes detailed analyses of how and why this is the case in Chapters 2 and 3. There is already a massive literature on how IT is utilized in organizations, and how the business performance of IT can be enhanced. Against the simple unilinear relation suggested by the IT productivity paradox, the more informed contributions suggest complex organizational linkages between IT use, productivity and business performance (see for example Harris, 1996; McKeen, Smith and Parent, 1997; Soh and Markus, 1995; Willcocks, Feeny and Islei, 1997—the latter also provides research into contributing management and organizational practices).

The position adopted throughout this book will be to focus on the organizational level, and in particular the issue of how assessment practices are implicated in variations in organizational performance. The book builds on the considerable evidence that seemingly indifferent IT performance may simply reflect difficulties experienced in measurement even at the organizational level (Byrd and Marshall, 1997; Graeser, Willcocks and Pisanias, 1998). It also accepts that there is plentiful evidence of many organizations and their stakeholders not directing IT expenditure into optimal areas, and of information and communication technologies not being developed, implemented or utilized to their full potential (van Nievelt and Willcocks, 1997). In other words, the indifferent IT performance may well be real. In all this, assessment practices become critical. Not only is it important to gain an accurate picture of the performance and impacts of IT, the metrics and assessment practices adopted also have an impact on whether or not that performance can be redirected or improved as necessary (Willcocks, 1994; 1996b).

In investigating these areas, the book seeks to complement many recent research contributions that have advanced our understanding of the assessment of IT performance at the organizational level. As some examples, Tallon, Kraemer and Gurbaxani (1997) have usefully directed attention away from productivity gains from IT at firm level, and towards a multidimensional assessment of IT business value involving measures of efficiency and effectiveness, combining economic and behavioural perspectives, and process-level and firm-level measures. Their initial findings suggest that IT business value can be measured across seven intermediate business processes (e.g. customer relations, product/service enhancement, marketing support). They also found support for positive IT impacts arising from its distinctive capability for coordinating value-adding activities across an organization's value chain.

Commenting on the IT productivity paradox, Soh and Markus (1995) suggest that mixed empirical results are always an invitation to seek better theory. For them, a productive approach is to move from the question of whether IT creates value to how, when and why benefits occur or fail to do so. In proposing a process theory of the relationships between IT investments and business value, they integrate much earlier theoretical work. They usefully point to the number of jumping-off points that can occur in the process of attempting to convert IT spend into business value. These are essentially: IT management process, type and quality of IT assets; specification of appropriate IT use; and IT impacts. One helpful effect of this focus on the effectiveness of the IT conversion process is to direct attention away from simple relationships between spending and performance. This also is the contribution of McKeen, Smith and Parent (1997) in proposing a resource-based approach that seeks to assess the leverage effect that IT deployment has on key, essentially human, resources in organizations.

Boar (1996) provides a different, but important, perspective on the comparative economics of different technologies. This is important in the IT field because technology platforms are continually being updated and new technologies/applications made available. The choice of one technology over another can have significant economic implications. Boar concentrates on client/server (C/S) computing. He refutes the common observation that C/S is more expensive than mainframe computing and will continue to be so indefinitely. One fundamental flaw has been the misapplication of a cost analysis model based on economies of scale. This is appropriate for mainframe computing, but not for C/S, whose cost structure is built around the economies of sharing, i.e. the decline in average cost per unit due to increased efficiencies of reuse (see below). Boar also shows that the mainframe computing cost studies have been conceptually and methodologically flawed and do not prove the mainframe superiority they assert. In practice, Boar demonstrates in detail that the value proposition/cost ratio of C/S can be significantly superior to mainframe computing, though others would still question whether the cost side would always work out as smoothly as Boar suggests (see Lacity, Willcocks and Subramanian, 1997; Strassmann, 1997b).

However, there have been enough hints in the story so far to believe that the economics of new technologies and their likely performance impacts may be no small, organizationally localized matter as we approach the end of the 1990s. In the next section we explore two possibilities. The first is that new types and uses of IT represent a paradigm shift that is already rendering inapplicable all notions of an IT productivity paradox as traditionally constructed. The consequent possibility is that this will have a number of large implications for IT assessment and measurement as conventionally conducted in organizations.

"CYBERNOMICS" AND IT PRODUCTIVITY: NOT BUSINESS AS USUAL?

Changing technologies, customer expectations, ways of doing business together with competitive dynamics—in combination, these place great pressures on, and represent large challenges for, IT evaluation practices. But in the face of complex changes, it becomes critical to have in place sense-making approaches that help to answer realistically and usefully the fundamental economic and value questions about IT. An understanding of the fundamental technology shifts from the 1960s to post-2000 provides a starting point for exploring the underlying economic implications.

Technology Shifts

Moschella (1997) has posited four main eras in IT adoption and use. These are shown in Figure I.1. Up to 1998 and the present "network-centric" era, each has seen within them roughly six- to seven-year cycles of investment in specific technologies. Strassmann (1997b) explains that although technology innovation cycles have shortened, computer adoption times have stayed at about seven years because it takes at least that long to institutionalize related managerial, social and organizational changes. Let us look at each era and its underlying economics. The basic shape of the argument follows Moschella (1997) and Strassmann (1997b). This is a necessarily simplified overview, but note that Figure I.1 depicts eras overlapping at many points.

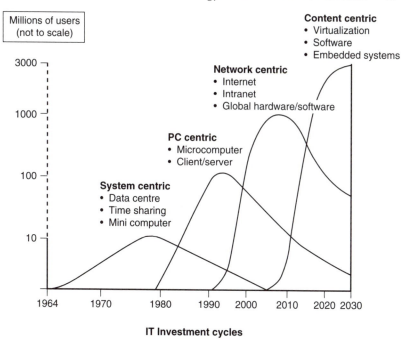

Figure I.1   *IT Investment Cycles 1964–2030 (adapted from Moschella, 1997)*

The Systems-Centric Era, 1964–81

It is generally accepted that this began with the IBM S/360 series, the computer industry's first broad group of steadily upgradable compatible systems. The dominating principle through most of this period was Grosch's law. Arrived at in the 1940s, this stated that computer power increases as the square of the cost—that is, a computer that is twice as expensive delivers four times the computing power. This law favoured large systems. Investment decisions were fairly simple initially and involved centralized data centres. IBM dominated supply and protected its prices: "one negotiated delivery schedules and technical support, not costs or budgets" (Strassmann, 1997b). In response to dissatisfaction with centralized control of computing by finance functions, there followed centralized time sharing arrangements with non-finance functions, some outsourcing by scientific, engineering and production departments to independent service suppliers, and subsequent moves towards small-scale computers to achieve local independence. This led to stealthy growth in equipment costs outside official central IT budgets, but also a dawning understanding of the high lifecycle support costs of systems acquired and run locally in a *de facto* decentralized manner.

From about 1975, the shift from centralized to business unit spending accelerated, aided by the availability of minicomputers. Also, in a competitive market, prices of software and peripherals fell rapidly and continuously, enabling local affordability, often outside IT budgets and embedded in other expenditures. Without centralized control, it became difficult to monitor IT costs.

The PC-Centric Era 1981–94

This era began with the arrival of the IBM PC in 1981. The sale of personal computers (PCs) went from $2 billion in 1980 to $160 billion in 1995. This period saw Grosch's law inverted: by the mid-1980s, the best price/performance was coming from PCs and other microprocessor-based systems. The underlying economics was summarized in Moore's law, named after one of the founders of Intel. This stated that semiconductor price/performance would double every two years for the foreseeable future. The prediction remained fairly accurate into the mid-1990s, helped by constantly improved designs and processing volumes of market-provided rather than in-house-developed microprocessor-based systems. The PC-centric era saw shifts from corporate, mostly proprietary to individual, commodity computing. The costs of switching from one PC vendor to another were low, while many peripherals and PC software took on commodity-like characteristics. A further shift in the late 1980s seemed to be towards open systems, with the promise of common standards and high compatibility. However, it became apparent that the move was not really from proprietary to open, but from IBM to Microsoft, Intel and Novell. Subsequently, many of the open systems initiatives were scaled back significantly.

These technical advances provided enormous access to cheap processing for business unit users. IT demand and expenditure were now coming from multiple points in organizations. One frequent tendency was a loosening of financial justification on the cost side, together with difficulties in, or lack of concern for, rigorously verifying the claimed benefits from computer spending. From 1988 on, technical developments in distributed computing architecture, together with organizational reactions against local, costly, frequently inefficient microcomputer-based initiatives, led to a client/server investment cycle. The economics of client/server have been much debated. The claim was that increased consolidation and control of local networks through client/server architectures would lower the costs of computing significantly.

However, Dec (1996), for example, argues that a client/server set-up for 5000 users costs 70 per cent more than a comparable mainframe/terminal configuration. Strassmann (1997b) suggests two reasons for this: the propensity to specify the latest technologies, resulting in continuous high-cost upgrades, and difficulties in anticipating the high personnel support costs associated with client/server. Further pressures on technology, support and training costs also come from users demanding instant keystrokes, rapid database access times and seamless network functionality.

The PC-centric era saw a massive explosion of personal computing, with for example some 63 million PCs built in 1995 alone. However, though the equipment and software were inexpensive on a price/performance calculation, this did not usher in a period of low-cost computing. Constant upgrades, rising user expectations and the knock-on costs over systems lifecycles saw to that (Willcocks, 1994). By the mid-1990s the cost per PC seat was becoming a worrying issue in corporate computing, especially as no consistent benchmarks on cost seemed to be emerging. Published estimates range regularly from $3000 to $18 000 per seat per year, probably because of differences in technology, applications, users, workloads and network management practices. From the late 1980s, one increasing response to rising computing costs, especially mainframe, network, telecommunications, support and maintenance, was outsourcing, mostly selective but in some cases "total", that is, handing over computing representing over 80 per cent of the IT budget to third-party management (see Chapter 10). This propensity has continued into the late 1990s (Willcocks and Lacity, 1997).

The Network-Centric Era 1994–2005

Although the Internet has existed for nearly 20 years, it was the arrival of the Mosaic graphical interface in 1993 that made possible mass markets based on the Internet and World Wide Web (WWW). This era is being defined by the integration of worldwide communications infrastructure and general-purpose computing. Restricting as it does WWW graphical capabilities, communications bandwidth begins to replace microprocessing power as the key commodity. Attention shifts from local area networks (LANs) to wide area networks, particularly intranets. There is already evidence of strong shifts of emphasis over time from graphical user interfaces to Internet browsers, from indirect to on-line channels, from client server to electronic commerce, from stand-alone PCs to bundled services, and from individual productivity to virtual communities (Dertouzos, 1997; Hagel and Armstrong, 1997; Moschella, 1997).

Economically, the pre-eminence of Moore's law is being replaced by Metcalfe's law, named after Bob Metcalfe (inventor of the Ethernet). Metcalfe's law states that the cost of a network rises linearly as additional nodes are added, but that the value can increase exponentially. Software economics has a similar pattern. Once software is designed, the marginal cost of producing additional copies is very low, potentially offering huge economies of scale for the supplier. Combining network and software economics produces vast opportunities for value creation. At the same time, the exponential growth in the number of Internet users from 1995 suggests that innovations that reduce use costs while improving ease of use will shape future developments, rather than, as previously, the initial cost of IT equipment (Strassmann, 1997b).

By 1998, fundamental network-centric applications were e-mail for messaging and the World Wide Web, the great majority of traffic on the latter being information access and retrieval. Transaction processing was also emerging in the forms of electronic commerce (EC) for businesses, shopping and banking for consumers and voting and tax collection for governments. The need to reduce transaction costs through EC may well result in a further wave of computer spending (Choi, Stahl and Whinston, 1997). Here also there are real challenges for the Internet's ability to provide levels of reliability, response times and data integrity comparable to traditional on-line transaction-processing expectations. Dealing with these challenges has large financial implications. Markets are also developing for audio and video applications. A key technological change throughout will be that most of the existing PC software base will need to become network enabled; there may well also be a shakeout in the ways in which transmission services are provided (Moschella, 1997).

Many of these developments and challenges depend on the number of people connected to the Internet, and there are significant national differences here. However, as more people join the general incentive to use the Internet increases, technical limitations notwithstanding. One possibility, implied earlier in this introduction for the USA from 1995, is that IT investment will lead to productivity. In turn, this will drive growth and further IT investments. The breakthrough, if it comes, may well be with corporations learning to focus computing priorities externally—on reaching customers, investors, and suppliers, for example—instead of the historical inclination primarily towards internal automation, partly driven by inherited evaluation criteria and practices (Willcocks, 1994; 1996b). Even so, as Moschella (1997) notes: "much of the intranet emphasis so far has been placed upon internal efficiencies, productivity and cost savings ... [and] has sounded like a replay of the client/server promises of the early 1990s, or even the paperless office claims of the mid-1980s".

A Content-Centric Era 2005–?

It is notoriously difficult to predict the future of information technologies. One plausible view has been put forward by Moschella (1997). The shifts would be from electronic commerce to virtual businesses; from the wired consumer to individualized services; from communications bandwidth to software, information and services; from on-line channels to customer pull; and from a converged computer/communications/consumer electronics industry value chain to one of embedded systems. A content-centric era of virtual businesses and individualized services would depend on the previous era delivering an inexpensive, ubiquitous and easy-to-use, high-bandwidth infrastructure. For the first time, demand for an application would define the range of technology usage rather than, as previously, also having to factor in what is technologically and economically possible. The IT industry focus would shift from specific technological capabilities to software, content and services. These are much less likely to be subject to diminishing investment returns. The industry driver would truly be "information economics", combining the nearly infinite scale economies of software with the nearly infinite variety of content.

Metcalfe's law would be superseded by the law of transformation. A fundamental consideration is the extent to which an industry/business is bit (information) based as opposed to atom (physical product) based. In the content-centric era, the extent of an industry's subsequent transformation would be equal to the square of the percentage of that industry's value added, accounted for by bit as opposed to atom-processing activity. The effect of the squared relationship would be to widen industry differentials. In all industries, but especially in the more "bit-based" ones, describing and quantifying the full IT value chain would become as difficult an exercise as assessing the full 1990s value chain for electricity.

Implications for IT Assessment Practices

Viewed retrospectively in the light of these four different perspectives and eras, it becomes fairly clear how time bound and limiting the assumptions embodied in the IT productivity paradox have been. And indeed, a constant criticism of traditional IT evaluation practices, especially at organizational level, has been their limiting effects, driving out strategic and externally focused IT investments (Graeser, Willcocks and Pisanias, 1998; Robson, 1997; Strassmann, 1990). This, of course, is not to make an argument for limitless spending, but rather for wider recognition of different types of IT investments and for more informed evaluation practices that also embody a quality and learning, as well as a financial control, agenda (Willcocks, 1996b).

Looking across these four eras, it also becomes clear that continuing shifts in the underlying economics make the assessment of IT investments a particularly fraught area requiring continuous careful revision. A particularly stark point emerges when Figure I.1 is reconsidered. It is not just that, in the late 1990s, we have been caught up in a fundamental shift from a PC-based to a network-based era. In fact, the period 1995–2000 represents the crossover point for three eras representing three different underlying sets of economics, each with subsets of types of investment. Not surprisingly, this will make the assessment of IT investments and payoffs particularly prone to confusion. While the need would remain to take into account different objectives for IT, to assess investments across systems lifecycles, and to assess impacts on the family of business, process, customer and learning measures (see Chapters 6, 7 and 11), a much deeper understanding of differing and changing economics, benefits and timescales would seem to be required.

The Internet/Intranet Business Case

It becomes particularly important to grasp the economics of the fast developing network-based era because it embodies a fundamental shift out of systems- and PC-centric thinking about IT investments and payoffs (see also Chapters 2 and 5). By 1997, the Internet interconnected over 50 million users and 16 million servers in more than 160 countries (Kambil, 1997). But although networks are pervasive, the benefits they promise can be maddeningly elusive. As at 1995, the problem seemed to lie less with the technology and more with corporate processes and IT assessment criteria. High-profile, successful, networked corporations like Wal-Mart Stores, Federal Express, Open Market Inc. and Sun Microsystems were untypical (*Business Week*, 1995; Gogan and Applegate, 1995). In the USA this positioning well behind the technology curve continued into 1997. According to Hamilton (1997), in 1996 more than half of US Internet users purchased merchandise on-line and sales totalled $500 million. However, such figures translate to only 5.4 per cent of the US population. Moreover, according to a survey of Fortune 500 organizations, the bulk of Web applications involved information sharing, document publishing, electronic mail and customer service; only 10 per cent involved sales transactions. The main reasons given included concerns over security, reliability, scalability, lack of infrastructure, common standards and audit trails, and unsuitable development tools (Gow, 1997).

The business case for Internet/intranet investment is not always clear. Even those, like Bank of America, that had gone forward with Web-enabled transactions perceived financial payback and time savings coming much later (Gow, 1997). One reason for caution would be the ability of the Internet to magnify mistakes and make them intensely public. Thus Machlis (1997) reports a major US credit-reporting agency sending 200 credit reports to the wrong customers, after 2000 requests to the Web site over an 11-hour period triggered a software error that misdirected the credit data. US firms showed less caution with intranets, with 85 per cent having installed them by mid-1997 or planning to do so. By comparison, in the UK the figure was 59 per cent by 1997, the fear of being left behind often being counteracted by difficulties in identifying "killer applications" for an intranet (Stammers, 1997).

We have already looked at some of the cost implications in the network-centric era, but what of the benefit opportunities? Considering the WWW and Internet, there can be several types of Web site. The primary drivers of the business model adopted are type of customer and preferred business impact (see Figure I.2).

Existing companies, for example Federal Express and 3M, have tended to evolve through using a site for image and product information purposes, to information collection/market research, customer support/service, internal support/service and then transactions/sales. On the other hand, simple economics require Internet start-ups, for

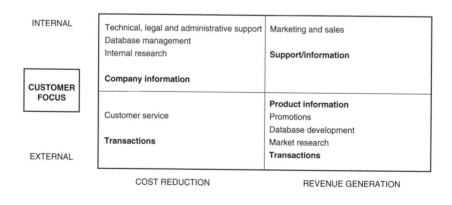

Figure I.2 *Drivers of Internet Business Models (source: Quelch and Klein, 1996)*

example Amazon.com and Software.net, to begin with transactions, then build customer support/service, provide a brand image and product information, then carry out information collection and market research to win repeat purchases (Quelch and Klein, 1996). These two different evolutionary models involve plotting different routes through the four quadrants shown in Figure I.2. Whatever the positioning, it is clear that a Web site business case needs to show how revenue can be generated, costs reduced, customers satisfied and/or business strategies underpinned.

Significant cost reductions are possible (Berryman et al., 1998). In the first 18 months of Web usage, US investment bank Morgan Stanley documented nearly $1 million in savings on internal access to routine information and electronic routing of key reports. By moving external customer support functions on to the Web, Cisco Connection Online saved $250 million in one year (Kambil, 1997). One immediate advantage and (following Metcalfe's law) exponential add-on value of a Web site is that it can reach a global audience, although this may not be its initial focus. This global product reach can offer multiple business opportunities, including faster new product diffusion, easier local adaptation and customization, overcoming import restrictions, reducing the competitive advantage of scale economies in many industries, and the effective marketing and selling of niche/speciality products to a critical mass of customers available worldwide. Clearly, the technology enables new business models, but these are a product of new business thinking and business cases that can recognize at least some of the longer-term benefits; although, from past evidence, many will also grow from use and learning (Feeny and Ives, 1997). At the same time, on the cost side Web sites, like other IT investments, are not one-off costs. Annual costs just for site maintenance (regardless of upgrades and content changes) may well be two to four times the initial launch cost (Bernoff and Ott, 1995).

Exploiting the Virtual Value Chain

Benefits may also arise from exploiting the information generated in the virtual value chain of a business. As Rayport and Sviokla (1995) have pointed out, if companies integrate the information they capture during stages of the physical value chain—from inbound logistics and production through sales and marketing—they can construct an information underlay for the business. To create value with information, organizations need to look to what Rayport and Sviokla call the "marketspace". One internal example is how Ford moved one key element of its physical value chain—product development of its "global car"—to much faster virtual team working. Externally, companies can also extract value by establishing space-based relationships with customers. Essentially, each extract from the flow of information along the virtual value chain could also consitute a new product or service. By creating value with digital assets, outlays on information technologies like intranets/Internets can be reharvested in an infinite number of combinations and transactions.

Exploitation of digital assets can have immense economic significance in a network-centric era. But organizations would need to rethink their previous ways of assessing benefits from IT investments. Rayport and Sviokla (1995) usefully summarize the five economic implications. Digital assets are not used up in their consumption but can be reharvested. Virtual value chains redefine economies of scale, allowing small firms to achieve low unit costs in markets dominated by big players. Businesses can also redefine economies of scope by utilizing the same digital assets across different and disparate markets. Digital transaction costs are low and continue to decline sharply. Finally, in combination these factors, together with digital assets, allow a shift from supply side to demand side, more customer-focused thinking and strategies.

Electronic Commerce

To add to this picture, Kambil (1997) shows how the Internet can be used in electronic commerce to lower the costs and radically transform basic trade processes of search, valuation, logistics, payment and settlement and authentication. Technical solutions to these basic trade processes have progressed rapidly. At the same time, the adoption of trade context processes to the new infostructure—processes that reduce the risks of trading e.g. dispute resolution, legitimizing agreements in the "marketspace"—has been substantially slower. This has also been one of the main barriers to wider adoption of electronic cash, along with the need for a critical mass of consumer acceptance, despite compelling arguments for e-cash's potential for improved service (Maat, 1997).

Some further insights into the new economics, and the power to create value in on-line markets, are provided by Hagel and Armstrong (1997). They too endorse the need for an understanding of the dynamics of increasing returns in electronic commerce (EC). EC displays three forms of increasing returns. First, an initial outlay to develop EC is required, but thereafter the incremental cost of each additional unit of the product/service is minimal (see the discussion above). Secondly, significant learning and cost-reduction effects are likely to be realized, with EC-based businesses driving down the experience curve much more quickly than more mature businesses. Thirdly, Metcalfe's law applies: network effects accrue exponential returns as membership increases and more units of product/service are deployed. As Microsoft showed spectacularly in software, harnessing the power of increasing returns means "the more you sell, the more you sell."

The New Economics of Electronic Communities

Hagel and Armstrong focus particularly on the commercial possibilities inherent in building electronic communities. Here networks give customers/members the ability to interact with each other as well as with vendors. In exchange for organizing the electronic community and developing its potential for increasing value for participants, a network organizer would extract revenues. A prime example of a network organizer is Open Market Inc. (Gogan and Applegate,1995; also Chapter 5). Revenues could be in the form of subscription, usage, content delivery or service fees charged to customers, and advertising and transaction commission from vendors. Customers would be attracted by a distinctive focus, for example consumer travel; the capacity to integrate content such as advertising with communication, e.g. through bulletin boards, both of which aggregate over time, access to competing publishers and vendors; and opportunities for commercial transactions. Vendors gain reduced search cost, increased propensity for customers to buy, enhanced ability to target, greater ability to tailor; and added value for existing products and services. They also benefit from elements more broadly applicable to networked environments: lower capital investment in buildings; broader geographic reach; and opportunities to remove intermediaries.

Hagel and Armstrong (1997) point out that it is the dynamics of increasing returns that drive revenue growth in virtual communities, but that these are easily missed by conventional financial analysis techniques. Using static revenue models and assumptions of straight-line growth, these conventional techniques can greatly underestimate the potential of virtual community investment. As a result, organizations may forgo investment altogether or underinvest, thereby increasing the risks of pre-emption by competitors and business failure.

Increasing returns depend on the achievement of four dynamic loops. The first is a content attractiveness loop, whereby member-based content attracts more members, who contribute more content. The second is a member loyalty loop. Thus more member-to-member interaction will build more member loyalty and reduce membership "churn". A third, member profile loop sees information gathered about members assisting in targeting advertising and customizing products/ services. The final, transaction offerings loop sees more vendors drawn into the community, more products/services being offered, thus attracting in more members and creating more commercial transactions. According to Hagel and Armstrong, it is the aggregate effect of these dynamic loops in combination that could create the exponential revenue growth pattern shown in Figure I.3.

To achieve these four dynamic loops, the evolutionary path is first to develop a critical mass of members. The other four growth assets are shown in Figure I.3. These may reach critical mass in a sequential manner, but community organizers may well seek to develop them much more in parallel, as shown in the Figure. The important point is that as each growth asset reaches critical mass and their effects combine, the revenue dynamic is exponentially influenced. However, despite Hagel and Armstrong's optimism, it should be emphasized that there is no inevitability about the scenario depicted in Figure I.3. Business and competitive risks do not disappear but are fundamental to the development and running of electronic communities.

In all this, as in more conventional businesses, the key economic asset is the member/customer, and critical activities revolve around his/her

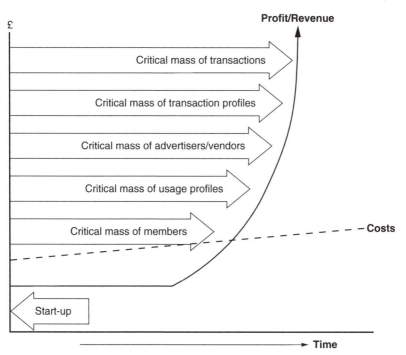

Figure I.3   *Revenue, Cost and Milestones for Virtual Communities (modified from Hagel and Armstrong, 1997)*

acquisition and retention. This can be costly on the WWW where "surfing" is much more typical than member loyalty. Up to 1998, even an experienced on-line service like America Online was losing up to 40 per cent of its members a year and spending up to $90 to acquire each new member. Other cost aspects need to be borne in mind. Start-up costs for an Internet site are commonly cited as low, typically between $1 and 2 million as at 1997 (Cronin, 1996; Kambil, 1997). On one model, technology-related costs in an electronic community may start as a small (say, 35 per cent) and declining proportion of total costs over a five-year period, being overwhelmed by member and advertiser acquistion and content-related costs (Hagel and Armstrong, 1997).

However, those making investment decisions do face a number of challenges. A look at Figure I.3 would suggest that fast returns on investment are unlikely, while short-term cost pressures are certain. Moreover, evidence from the Internet has been that early revenue sources such as membership subscription, usage fees and advertising charges, act as dissuaders and can slow long-term growth substantially. Moreover, Kambil's warnings (see above) indicate that even by 1998 the Internet was still not a commerce friendly environment, with key robust technologies on payment, authentication, security and information-usage capture still to be put in place. At the same time, early entrants will probably secure the markets, through the dynamics of increasing returns, but also for historically familiar reasons with competitive edge IT applications: low barriers to entry, accumulation of unique assets, lock-in of customers and vendors, but also concentration and economies of scale and scope effects (Feeny and Ives, 1997).

THIS BOOK: STRUCTURE AND ARGUMENT

These developments have considerable implications for assessment approaches to information technology-based investments, and are detailed here as an adjunct to and to provide context for the chapters in this book. The book limits its focus to contributions that enhance our understanding of the relationships between IT investments, productivity and performance and how these can be assessed. This begins in Section I, where attention is drawn away from the macroeconomic debate and focused on more useful and meaningful assessments of organizational-level IT adoption and use. In Section II there are four chapters devoted to considering how organizations typically carry out IT investment appraisals, and how these practices may need to be reconstructed.

Section III extends the exploration across the systems lifecycle model presented in Chapter 2, including assessment of on-going operations (Chapter 10). However, its distinctive contributions are to the assessment of IT project development, the evaluation of IT sourcing options and likely subsequent outsourcing arrangements, and the assessment of IT infrastructure investments. Finally, Section IV provides two chapters as a key reminder that all too much IT assessment makes assumptions about accuracy and objectivity that are defeated time and again by the social, political and stakeholder factors and issues inherent in any attempt at evaluation in organizations. Interpretive approaches are strongly argued for, and these arguments remain valid across the eras delineated earlier in this introduction. Let us now consider the content of each chapter in more detail.

The IT Productivity Paradox in Organizations

In Chapter 1 Erik Brynjolfsson and Lorin Hitt tackle the the IT productivity paradox with firm-level evidence. Their exploratory study is one of several by the same authors (see also Brynjolfsson and Hitt, 1994, 1996). It uses firm-level data on several components of information systems (IS) spending for 1987–91. The dataset includes 367 large firms which generated approximately $1.8 trillion dollars in output in 1991. Brynjolfsson and Hitt supplemented the IS data with data on other inputs, output and price deflators from other sources. As a result, they could assess several econometric models of the contribution of IS to firm-level productivity.

Their results suggest that IS spending made a substantial and statistically significant contribution to firm output in the period investigated. In particular, the gross marginal product (MP) for computer capital averaged 81 per cent for the firms in their sample. The MP for computer capital was found to be at least as large as the marginal product of other types of capital investment and that, dollar for dollar, IS labour spending generated at least as much output as spending on non-IS labour and expenses. Because the models they applied were similar to those that have been previously used to assess the contribution of IS and other factors of production, Brynjolfsson and Hitt attribute the different results to the fact that the present data set was more current and larger than others explored. The authors conclude that there is significant evidence that the "productivity paradox" disappeared by 1991, at least in their sample of firms (see also the discussion above).

Chapter 2 follows on from the Introduction and provides an additional detailed critical assessment of the fact that, despite the massive investments in IT in the developed economies, the IT impact on productivity and business performance continues to be questioned. Leslie

Willcocks and Stephanie Lester suggest that important elements in the uncertainty about IT payoffs relate to deficiencies in measurement at the macroeconomic level, but also to weaknesses in organizational evaluation practice. The chapter reports evidence from a 1996 UK survey pointing to such weaknesses. Focusing at the more meaningful organizational level, an integrated systems lifecycle approach is put forward as a long-term way of strengthening evaluation practice. This incorporates a cultural change in evaluation from "control through numbers" to a focus on quality improvement. The approach is compared against late 1990s research findings in a multinational insurance company, where senior managers in a newly created business division consciously sought related improvements in evaluation practice and IT productivity.

Chapter 3 provides statistically analysed evidence on over 300 business units in the USA and Europe to show that the notion of the application of IT in business organizations failing to affect productivity must be rejected as faulty. The analysis strongly substantiates a significant and multifaceted effect of IT on productivity and performance. However, the study demonstrates that IT is unable to add value itself, but does so only in interaction with other factors. Type, timing and focus of the IT investment are critical. Gus van Nievelt makes several significant contributions. First, he develops a highly useful measure of organizational performance in the form of an overhead productivity ratio based on economic value added (EVA). Secondly, he relates organizational performance and a range of organizational variables, including IT expenditure, to competitive positioning and relative customer satisfaction. Thirdly, the powerful model built from the 300-plus case database helps to locate the conditions under which different types of IT investment will be effective or ineffective. All this represents an empirically based, in several ways superior, approach to analysing and understanding the way in which IT, productivity and organizational performance relate.

IT and Investment Appraisal

In Section II the focus is very much more on how IT investments are justified and directed in organizations. In Chapter 4, Joan Ballantine, Robert Galliers and Stephanie Stray add to the long-standing debate over IT investment appraisal (see Robson, 1997 and Willcocks, 1994 for overviews) by discussing the IS/IT project evaluation practices of a sample of the top 1000 UK companies. The study sheds light on a number of evaluation issues, including the extent to which formal procedures of evaluation exist within organizations and how far consultation with stakeholders takes place. In addition, it identifies the many problems inherent in evaluating IS/IT investments. The implications of the findings are discussed in the light of previous research, in addition to pinpointing a number of key issues where further research is needed.

Philip Powell follows this in Chapter 5 by investigating whether IT investments require to be assessed any differently from other major investments made by organizations. He shows that all investment decisions are problematic, but that the information systems and information technology (IS/IT) community seems particularly nervous and uncertain on the subject of evaluation of its investments. The chapter contains a comparative perspective on historic and non-IT as well as IT-based investments. The author contributes an analysis of types and problems with different investment appraisal techniques, and compares their applicability in different investment fields. He finds some evidence for the lack of use of formal techniques in the IT field, and posits that this may be due not to a deficiency in the tools available to the evaluator, but to other political, organizational or competitive factors. These factors are appraised and possible ways forward considered. Finally, citing case studies, the author ties the argument to this introduction by considering the extent to which the need to make network-based investments ushers in an era when evaluation practice cannot be business as usual.

In Chapter 6, Barbara Farbey, Frank Land and David Targett review 14 main techniques available for front-end evaluation, and their usefulness and limitations. They then report on a 16-case study research project into implemented projects to find out how these had been evaluated at investment appraisal stage. Supporting concerns registered elsewhere in this book (see above and Chapters 2 and 5), in fact they found *ad hoc* procedures used in the majority of cases. These procedures are classified by the authors as "top-down strategic", "top-down dictat", "incremental change" and "competitive imperative". Farbey, Land and Targett then contribute a detailed and highly useful contingency framework derived from their research.

N. Venkatraman brings together the Section II themes with a compelling case for rethinking the administrative logic of assessing and managing IT resources (Chapter 7). He introduces the concept of IT as a value centre with four components. Depending on purpose and risk propensity, IT investments need to be classified differently as focused on cost efficiency, service, profit or investment contribution. Each type of contribution is distinct and requires different metrics and management approaches. The author provides a detailed discussion of these four value centres and the management options within each. He also argues that asking certain vital questions about IT purpose will help to reframe the discussion between business and IT managers on the value centre concept. Is the objective to create business capabilities or rectify operational weaknesses? How should a firm invest in IT to support the preferred value centre profile? How should capabilities be sourced (see also Chapter 10)? Should single or multifaceted assessment criteria be adopted (see also Chapters 2, 3 and 6)? What is the consequent logic of IT organization—internal captive monopoly or solutions integrator? These remain perennial questions in IT but, as argued above, become particularly vital to ask in the period of mixed eras that we entered in the mid-1990s.

IT Development, Sourcing and Infrastructure: Assessment Issues

The first two chapters in Section III deal with the assessment of IT development projects, with Chapter 9 also relating control of the development process to the business benefits produced by implemented systems.

Janne Ropponen, in Chapter 8, points out the perennial and high risks associated particularly with software development, and the need for these to be managed. Software risk management can be defined as an attempt to formalize risk-oriented correlates of development success into a readily applicable set of principles and practices. His earlier research provides a prioritized list of software risks and risk management methods in relation to them. Using a survey of over 80 experienced project managers, the author investigates these issues further. In particular, the study addresses two main questions: which software risks are critical in different contexts; how widely are various risk management methods used and what experiences have been gained from their use? In the study project managers agreed significantly that the most critical risk items lay with the stream of continuous requirement changes and unrealistic budgets and schedules. A comparison of cross-country data showed that software risks tend to differ from one context to another. The study also reveals that project managers rarely applied specific risk management methods due to their low understanding and knowledge of software risks. Many, however, did engage in activities to combat software risks. Those who instigated risk management methods found them useful subsequently and continued to apply them.

The next chapter extends the area of study to cover investment appraisal, development and realization of benefits from IT applications. Valerie Graeser and Leslie Willcocks use a detailed case study of benefits funding at the California Franchise Tax Board to illuminate these issues and show an integrated lifecycle approach to IT evaluation in action. A substantial literature now shows that IT projects, IT assessment and the use of external IT vendors are fraught with difficulties. The chapter explores these themes through the case history of projects at the $30 billion revenue US public-sector agency in the 1993–7 period. Against a background of failed projects, a new benefits-funding mechanism was developed. The chapter describes its implementation and its use in two major projects. The levels of success achieved in these projects are analysed and the critical success factors identified and compared with those emerging from the wider literature.

In Chapter 10, Leslie Willcocks, Guy Fitzgerald and Mary Lacity extend the theme of assessment and use of external IT vendors. The chapter is based on findings from 26 researched longitudinal case studies of IT outsourcing conducted in the 1993–6 period. The primary focus is on evaluation practices in the lead-up to making IT sourcing decisions. The pre-existing IT evaluation system was found to be a help or a major hindrance as a basis from which to assess outsourcing vendor bids. Difficulties experienced in evaluating in-house performance are highlighted. Issues included evaluating total IT contribution, identifying full costs, benchmarking and external comparisons, the role of charging systems, and the adoption of service-level agreements by the in-house operation. Organizational experiences of assessing vendor bids against in-house options are then detailed. These are presented in codified form as a detailed case study and additional lessons derived from the research. Finally, the chapter highlights the emerging evaluation approach shared by organizations that made effective sourcing decisions.

By 1998, many organizations on the edge of the network-centric era were having to revisit the issue of infrastructure investment. In Chapter 11, Peter Weill and Marianne Broadbent point out that alignment between strategic context and the information technology portfolio requires planned and purposeful management processes, within both business and information technology disciplines. In practice, the natural state is non-alignment. Building on the picture in Chapter 7, the authors argue that, to pursue alignment, organizations invest in four fundamentally different types of IT with different management objectives: strategic, informational, transactional and infrastructure. IT infrastructure is the base foundation of budgeted-for IT capability (both technical and human), shared throughout an organization in the form of reliable services and usually managed by the IT/IS group.

IT infrastructure investments are typically large, long term in nature and underpin the future competitiveness of firms. The direct business benefits of IT infrastructure are difficult to specify and an analogy can be drawn with investments in public infrastructure at national and regional levels. All IT investment is not alike, and the IT infrastructure component of an organization's IT portfolio is a significant contributor to long-term business advantage. What organizations expect to get from their IT infrastructure investments depends on their view of the role of IT infrastructure. Drawing on recent research in large firms in seven countries, this chapter identifies and describes four different views of infrastructure in firms: none, utility, dependent and enabling. The investment, benefit expectations, top management involvement and value of IT infrastructure was found to vary markedly depending on the view of IT infrastructure. The ability of firms to achieve their strategic intent and implement their vision through different views of infrastructure is illustrated by examples in four firms. A discussion of the characteristics and necessary conditions of the four views of IT infrastructure complete the chapter.

The Need for Interpretive Approaches

The final section of the book seeks to highlight social, political and interpretive issues inherent in IT evaluation. These issues have been consistently neglected, to the detriment of evaluation processes and their outcomes. Chapter 12, by Geoff Walsham, argues for the more extensive use of an interpretive approach to the evaluation of information systems, involving a dynamic process of evaluation throughout the systems lifecycle, in which the interpretations of individuals and stakeholder groups are mobilized to influence systems design and implementation. The broad purpose of an interpretive IS evaluation is to deepen understanding and to generate motivation and commitment. Evidence to support the arguments of the chapter is drawn both from the general literature on evaluation and from conceptual and empirical work in the IS field itself. Some specific proposals are put forward for designing interpretive IS evaluation, and the chapter concludes with a discussion of the prospects for more widespread future use of this type of evaluation approach.

In the last chapter, Rudy Hirschheim and Steve Smithson provide a retrospective, critical assessment of IT evaluation approaches. They argue that much of what has been done under the umbrella of IS/IT evaluation from the 1980s to date has been ill-conceived. Much of the time an overly rational, simplistic notion of evaluation has been applied, turning out all too frequently to be dysfunctional in the long run due to the inherent unintended consequences it has invariably brought about. In reviewing the IT evaluation literature, the authors note the predominant focus on quantification, objectivity and efficiency critieria, reflecting the strongest concerns actually found in IT evaluation practices (see also Chapters 4 and 5). Such approaches have not only tended to exclude large number of stakeholders from the evaluation process; as one consequence, they have also tended not to capture the multiple effects of IT not just in economic, but also organizational, political, social, political and managerial terms. The authors provide a classification of IT evaluation approaches and then provide an important reminder that IT assessment in organizations is inherently a political process.

Taken together, the two chapters in this final section present a strong thesis and a number of important challenges to those concerned with IT evaluation. As such, it is to be hoped that they are typical of the contributions made by each of the other chapters, and represent a fitting way to conclude the book.

REFERENCES

Allen, D. (1997). Where's the Productivity Growth (from the Information Technology Revolution)? *Federal Reserve Bank of St. Louis Review*, March/April, 79, 2, 15–25.

Baily, M. and Gordon, J. (1988). The Productivity Slowdown, Measurement Issues, and The Explosion of Computer Power. In Brainard, W. and Perry, G. (eds) *Brookings Papers On Economic Activity*. The Brookings Institution Washington DC.

Baker, G. (1997). Anatomy of a Miracle. *Financial Times*, June 20th, 17.

Banker, R., Kaufman, R. and Mahmood, M. (eds) (1993). *Strategic Information Technology Management: Perspectives on Organizational Growth and Competitive Advantage*. Idea Group Publishing, Harrisburg.

Barua, A., Kriebel, C. and Mukhopahyay, T. (1991). Information Technology and Business Value: An Analytic and Empirical Investigation. *University of Texas at Austin Working Paper*, Austin Texas.

Bernoff, J. and Ott, A. (1995). *People and Technology: What Web Sites Cost*. The Forrester Report, Volume 2. Forrester Consulting, Cambridge, Mass.

Berryman, K., Harrington, L., Layton-Rodin, D. and Rerolle, V. (1998). Electronic Commerce: Three Emerging Strategies. *McKinsey Quarterly*, 1, 152–9.

Boar, B. (1996). *Cost-Effective Strategies for Client/Server Systems*. John Wiley, New York.

Brynjolfsson, E. and Hitt, L. (1993). Paradox Lost? Firm-Level Evidence on the Returns to Information Systems Spending. *Center for Coordination Science Working Paper*, MIT, Boston.

Brynjolfsson, E. and Hitt, L. (1994). Information Technology as a Factor of Production: the Role of Difference among Firms. *Working Paper 3715*, MIT Sloan School of Management, Boston.

Brynjolfsson, E. and Hitt, L. (1996). Productivity, Business Profitability and

Consumer Surplus: Three Different Measures of Information Technology Value. *MIS Quarterly*, June, 121–42.

Business Week (1993). The Technology Payoff—Special Report. *Business Week*, July 24th, 37–46.

Business Week (1995). Annual Report on Information Technology: the Networked Corporation. *Business Week*, June 26th, 45–67.

Byrd, T. and Marshall, T. (1997). Relating Information Technology Investment to Organizational Performance: a Causal Model Analysis. *Omega*, 25, 1, 43–56.

Choi, S.-Y., Stahl, D. and Whinston, A. (1997). *The Economics of Electronic Commerce*. Macmillan Technical, Indianopolis.

Cronin, M. (1996). *Global Advantage on the Internet*. Van Nostrand Reinhold, New York.

David, P. (1990). The Dynamo and the Computer: an Historical Perspective on the Modern Productivity Paradox. *American Economic Review*, May, 355–61.

Dec, K. (1996). *Client/Server: Fiscal Benefits and Justification*. Gartner Group Symposium, Lake Buena Vista, Florida, October.

Dertouzos, M. (1997). *What Will Be: How the New World of Information Will Change our Lives*. HarperEdge, New York.

Economist, The (1996). The Hitchhiker's Guide to Cybernomics. *The Economist*, September 28th.

Feeny, D. and Ives, B. (1997). IT as a Basis for Sustainable Competitive Advantage. In Willcocks, L., Feeny, D. and Islei, G. (eds) *Managing IT as a Strategic Resource*. McGraw-Hill, Maidenhead.

Gillin, P. (ed.) (1994). The Productivity Payoff: the 100 Most Effective Users of Information Technology. *Computerworld*, September 19th, Section 2, 4–55.

Gogan, J. and Applegate, L. (1995). *Open Market Inc. (A)*. Harvard Business School Publishing, Boston.

Gow, G. (1997). Risk versus Opportunity. *Computerworld*, February 24th, 14–20.

Graeser, V., Willcocks, L. and Pisanias, N. (1998). *Developing the IT Scorecard: a Study of Evaluation Practices and Integrated Performance Measurement*. Business Intelligence, London.

Greenspan, A. (1997). Quoted in: Feds Link IT, Productivity, but Hard Evidence Lacking. *Computerworld*, August 25th, 1.

Griffith, V. (1997). Freedom Fantasy: Interview with Stephen Roach. *Financial Times*, August 13th, 10.

Griliches, Z. (1994). Productivity, R&D and the Data Constraint. *American Economic Review*, March, 1–23.

Hagel, J. and Armstrong, A. (1997). *Net Gain: Expanding Markets through Virtual Communities*. Harvard Business School Press, Boston.

Harris, D. (ed.) (1996). *Organizational Linkages: Understanding the Productivity Paradox*. National Academy Press, Washington DC.

Hamilton, S. (1997). E-Commerce in the 21st Century. *Computer*, 30, 5, 44–7.

Hu, Q. and Plant, R. (1998) Does IT Spending Impact Firm Productivity and Performance? *University of Miami Working Paper*, University of Miami, Florida.

Kambil, A. (1997). Doing Business in the Wired World. *Computer*, 30, 5, 56–62.

Kraemer, K. and Dedrick, J. (1996). IT and Economic Development: International Competitiveness. In Dutton, W. (ed.) *Information and Communication Technologies*. Oxford University Press, Oxford.

Lacity, M., Willcocks, L. and Subramanian, A. (1997). A Strategic Client Server

Implementation: Plus Ça Change? In Willcocks, L., Feeny, D. and Islei, G. (eds) *Managing IT as a Strategic Resource*. McGraw-Hill, Maidenhead.

Landauer, T. (1995). The Trouble with Computers: Usefulness, Usability and Productivity. MIT Press, Cambridge, Mass.

Loveman, G. (1988). An Assessment of the Productivity Impact of Information Technologies. *MIT Management In The Nineties Working Paper*, 88-054. MIT, Cambridge, USA.

Maat, M.T. (1997). The Economics of E-Cash. *IEEE Spectrum*, February, 68–73.

Machlis, S. (1997). Internet Can Magnify Mistakes. *Computerworld*, August 25th, 5.

Mandel, M., Naughton, K., Burns, G. *et al.* (1997). How Long Can this Last? *Business Week*, May 19th, 38–42.

McKeen, J., Smith, H. and Parent, M. (1997). Assessing the Value of Information Technology: the Leverage Effect. *Proceedings of the Fifth European Conference on Information Systems*, Cork, June 9–12th.

Mokyr J. (1990). The Lever of Riches: Technological Creativity and Economic Progress. Oxford University Press, Oxford.

Moschella, D. (1997). *Waves of Power: Dynamics of Global Technology Leadership 1964–2010*. Amacom, New York.

Nievelt, M.C.A. van (1997). Personal communication, March 24th.

Nievelt, M.C.A. van and Willcocks, L. (1997). *Benchmarking Organisational and IT Performance*. Oxford Executive Research Briefing, Templeton College, Oxford.

Oliner, S. and Sichel, D. (1994). Computers and Output Growth Revisited: How Big is the Puzzle? *Brooking Papers on Economic Activity*, 2, 273–334.

Quelch, J. and Klein, L. (1996). The Internet and International Marketing. *Sloan Management Review*, Spring, 60–75.

Quinn, J. and Baily, M. (1994). Information Technology: Increasing Productivity in Services. *Academy of Management Executive*, 8, 3, 28–51.

Rayport, J. and Sviokla, J. (1995). Exploiting the Virtual Value Chain. *Harvard Business Review*, November–December, 75–85.

Roach, S. (1986). *Macro-Realities of the Information Economy*. National Academy of Sciences, New York.

Roach, S. (1994). Lessons of the Productivity Paradox. In Gillin, P. (ed.) *The Productivity Payoff: the 100 Most Effective Users of Information Technology*. Computerworld, September 19th, Section 2, 55.

Roach, S. (1997). Quoted in Griffith, V. Freedom Fantasy. Interview in *Financial Times*, August 13th, p. 10.

Robson, W. (1997). *Strategic Management and Information Systems*. Pitman, London.

Skyrme, D. and Amidon, D. (1997). *Creating the Knowledge-Based Business*. Business Intelligence, London.

Soh, C. and Markus, L. (1995). How IT Creates Business Value: a Process Theory Synthesis. *Proceedings of the International Conference in Information Systems*, Amsterdam, December 10–13th.

Stammers, T. (1997). Intranets: Proceed with Caution. *Computing*, September 25th, 26.

Strassmann, P. (1990). *The Business Value of Computers*. Information Economics Press, New Canaan.

Strassmann, P. (1997a). Do US Firms Spend too much on Information Technology? Interview by Norm Alster. *Investor's Business Daily*, April 3rd.

Strassmann, P. (1997b). *The Squandered Computer*. Information Economics Press, New Canaan.

Tallon, P., Kraemer, K. and Gurbaxani, V. (1997). A Multidimensional Assessment of the Contribution of Information Technology to Firm Performance. *Proceedings of the Fifth European Conference on Information Systems*, Cork, June 9–12th.

Teresko, J. (1997). Probing the Digital Future, *Industry Week*, April 7th, 113–18.

Willcocks, L. (ed.) (1994). *Information Management: Evaluation of Information Systems Investments*. Chapman and Hall, London.

Willcocks, L. (1996a). Interview in debate with Landauer, Roach and Strassmann, *"IT doesn't add up"*, BBC Radio 4, London, June 16th.

Willcocks, L. (ed.) (1996b). *Investing in Information Systems: Evaluation and Management*. Thomson Business Press/Chapman and Hall, London.

Willcocks, L., Feeny, D. and Islei, G. (eds) (1997). *Managing IT as a Strategic Resource*. McGraw-Hill, Maidenhead.

Willcocks, L. and Lacity, M. (eds) (1997). *The Strategic Sourcing of Information Systems*. John Wiley, Chichester.

Willcocks, L. and Lester, S. (1996). Beyond the IT Productivity Paradox. *European Management Journal*, 14, 3, 279–90.

SECTION I

Is There a Productivity Paradox?

1

Paradox Lost? Firm-Level Evidence on the Returns to Information Systems Spending

ERIK BRYNJOLFSSON AND LORIN HITT
MIT Soan School of Management and Wharton School,
University of Pennsylvania

INTRODUCTION

Spending on information systems (IS), and in particular information technology (IT) capital, is widely regarded as having enormous potential for reducing costs and enhancing the competitiveness of US firms. Although spending has surged in the past decade, there is surprisingly little formal evidence linking it to higher productivity. Several studies, such as those by Loveman (1994) and by Barua, Kriebel and Mukhopadhyay (1991) have been unable to reject the hypothesis that computers add nothing at all to total output, while others estimate that the marginal benefits are less than the marginal costs (Morrison and Berndt, 1990).

As discussed in the Introduction, this "productivity paradox" has alarmed managers and puzzled researchers. US corporations—the focus of this chapter—have spent billions of dollars on computers and many firms have radically restructured their business processes to take advantage of computers. If these investments have not increased the value produced or reduced costs, then managements must rethink their IS strategies.

Beyond the IT Productivity Paradox.
Edited by L. P. Willcocks and S. Lester © 1999 John Wiley & Sons Ltd.

In this chapter we present an initial look at some recent evidence and find results that differ from previous studies. Our data set is based on five annual surveys of several hundred large firms for a total of 1121 observations[1] over the period 1987–91. The firms in our sample generated approximately $1.8 trillion worth of gross output in the USA in 1991, and their value added of $630 billion accounted for about 13% of the 1991 US gross domestic product of $4.86 trillion (Council of Economic Advisors, 1992). Because the identity of each of the participating firms is known, we were able to supplement the IS data with data from several other sources. As a result, we could assess several econometric models of the contribution of IS to firm-level productivity.

Our examination of these data indicates that IS spending has made a substantial and statistically significant contribution to the output of firms. Our point estimates indicate that, dollar for dollar, spending on computer capital created more value than spending on other types of capital. We find that the contribution of IS to output does not vary much across years, although there is weak evidence of a decrease over time. In addition, we find some evidence of differences across various sectors of the economy. Technology strategy also appears to affect returns. For instance, we find that neither firms that relied heavily on mainframes nor firms which emphasized personal computer (PC) usage performed as well as firms that invested in a mix of mainframes and PCs.

In each of the specifications we examine, estimates of the gross marginal product for computers exceeds 50% annually. Considering a 95% confidence interval around our estimates, we can reject the hypothesis that computers add nothing to total output. Furthermore, several of our regressions suggest that the marginal product for computers is significantly higher than the return on investment for other types of capital, although this comparison is dependent on the assumed cost of computer capital. Overall, our inital examination of this sample of large firms suggests that the "productivity paradox" disappeared in the 1987–91 period. However, further analysis is clearly called for to resolve the differences between these findings and those of earlier studies (see also Hitt and Brynjolfsson, 1996; Byrd and Marshall, 1997; Introduction).

Previous Research on IT and Productivity

There is a broad literature on IT value which is reviewed in detail in the Introduction and Chapter 2 (see also Brynjolfsson, 1993; Wilson, 1993). Many of these studies examined correlations between IT spending ratios and various performance measures, such as profits or stock returns (Dos Santos, Peffers and Mauer, 1993; Harris and Katz, 1988;

Strassmann, 1990) and some found that the correlation was either zero or very low, which has led to the conclusion that computer investment has been unproductive. However, in interpreting these findings, it is important to bear in mind that economic theory predicts that in equilibrium, companies that spend more on computers would not, on average, have higher profitability or stock market returns. Managers should be as likely to overspend as to underspend, so high spending should not necessarily be "better". Where non-zero correlations are found, they should be interpreted as indicating either an *unexpectedly* high or low contribution of information technology, as compared to the performance that was anticipated when the investments were made. Thus, perhaps counter-intuitively, the common finding of zero or weak correlations between the percentage of spending allocated to IT and profitability does not necessarily indicate a low payoff for computers.

To examine the contribution of IT to output, it is helpful to work within the well-defined framework of the economic theory of production. In fact, Alpar and Kim (1991) found that methods based on production theory could yield insights that were not apparent when more loosely constrained statistical analyses were performed. The economic theory of production posits that the output of a firm is related to its inputs via a production function and predicts that each input should make a positive contribution to output. A further prediction of the theory is that the marginal cost of each input should just equal the marginal benefit produced by that input. Hundreds of studies have estimated production functions with various inputs, and the predictions of economic theory have generally been confirmed (see Berndt (1991), especially Chapters 3 and 9, for an excellent review of many of these studies).

The "productivity paradox" of IT is most accurately linked to a subset of studies based on the theory of production which either found no positive correlation overall (Barua, Kriebel and Mukhopadhyay, 1991; Loveman, 1994) or found that benefits fell short of costs (Morrison and Berndt, 1990). Using the Management of the Productivity of Information Technology (MPIT) database,[2] Loveman (1994) concluded: "Investments in IT showed no net contribution to total output." While his elasticity estimates ranged from -0.12 to 0.09, most were not statistically distinguishable from zero. Barua, Kriebel and Mukhudpadhyay (1991) found that computer investments are not significantly correlated with increases in return on assets (but see Introduction). Similarly, Morrison and Berndt (1990) examined industry-level data using a production function and found that each dollar spent on "high-tech" capital (computers, instruments and telecommunications equipment) increased measured output by only 80 cents on the margin.

Although previous work provides little econometric evidence that computers improve productivity, Brynjolfsson's (1993) review of the overall literature on this "productivity paradox" concludes that the "shortfall of evidence is not necessarily evidence of a shortfall". He notes that increases in product variety and quality should properly be counted as part of the value of output, but that the price deflators that the government currently uses to remove the effects of inflation are imperfect. These deflators are computed assuming that quality and other intangible characteristics do not change for most goods. As a result, inflation is overestimated and real output is underestimated by an equivalent amount (because real output is estimated by multiplying nominal output by the price deflator). In addition, as with any new technology, a period of learning, adjustment and restructuring may be necessary to reap its full benefits, so that early returns may not be representative of the ultimate value of IT. Accordingly, he argues that "mismeasurement" and "lags" are two of four viable explanations (along with "redistribution" and "mismanagement") for the collected findings of earlier studies (see also Chapter 2). This leaves the question of computer productivity open to continuing debate.

Data Issues

The measurement problem has been exacerbated by weaknesses in available data. Industry-level output statistics have historically been the only data that are available for a broad cross-section of the economy. In a related study using much of the same data as the Morrison and Berndt (1990) study, Berndt and Morrison (1995) conclude: "there is a statistically significant negative relationship between productivity growth and the high-tech intensity of the capital". However, they also point out: "it is possible that the negative productivity results are due to measurement problems". Part of the difficulty is that industry-level data does allow us to distinguish firms *within* a particular industry which invest heavily in IT from those with low IT investments. Comparisons can only be made among industries, yet these comparisons can be sensitive to the price deflators used, which in turn depend on the assumptions about how much quality improvement has occurred in each industry. Firm-level production functions, on the other hand, will better reflect the "true" outputs of the firm, insofar as the increased sales at each firm can be directly linked to its use of computers and other inputs, and all the firms are subject to the same industry-level price deflator.

On the other hand, a weakness of firm-level data is that it can be painstaking to collect, and therefore studies with firm-level data have historically focused on relatively narrow samples. This has made it difficult to draw generalizable results from these studies. For instance, Weill (1992) found some positive impacts for investments in some categories of IS but not for overall IS spending. However, the 33 strategic business units (SBUs) in his sample from the valve manufacturing industry accounted for less than $2 billion in total sales, and he notes: "The findings of the study have limited external validity" (Weill, 1992). By the same token, the Loveman (1994) and Barua, Kriebel and Mukhudpadhyay (1991) studies were based on data from only 20 firms (60 SBUs) in the 1978–82 period and derived only rather imprecise estimates of IT's relationship to firm performance.

The imprecision of previous estimates highlights an inherent difficulty of measuring the benefits of IT investment. To better understand the perceived benefits, we conducted a survey of managers to find out the relative importance of reasons for investing in IT (see Brynjolfsson, 1994). Our results indicate that the primary reason for IT investment was customer service, followed by cost savings. Close behind were timeliness and quality. In practice, the value of many of the benefits of IT, other than cost savings, is not well captured in aggregate price deflators or output statistics (Baily and Gordon, 1988)

Given the weaknesses of existing data, it has been very difficult to distinguish the contribution of IT from random shocks that affect productivity even when sophisticated analytical methods are applied. As Simon (1984) has observed:

> In the physical sciences, when errors of measurement and other noise are found to be of the same order of magnitude as the phenomena under study, the response is not to try to squeeze more information out of the data by statistical means; it is instead to find techniques for observing the phenomena at a higher level of resolution. The corresponding strategy for economics is obvious: to secure new kinds of data at the micro level.

A convincing assessment of IS productivity would ideally employ a sample which included a large share of the economy (as in the Berndt and Morrison studies), but at a level of detail that disaggregated inputs and outputs for individual firms (as in Loveman, 1994; Barua, Kriebel and Mukhudpadhyay 1991; and Weill, 1992). Furthermore, because the recent restructuring of many firms may have been essential to realizing the benefits of IS spending, the data should be as current as possible. Lack of such detailed data has hampered previous efforts. While our chapter applies essentially the same models as those used in earlier studies, we use new, firm-level data which is more recent, more detailed and includes more companies. We believe that this accounts for our sharply different results.

Theoretical Issues

As discussed above, there are a number of hypotheses for explaining the productivity paradox, including the possibility that it is an artifact of mismeasurement. We consider this possibility in this chapter.

More formally, we examine the following hypotheses using a variety of statistical tests:

H1) The output contributions of computer capital and IS staff labour are positive;

H2) The net output contributions of computer capital and IS staff labour are positive after accounting for depreciation and labour expense respectively.

In our analysis, we build on a long research stream which applies production theory to determine the contributions of various inputs to output. This approach uses economic theory to determine the set of relevant variables and to define the structural relationships among them. The relationship can then be estimated econometrically and compared with the predictions of economic theory. In particular, for any given set of inputs, the maximum amount of output that can be produced, according to the known laws of nature and existing "technology", is determined by a *production function*. As noted by Berndt (1991), various combinations of inputs can be used to produce a given level of output, so a production function can be thought of as pages of a book containing alternative blueprints. This is essentially an engineering definition, but business implications can be drawn by adding an assumption about how firms behave, such as profit maximization or cost minimization. Under either assumption, no inputs will be "wasted", so the only way to increase output for a given production function is to increase at least one input.

The theory of production not only posits a relationship among inputs and output, but also posits that this relationship may vary depending on particular circumstances. Many of these differences can be explicitly modelled by a sufficiently general production function without adding additional variables. For instance, it is common to assume that there are constant returns to scale, but more general models will allow for increasing or decreasing returns to scale. In this way, it is possible to see whether large firms are more or less efficient than smaller firms. Other differences may have to do with the economic environment surrounding the firm and are not directly related to inputs. Such differences are properly modelled as additional "control" variables. Depending on prices and desired levels of output, different firms may choose different combinations of inputs and outputs, but they will all adhere to the set defined by their production function. The neoclassical economic theory of production has been fairly successful empirically, despite the fact that it treats firms as "black boxes" and thus ignores history or details of the internal organization of firms. Of course, in the real world, such factors can make a significant difference and recent advances in the theory of the firm may enable them to be more rigorously modelled as well.

To operationalize the theory for our sample, we assume that the firms in our sample produce a quantity of OUTPUT (Q) via a production function (F), whose inputs are COMPUTER CAPITAL (C), NON-COMPUTER CAPITAL (K), IS STAFF labour (S), and OTHER LABOUR AND EXPENSES (L).[3] These inputs comprise the sum total of all spending by the firm and all capitalized investment. Economists historically have not distinguished computer capital from other capital, lumping them together as a single variable. Similarly, previous estimates of production functions have not distinguished IS staff labour from other types of labour and expenses. However, for our purposes, making this distinction will allow us directly to examine hypotheses such as H1 and H2 above. We seek to allow for fairly general types of influences by allowing for any type of environmental factors which affect the business sector (*j*) in which the company operates and year (*t*) in which the observation was made.[4] Thus, we can write:

$$Q = F(C, K, S, L; j,t) \qquad\qquad 1$$

Output and each of the input variables can be measured in either physical units or dollars. If measured in dollar terms, the results will more closely reflect the ultimate objective of the firm (profits, or revenues less costs). However, this approach requires the deduction of inflation from the different inputs and outputs over time and in different industries. This can be done by multiplying the nominal dollar value of each variable in each year by an associated deflator to get the real dollar values. Unfortunately, as mentioned earlier, this appproach will probably underestimate changes in product quality or variety since the deflators are imperfect.

The amount of output that can be produced for a given unit of a given input is often measured as the marginal product (MP) of the input, which can be interpreted as a rate of return. When examining differences in the returns of a factor across firms or time periods, it is important to control for the effects of changes in the other inputs to production. Since the production function identifies both the relevant variables of interest as well as the controls, the standard approach to conducting productivity analyses is to assume that the production function, F, has some functional form, and then estimate its parameters (Berndt, 1991, pp. 449–60).

The economic theory of production places certain technical constraints on the choice of functional form, such as quasi-concavity and monotonicity (Varian, 1992). In addition, we observe that firms use multiple inputs in production, so the functional form should also include the flexibility to allow continuous adjustment between inputs as the relative prices of inputs change (ruling out a linear form). Perhaps the simplest functional form that relates inputs to outputs and is consistent with these constraints is the Cobb-Douglas specification, variants of which have been used since 1896 (Berndt, 1991). This specification is probably the most common functional form used for estimating production functions and remains the standard for studies such as ours, which seek to account for output growth by looking at inputs and other factors.[5]

$$Q = e^{\beta_0} C^{\beta_1} K^{\beta_2} S^{\beta_3} L^{\beta_4} \qquad\qquad 2$$

In this specification, β_1 and β_3 are the output elasticity of COMPUTER CAPITAL and information systems staff (IS STAFF) respectively.[6] If the coefficients β_0–β_4 sum to 1, then the production function exhibits constant returns to scale. However, increasing or decreasing returns to scale can also be modelled with the above function. The principal restriction implied by the Cobb-Douglas form is that the elasticity of substitution between factors is constrained to be equal to -1. This means that as the relative price of a particular input increases, the amount of the input employed will decrease by a proportionate amount, and the quantities of other inputs will increase to maintain the same level of output. As a result, this formulation is not appropriate for determining whether inputs are substitutes or complements.

The remainder of the chapter is organized as follows: in the next section we describe the statistical methodology and data of our study. The results are then presented. We conclude with a discussion of the implications of our results.

METHODS AND DATA

Estimating Procedures

The basic Cobb-Douglas specification is obviously not linear in its parameters. However, by taking logarithms of equation 2 and adding an error term (ε), one can derive an equivalent equation that can be estimated by linear regression. For estimation, we have organized the equations as a *system* of five equations, one for each year:

$$\text{Log } Q_{i,87} = \beta_{87} + \beta_j + \beta_1 \text{ Log } C_{i,87} + \beta_2 \text{ Log } K_{i,87} + \beta_3 \text{ Log } S_{i,87} + \beta_4 \text{ Log } L_{i,87} + \varepsilon_{87} \qquad 3a$$

$$\text{Log } Q_{i,88} = \beta_{88} + \beta_j + \beta_1 \text{ Log } C_{i,88} + \beta_2 \text{ Log } K_{i,88} + \beta_3 \text{ Log } S_{i,88} + \beta_4 \text{ Log } L_{i,88} + \varepsilon_{88} \qquad 3b$$

$$\text{Log } Q_{i,89} = \beta_{89} + \beta_j + \beta_1 \text{ Log } C_{i,89} + \beta_2 \text{ Log } K_{i,89} + \beta_3 \text{ Log } S_{i,89} + \beta_4 \text{ Log } L_{i,89} + \varepsilon_{89} \qquad 3c$$

$$\text{Log } Q_{i,90} = \beta_{90} + \beta_j + \beta_1 \text{ Log } C_{i,90} + \beta_2 \text{ Log } K_{i,90} + \beta_3 \text{ Log } S_{i,90} + \beta_4 \text{ Log } L_{i,90} + \varepsilon_{90} \qquad 3d$$

$$\text{Log } Q_{i,91} = \beta_{91} + \beta_j + \beta_1 \text{ Log } C_{i,91} + \beta_2 \text{ Log } K_{i,91} + \beta_3 \text{ Log } S_{i,91} + \beta_4 \text{ Log } L_{i,91} + \varepsilon_{91} \qquad 3e$$

where: Q, C, K, S, L and β_1–β_4 are as before; 87, 88, 89, 90 and 91 index each year; j indexes each sector of the economy; and i indexes each firm in the sample

Under the assumption that the error terms in each equation are independently and identically distributed, estimating this system of equations is equivalent to pooling the data and estimating the parameters by ordinary least squares (OLS). However, it is likely that the variance of the error term varies across years, and that there is some correlation between the error terms across years. It is therefore possible to get more efficient estimates of the parameters by using the technique of iterated seemingly unrelated regressions (ISUR).[7]

As equations 3a–3e are written, we have imposed the usual restriction that the parameters are equal across the sample, which allows the most precise estimates of the parameter values. We can also allow some or all of the parameters to vary over time or by firm characteristics, although this additional information is generally obtained at the expense of lowering the precision of the estimates. We will explore some of these alternative specifications in the results section; however, the main results of this chapter are based on the system of equations shown in 3a–3e.

Data Sources and Variable Construction

This study employs a unique data set on IS spending by large US firms which was compiled by International Data Group (IDG). The information is collected in an annual survey of IS managers at large firms[8] conducted since 1987. Respondents are asked to provide the market value of central processors (mainframes, minicomputers, supercomputers) used by the firm in the USA, the total central IS budget, the percentage of the IS budget devoted to labour expenses, the number of PCs and terminals in use and other IT-related information.

Since the names of the firms are known and most of them are publicly traded, the IS spending information from the IDG survey could be matched to Standard and Poors' Compustat II[9] to obtain measures of output, capital investment, expenses, number of employees and industry classification. In addition, these data were also combined with price deflators for output, capital, employment costs, expenses and IT capital.

There is some discretion as to how the years are matched between the survey and Compustat. The survey is completed at the end of the year for data for the following year. Since we are primarily interested in the value of computer capital stock, and the survey is timed to be completed by the beginning of the new fiscal year, we interpret the survey data as a beginning of period value, which we then match to the end of year data on Compustat (for the previous period). This also allows us to make maximum use of the survey data and is the same approach used by IDG for its reports based on these data, e.g. Maglitta and Sullivan-Trainor (1991).[10]

IDG reports the "market value of central processors" (supercomputers, mainframes and minicomputers) but only the total *number* of "PCs and terminals". Therefore, the variable for COMPUTER CAPITAL was obtained by adding the "market value of central processors" to an estimate of the value of PCs and terminals, which was computed by multiplying the weighted average value for PCs and terminals by the number of PCs and terminals.[11] This approach yields roughly equal values, in aggregate, for central processors ($33.0 billion) as for PCs and terminals ($30.4 billion) in 1991. These values were corroborated by a separate survey by International Data Corporation (IDC, 1991) which tabulates shipments of computer equipment by category. This aggregate computer capital is then deflated by the computer systems deflator reported in Gordon (1990).

The variables for IS STAFF, NON-IS LABOUR AND EXPENSE and OUTPUT were computed by multiplying the relevant quantity from the IDG survey or Compustat by an appropriate government price deflator. IS STAFF was computed by multiplying the IS Budget figure from the IDC survey by the "percentage of the IS budget devoted to labour expenses", and deflating this figure. NON-IS LABOUR AND EXPENSE was computed by deflating total expense and subtracting deflated IS STAFF from this value. Thus, all the expenses of a firm are allocated to either IS STAFF or NON-IS LABOUR AND EXPENSE.

Total capital for each firm was computed from book value of capital stock, adjusted for inflation by assuming that all investment was made at a calculated average age (total depreciation/current depreciation) of the capital stock.[12] From this total capital figure, we subtract the deflated value of COMPUTER CAPITAL to get NON-COMPUTER CAPITAL. Thus, all capital of a firm is allocated to either COMPUTER CAPITAL or NON-COMPUTER CAPITAL. The approach to constructing total capital follows the methods used by other authors who have studied the marginal product of specific production factors using a similar methodology (Hall, 1990; Mairesse and Hall, 1993).

The firms in this sample are quite large. Their average sales over the sample period were nearly $7.4 billion. However, in many other respects, they are fairly representative of the US economy as a whole. For instance, their computer capital stock averages just over 2% of total sales, or about $155 million, which is roughtly consistent with the capital flow tables for the US economy published by the Bureau of Economic Analysis (BEA). Similarly, the average IS budget as a share of sales was very close to the figure reported in a distinct survey by CSC/Index (Quinn *et al.*, 1993). A summary of the sources, construction procedure and deflator for each variable is provided in Table 1.1, and sample statistics are shown in Tables 1.2a and 1.2b.

Potential Data Problems

There are a number of possible errors in the data, either as a result of errors in source data or inaccuracies introduced by the data-construction methods employed. First, the IDG data on IS spending are largely self-reported and therefore the accuracy depends on the diligence of the respondents. Some data elements require a degree of judgment—particularly the market value of central processors and the total number of PCs and terminals. Also, not all companies responded to the survey, and even those that did respond in one year may not have responded in every other year. This may result in sample selection bias. For instance, high-performing firms (or perhaps low-performing firms) may have been more interested in participating in the survey.

However, the effect of these potential errors will probably be small. The information is reasonably consistent from year to year for the same firm and we have checked the aggregate values against other independent sources. We used a different independent source (Compustat) for our output measures and for our non-IT variables, eliminating the chance of respondent bias for these measures. We also examined whether the performance of the firms in our sample (as measured by return on equity (ROE)) differ from the population of the largest half of Fortune 500 manufacturing and Fortune 500 service firms. Our results indicate that there are no statistically significant differences between the ROE of firms in our sample and those that are not (t-statistic = 0.7), which suggests that our sample is not disproportionately comprised of "strong" or "weak" firms. Furthermore, the average size of the firms of our sample is not significantly different from the average size of firms in the top half of the Fortune 500 listings (t-statistic = 0.8). Finally, the response rate of the sample is relatively high at over 75%, suggesting that sample selection bias is probably not driving the results.

Second, there are a number of reasons for IS STAFF and COMPUTER CAPITAL possibly being understated, although by construction these

Table 1.1   Data Sources, Construction Procedures and Deflators

Series	Source	Construction procedure	Deflator
COMPUTER CAPITAL	IDG Survey	"Market Value of Central Processors" converted to constant 1987 dollars, plus the total number of PCs and terminals multiplied by an average value of a PC/terminal, also converted to constant 1987 dollars.	Deflator for Computer Systems (Gordon, 1993). Extended through 1991 at a constant rate.
NON-COMPUTER CAPITAL	Compustat	Total Property, Plant and Equipment Investment converted to constant 1987 dollars. Adjusted for retirements using Winfrey S-3 Table (10-year service life) and aggregated to create capital stock. Computer capital as calculated above was subtracted from this result.	GDP Implicit Deflator for Fixed Investment (Council of Economic Advisors, 1992).
IS STAFF	IDG Survey	Total IS Budget times percentage of IS Budget (by company) devoted to labour expense. Converted to constant 1987 dollars.	Index of Total Compensation Cost (Private Sector) (Council of Economic Advisors, 1992).
NON-IS LABOUR AND EXPENSE	Compustat	Total Labour, Materials and other non-interest expenses converted to constant 1987 dollars. IS labour as calculated above was subtracted from this result.	Producer Price Index for Intermediate Materials, Supplies and Components (Council of Economic Advisors, 1992).
OUTPUT	Compustat	Total sales converted to constant 1987 dollars.	Industry Specific Deflators from *Gross Output and Related Series by Industry, BEA (1977–89)* where available (about 80 per cent coverage)—extrapolated for 1991 assuming average inflation rate from previous five years. Otherwise, sector-level Producer Price Index for Intermediate Materials Supplies and Components (Gorman, 1992).

Table 1.2a *Summary Statistics*

Sample statistics–average over all points
(constant 1987 dollars)

	Total $ (annual average)	As a % of output	Per firm average
OUTPUT	$1661 bn	100%	$7.41 bn
COMPUTER CAPITAL (stock)	$34.7 bn	2.09%	$155 MM
NON-COMPUTER CAPITAL (stock)	$1614 bn	97.2%	$7.20 bn
IS BUDGET (flow)	$27.1 bn	1.63%	$121 MM
IS STAFF (flow)	$11.3 bn	0.68%	$50.4 MM
NON-IS LABOUR AND EXPENSES (flow)	$1384 bn	83.3%	$6.17 bn
Avg. number of companies per year	224	224	224
Total observations	1121	1121	1121

Table 1.2b *Sample Composition Relative to Fortune 500 Population*

Sample composition
Number of firms

	Fortune 500 Manufacturing	Fortune 500 Service	Other
1991 sample breakdown			
Top half Fortune 500	157	61	
Lower half Fortune 500	*39*	*22*	
Total	196	83	14
All Fortune 500 firms in Compustat			
Top half Fortune 500	240	228	
Lower half Fortune 500	*226*	*196*	n.a.
Total	466	424	

errors do not reduce total capital and total expense for the firm. The survey is restricted to central IS spending in the USA plus PCs and terminals both inside and outside the central department. Some firms may have significant expenditures on information systems outside the central department or outside the USA. In addition, the narrow definitions of IS spending employed in this study may exclude significant costs that could be legitimately counted as COMPUTER CAPITAL, such as software and communication networks. Furthermore, by including only the labour portion of IS expenses in IS STAFF as a separate variable (in order to prevent double counting of capital expenditure), other parts of the IS budget are left in the NON-IS LABOUR AND EXPENSE category.

The effects of these problems on the final results are discussed in the results section below.

A third area of potential inaccuracy comes from the price deflators. Numerous authors (for example Baily and Gordon, 1988; Siegel, Donald and Griliches, 1992) have criticized the current methods employed by the BEA for constructing industry-level price deflators. It has been argued that these methods substantially underestimate quality change or other intangible product improvements. If consumer purchases are in part affected by intangible quality improvements, the use of firm-level data should provide a closer approximation to the true output of a firm, because firms which provide quality improvement will have higher sales and can be directly compared to firms in the same industry.

Finally, the measurement of OUTPUT and COMPUTER CAPITAL input in certain service industries appeared particularly troublesome. For financial services, we found that OUTPUT was poorly predicted in our model, presumably because of problems in defining and quantifying the output of financial institutions. In the telecommunications industry, it has been argued (Popkin, 1992) that many of the productivity gains have come from very large investments in computer-based telephone switching gear, which is primarily classified as communications equipment and not COMPUTER CAPITAL, although it may be highly correlated with measured computer capital. We therefore excluded all firms in the financial services industries (SIC60–SIC69) and telecommunications (SIC48).[13]

RESULTS

Basic Results

The basic estimates for this study are obtained by estimating the system of equations 3a–3e by ISUR. Note that we allow the intercept term to vary across sectors and years.

As reported in column 1 of Table 1.3, our estimate of β_1 indicates that COMPUTER CAPITAL is correlated with a statistically significant increase in OUTPUT. Specifically, we estimate that the elasticity of output for COMPUTER CAPITAL is 0.0169 when all the other inputs are held constant. Because COMPUTER CAPITAL accounted for an average of 2.09% of the value of output each year, this implies a gross MP (increase in dollar output per dollar of capital stock) for COMPUTER CAPITAL of approximately 81%[14] per year. In other words, an additional dollar of computer capital stock is associated with an increase in output of 81 cents per year on the margin.[15]

Table 1.3 *Base Regressions—Coefficient Estimates and Implied Gross Rates of Return. All Parameters (except Year Dummy) Constrained to Be Equal across Years*

Parameter	Coefficients	Marginal product
β_1 (COMPUTER CAPITAL)	0.0169***	81.0%
	(0.00431)	
β_2 (NON-COMPUTER CAPITAL)	0.0608***	6.26%
	(0.00466)	
β_3 (IS STAFF)	0.0178***	2.62
	(0.00526)	
β_4 (OTHER LABOUR & EXP.)	0.883***	
	(0.00724)	1.07
Dummy variables	Year*** & Sector***	
R^2 (1991)	97.5%	
N (1991)	293	
N (total)	1121	

Key: *** – $p < 0.01$, ** – $p < 0.05$, * – $p < 0.1$, standard errors in parenthesis

The estimate for the output elasticity for IS STAFF was 0.0178, which indicates that each dollar spent here is associated with a marginal increase in OUTPUT of $2.62. The surprisingly high return to information systems labour may reflect systematic differences in human capital,[16] since IS staff are likely to have more education than other workers. The high return may partially explain Krueger's (1993) finding that workers who use computers are paid a wage premium.

The above estimates strongly support hypothesis H1, that the contribution of IT is positive. The t-statistics for our estimates of the elasticity of COMPUTER CAPITAL and IS STAFF are 3.92 and 3.38 respectively, so we can reject the null hypothesis of zero contribution of IT at the 0.001 (two-tailed) confidence level for both. We can also reject the joint hypothesis that they are both equal to zero ($\chi^2(2) + 43.9$, $p < .0001$).

To assess H2 (that the contribution of IT is greater than its cost), it is necessary to estimate the cost of COMPUTER CAPITAL and IS STAFF. After these costs are subtracted from the gross benefits reported above, we can then assess whether the remaining "net" benefits are positive. Because IS STAFF is a flow variable, calculating net benefits is straightforward: a dollar of IS STAFF costs one dollar, so the gross marginal product of $2.62 implies a net marginal product of $1.62. For IS STAFF, we can reject the null hypothesis that the returns equal costs in favour of the hypothesis that returns exceed costs at the .05 confidence level ($\chi^2(1) = 4.4$, $p < .035$).

Assessing H2 for COMPUTER CAPITAL, which is a stock variable, requires that we determine how much of the capital stock is "used up" each year and must be replaced just to return to the level at the beginning of the year. This is done by multiplying the annual depreciation[17] rate for computers by the capital stock in place. According to the Bureau of Economic Analysis, the average service life of "Office, Computing and Accounting Machinery" is seven years (Bureau of Economic Analysis, 1987). If a seven-year service life for computer capital is assumed, then the above gross marginal product should be reduced by subtracting just over 14% per year, so that after seven years the capital stock will be fully replaced. This procedure yields a *net* marginal of 67%. However, a more conservative assumption is that COMPUTER CAPITAL (in particular PCs) could have an average service life as short as three years, which implies that the net rate of return should be reduced by 33%. This would yield a *net* MP estimate of 48%. In either case, we can reject the null hypothesis that the net marginal returns to computers are zero (p < .01).

However, it should be noted that the full cost of computers involves other considerations than just the decline in value of the asset itself. For instance, calculating a Jorgensonian cost of capital (Christensen and Jorgenson, 1969) would also attempt to account for the effects of taxes, adjustment costs and capital gains or losses, in addition to depreciation costs. On the other hand, firms invest in IT at least partly to move down the learning curve (Brynjolfsson, 1993) or create options (Kambil, Henderson and Mohsenzadeh, 1993) and these effects may create "assets" offsetting some of the losses to depreciation. The high gross marginal product of COMPUTER CAPITAL suggests that if the total annual cost of COMPUTER CAPITAL were as much as 40%, its net marginal product would be greater than zero by a statistically significant amount.

An alternative approach to assessing H2 is to consider the *opportunity cost* of investing in COMPUTER CAPITAL or IS STAFF. A dollar spent in either of these areas could have generated a gross return of over 6% if it had instead been spent on NON-COMPUTER CAPITAL, or a net return of 7% if it were spent on OTHER LABOUR AND EXPENSE. In this interpretation, there are only excess returns to COMPUTER CAPITAL or IS STAFF if the returns exceed the return of the respective non-IS component.

As shown in Table 1.4, we can reject the hypothesis that the *net* MP for COMPUTER CAPITAL is equal to the MP for NON-COMPUTER CAPITAL, assuming a service life of as little as three years for COMPUTER CAPITAL (and none for NON-COMPUTER CAPITAL) at the .05 confidence level. Similarly, we can reject the hypothesis that IS STAFF generates the same returns as spending on OTHER LABOUR AND EXPENSE (p < .05).

Our confidence in the regression taken as a whole is increased by the fact that the estimated output elasticities for the other, non-IT, factors of

Table 1.4 χ^2 Tests for Differences in Marginal Product between COMPUTER CAPI-
TAL and OTHER CAPITAL (return on COMPUTER CAPITAL greater than return on OTHER
CAPITAL)

Return difference tests COMPUTER CAPITAL vs. OTHER CAPITAL	Return	χ^2 Statistic	Significance
Gross return	81%	15.5	$p < .001$
Net—7-year service life	67%	10.6	$p < .01$
Net—3-year service life	48%	5.5	$p < .02$

production were all positive and each was consistent not only with economic theory (i.e. they imply a real rate of return on non-IT factors of 6–7%), but also with estimates of other researchers working with similar data (for example Hall, 1993; Loveman, 1994). Furthermore, the elasticities summed to just over one, implying constant or slightly increasing returns to scale overall, which is consistent with the estimates of aggregate production functions by other researchers (Berndt, 1991). The R^2 hovered around 99%, indicating that our independent variables could "explain" most of the variance in output.

What Factors Affect the Rates of Return for Computers?

The estimates described above were based on the assumption that the parameters did not vary over time, in different sectors, or across different subsamples of firms. Therefore, they should be interpreted only as overall averages. However, by using the multiple equations approach, it is also possible to address questions such as: "Has the return to computers been consistently high, or did it vary over time?" and "Have some sectors of the economy had more success in using computers?" We address these questions by allowing the parameters to vary by year or by sector.

Economic theory predicts that managers will increase investments in any inputs that achieve higher than normal returns and that as investment increases, marginal rates of return eventually fall to normal levels. This pattern is supported by our findings for COMPUTER CAPITAL, which exhibited higher levels of investment (stock increases > 25% per year) and lower returns over time. We find that the rates of return are fairly consistent over the period 1987–9 and then drop in 1990–91. We can reject the null hypothesis of equality of returns over time in the full sample ($\chi^2(4) = 11.2$, $p < .02$). Nonetheless, even at the end of the period, the returns to COMPUTER CAPITAL still exceed the returns to NON-COMPUTER CAPITAL. However, these results should be interpreted with caution since they are particularly sensitive to sample changes and time-specific exogenous events such as the 1991 recession.[18]

Roach (1987) has argued that the service sector uses computers much less efficiently than manufacturing and points to aggregate statistics which report higher overall productivity growth for manufacturing than for services. Our data set allows us to reconsider this claim in the light of more disaggregated data. The marginal product (ignoring the mining sector which includes only 10 firms and has a large standard error) varies from 10% in transportation and utilities to 127% in non-durable manufacturing. While there have been some suggestions that reorganizing service processes around a "factory" model may help services achieve productivity gains comparable to manufacturing, we cannot confirm that the differences in measured returns are due to fundamental differences, or simply to "noise" in the data. Although the returns to computers in durable and non-durable manufacturing are as high or higher than the returns in any other sector, we are unable to reject the hypothesis that these rates of return are the same across most sectors due to the imprecision of the estimates (without mining, $\chi^2(4) = 6.6$, p $< .16$).

A second area that can be addressed by our data and method is technology strategy. We have already found that firms with more computer capital will, *ceteris paribus*, have higher sales than firms with less computer capital, but do the *types* of computer equipment purchased make a difference? We have data on two categories of equipment: central processors, such as mainframes, and PCs and terminals. For this analysis, we divide the sample into three equal groups based on the ratio of central processor value to PCs and terminals. We find that the rate of return is highest for firms using a more balanced mix of PCs and mainframes (see Table 1.5), and lower for firms at either extreme. One interpretation of this finding is that an IS strategy which relies too heavily on one category of equipment and users will be less effective than a more even-handed approach which allows a better "division of labour".

Sensitivity Analysis and Possible Biases—Econometric Issues

Our estimates of the return to COMPUTER CAPITAL required that a number of assumptions be made about the econometric specification and the construction of the data set. This and the following section explore the validity of our assumptions and generally find that the results are robust.

The econometric assumptions required for ISUR to produce unbiased estimates of both the parameters and the standard errors are similar

Table 1.5 *Split Sample Regression Results—Mainframes as a Percentage of Total* COMPUTER CAPITAL

Coefficient estimates and marginal product for COMPUTER CAPITAL
Grouping based on mainframes as a percentage of total COMPUTER CAPITAL

Sample split	Highest	Middle	Lowest	Statistical ordering[1]
Elasticity estimate (β_1)	0.0113**	0.0159***	0.0117**	
Standard error	(0.00500)	(0.00528)	(0.00521)	Med > (High,Low)
Marginal product (MP$_c$)	49.1%	79.5%	58.2%	($p < 0.03$)
Mean % mainframes	74%	54%	34%	
Group std. Dev.	9%	5%	8%	

Key: *** – $p < 0.01$, ** – $p < 0.05$, * – $p < 0.1$, standard errors in parenthesis
Note: 1   Ordering by χ^2 tests of *return* differences. P-value shown represents null hypothesis of equality across groups.

to those for OLS: the error term must be uncorrelated with the regressors (inputs) and homoskedastic in the cross-section.[19] ISUR implicitly corrects for serial correlation and heteroskedasticity over time in our formulation, so that additional restrictions on the error structure are not necessary. Nonetheless, we computed single-year OLS estimates both with and without heteroskedasticity-consistent standard errors to test for heteroskedasticity, and plotted the residuals from the basic specification to assess normality. These analyses suggest that neither of these assumptions was violated, although even if they were coefficient estimates (even for OLS) they would still be unbiased and consistent (but standard errors would be incorrect).

However, the assumption that the error term is uncorrelated with the inputs (orthogonality) is potentially an issue. One way in which this assumption could be violated is if the causality is reversed: instead of increases in purchases of inputs (e.g. computers) leading to higher output, an increase in output could lead to further investment (for example, a firm spends the proceeds from an unexpected increase in demand on more computer equipment). The orthogonality assumption can also be violated if the input variables are measured with error. The direction of bias of the coefficients from measurement error is dependent on both the correlation between the variables as well as the correlation between measurement errors (see Kmenta (1986) for a complete discussion).[20]

Regardless of the source of the error, it is possible to correct for the potential bias using instrumental variables methods, or two-stage least squares (2SLS). We use once-lagged values of variables as instruments, since by definition they cannot be associated with unanticipated shocks in the dependent variable in the following year.[21] Table 1.6 reports a comparison of pooled OLS estimates with 2SLS estimates and shows that the coefficient estimates are similar, although somewhat higher for COMPUTER CAPITAL and lower for IS STAFF. In both cases the standard errors were substantially larger, as is expected when instrumental variables are used. Using a Hausman specification test, we cannot reject the null hypothesis that the error term is uncorrelated with the regressors (see bottom of Table 1.6 for test statistics) and therefore do not reject our initial specification.

Sensitivity Analysis and Possible Biases–Data Issues

To explore further the robustness of our results, we examined the impact of the possible data errors discussed above that can be tested: error in the valuation of PCs and terminals; errors in the price deflators; and understatement or misclassification of computer capital.

To assess the sensitivity of the results to possible errors in the valuation of PCs and terminals, we recalculated the basic regressions, varying the assumed average PC and terminal value from $0 to $6K.

Table 1.6 *Specification Test—Comparison of OLS and Two-Stage Least Squares. All Parameters (except Year Dummy) Constrained to Be Equal across Years*

Parameter	OLS estimates	2SLS estimates
β_1 (COMPUTER CAPITAL)	0.0284***	0.0435***
	(0.00723)	(0.0126)
β_2 (NON-COMPUTER CAPITAL)	0.0489***	0.0481***
	(0.00668)	(0.00702)
β_3 (IS STAFF)	0.0191***	0.00727
	(0.00795)	(0.0116)
β_4 (NON-IS LABOUR & EXP.)	0.881***	0.879***
	(0.0113)	(0.0125)
Dummy variables	Year*** & Sector***	Year*** & Sector***
R^2	98.3%	98.3%
N (total)	702	702

Key: *** – $p < 0.01$, ** – $p < 0.05$, * – $p < 0.1$, standard errors in parentheses
Note: OLS estimates are for sample of same firms as were available for 2SLS regression ($n = 702$).

Hausman test results (instruments are lagged independent variables):
$\chi^2 (4) = 6.40$, ($p < 0.17$)—cannot reject exogeneity

Note that as the assumed value of PCs and terminals increases, the increase in COMPUTER CAPITAL will be matched by an equal decrease in NON-COMPUTER CAPITAL, which is calculated as a residual. Interestingly, the return to COMPUTER CAPITAL in the basic regression is not very sensitive to the assumed value of PCs and terminals, ranging from 77% if they are not counted to 59% if PCs and terminals are counted at $6K (peaking at about 85%).

A second contribution to error is the understatement of output due to errors in the price deflators. While it is difficult to correct directly for this problem, we estimated the basic equations year by year, so that errors in the relative deflators would have no impact on the elasticity estimates. The estimated marginal products ranged from 109% to 197% in the individual year regressions versus 81% when all five years were estimated simultaneously. The standard error on the estimates was significantly higher for all estimates, which can account for the greater range of estimates. Overall, this suggests that our basic findings are not a result of the assumed price deflators. However, if the price deflators systematically underestimate the value of intangible product change over time or between firms, our measure of output will be understated, implying that the actual return for computer capital is higher than our estimates.

To assess the third source of error, possible understatement or misclassification of computer capital, we consider three cases: hidden computer spending exists, but does not show up elsewhere in the data; hidden computer spending exists and shows up in the "NON-IS LABOUR AND EXPENSE" category; or hidden computer spending exists and shows up in the "OTHER CAPITAL" category. If the hidden IS costs do not show up elsewhere in the firm (e.g. software development or training costs from previous years), then the effect on the estimated returns is dependent on how closely correlated these costs are to our measured COMPUTER CAPITAL. If they are uncorrelated, our estimate for the elasticity and the return to COMPUTER CAPITAL is unbiased. If the missing costs are perfectly correlated with the observed costs, then, because of the logarithmic form of our specification, they will result only in a multiplicative scaling of the variables, and the estimated elasticities and the estimated standard error will be unchanged.[22] For the same reason, the sign and statistical significance of our results for the returns to COMPUTER CAPITAL and IS STAFF will also be unaffected. However, the denominator used for the MP calculations will be affected by increasing computer capital, so the estimated MP will be proportionally lower or higher. For instance, if the hidden costs were to lead to a doubling of the true costs of computer capital, then the true MP would fall from 81% to just over 40%. Finally, if the hidden costs were negatively correlated with the observed costs, then the true returns would be higher than our estimates.

A second possible case is that hidden IS capital expenses (e.g. software) show up in the NON-IS LABOUR AND EXPENSE category. To estimate the potential impact of these omissions, we estimate the potential size of the omitted, misclassified IS capital relative to COMPUTER CAPITAL using data from another IDG survey (IDC, 1991) on aggregate IS expenditures, including software as well as hardware. To derive a reasonable lower bound on the returns to COMPUTER CAPITAL, we assume that the misclassified IS capital had an average service life of three years, and further make the worst-case assumption of perfect correlation between misclassified IS capital and COMPUTER CAPITAL (and reduce proportionally the amount of NON-IS LABOUR AND EXPENSE). In this scenario, our estimates for the amount of COMPUTER CAPITAL in firms roughly double, yet the rates of return are little unchanged from the basic analysis that does not include misclassified IS capital (68% vs 81%). This surprising result appears to be due to the fact that the return on NON-IS LABOUR AND EXPENSE is at least as high as the return on COMPUTER CAPITAL, so moving costs from one category to another does not change overall returns a great deal.

Alternatively, a third possible case is that the hidden IS capital expenditures show up in OTHER CAPITAL. This would apply to items such as telecommunications hardware which would normally be classified as capital expenditure. In this case, the marginal product of COMPUTER CAPITAL will be reduced proportionally to the amount of the misclassification. Intuitively, this case is similar to the case discussed earlier in which the hidden costs are perfectly correlated with measured costs but do not appear elsewhere. Our simulation results indicate that the elasticities on computer capital vary less than 5%, even between assumptions of 0% to 100% of computer capital being misclassified.

Irrespective of these sensitivity calculations, it should be noted that the definition of COMPUTER CAPITAL used in this study was fairly narrow and did not include items such as telecommunications equipment, scientific instruments or networking equipment. The findings should be interpreted accordingly and do not necessarily apply to broader definitions of IT. However, to the extent that the assumptions of our sensitivity analysis hold, the general finding that IT contributes significantly to output is robust (H1), although the actual point estimates of marginal product may vary, possibly resulting in no statistical difference between returns to computer capital and returns to other capital.

DISCUSSION

Comparison with Earlier Research

Although we found evidence that computer capital and IS labour increase output significantly under a variety of formulations (see summary Table 1.7), several other studies have failed to find evidence that IT increases output. Because the models we used were similar to those used by several previous researchers, we attribute our different findings primarily to our larger and more recent data set. Specifically, there are at least three reasons for our results differing from previous results.

First, we examined a later time period (1987–91) than did Loveman (1978–82), Barua, Kriebel and Mukhopadhyay (1978–82) or Berndt and Morrison (1968–86). The massive build-up of computer capital is a

Table 1.7 *Summary of Hypothesis Tests*

Hypothesis	Description of test (alternative hypothesis)	Test statistic
H1	Positive marginal product for COMPUTER CAPITAL	$t = 3.92$, $p < 0.01$
H1	Positive marginal product for IS STAFF	$t = 3.38$, $p < 0.01$
H1	Simultaneous test for positive marginal product for COMPUTER CAPITAL and IS STAFF	$\chi^2(2) = 43.9$, $p < 0.01$
H2	Positive net marginal product for COMPUTER CAPITAL (see Table 1.6), cost @ 14% (7-year average life)	$t = 3.24$, $p < 0.01$
H2	Positive net marginal product for COMPUTER CAPITAL (see Table 1.6), cost @ 33% (3-year average life)	$t = 2.32$, $p < 0.05$
H2	Positive net marginal product for IS STAFF	$\chi^2(1) = 4.4$, $p < 0.05$
H2	Marginal product of COMPUTER CAPITAL exceeds marginal product of OTHER CAPITAL	see Table 1.6
H2	Marginal product of IS STAFF exceeds marginal product of OTHER LABOUR and EXPENSE	$\chi^2(1) = 4.0$, $p < 0.05$
Extension of H1	Marginal product of COMPUTER CAPITAL changes across time	$\chi^2(4) = 11.2$, $p < 0.02$
Extension of H1	Marginal product of COMPUTER CAPITAL varies across sectors	$\chi^2(4) = 6.6$, $p < 0.2$
Extension of H1	Marginal product varies by mainframes as a percentage of total COMPUTER CAPITAL	$\chi^2(2) = 6.9$, $p < 0.03$

relatively recent phenomenon. Indeed, the delivered amount of computer power in the companies in our sample is likely to be at least an order of magnitude greater than that in comparable firms from the period studied by the other authors. Brynjolfsson (1993) argues that even if the MP of IT were twice that of non-IT capital, its impact on output in the 1970s or early 1980s would not have been large enough to be detected with available data by conventional estimation procedures. Furthermore, the changes in business processes needed to realize the benefits of IT may have taken some time to implement, so it is possible that the actual returns from investments in computers were at first fairly low. In particular, computers may have initially created organizational slack which was only recently eliminated, perhaps hastened by the increased attention engendered by earlier studies that indicated a potential productivity shortfall and suggestions that "to computerize the office, you have to reinvent the office" (Thurow, 1990). Apparently, an analogous period of organizational redesign was necessary to unleash the benefits of electric motors (David, 1990).

A pattern of low initial returns is also consistent with the strategy for optimal investment in the presence of "learning by using": short-term returns should initially be lower than returns for other capital, but subsequently rise to exceed the returns to other capital, compensating for the "investment" in learning (Lester and McCabe, 1993). Under this interpretation, our high estimates of computer MP indicate that businesses are beginning to reap rewards from the experimentation and learning phase in the early 1980s.

Secondly, we were able to use different and more detailed firm-level data than had been available before. We argue that the effects of computers in increasing variety, quality or other intangibles are more likely to be detected in firm-level data than in the aggregate data. Unfortunately, all such data, including ours, is likely to include data errors. It is possible that the data errors in our sample happened to be more favourable (or less unfavourable) to computers than those in other samples. We attempted to minimize the influence of data errors by cross-checking with other data sources, eliminating outliers, and examining the robustness of the results to different subsamples and specifications. In addition, the large size of our sample should, by the law of large numbers, mitigate the influence of random disturbances. Indeed, the precision of our estimates was generally much higher than those of previous studies; the statistical significance of our estimates owes as much to the tighter confidence bounds as to higher point estimates.

Thirdly, our sample consisted entirely of relatively large, Fortune 500 firms. It is possible that the high IS contribution we find is limited to these larger firms. However, an earlier study (Brynjolfsson *et al.*, 1994) found evidence that smaller firms may benefit disproportionately from investments in information technology. In any event, because firms in the sample accounted for a large share of the total US output, the economic relevance of our findings is not heavily dependent on extrapolation of the results to firms outside of the sample.

Managerial Implications

If the spending on computers is correlated with significantly higher returns than spending on other types of capital, it does not necessarily follow that companies should increase spending on computers. The firms with high returns and high levels of computer investment may differ systematically from the low performers in ways that cannot be rectified simply by increasing spending. For instance, recent economic theory has suggested that "modern manufacturing", involving high intensity of computer usage, may require a radical change in organization (Milgrom and Roberts, 1990). This possibility is emphasized in numerous management books and articles (see for example Malone and Rockart, 1991; Scott Morton, 1991) and supported in our discussions with managers, both at their firms and during a workshop on IT and Productivity attended by approximately 30 industry representatives.[23]

Furthermore, our results showing a high gross marginal product may be indicative of the differences between computer investment and other types of investment. For instance, managers may perceive IS investment as riskier than other investments, and therefore require higher expected returns to compensate for the increased risk. Finally, IS is often cited as an enabling technology which does not just produce productivity improvements for individuals, but provides benefits by facilitating business process redesign or improving the ability of groups to work together. In this sense, our results may be indicative of the substantial payoffs of reengineering and other recent business innovations.

CONCLUSION

We have conducted a preliminary examination of over 1000 observations on output and several inputs at the firm level for 1987–91. The firms in our sample had aggregate sales of over $1.8 trillion in 1991 and thus account for a substantial share of the US economy. We examined several specifications, different subsamples of the data, and attempted to validate some of the assumptions of our econometric procedures to the extent possible. Overall, we found that computers contribute significantly to firm-level output, even after accounting for depreciation, measurement error and some data limitations.

Given that this is the first look at this new data, there are a number of other directions in which this work could be extended. First, the data set could be extended to include alternative measures of output, such as value added, and to include additional inputs, such as R&D, that have been explored in other literature (see Brynjolfsson and Hitt, 1995). Secondly, although our approach allowed us to infer the value created by intangibles like product variety by looking at changes in the revenues at the firm level, more direct approaches might also be promising, for example directly accounting for intangible outputs such as product quality or variety.

Finally, the type of extension which is likely to have the greatest impact on practice is further analysis of the factors which differentiate firms with high returns to IT from low performers. For instance, is the current "downsizing" of firms leading to higher IT productivity? Are the firms that have undertaken substantial "reengineering efforts" also the ones with the highest returns? Since this study has presented evidence that the computer "productivity paradox" is a thing of the past, it seems appropriate that the next round of work should focus on identifying the strategies which have led to large IT productivity.

ACKNOWLEDGEMENTS

This research has been generously supported by the MIT Center for Coordination Science, the MIT Industrial Performance Center and the MIT International Financial Services Research Center. We thank Martin Neil Baily, Rajiv Banker, Ernst Berndt, Geoff Brooke, Zvi Griliches, Bronwyn Hall, Susan Humphrey, Dan Sichel, Robert Solow, Paul Strassmann, Diane Wilson, three anonymous referees and seminar participants at Boston University, Citibank, Harvard Business School, the International Conference on Information Systems, MIT, National Technical University in Singapore, Stanford University, the University of California at Irvine and the US Federal Reserve for valuable comments, while retaining responsibility for any errors that remain. We are also grateful to International Data Group for providing essential data. An earlier, abbreviated version of this paper was published in the *Proceedings of the International Conference on Information Systems, 1993*, under the title "Is Information Systems Spending Productive? New Evidence and New Results".

NOTES

1 An observation is one year of data on all variables for a specific firm. We did not have all five years of data for every firm, but the data set does include at least one year of data for 367 different firms.

2 The database contains standard financial information, IT spending data and other economic measures such as product prices and quality for 60 business units of 20 firms over the period 1978–84. See Loveman (1994) for a more detailed description.

3 Another common way to operationalize the theory is to use the production function to derive a "cost function" which provides the minimum cost required for a given level of output. While cost functions have some attractive features, they require access to firm-level price information for each input, which are data we do not have.

4 A more complete model might include other variables describing management practices or lags of IT spending. We do not consider lags because we already use an IT stock variable and the panel is too short to consider lags.

5 For instance, Hall (1993) introduces her Cobb-Douglas production function with the words: "using the by now standard growth accounting framework".

6 Formally, the output elasticity of computers, E_C, is defined as: "For our production function, F, this reduces to:" The MP for computers is simply the output elasticity multiplied by the ratio of output to computer input.

7 Sometimes also called IZEF, the iterated version of Zellner's efficient estimator. By leaving the covariance matrix across years unconstrained this procedure implicitly corrects for serial correlation among the equations, even when there are missing observations for some firms in some years.

8 Specifically, the survey targets Fortune 500 manufacturing and Fortune 500 service firms that are in the top half of their industry by sales (see Table 1.2a).

9 Compustat II provides financial and other related information for publicly traded firms, primarily obtained through annual reports and regulatory filings.

10 This matching procedure may be sensitive to possible reverse causality between OUTPUT and IS LABOUR, as is shown by our Hausman test in Table 1.6.

11 Specifically, we estimated the value of terminals and the value of PCs and then weighted them by the proportion of PCs versus terminals. For terminals, we estimated the value as the average list price of an IBM 3151 terminal in 1989, which is $609 (Pelaia, 1993). For PCs, we used the average nominal PC cost over 1989–91 of $4447, as reported in Berndt and Griliches (1990). These figures were then weighted by the proportion of PCs to terminals in the 1993 IDG survey (58% terminals). The resulting estimate was .42*$609 + .58* $4447 = $2835.

12 An alternative measure of capital stock was computed by converting historical capital investment data into a capital stock using the Winfrey S-3 table. This approach was used in earlier versions of this paper (Brynjolfsson and Hitt 1993), with similar results. However, the calculation shown above is more consistent with previous research (see for example Hall, 1993).

13 The impact of these changes in both cases was to lower the return to

COMPUTER CAPITAL slightly as compared to the results on the full sample.
14 As outlined in note 6, which in this case is .0169/.0209 = .8086 or about 81%.
15 It is worth noting that our approach provides estimates of the *marginal* product of each input: how much the last dollar of stock or flow added to output. In general, infra-marginal investments have higher rates of return than marginal investments, so the return to the first dollar invested in computers is likely to be even higher than the marginal returns we reported.
16 We thank Dan Sichel for pointing this out.
17 Technically, "negative capital gains" may be a more accurate term than "depreciation", since computer equipment is more likely to be replaced because of the arrival of cheaper, faster alternatives than because it simply wears out.
18 A decline in the returns to COMPUTER CAPITAL between 1989 and 1990 is also evident in a balanced panel of 201 firms in the sample for 1989–91.
19 Note that if we had used OLS, further assumptions would be required: that all error terms are independent and that there is constant variance over time.
20 If an input variable is systematically understated by a constant multiplicative factor, then the coefficient estimates would be unchanged.
21 However, in the presence of individual firm effects, lagged values are not valid instruments. While we did not test for firm effects, we suspect that they may be important and so the results of our 2SLS estimates should be interpreted with caution.
22 This is because multiplicative scaling of a regressor in a logarithmic specification will not change the coefficient estimate or the standard error. All the influence of the multiplier will appear in the intercept term which is not crucial to our analysis.
23 The MIT Center for Coordination Science and International Financial Services Research Center jointly sponsored a Workshop on IT and Productivity which was held in December 1992.

REFERENCES

Alpar, P. and Kim, M. (1991). A Microeconomic Approach to the Measurement of Information Technology Value. *Journal of Management Information Systems*, Fall, 7, 2, 55–69.

Baily, M.N. and Gordon, R.J. (1988). The Productivity Slowdown, Measurement Issues, and the Explosion of Computer Power. In Brainard, W.C. and Perry, G.L. (eds) *Brookings Papers on Economic Activity*, The Brookings Institution, Washington, DC, 347–431.

Barua, A., Kriebel, C. and Mukhopadhyay, T. (1991). Information Technology and Business Value: an Analytic and Empirical Investigation. *University of Texas at Austin Working Paper*, Texas (May).

Berndt, E. (1991). *The Practice of Econometrics: Classic and Contemporary*, Addison-Wesley, Reading, MA.

Berndt, E.R. and Morrison, C.J. (1995). High-tech Capital Formation and Economic Performance in U.S. Manufacturing Industries: an Exploratory Analysis, *Journal of Econometrics*, 1, 65, 9–43.

Brynjolfsson, E. (1993). The Productivity Paradox of Information Technology, *Communications of the ACM*, 35, 66–77.

Brynjolfsson, E. (1994). Technology's True Payoff, *Informationweek*, October 10, 34–6.

Brynjolfsson, E. and Hitt, L. (1993). Is Information Systems Spending Productive? New Evidence and New Results. *Proceedings of the 14th International Conference on Information Systems*, Orlando, Florida.

Brynjolfsson, E. and Hitt, L. (1995). Information Technology as a Factor of Production: the Role of Differences Among Firms. *Economics of Innovation and New Technology*, 3, 4, 183–200.

Brynjolfsson, E., Malone, T., Gurbaxani, V. and Kambil, A. (1994). Does Information Technology Lead to Smaller Firms? *Management Science*, 40, 12.

Bureau of Economic Analysis, U.S. D.o.C. (1987). *Fixed Reproducible Tangible Wealth in the United States, 1925–85*, US Government Printing Office, Washington, DC.

Byrd, T. and Marshall, T. (1997). Relating Information Technology Investment to Organizational Performance. *Omega*, 25, 1, 43–56.

Christensen, L.R. and Jorgenson, D. (1969). The Measurement of U.S. Real Capital Input, 1929–1967. *Review of Income and Wealth*, 15, 4, 293–320.

Council of Economic Advisors (ed.) (1992). *Economic Report of the President*. US Government Printing Office, Washington DC.

David, P.A. (1990). The Dynamo and the Computer and Dynamo: a Historical Perspective on the Modern Productivity Paradox. *American Economic Review Papers and Proceedings*, 80, 2, 355–61 (May).

Dos Santos, B.L., Peffers, K.G. and Mauer, D.C. (1993). The Impact of Information Technology Investment Announcements on the Market Value of the Firm. *Information Systems Research*, 4, 1, 1–23.

Gordon, Robert J. (1990). *The Measurement of Durable Goods Prices*. University of Chicago Press, Chicago.

Gorman, J.A. (1992). *Personal communication*. Output deflators by industry. Raw data provided on computer disk from Bureau of Economic Analysis, Washington.

Hall, B.H. (1990). *The Manufacturing Sector Master File: 1959–1987, Documentation*. NBER Working Paper 3366.

Hall, B.H. (1993). The Stock Market's Valuation of R&D Investment During the 1980's. *American Economic Review*, 83, 2, 259–64.

Harris, S.E. and Katz, J.L. (1988). Profitability and Information Technology Capital Intensity in the Insurance Industry. *In Proceedings of the Twenty-First Hawaii International Conference on System Science*, 124–30.

Hitt, L. and Brynjolfsson, E. (1996). Productivity, Business Profitability and Consumer Surplus: Three Different Measures of IT Value. *MIS Quarterly*, 20, 2, 121–42.

International Data Corporation (IDC) (1991). *U.S. Information Technology Spending Patterns, 1969–1994*, IDC Special Report 5368, IDC, New York.

Kambil, A., Henderson, J. and Mohsenzadeh, H. (1993). Strategic Management of Information Technology Investments: an Options Perspective. In Banker, R., Kaufman, R. and Mahmood, M. (eds) *Strategic Information Technology Management: Perspectives on Organizational Growth and Competitive Advantage*, Idea Group Publishing, Harrisburg, PA, 161–78.

Krueger, A. (1993). How Computers Have Changed the Wage Structure: Evidence from Micro-data, 1984–1989. *Quarterly Journal of Economics*, 108, 1, 33–60.

Lester, R. and McCabe M.J. (1993) The Effect of Industrial Structure on Learning by Doing in Nuclear Power Plant Performance. *Rand Journal of Economics*, 24, 3, 418–38.

Loveman, G.W. (1994). An Assessment of the Productivity Impact on Information Technologies. In Allen, T.J. and Scott Morton, M. (eds) *Information Technology and the Corporation of the 1990s: Research Studies*. MIT Press, Cambridge, MA, 84–110.

Maglitta, J. and Sullivan-Trainor, M. (eds) (1991). *The Premier 100*. CW Publishing, Framingham, MA.

Mairesse, J. and Hall, B. (1993). *R&D Investment and Productivity Growth in the 1980s: a First Look at the United States and French Manufacturing Sectors*. Prepared for the AEA Meetings, Anaheim, CA.

Malone, T. and Rockart, J. (1991). Computers, Networks and the Corporation. *Scientific American*, 265, 3, 128–36.

Milgrom, P. and Roberts, J. (1990). The Economics of Modern Manufacturing: Technology, Strategy and Organization. *American Economic Review*, 80, 3, 511–28.

Morrison, C.J. and Berndt, E.R. (1990). Assessing the Productivity of Information Technology Equipment in the U.S. Manufacturing Industries, *National Bureau of Economic Research Working Paper 3582*, New York (January).

Pelaia, E. (1993). IBM terminal prices, personal communication with IBM representative.

Popkin, J. and Company (1992). *The Impact of Measurement and Analytical Issues in Assessing Industry Productivity and its Relation to Computer Investment*. mimeo, Washington DC, October.

Quinn, M.A. *et al.*, (1993). Critical Issues of Information Systems Management for 1993. *The Sixth Annual Survey of Information Systems Management Issues*. CSC Index, Cambridge, MA.

Roach, S. (1987). *America's Technology Dilemma: a Profile of the Information Economy*. Morgan Stanley Special Economic Study, New York (April).

Scott Morton, M. (ed.) (1991). *The Corporation of the 1990s: Information Technology and Organizational Transformation*. Oxford University Press, New York.

Siegel, D., Donald, R. and Griliches, Z. (1992). Purchased Services, Outsourcing, Computers, and Productivity in Manufacturing. In Griliches *et al.* (eds) *Output Measurement in the Service Sectors*, University of Chicago Press, Chicago.

Simon, H. (1984). On the Behavioral and Rational Foundations of Economic Dynamics. *Journal of Economic Behavior and Organizations*, 1, 5, 35–66.

Strassmann, P.A. (1990). *The Business Value of Computers*. Information Economics Press, New Canaan, Connecticut.

Thurow, L. (1990). Are Investments in Information Systems Paying off? *MIT Management*, Spring.

Varian, H. (1992). *Microeconomic Analysis*, 3rd edn. W.W. Norton & Company, New York.

Weill, P. (1992). The Relationship Between Investment in Information Technology and Firm Performance: a Study of the Valve Manufacturing Sector. *Information Systems Research*, 3, 4, 307–33.

Wilson, D. (1993). Assessing the Impact of Information Technology on Organizational Performance. In Banker, R., Kauffman, R. and Mahmood, M.A. (eds) *Strategic Information Technology Management: Perspectives on Organizational Growth and Competitive Advantage*. Idea Group, Harrisburg, PA.

2
In Search of Information Technology Productivity: Assessment Issues

LESLIE P. WILLCOCKS AND STEPHANIE LESTER
Oxford Institute of Information Management

Computers everywhere, except in the productivity statistics. (Solow, 1987)

INTRODUCTION

The history of numerous failed and disappointing information technology (IT) investments in work organizations has been richly documented. The 1993 abandonment of the five-year Taurus project in the London financial markets, in this case at a cost of £80 million to the Stock Exchange and possibly £400 million to City institutions, provides only high-profile endorsement of underlying disquiet on the issue (Currie, 1994). In the USA the Confirm and California Department of Motor Vehicles project failures are also often cited as similar high-profile disasters (Flowers, 1996). In practice, survey and case research has consistently established IT investment as a high-risk, hidden-cost business, with a variety of factors, including the size and complexity of the project, the "newness" of the technology, the degree of "structuredness" in the project, and major human, political and cultural factors compounding the risks (Willcocks and Lester, 1996; Willcocks and Margetts, 1993). Alongside, indeed we would argue contributing to, the performance issues surrounding IT is accumulated evidence of problems in IT evaluation, together with a history of general indifferent

Beyond the IT Productivity Paradox.
Edited by L. P. Willcocks and S. Lester © 1999 John Wiley & Sons Ltd.

organizational practice in the area (as examples only see Farbey, Land and Targett, 1992; Strassmann, 1990, 1997).

Continuing from the Introduction and Chapter 1, here we focus first on the relationship between IT performance and its evaluation as it is expressed in the "IT productivity paradox" debate. We shall find that, while much of the sense of disappointment may be justified, at the same time it is fed by limitations in evaluation techniques and processes, and by misunderstandings of the contribution that IT can and does make to organizations, as much as by actual experience of poorly performing information systems. The focus then moves to how organizations may seek to improve their IT/IS evaluation procedures and processes. Taking into account the many limitations in evaluation practice continuing to be identified by a range of the more recent research studies, a high-level framework is advanced for how evaluation can and needs to be applied across the systems lifecycle. The relevance of this composite approach is then tested against events, managerial intentions and evaluation practices in a UK-based multinational during the 1995–6 period.

Throughout the chapter, information technology (IT) refers to hardware, software and related technical routines, and information systems (IS) to organizational applications, increasingly IT based, that deliver on the information needs of an organization's stakeholders. Note, however, that some sources referred to in this chapter use "IT" to mean both IT and IS.

"WHAT GETS MEASURED GETS MANAGED"—THE WAY FORWARD?

With regard to IT investments, evaluation and management efforts regularly run into difficulties of three generic types. First, many organizations find themselves in a "Catch-22" (Willcocks, 1992). For competitive reasons they cannot afford not to invest in IT, but economically they cannot find sufficient justification, and evaluation practice cannot provide enough underpinning for making the investment. Secondly, for many of the more advanced and intensive users of IT, as the IT infrastructure becomes an inextricable part of the organization's processes and structures, it becomes increasingly difficult to separate out the impact of IT from that of other assets and activities. This may be particularly the case, for example, with start-up companies on the Internet (see Introduction). Thirdly, and despite the high levels of expenditure, there is widespread lack of understanding of IT and information systems (IS) as major capital assets. While senior managers regularly give detailed attention to annual expenditure on IT/IS, there is little awareness of the size of the capital asset that has been bought over the years (Keen, 1991; Willcocks, 1994). Failure to appreciate the size of this investment leads to IT/IS being undermanaged, a lack of serious attention being given to IT/IS evaluation and control, and also a lack of concern for discovering ways of utilizing this IT/IS asset base to its full potential.

Solutions to these difficulties have most often been sought through variants on the mantra: "what gets measured gets managed". As a dominant guiding principle more—and more accurate—measurement has been advanced as the panacea to evaluation difficulties. In a large body of literature, while some consideration is given to the difficulties inherent in quantifying IT impacts, a range of other difficulties are downplayed or even ignored. These include, for example:

- the fact that measurement systems are prone to decay;
- the goal displacement effects of measurement;
- the downside that only that which is measured gets managed;
- the behavioural implications of measurement and related reward systems; and
- the politics inherent in any organizational evaluation activity.

In practice, counter evidence against a narrow focus on quantification for IT/IS evaluation has been gathering. Thus some recent studies point to how measurement can be improved, but also to the limitations of measurement and areas where sets of measures may be needed because of the lack of a single reliable measure (Banker, Kauffman and Mahmood, 1993; Farbey, Land and Targett, 1993; Willcocks, 1996a; Graeser, Willcocks and Pisanias, 1998). They also point to the key role of stakeholder judgement throughout any IT/IS evaluation process. Furthermore, some published research studies point to the political-rational as opposed to the straightforwardly rational aspects of IT measurement in organizations. For example, Lacity and Hirschheim (1996) provide an important insight into how measurement, in this case benchmarking IT performance against external comparators, can be used in political ways to influence senior management judgement. Currie (1989) detailed the political uses of measurement in a paper entitled "The art of justifying new technology to top management"; others focused on a similar issue (Walsham, 1993; Willcocks, Currie and Mason, 1999; see also Chapters 12 and 13).

Additionally, there are signs that the problems with overfocusing on measurement are being recognized, albeit slowly, with moves toward emphasizing the demonstration of the value of IS/IT, not merely its measurement (see Chapters 7, 9 and 11; Banker, Kauffman and Mahmood, 1993; Gillin, 1994ab; LaPlante, 1994; LaPlante and Alter, 1994). Elsewhere we have argued for the need to move measurement itself from a focus on the price of IT to a concern for its value; and for a concomitant shift in emphasis in the measurement regime from control to quality improvement (Willcocks and Lester, 1996). The Introduction to this book also implies that a network-based era requires renewed understanding of both quantitative and qualitative aspects of IT assessment.

These difficulties and limitations in evaluation practice have become bound up with the notion that, despite large investments in IT over many years, it has been difficult to discover where the IT payoffs have occurred, if indeed there have been many (see Introduction and Chapter 1). We now address critically this overall sense that many have that, despite huge investments in IS/IT so far, these have been producing disappointing returns.

REVISITING THE "IT PRODUCTIVITY PARADOX"

As indicated in the Introduction, alongside the seemingly inexorable rise of IS/IT investment in the last 15 years, there have been considerable uncertainty and concern about the productivity impact of IT being experienced in work organizations. This has been reinforced by several high-profile studies at the levels of both the national economy and industrial sector suggesting in fact that if there has been an IS/IT payoff it has been minimal, and hardly justifies the vast financial outlays incurred. Two early influential studies embodying this theme were by Roach and Loveman, while the most recent advocate of this argument was Landauer (Landauer, 1995; Loveman, 1988; Roach, 1986). A key, overarching point needs to be made immediately. It is clear from the review in the Introduction of the many research studies conducted at national, sectoral and organization-specific levels that the failure to identify IS/IT benefits and productivity says as much about the deficiencies in assessment methods and measurement, and the rigour with which they are applied, as about mismanagement of the development and use of information-based technologies (see also Brynjolffson, 1993; Glazer, 1993; Willcocks, 1994). Chapter 1 provided some recent evidence on this theme, and the Introduction offered a detailed overview, but it is useful to chase this hare of the IT productivity paradox further, because the issue goes to the heart of the subject of this Chapter.

Interestingly, the IT productivity paradox is rarely related in the literature to manufacturing sectors for which, in fact, there are a number of studies from the early 1980s on showing rising IT expenditure correlating with sectoral and firm-specific productivity rises (Brynjolffson and Hitt, 1993; Loveman, 1988; Weill, 1990). The high-profile studies raising concern also tend to base their work predominantly on statistics gathered in the US context. Their main focus, in fact, tends to be limited to the service sector in the USA (Hackett, 1990; Roach, 1988, 1991). Recently a number of studies have questioned the data on which such studies were based, suggesting that they are sufficiently flawed to make simple conclusions misleading (Brynjolffson, 1993; Quinn and Baily, 1994). It has been pointed out, for example, that in the cases of Loveman (1988) and Roach (1986) neither personally collected the data that they analysed, thus their observations describe numbers rather than actual business experiences (see Chapter 3; also van Nievelt, 1992).

Still others argue that the productivity payoff may have been delayed but, by the mid-1990s, recession and global competition have forced companies finally to use the technologies they put in place over the last decade, with corresponding productivity leaps (Gillin, 1994a; Roach, 1994; Sager and Gleckman, 1994; also Introduction). This explanation fits quite well with the fact that, as pointed out in Chapter 1, the research periods of many of the studies uncovering lack of IT productivity were restricted to the early 1980s or before. By way of example, Barua, Kriebel and Mukhopadhyay (1991) studied 20 firms in the 1978–82 period, Loveman's (1988) study covered 1978–82; while Morrison and Berndt (1990) covered 1968–86. Gillin (1994ab) makes the additional point that, in any case, productivity figures always failed to measure the cost avoidance and savings on opportunity costs that IS/IT can help to achieve.

Others also argue that the real payoffs occur when IS/IT development and use are linked with the business reengineering (BPR) efforts coming onstream in the 1990s (see Chapter 1; also Davenport, 1993; Hammer and Champy, 1993). However, recent UK evidence develops this debate by finding that few organizations were actually getting "breakthrough" results through IT-enabled BPR. Organizations were "aiming low and hitting low" and generally not going for the radical, high-risk reengineering approaches advocated by many commentators. Moreover, there was no strong correlation between size of IT expenditure on reengineering projects and resulting productivity impacts. In business process reengineering, as elsewhere (see below), it is the management of IT, and what it is used for, rather than the size of IT spend that counts (Willcocks, 1996b).

Relatedly, Bakos and Jager (1995) provide interesting further insight. They argue that computers are not boosting productivity, but the fault lies not with the technology but with its management and how computer use is overseen. Along with Quinn and Baily (1994), they question the reliability of the productivity studies and, supporting the positive IT productivity findings in the study by Brynjolfsson and Hitt in Chapter 1, posit a new productivity paradox: "how can computers be so productive?"

In the face of such disputation, Brynjolfsson's 1993 paper makes salutary reading. He suggests four explanations for the seeming IT productivity paradox. The first is measurement errors. In practice, the measurement problems appear particularly acute in the service sector and with white-collar worker productivity—the main areas investigated by those pointing to a minimal productivity impact from IT use in the 1980s and early 1990s. Brynjolfsson concludes from a close examination of the data behind the studies of IT performance at national and sectoral levels that mismeasurement is at the core of the IT productivity paradox. A second explanation is timing lags due to learning and adjustment. Benefits from IT can take several years to show through in significant financial terms, a point made by others when arguing for newer ways of evaluating IS/IT performance at the organizational level (Keen, 1991; Strassmann, 1990). While Brynjolffson largely discounts this explanation in his 1993 paper, there is evidence to suggest that he is somewhat overoptimistic about the ability of managers to account rationally for such lags and include them in their IS/IT evaluation system (Willcocks, 1994; Graeser, Willcocks and Pisanias, 1998). Moreover, in Chapter 1 Brynjolffson and Hitt do offer an "investment in learning" explanation for lack of productivity in the early 1980s, feeding through into a "substantial and significant" IS contribution to firm output in the 1987–91 period that they studied.

A third possible explanation, suggested also in the Introduction to this book, is that of redistribution. IT may be beneficial to individual firms but unproductive from the standpoint of the industry, or the economy, as a whole. IT rearranges the share of the pie, with the bigger share going to those heavily investing in IT, without making the pie bigger. Brynjolfsson suggests, however, that the redistribution hypothesis would not explain any shortfall in IT productivity at the firm level. To add to his analysis, one can note that in several sectors, for example banking and financial services, firms seemingly compete by larger spending on IT-based systems that are, in practice, increasingly becoming minimum entry requirements for the sector, and commodities rather than differentiators of competitive performance. As a result, in some sectors, for example the oil industry, organizations are increasingly seeking to reduce such IS/IT costs by accepting that some systems are industry standard and can be developed together.

A fourth explanation is that IS/IT is not really productive at the firm level. Brynjolfsson (1993) posits that despite the neoclassical view of the firm as a profit maximizer, it may well be that decision makers are, for whatever reason, often not acting in the interests of the firm: "instead they are increasing their slack, building inefficient systems, or simply using outdated criteria for decision-making" (p. 75). The implication of Brynjolfsson's argument is that political interests and/or poor evaluation practice may contribute to failure to make real, observable gains from IS/IT investments. However, Brynjolfsson appears to discount these possibilities citing a lack of evidence either way, though here he seems to be restricting himself to the economics literature. Against his argument, however, there are in fact frequent study findings showing patchy strategizing and implementation practice where IT/IS is concerned (for overviews see Currie, 1995; Robson, 1997). Furthermore, recent evidence in the IT/IS evaluation literature suggests more evidence showing poor evaluation practice than Brynjolfsson has been willing to credit (see below; also Chapters 4, 12 and 13).

ORGANIZATIONAL VARIATIONS IN IS/IT PERFORMANCE

It is on this point that the real debate on the apparent "IT productivity paradox" needs to hinge. Studies at the aggregate levels of the economy or industrial sector conceal important questions and data about variations in business experiences at the organizational and intra-organizational levels. Chapter 1 consists of Brynjolffson and Hitt's study of 367 large US firms generating $1.8 trillion in 1991 output. For 1987–91 they found "IS spending making a substantial and statistically significant contribution to firm output". They conclude that the IT productivity paradox, if it ever existed, had disappeared by 1991 for their sample firms, which together represented a large share of total US output. Although they used similar models as previous researchers, Brynjolfsson and Hitt attribute their different findings mainly to the larger and more recent data set they used. Even so, they point to further analysis being needed of the factors which differentiate firms with high returns to IT from low performers. Our case study will help locate some of these reasons as relating to IT/IS evaluation as well as IT/IS management practices.

In practice, organizations seem to vary greatly in their ability to harness IS/IT for organizational purposes (see also Introduction). In an early study, Cron and Sobol (1983) pointed to what has since been called the "amplifier" effect of IT. Its use reinforces existing management approaches, dividing firms into very high or very low performers.

This analysis has been supported by later work that also found no correlation between size of IT spend and firms' return on investment (Kobler Unit, 1987; Strassmann, 1990). Subsequently, a 1994 analysis of the information productivity of 782 US companies found that the top 10 spent a smaller percentage (1.3% compared to 3% for the bottom 100) of their revenue on IT, increased their IT budget more slowly (4.3% in 1993–4, the comparator being the bottom 110 averaging 10.2%), thus leaving a greater amount of finance available for non-IT spending (Sullivan-Trainor, 1994).

The calculation of information productivity in this study does make a rather large assumption—that management productivity is synonymous with information productivity because management is so highly dependent on information. This is probably not sustainable (Willcocks, 1994). Notwithstanding this, not only did the the top performers seem to spend less proportionately on their IT; they also tended to keep certain new investments as high as business conditions permitted while holding back on infrastructure growth. Thus, on average, hardware investments were only 15% of the IT/IS budget while new development took more than 50%, with 41% of systems development spending incurred on client/server investment (Sullivan-Trainor, 1994). Clearly, the implication of this analysis is that top performers spend relatively less money on IS/IT, but focus their spending on areas where it will make more difference in terms of business value. An important aspect of their ability to do this must lie with their evaluation techniques and processes.

Van Nievelt in Chapter 3 adds to this picture (see also van Nievelt and Willcocks, 1997). Analysing database information on over 300 organizations, he found empirically that IT as a coordinating, communicating and leveraging technology was capable of enhancing customer satisfaction, flattening organizational pyramids and supporting knowledge workers in the management arena. At the same time, many organizations did not direct their IT expenditure into appropriate areas at the right time, partly because of inability to carry out evaluation of where they were with their IT expenditure and IT performance relative to business needs in a particular competitive and market context. Van Nievelt's work is worth pursuing, based as it is on strong empirical and statistical analysis, and because it shows ways out of the IT productivity paradox. His work in Chapter 3 shows the paradox to be faulty. His statistical analysis of business-unit-level data provides strong evidence for a significant, positive but multifaceted IT effect on productivity. However, the timing and placement of IT expenditure emerge as all important. As one example, he found that when customer perceptions of the firm are unfavourable relative to competitors, executing such a broadly recommended move as making large investments in "strategic IS" has a strong probability of causing significant economic damage to the firm.

The work reported here shows how complex it is to identify IT impacts and effects, and points to the need to examine a range of correlated factors before rushing to judgement. It also serves to highlight how macroeconomic studies of IT productivity can mislead, and how microeconomic studies of the ways in which individual organizations and markets behave are altogether more helpful. At the same time, it becomes clear that IT events must become continually correlated to business performance in ways frequently not represented in existing assessment practice, as we now turn to examine.

IT EVALUATION PRACTICE: REINVENTING THE WHEEL?

Many recent UK studies show both difficulties in establishing the business value of IT and also indifferent evaluation practice (Grindley, 1995; Willcocks and Lester, 1996; Graeser, Willcocks and Pisanias, 1998; see also Chapters 4, 5 and 6). One 1995/96 study points to sectoral differences, with a majority of financial companies getting "good" or "very good" value from IT, while manufacturing and distributive trades are less certain about the IT payoff now and less optimistic about IT payoffs in the next five years (Kew Associates, 1995). One noticeable—and worrying—feature of such studies is how often their findings on weaknesses in evaluation practice replicate those of much earlier studies (Butler Cox, 1990; Hochstrasser, 1994; Strassmann, 1990).

Our own recent research reinforces and extends these points (Harvey, Islei and Willcocks, 1996). A survey of 150 senior IT managers in February–March 1996 attracted a 70% response rate, with 37% of the total sample being usable. The three main reasons cited by those returning but not filling in the questionnaire can be summarized as (a) not enough time; (b) not company policy; and (c) not a major issue for the organization. The sample was drawn from organizations in a cross-section of the main economic sectors, with respondents being mainly in financial services, energy, pharmaceuticals, publishing, manufacturing and public and private service sectors. Two-thirds of IT departments admitted that they encountered scepticism when trying to demonstrate the effectiveness of IT services. The majority of the survey sample expressed their assessment of performance predominantly in terms of technical efficiency or project evaluation, sometimes a mix of the two. By contrast, IT's overall contribution to the business was the predominant focus in only 16% of organizations. Of the business-related performance measures covered by the survey, the most frequently used was customer/user satisfaction with the business impact of IT services. But this was applied in only 40% of organizations. The next most commonly used—by a quarter of respondents respectively—were measures that reflect the effectiveness in meeting specific business goals, broad-based quality rating of IT services and improvements in business process operations. The most frequently mentioned (50%) "most useful" measures fell into the business improvement category. While 36% claimed that customer satisfaction ratings were valuable, only two respondents extended this beyond the boundaries of the organization to include external customers.

Much of this points to continuing patterns of indifferent evaluation practice, a conclusion reinforced by 1998 survey findings (Graeser, Willcocks and Pisanias, 1998). The reasons cited for this in 1996 were diverse, but a number had to do with corporate circumstances of a long-standing and intractable nature. For example, 55% of respondents pointed out that the absence of a clearly articulated business strategy, or a poorly defined business goal, was fundamental to their problems in closing the loop between IT and its contribution to business performance. Thirty per cent complained of the absence of good working relationships with the rest of the organization. This absence of close liaison was reflected by the relative scarcity of forums for IT and business managers to discuss IT performance measurement issues.

At the same time, the survey indicated changes in the use of measurement systems. While business-related measures were still the least commonly used, they were the fastest evolving. Almost three-quarters of these types of measures had been introduced within the last 12 months. However, by far the most widely cited set of problems were associated with developing such new sets of measures; 80% cited difficulties in this area. Some IT managers were clearly low down on the learning curve and handicapped by ignorance of options: "lack of understanding of possible methods", "identifying what to measure" or, more plaintively, "how to measure performance" exemplified their difficulties. In other cases, the problems were information based and related to concerns about "the accuracy of source data" or "the availability of data on business performance enhanced by IT". Elsewhere, it was the indirect contribution of IT investment entailed in "assessing the benefits of infrastructure projects" and "trying to quantify soft measures" that blocked faster progress. Obviously, the many difficulties associated with these efforts are compounded when the implications of the technology shifts detailed in the Introduction to this book are confronted.

Much of this section points to the need for a family of measures that cover technical and business performance of IT in an integrated manner. Measures are needed that point to cost effectiveness and containment, but that embrace additional key IT/business performance criteria. In this respect, there is potential value in drawing on emerging practice in applying models developed to extend the range of corporate performance measurement (for example Kaplan and Norton, 1992; Peters, 1996). The second issue is to integrate these measures over time, right into decisions about whether existing IT needs to be replaced, enhanced or dropped. Past studies have shown this to be a particularly weak area in evaluation practice (for summaries see Willcocks, 1994, 1996a). A third intractable area is building evaluation as a process that includes a large range of stakeholders, and that improves IT/business relationships over time by sharpening understanding of IT's business value, while not just monitoring but also improving IT's business use. An attempt to address these concerns is made in the remainder of this chapter.

EVALUATION—A SYSTEMS LIFECYCLE APPROACH

At the heart of one way forward for organizations is the notion of an IT/IS evaluation and management cycle. A simplified diagrammatic representation of this is provided in Figure 2.1.

Earlier research found that few organizations actually operated evaluation and management practice in an integrated manner across systems lifecycles (Willcocks and Lester, 1991, 1996). This seemed to continue into 1998 (Graeser, Willcocks and Pisanias, 1998). The evaluation cycle attempts to bring together a rich and diverse set of ideas, methods and practices that are to be found in the evaluation literature to date. Such an approach would consist of several interrelated activities:

1. Identifying net benefits through strategic alignment and prioritization.
2. Identifying types of generic benefit and matching these to assessment techniques.
3. Developing a family of measures based on financial, service, delivery, learning and technical criteria.
4. Linking these measures to particular measures needed for development, implementation and post-implementation phases.
5. Ensuring each set of measures runs from the strategic to the operational level.

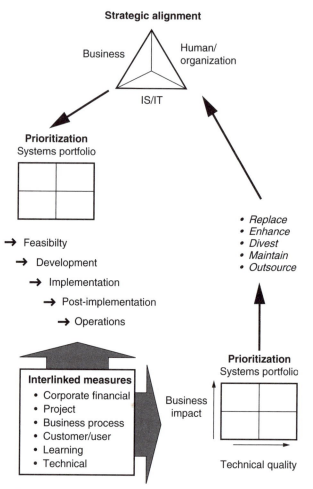

Figure 2.1   *Investing in IT/IS: an Evaluation Lifecycle*

6. Establishing responsibility for tracking these measures and regularly reviewing results.
7. Regularly reviewing the existing portfolio and relating this to business direction and performance objectives.

A key element in making the evaluation cycle dynamic and effective is the involvement of motivated, salient stakeholders in processes that operationalize the evaluation criteria and techniques. Our previous research points to the need to operationalize these practices across a lifecycle of six interrelated phases—alignment, prioritization, feasibility, development and implementation, post-implementation and operations. Some detail of previous findings on evaluation at these different phases now follows. The framework will then be used as a template to analyse a case study.

Alignment

In an earlier review of front-end evaluation, Willcocks (1992) pointed out how lack of alignment between business, information systems and human resource/organizational strategies inevitably compromised the value of all subsequent IS/IT evaluation effort, to the point of rendering it of marginal utility and, in some cases, even counter-productive. In this respect he reflected the concerns of many authors on the subject (Earl, 1989; Hares and Royle, 1994; Peters, 1994. See also Chapters 6, 7 and 11). At the same time, the importance of recognizing evaluation as a process imbued with inherent political characteristics and ramifications was emphasized, reflecting a common finding among empirical studies (Currie, 1995; Symons, 1994). Many tools have been advanced to enable the evaluation and achievement of alignment. Among the better known are McFarlan and McKenney's (1983) strategic grid, Porter and Millar's (1991) value chain analysis, and Earl's (1989) multiple methodology.

Prioritization

The notion of a systems portfolio implies that IT/IS investment can have a variety of objectives. The practical problem becomes one of prioritiz-ation—of resource allocation among the many objectives and projects that are put forward. Several classificatory schemes for achieving this appear in the extant literature, among them those of Hochstrasser (1994) and Information Economics (Norris, 1996; Parker, Benson and Trainor, 1988). Others have suggested classificatory schemes that match business objectives with types of IS/IT project (Butler Cox Foundation, 1990; Willcocks, 1994; see also Chapters 6 and 7). Thus, on one schema, projects could be divided into six types: efficiency, effectiveness, must-do, architecture, competitive edge, and research and development. The type of project could then be matched to one of the more appropriate evaluation methods available, a critical factor being the degree of tangi-bility of the costs and benefits being assessed. A useful categorization of types of investments and the main tools available for evaluating priori-ties is provided by Norris (1996).

Our own approach is to relate IT usage to fundamental purposes. We see these as fivefold (Figure 2.2). Historically, the first purpose of IT contribution—cost efficiency—has predominated in organizations. In practice, there are a series of IT investments that have to be made for identifiably valid business reasons, but for which direct business bene-

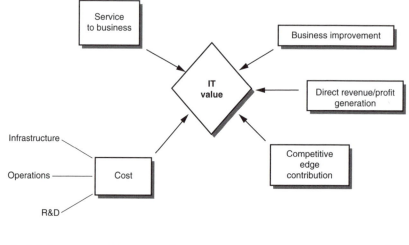

Note: Development costs are allocated directly to each contribution focus   *Source: L.P. Willcocks, 1997*

Figure 2.2   *Finding IT Value: a Cost/Contribution Framework*

fits cannot be easily attributed. The three most typical forms of IT investment here are on infrastructure (see Chapter 11), operations and R&D systems. At this stage, such IT investments wil be assessed on IT efficiency criteria, but typically with ring-fenced budgets for R&D and for certain infrastructure investments.

The second contribution that the IT function and systems can make is as a service to the business. Here IT will be assessed against current business unit objectives, business manager perceptions and quality of service, for example. Thirdly, IT well may enable or support business change and improvement, for example when applied to new business processes. Here assessment will be predominantly on impact on business performance metrics. Fourthly, IT applications and services may well be sold externally in order to deliver direct revenue and profit to the organization. Fifthly, IT may be channelled into differentiating the business competitively in relationship to customers, suppliers and/or through partnering arrangements. The point is that each of these five options requires distinctive, but connnected, evaluation regimes (see also Chapter 7 for a further discussion and model).

Feasibility

After alignment and prioritization, the feasibility of each IS/IT investment needs to be examined. All the research studies show that the main weakness here has been overreliance on and/or misuse of traditional, finance-based cost-benefit analysis (Farbey, Targett and Land, 1995; Willcocks and Lester, 1996; see also Chapter 4). The contingency approach outlined above helps to deal with this, but such approaches need to be allied with active involvement of a wider group of stakeholders than those being identified at the moment in the research studies (Willcocks and Lester, 1991, 1996; see also Chapters 6, 7, 12 and 13). Following this, Figure 2.1 suggests that evaluation needs to be conducted in a linked manner across feasibility, systems development and into systems implementation and operational use. A key issue here is the establishment at the feasibility stage of interlinked, anchor measures (Butler Cox Foundation, 1990; Strassmann, 1990; Willcocks, 1992; Chapter 7).

Development and Implementation

The evaluation cycle posits the development of a series of interlinked measures that reflect various aspects of IS/IT performance, and that are applied across the system's lifetime. These are tied to processes and people responsible for monitoring performance, improving the evaluation system and also helping to "flush out" and manage the benefits from the investment. Figure 2.1 suggests, in line with prevailing academic and practitioner thinking by the mid-1990s, that evaluation cannot be based solely or even mainly on technical efficiency criteria. For other criteria there may be debate on how they are to be measured, and this will depend on the specific organizational circumstances.

Kaplan and Norton (1992) were highly useful for popularizing the need for a number of perspectives on evaluation of business performance. Willcocks (1994) showed how the Kaplan and Norton balanced scorecard approach could be adapted fairly easily for the case of assessing IT/IS investments. To add to that picture, most recent research, for example by Norris (1996) and Peters (1996), suggests the need for six sets of measures. These would cover the corporate financial perspective (e.g. profit per employee); the systems project (e.g. time, quality, cost); business process (e.g. purchase invoices per employee); the customer/user perspective (e.g. on-time delivery rate); an innovation/learning perspective (e.g. rate of cost reduction for IT services); and a technical perspective (e.g. development efficiency, capacity utilization). Each set of measures would run from strategic to operational levels, each measure being broken down into increasing detail as it is applied to actual organizational performance. For each set of measures the business objectives for IT/IS would be set. Each objective would then be broken down into more detailed measurable components, with a financial value assigned where practicable.

Responsibility for tracking these measures, together with regular reviews that relate performance to objectives and targets, are highly important elements in delivering benefits from the various IS investments (for benefits realization see also Chapter 9). It should be noted that such measures are seen as helping to inform stakeholder judgements, and not as a substitute for such judgements in the evaluation process (Grindley, 1995; Norris, 1996; Peters, 1996; Willcocks and Lester, 1996).

Post-implementation

One all too often routinized phase of review is that of post-implementation (see Figure 2.1). Our own research suggests that this is one of the most neglected, yet one of the more important areas, as far as IS evaluation is concerned. An advantage of the above schema, in practice, is that post-implementation evaluation arises naturally out of implementation assessment on an on-going basis, with an already existing set of evaluators in place. This avoids the ritualistic, separated review that usually takes place in the name of post-implementation assessment (Kumar, 1990; Willcocks and Lester, 1996). A detailed discussion on how to perform an effective post-implementation review cannot be provided here, but see Norris (1996).

On-going Operations

There remains the matter of assessing the on-going systems portfolio on a regular basis. Notoriously, when it comes to evaluating the existing IT/IS investment, organizations are not good at making decisions to terminate a systems development or an existing system. There may be several related ramifications. The IT inheritance of "legacy systems" can deter investment in new systems—it can, for example, be all too difficult to take on new work when IT/IS staff are awash in a rising tide of maintenance arising from the existing investment. Existing IT/IS-related activity can also devour the majority of the financial resources available for IS investment (Robson, 1997; Strassmann, 1997; Swanson and Beath, 1988). All too often, such failures derive from not having in place, or not operationalizing, a robust assessment approach that enables timely decisions on systems and service divestment, outsourcing, replacement, enhancement and/or maintenance. As Figure 2.1 shows, such decisions need to be based on at least two criteria—the technical quality of the system/service and its business contribution—as well as being related back to the overall strategic direction and objectives of the organization (Willcocks, Feeny and Islei, 1997).

A further element in assessment of the on-going systems portfolio is the relevance of external comparators. External benchmarking firms, for example RDC and Compass, have already been operating for several years, and offer a range of services that can be drawn on, but mainly for technical aspects of IT performance. There is, however, a growing demand for extending external benchmarking services more widely to include business and other performance measures (see, for example, Chapter 3). It is worth remarking that external IT benchmarking, like all measures, can serve a range of purposes within an organization. Lacity and Hirschheim (1995, 1996) detail from their research how benchmarking services were used to demonstrate to senior executives the usefulness of the IT department. In some cases, external benchmarking subsequently led to the rejection of outsourcing proposals from external vendors.

Evaluating IT Sourcing Options

Evaluation of on-going operations will point to the need to replace, enhance, divest or maintain particular systems. This leads into the final point. An increasingly important part of assessing the existing and any future IT/IS investment is the degree to which the external IT services market can provide better business, technical and economic options for an organization. By 1996, for example, over 55% of UK organizations were outsourcing 10% or more of their IT budget (Willcocks and Lacity, 1997). In practice, recent survey and case research by the authors and others found few organizations taking a strategic approach to IT/IS sourcing decisions, although many derived economic and other benefits from incremental, selective, low-risk, as opposed to high-risk, "total" approaches to outsourcing (Lacity, Willcocks and Feeny, 1995; Willcocks and Fitzgerald, 1994). In Figure 2.1 we show how IT sourcing decisions need to link not just with evaluation of existing operations but also with issues of strategic alignment (see also Chapter 10).

Evaluation of IT/IS sourcing options, together with assessment of on-going vendor performance in any outsourced part of the IT/IS service, needs to be integrally imbedded into the systems lifecycle approach detailed above. This is not least because an external vendor bid, if carefully analysed against one's own detailed in-house assessment of IT performance, can be a highly informative form of benchmarking. Recent research gives more detail on the criteria that govern successful and less successful sourcing decisions.

In case and survey research, Willcocks and Fitzgerald (1994) found six key factors. Three are essentially business related. First, IT can contribute to differentiate a business from its competitors, or be merely a commodity. Secondly, IT may be strategic in underpinning the firm's achievement of goals and critical to its present and future strategic direction, or be merely useful. "Useful commodities" provide the lowest risk among outsourcing candidates. Thirdly, a high degree of uncertainty about future business environment and needs affects longer-term IT needs. High uncertainty suggests in-house sourcing as a better option. Three technical considerations are also important. It would seem less preferable for an organization to outsource in a situation of low technology maturity, where there is a high level of integration of the system or activity with other parts of the technical platform, and/or where in-house capability is equivalent to or better than that available on the external market. Making sourcing decisions, in practice, involves making tradeoffs among the preferences suggested by these factors. Other important factors we uncovered were:

- Does the decision make economic sense?
- How does the decision fit with the rate of technological change?
- Are there issues around ownership when transferring people and assets?
- Is a suitable vendor available?
- Does the organization have the management capability to deliver on the decision?
- Will significant human resource issues arise?

Even where an organization does not outsource IT, our case evidence is that increasingly it is good practice to assess in-house performance against what a potential vendor bid might be, even if, as is increasingly the case, this means paying a vendor for the assessment. Benchmarking IT/IS performance against external comparators can also be highly useful in providing insight not only into in-house IT/IS performance, but also into the efficacy of internal evaluation criteria, processes and the availability or otherwise of detailed, appropriate assessment information (for more detail on IT outsourcing evaluation, see Chapter 10).

CASE STUDY: INSURANCE INC.—DEVELOPING EVALUATION PRACTICES

The relevance of the above discussions on the IT productivity paradox and on evaluation practice will now be tested against case study data. Between the beginning of September 1995 and the end of February 1996, evaluation practice was investigated in the business and systems contexts provided by a newly formed business division of a major insurance company. We interviewed eight managers drawn from the senior team, business change and systems departments, and line management. This provided a triangulation of perspectives. The managers were also chosen as those people most involved and knowledgeable about information systems and its evaluation at the company. Semi-structured questionnaires were used and four managers from senior management, systems and line areas were interviewed twice, at the beginning and end of the period.

We also made four site visits during this period to observe how information systems and management operated. These visits included shorter semi-structured interviews of between 15 and 30 minutes each with business and systems staff (12 in total). In addition to attending two IS strategy meetings in the research period, we were also given access to considerable company documentation, including IS strategy documents, budgets, business strategy details, minutes of relevant meetings and systems progress reports. In total we collected over 400 pages of documentation and over 300 pages of interview transcripts. This enabled us to establish the business and systems contexts and analyse IT/IS evaluation practices against the impacts that the systems were having in the organization.

Business Context

Insurance Inc. is a large insurance company with headquarters in the UK. In 1995, it held £4833 million in insurance premiums and employed over 17 000 people. In 1994 the company was organized along product lines. From a customer's perspective it had to deal with different divisions for different products. During 1995, the company was reorganized from geographic regions into customer type, for example UK to motor insurance and personal insurance. The case concentrates on one UK division called Corporate Alliances (CA).

CA primarily sells housing, health, legal and emergency insurance, worth about £650 million. The majority of its business is with five large financial institutions—building societies and banks. These customers in turn sell on CA's products to end-customers, most typically their own employees. CA works in a highly competitive market where profits are difficult to achieve. In early 1996, it was challenged by the decision of a major customer to provide its own insurance. To increase revenues, throughout 1995–6 CA looked to expand into Europe, but ran the danger of intruding on the customer base of Insurance Inc.'s Europe-based Business Division. Another set of problems in CA was poor processing of end-customer claims, resulting in fraud, exaggerated claims and excess payments. Reducing the cost of operations became a critical necessity and an IT-based reengineering project had been started more than a year before.

Information Technology/Systems Context

By 1995, CA had a functional organizational design, including underwriting, marketing, account managers, core and support services. There were two departments in the support service unit: Business Technology and Service Delivery. Business Technology had a £15 million budget and directly employed 180 people, mainly systems developers. In late 1995, another 300 staff were being devolved into the business units to integrate applications development more effectively. These included network support and IT operations staff, but increasingly these business units and group IT division were opting for outsourcing. In February 1996, the network activity was outsourced to IBM and the group-run mainframe operation was about to be outsourced, the effect anticipated being a reduction of 150 in staff numbers. On initial figures, the perception among senior management was that outsourcing the mainframe would save £46 million over five years.

At the time of the interviews, the Business Technology department was developing five major projects:

1. A business reengineering project for core processes, including claims processing.
2. A system to replace the insurance policy administration system on the mainframe.
3. A system to apply imaging technology to scan policies, forms and letters.
4. A system to implement telephony, integrating computers and telephones.
5. A client/server system for claims processing.

The service delivery department ran seven regional data centres throughout the UK. There were 800 staff, primarily dealing with operations support and data entry for policies and claims. Insurance Inc. had no plans to outsource these data centres.

According to senior IS managers, the main challenges facing IT/IS staff were managing user expectations, prioritizing work and managing large-scale projects. Much of this was a balancing act—high IT spending would annoy senior management and business sponsors of systems, while spending too little on IT could cut services and functionality and increase user dissatisfaction. Some sense of the pressures, how different stakeholders might perceive an IT productivity paradox and how this might be related to the lack of commonly held evaluation practices was conveyed by the Business Technology manager:

Between 1992 and 1995 we saw a dramatic headcount rise and a £10 million budget rising to £15 million. A lot of people do not understand why this amount of spend occurs and how it compares with other companies. For example, they do not understand that it takes four person-years just to handle the systems changes to the date year 2000. In fact, the business decisions explain the spend. For example, a decison to diversify means new systems. Moreover, in practice there are no mechanisms in place to reduce this spend by synergies across the group and standardizing and identifying commonalities across [Insurance Inc.].

Evaluation Practices

The managing director of CA previously headed Insurance Inc. Group Management Services. Several senior managers had come from IT-related functions. This meant that there was a strong belief in the importance of IT among the senior management team. However in the 1980s and early 1990s, in the old company from which CA had been split off, IT had had low credibility among line managers. In some cases, systems failures had resulted directly in financial losses. Part of the problems stemmed from omissions in evaluation practice, with little attempt to tie investments to business needs and measure and demonstrate business impacts. By the early 1990s, there was a disciplined, centralized evaluation procedure, but this created a very bureaucratic way of raising a request for IT. This created tensions between IT and business staff, together with accusations of IT being unresponsive. The IT function was reorganized into customer-facing teams. While this improved customer service, it meant that, by 1995, an increasing number of requests escaped central prioritization. As we shall see, this fractured an integrated lifecycle approach at a vital point, as respondents readily admitted.

Alignment

By 1995, senior managers primarily evaluated IT in terms of financial benefit, either directly through productivity improvements or indirectly through ability to win clients—a critical issue in the 1995–6 period. However, respondents indicated ways in which alignment of IT expenditure with business strategy did not always occur:

> With the strategic projects we go through a proper lifecycle of measuring what the benefit was when ... implemented, and do a customer satisfaction survey. But that is only really for the top three or four projects. For a lot of the other work we are not doing that kind of activity ... there are satisfaction surveys but not so much of a business benefit analysis ... it's being given a test before it's adopted—is it important to the business—but it's not really being given a cost-benefit analysis. (Senior manager)

Prioritization

Much of the problem seemed to stem from weaknesses in prioritization processes and in the type of criteria used:

> What we tend not to do is prioritize the low-level requests properly ... when they are doing useful IT rather than strategic IT, because of our desire to get close to the users and deliver what they want, we tend to deliver everything they ask for and there is a long list of the things we can do... People can actually ask for new IT relatively easily and that ... may actually be wasting money. (Senior manager)

From Feasibility to On-going Operations

The ways in which IT productivity—in terms of business, as opposed to user, benefit—can escape through weaknesses in evaluation practices are indicated by the following comment:

> The things that come through with five person-days, two person-days, ten person-days we call "business normal". We would expect to get a lot of those things because once you've put in a system it's like a living system. But I think it covers about 40% of our budget spend ... if we could get the executives responsible for different areas to understand their net costs and if we could put down an invoice and say this is what we have delivered and it costs, say £100 000, and the benefit is £250 000 and may be closer to £500 000, they will look at that and feel good about it. But then we also need to follow through and say well, now deliver the £250 000 worth of benefit. (IT project manager)

What the IT manager is recommending here fits in well with the notion of an evaluation approach integrated across the systems life-cycle, with a range of measures, not just technical criteria, being applied. It should also be realized that, as with other organizations, IT resource in terms of people is both expensive and not unlimited. IT resource used in CA for the type of work detailed by the IT project manager creates an opportunity cost for more strategic work with much higher business impact, thus affecting the IT productivity equation, potentially quite radically.

Benchmarking and Outsourcing

Two other evaluation areas at CA can be compared against our proposals for evaluating across the systems lifecycle. These areas are benchmarking and outsourcing. Respondents generally agreed that CA systems in the health and creditor areas were at the leading edge in Europe. But in the household area there was definite feedback from clients that CA systems were not up to the level of competitors. However, respondents indicated that CA did not possess enough good benchmarking information to make detailed assessments against competitors:

> In the past we've tried to gain more information about our competitors through visits and attending seminars, but some more formal benchmarking we believe is now appropriate. (IT manager)

On IT/IS outsourcing, the most recent decision to outsource IBM mainframes on a five-year contract was actually arrived at at corporate level. The mainframes in fact took in work from a number of business divisions. The business divisions did not drive the decision, although they related it to their own strategic plans. However, subsequently there was some concern in CA:

> Having been on the receiving end, we are looking at it in terms of cost management and how we make sure we get all the benefits ... there is a cost in having to manage that ... at CA we may not save a lot of money by the deal ... we've got to live with the decision and minimize the impacts on the business and maximize any benefit ... this creates new tasks—monitoring the vendor performance and user satisfaction, for example. (Senior manager)

Summary Points

In terms of the systems lifecycle approach detailed earlier, the case history shows up a number of strong evaluation practices and a number of weaknesses. These practices also relate to IT productivity issues in a number of interesting ways. A history of indifferent evaluation practice and—in business terms—uncertain IT productivity had been challenged by restructuring, a highly competitive business climate, and new senior management personnel. By 1996, evaluation practice was strong on identifying some strategic projects. However, respondents indicated that a difficulty lay with the lack of precision within the business strategy itself. In March 1996, senior management had embarked on a review of both business and IS strategy with a view to achieving more precise alignment.

Feasibility and prioritization procedures seemed weak for what in fact covered some 40% of total IT/IS expenditure. Respondents also indicated that they were actively looking at ways in which interlinked measures could be set up across development and implementation of systems so that IT/IS business benefit could be more easily assessed. Another concern lay with improvements in the process of evaluation, with business managers to be made more responsible for evaluating and managing benefits.

External benchmarking was also on the new agenda. The original outsourcing evaluation was out of the hands of CA managers, but it became clear that there were a number of concerns about how productive the results would be for CA itself. One way forward seemed to be to put in place close monitoring of vendor performance, while one manager intimated that if this monitoring indicated low value for CA division, the option to withdraw from the outsourcing arrangement needed to be considered.

Evaluation practices influenced IT productivity in a number of ways. First, from the 1980s stakeholder perceptions of the value of IT could be seen to have been influenced by how IT evaluation was conducted and the ability, or otherwise, of evaluation procedures to demonstrate business value. Secondly, CA division was beginning to align IT expenditure with strategic business necessities and this would, in the assessment of the senior and IT/IS managers, enhance IT productivity in business terms. Thirdly, weaknesses in feasibility evaluation and prioritization were channelling substantial IT expenditure into less productive areas. Fourthly, weaknesses in interlinked measures and assignment of responsibility for monitoring development and implementation meant that benefits from the IT/IS expenditure were less significant than they could have been. Fifthly, more detailed benchmarking might also have induced a clearer focus on where to make IT expenditure and what level of IT productivity should be attainable. These fourth and fifth points of our analysis were subsequently acknowledged by senior IT/IS managers, who made active moves to change evaluation practice in these areas. Sixthly, the non-involvement in the original IT outsourcing evaluation, in our analysis, tied CA to a less than productive arrangement, while incurring subsequent management and monitoring time and effort, deflecting IT/IS skills and capabilities better used elsewhere.

It would seem that so far as the IT productivity paradox exists in organizations, it is best explained by such practical considerations. Moreover, as the case history helps to illustrate to some degree, improvements in evaluation practice can have a significant role to play in the resolution of IT productivity issues.

CONCLUSION

There are several ways out of the IT productivity paradox discussed here and in the Introduction. Several of the more critical relate to improved ways of planning for, managing and using IT/IS. However, part of the IT productivity paradox has been configured out of difficulties and limitations in measuring and accounting for IT/IS performance.

Bringing the so-called paradox into the more manageable and assessable organizational realm, it is clear from our overview of recent research, our own survey and the case study detailed in this chapter that there was still, as at 1998, much indifferent IT/IS evaluation practice to be found in work organizations. This chapter has detailed how far a sense of the IT productivity paradox can be engendered by indifferent evaluation practice and measurement at national, sectoral and organizational levels. It has argued that the issue of IT productivity needs to be examined at the more meaningful intra-organizational level. Here we pointed to much indifferent evaluation practice, not least in the case study of Insurance Inc. At the same time, we have uncovered ways in which poor evaluation practice can lead to not just perceptions of, but also to the reality of low IT productivity.

In detailing an integrated lifecycle approach to IT/IS evaluation, we have utilized our own and others' research findings to suggest one way forward. The "cradle to grave" framework is holistic and dynamic and relies on a judicious mixture of the "business case", appropriate criteria and metrics, managerial and stakeholder judgement and processes, together with motivated evaluators. It also signals a move from a restricted "control through numbers" assessment culture to one that utilizes measurement and judgement in a more integrated manner across the systems lifecycle in order to promote quality improvement. The relevance and usefulness of the approach, at least as an analytical tool, were revealed by applying it as a template against evaluation practices at Insurance Inc. On reviewing our analysis, case participants also endorsed the practicality of the approach by subsequently undertaking some changes to bring aspects of evaluation practice in line with the framework. This provides limited, but encouraging, evidence that the practices detailed in the central sections of this chapter do, when combined, offer one of the better routes out of the IT productivity paradox, not least in the ability of the approach we have detailed to link evaluation with how IT is planned for, managed and used. We would also suggest that the basic parameters of this approach remain robust in the face of the discussion of the network-based era in the Introduction, but that processes and procedures can only provide a framework, and not substitute for a real grasp of the underlying economics of, and pertinent metrics for, different types of IT investment.

REFERENCES

Bakos, Y. and Jager, P. de. (1995). Are computers boosting productivity? *Computerworld*, March 27th, 128–130.

Banker, R., Kauffman, R. and Mahmood, M. (eds) (1993). *Strategic Information*

Technology Management: Perspectives on Organizational Growth and Competitive Advantage. Idea Publishing, Harrisburg.

Barua, A., Kriebel, C. and Mukhopadhyay, T. (1991). Information Technology and Business Value: an Analytic and Empirical Investigation. *University of Texas Working Paper*, Austin. Texas, May.

Brynjolfsson, E. (1993). The Productivity Paradox of Information Technology. *Communications of The ACM*, 36, 12, 67–77.

Brynjolfsson, E. and Hitt, L. (1993). Is Information Systems Spending Productive? *Proceedings of the International Conference in Information Systems*, Orlando, December.

Butler Cox Foundation (1990). *Getting Value from Information Technology*. Research Report 75, June. Butler Cox, London.

Cron, W. and Sobol, M. (1983). The Relationship between Computerization and Performance: a Strategy for Maximizing the Economic Benefits of Computerization. *Journal of Information Management*, 6, 2, 171–81.

Currie, W. (1989). The Art of Justifying New Technology to Top Management. *Omega*, 17, 5, 409–18.

Currie, W. (1994). The Strategic Management of a Large-Scale IT Project in the Financial Services Sector. *New Technology Work and Employment*, 9, 1, 19–29.

Currie, W. (1995). *Management Strategy for IT: an International Perspective*. Pitman Publishing, London.

Davenport, H. (1993). *Process Innovation: Reengineering Work through Information Technology*. Harvard Business School Press, Boston, MA.

Earl, M. (1989). *Management Strategies for Information Technology*. Prentice Hall, Hemel Hempstead.

Farbey, B., Land, F. and Targett, D. (1992). Evaluating Investments in IT. *Journal of Information Technology*, 7, 2, 100–12.

Farbey, B., Land, F. and Targett, D. (1993). *How to Assess Your IT Investment*. Butterworth-Heinemann, Oxford

Farbey, B., Targett, D. and Land, F. (eds) (1995). *Hard Money, Soft Outcomes*. Alfred Waller/Unicom, Henley.

Flowers, S. (1996). *Software Failure: Management Failure*. John Wiley, Chichester.

Gillin, P. (1994a). Is IS Making us More Productive? *Computerworld*, September 19th, 10–12.

Gillin, P. (ed.) (1994b). The Productivity Payoff: The 100 Most Effective Users of Information Technology. *Computerworld*, September 19th, Section 2, 4–55.

Glazer, R. (1993). Measuring the Value of Information: the Information-Intensive Organization. *IBM Systems Journal*, 32, 1, 99–110.

Graeser, V, Willcocks, L. and Pisanias, N. (1998). *Developing the IT Scorecard: a Study of Evaluation Practice and Integrated Performance Measurement*. Business Intelligence, London.

Grindley, K. (1995). *Managing IT at Board Level*. Pitman Publishing, London.

Hackett, G. (1990). Investment in Technology—the Service Sector Sinkhole? *Sloan Management Review*, Winter, 31, 2, 97–103.

Hammer, M. and Champy, J. (1993). *Reengineering the Corporation: a Manifesto for Business Revolution*. Nicholas Brealey, London.

Hares, J. and Royle, D. (1994). *Measuring the Value of Information Technology*. John Wiley, Chichester.

Harvey, D., Islei, G. and Willcocks, L. (1996). *Measuring the Performance of Corporate Information Technology Services*. OXIIM/BI Report. Business Intelligence, London.

Hochstrasser, B. (1994). Justifying IT Investments. In Willcocks, L. (ed.) *Information Management: Evaluation of Information Systems Investments.* Chapman and Hall, London, 151–69.

Kaplan, R. and Norton, D. (1992). The Balanced Scorecard: Measures that Drive Performance. *Harvard Business Review*, January–February, 70, 1, 71–9.

Keen, P. (1991). *Shaping the Future: Business Design through Information Technology.* Harvard Business Press, Boston, MA.

Kew Associates (1995). *User IT Expenditure Survey 1995.* Computer Weekly/Kew Associates, London.

Kobler Unit (1987). *Is Information Technology Slowing You Down?* Kobler Unit report, Imperial College, London.

Kumar, K. (1990). Post-Implementation Evaluation of Computer-Based Information Systems: Current Practices. *Communications of the ACM*, 33, 2, 203–12.

Lacity, M. and Hirschheim, R. (1995). *Beyond the Information Systems Outsourcing Bandwagon.* John Wiley, Chichester.

Lacity, M. and Hirschheim, R. (1996). The Role of Benchmarking in Demonstrating IS Performance. In Willcocks, L. (ed.) *Investing in Information Systems: Evaluation and Management.* Chapman and Hall, London, 313–32.

Lacity, M., Willcocks, L. and Feeny, D. (1995). IT Outsourcing: Maximize Flexibility and Control. *Harvard Business Review*, May–June, 73, 3, 84–93.

Landauer, T. (1995). *The Trouble with Computers: Usefulness, Usability and Productivity.* MIT Press, Cambridge.

LaPlante, A. (1994). No Doubt about IT. *Computerworld*, August 15th, 79–86.

LaPlante, A. and Alter, A. (1994). IT all Adds up. *Computerworld*, October 31st, 76–84.

Loveman, G. (1988). An Assessment of the Productivity Impact of Information Technologies. *MIT Management in the Nineties Working Paper 88-054.* Massachusetts Institute of Technology, Cambridge, MA.

McFarlan, W. and McKenney, J. (1983). *Corporate Information Systems Management: the Issues Facing Executives.* Dow Jones Irwin, New York.

Morrison, C. and Berndt, E. (1990). Assessing the Productivity of Information Technology Equipment in the US Manufacturing Industry. *National Bureau of Economic Research Working Paper 3582*, Washington, January.

Nievelt, M.C.A. van (1992). Managing with Information Technology—a Decade of Wasted Money? *Compact*, Summer, 15–24.

Nievelt, M.C.A. van and Willcocks, L. (1997). *Benchmarking Organizational and IT Performance.* Templeton Executive Research Briefing 6, Templeton College, Oxford.

Norris, G. (1996). Post-Investment Appraisal. In Willcocks, L. (ed.) *Investing in Information Systems: Evaluation and Management.* Chapman and Hall, London, 193–223.

Parker, M., Benson, R. and Trainor, H. (1988). *Information Economics.* Prentice Hall, London.

Peters, G. (1994). Evaluating your Computer Investment Strategy. In Willcocks, L. (ed.), *Information Management: Evaluation of Information Systems Investments.* Chapman and Hall, London, 99–112.

Peters, G. (1996). From Strategy to Implementation: Identifying and Managing Benefits of IT Investments. In Willcocks, L. (ed.) *Investing in Information Systems: Evaluation and Management.* Chapman and Hall, London, 225–41.

Porter, M. and Millar, V. (1991). How Information Gives you Competitive Advantage. In McGowan, W. (ed.) *Revolution in Real Time: Managing Informa-*

tion Technology in the 1990s. Harvard Business School Press, Boston, MA.

Quinn, J. and Baily, M. (1994). Information Technology: Increasing Productivity in Services. *Academy of Management Executive*, 8, 3, 28–47.

Roach, S. (1986). *Macro-Realities of the Information Economy*. National Academy of Sciences, New York.

Roach, S. (1988). Technology and the Services Sector: the Hidden Competitive Challenge. *Technological Forecasting and Social Change*, 34, 4, 387–403.

Roach, S. (1991). Services under Siege—The Restructuring Imperative. *Harvard Business Review*, September–October, 69, 5, 82–92.

Roach, S. (1994). Lessons of the Productivity Paradox. In Gillin, P. (ed.) *The Productivity Payoff: the 100 Most Effective Users of Information Technology. Computerworld*, September 19th, Section 2, 55.

Robson, W. (1997). *Strategic Management and Information Systems*. Pitman Publishing, London.

Sager, I. and Gleckman, H. (1994). The Information Revolution. *Business Week*, June 13th, 35–9.

Strassmann, P. (1990). *The Business Value of Computers*. Information Economics Press, New Canaan.

Strassmann, P. (1997). *The Squandered Computer*. Information Economics Press, New Canaan.

Sullivan-Trainor, M. (1994). Best of Breed. In Gillin, P. (ed.) *The Productivity Payoff: The 100 Most Effective Users of Information Technology. Computerworld*, September 19th, 8–9.

Swanson, E. and Beath, C. (1988). *Maintaining Information Systems in Organizations*. John Wiley, Chichester.

Symons, V. (1994). Evaluation of Information Systems Investments: Towards Multiple Perspectives. In Willcocks, L. (ed.) *Information Management: Evaluation of Information Systems Investments*. Chapman and Hall, London, 253–68.

Walsham, G. (1993). *Interpreting Information Systems in Organizations*. John Wiley, Chichester.

Weill, P. (1990). *Do Computers Pay off?* ICIT Press, Washington.

Willcocks, L. (1992). IT Evaluation: Managing the Catch-22. *European Management Journal*, 10, 2, 220–29.

Willcocks, L. (ed.) (1994). *Information Management: Evaluation of Information Systems Investments*. Chapman and Hall, London.

Willcocks, L. (ed.) (1996a). *Investing in Information Systems: Evaluation and Management*. Chapman and Hall, London.

Willcocks, L. (1996b). Does IT-Enabled BPR Pay off? Recent Findings on Economics and Impacts. In Willcocks, L. (ed.) *Investing in Information Systems: Evaluation and Management*. Chapman and Hall, London, 171–92.

Willcocks, L., Currie, W. and Mason, D. (1999). *Information Systems at Work: People, Politics and Technology*. McGraw-Hill, Maidenhead.

Willcocks, L., Feeny, D. and Islei, G. (eds) (1997). *Managing IT as a Strategic Resource*. McGraw-Hill, Maidenhead.

Willcocks, L. and Fitzgerald, G. (1994). *A Business Guide to IT Outsourcing*. Business Intelligence, London.

Willcocks, L. and Lacity, M. (1997). *The Strategic Sourcing of Information Systems*. John Wiley, Chichester.

Willcocks, L. and Lester, S. (1991). Information Systems Investments: Evaluation at the Feasibility Stage of Projects. *Technovation*, 11, 5, 243–68.

Willcocks, L. and Lester, S. (1996). The Evaluation and Management of Information Systems Investments: from Feasibility to Routine Operations. In Willcocks, L. (ed.) *Investing in Information Systems: Evaluation and Management.* Chapman and Hall, London, 15–36.

Willcocks, L. and Margetts, H. (1993). Risk Assessment and Information Systems. *European Journal of Information Systems*, 3, 2, 127–38.

3
Benchmarking Organizational and IT Performance

M.C. AUGUSTUS VAN NIEVELT
VN International

INTRODUCTION

During the past decade, particularly since the launch of the personal computer (PC), business spending on information systems (IS) has increased significantly. It is perfectly reasonable that management boards now request some proof that the IS investments which they approved have actually led to increased productivity and profitability.

Rationally, we expect applications of information technology (IT) to improve economic performance by increasing efficiency through automation and by enhancing effectiveness through information. The business literature certainly provides ample anecdotal evidence of benefits derived from IT. But, as described in the Introduction and Chapter 2, some well-publicised macroeconometric analyses threaten to spoil our euphoria by essentially concluding that "IT does not appear to have improved the economy as a whole" (for a collection of related papers, see Harris, 1996).

Is it possible to resolve the apparent inconsistencies in this so-called IT productivity paradox? The macroeconomic findings can be interpreted in two ways:

1. IT contributes effectively nothing to performance, or
2. IT has effects, but *in the aggregate* the negative experiences of some businesses cancel out the benefits obtained by others.

Beyond the IT Productivity Paradox.
Edited by L. P. Willcocks and S. Lester © 1999 John Wiley & Sons Ltd.

Option 2 implies the existence of one or more additional factors, that determine if IT will boost or depress performance.

Since *aggregate* national or industry-level data cannot be used to distinguish between these alternatives, we must investigate the economic effects of IT at the microeconomic level, i.e. at the level of distinct business units subject to competitive market conditions. And the organizational effectiveness of these units must be measured with an appropriately designed productivity gauge.

The Benchmarking Organizational Performance (BOP)™ research programme has analysed 300 cases in Europe and North America, and the results statistically demonstrate that applications of IT can have strongly positive or strongly negative effects. Among the critically important factors shown to separate success from failure are customer perceptions and organizational structure. The finding that customer satisfaction is the key determinant of economic success confirms the validity of the management literature's near-unanimous recommendation to pursue a customer-oriented strategy. Nevertheless, it was surprising also to find that, when customer perceptions are unfavourable relative to competitors, executing such a broadly recommended move as investing in "strategic IS" has a strong probability of causing significant economic damage.

WHY IS THERE AN IT PRODUCTIVITY PARADOX?

Opening their 1993 paper on strategic alignment, Henderson and Venkatraman summarized the IT productivity paradox as follows:

> How do we reconcile the dramatic increase in the role of IT in organizations and markets with the evidence of minimal productivity gains at an aggregate level of the economy?

The aggregate level of the economy is the focus of macroeconomics—the study of business cycles, inflation and unemployment. Microeconomics, on the other hand, investigates how individual organizations and markets behave, and includes examining the role of IT in this behaviour. Why, then, did macroeconomists feel compelled to examine this productivity conundrum, in the process generating so much negative publicity?

Obviously, the perceived slowdown in economic growth and productivity during the 1970s and 1980s—just when investments in IT were sharply increasing—was a legitimate subject for macroeconomists to study. Moreover, the economic data required for such a study is made available predominantly at the aggregate level. Unfortunately, macroeconomists tend to treat IT as a "factor of production", searching for the direct relationship between an input—in this case investments in IT—and the output of the economy (for example gross domestic product). When the aggregate-level data could not reveal that such a relationship existed, the IT productivity paradox was upon us.

As discussed in the Introduction and previous chapter, Brynjolfsson (1993) and others have suggested several ways to explain this paradox. The simplest explanation is a time lag between input and output, due to the slow process of learning how to apply the novel technologies. In other words, IT does produce beneficial effects, but these may take years to show up. Such a time lag may well have played a role in the late 1970s and early 1980s, but user-friendly interfaces and improved IS development tools should have substantially eliminated this delaying effect.

The second argument is mismeasurement, since IT-enabled organizational productivity ought to have been measured at the business unit or product-market level. This argument invalidates all research based on data at the total economy level, at the industry level and even at the multibusiness firm level. Consequently, publicly or commercially available databases cannot be used to investigate IT effects, necessitating the time-consuming collection of unpublished information from individual business units.[1]

Finally, the redistribution hypothesis implies the existence of gainers and losers. This argues that an industry-wide application of IT indeed increases efficiency and productivity in that branch of the economy, but simultaneously intensifies competition, thus preventing the translation of productivity gains into industry-wide profitability increases. The result is a zero-sum game whereby some competitors experience economic improvements from the application of IT, but at the expense of others in the same market.

Long before the productivity paradox spectre was raised, we reported the following initial results of the BOP research programme at that time called Management Productivity and Information Technology (van Nievelt, 1984, pp. 13–14):

> surprisingly, the effects of IT-related expenditures on management productivity [i.e. economic performance] appeared random at best ... [but] a closer scrutiny of the data revealed the existence of a bimodal population, which was then pre-sorted by strategic position [a multifactor composite indicating profit potential].

Subsequent analysis of the pre-sorted data[2] demonstrated:

> the application of IT improves management productivity only in businesses in ... an average or superior strategic position, [conversely] a significant

damaging effect from rising IT expenditures emerged for businesses in inferior strategic positions.

Evidently, the earliest BOP findings already suggested a redistribution mechanism. At about the same time, Cron and Sobol (1983) also reported finding a bimodal distribution within a single industry, when they tabulated the effect of IT investments on the profitability of medical supply wholesalers. When they pre-sorted by annual revenues, it was found that the larger companies profited from IT, while the smaller ones were adversely affected. Since within a single market revenue becomes a proxy for market share, Cron and Sobol observed likewise that competitive position affects the economic benefits from IT.

To advance the BOP research programme further, it next became crucially important to identify the key operative factor in this "strategic" or "competitive" position: was it share of market, product quality, or possibly something else? Through systematic statistical comparison of the different variables, the research empirically established that *Customer satisfaction* (relative to competitors) is the determining factor.

The above finding is certainly not counter-intuitive, given the ubiquitous counsel for businesses to become more market driven and customer oriented or, in the terminology of Henderson and Venkatraman (1993), to practise "strategic alignment".[3]

> Our concept of strategic alignment is based on [the] fundamental assumption [that] economic performance is directly related to the ability of management to create a strategic fit between the position of an organization in the competitive product-market arena and the design of an appropriate administrative structure to support [strategy] execution.

And, as also discussed in Chapter 2, others have urged the need to bring quality and customer service into the IT productivity equation (Brynjolfsson, 1993):

> The closer one examines the data behind the studies of IT performance, the more it looks like mismeasurement is at the core of the "productivity paradox" ... Rapid innovation has made IT intensive industries particularly susceptible to the problems associated with measuring quality changes ... Increased variety, improved timeliness of delivery and personalized customer service are additional benefits that are poorly represented in productivity statistics. These are all qualities that are particularly likely to be enhanced by IT.

THE RESEARCH BASE

The BOP research programme was launched in 1983, initially as the framework for a systematic and facts-based investigation of the way in which the application of IT was affecting the economic performance of individual businesses. Since BOP was relatively unburdened by any pre-conceived hypotheses to be proven or disproven, the programme collected numerical data on an extremely broad spectrum of over 100 financial and organizational variables, including market characteristics, personnel headcount, structure (e.g. number of organizational layers), employment costs and purchased services by core process, balance sheet items, corporate allocations and information systems expenditures. It should be noted that BOP collects data on all IT-related expenditures (including purchased data and communications services) and not just on capital investments.

Individual business units contribute the data, receiving a benchmarked diagnostic performance audit in return. BOP defines a business unit as a single line of products or services or similar operating component with an identifiable set of customers and competitors for which an income statement can be constructed.

The programme is currently (1998) in its 16th year and the BOP database has grown to well over 300 cases—far in excess of minimum statistical requirements—of more than 100 variables each. On-going fundamental research applies sophisticated statistical techniques to identify and validate the significant single-factor correlations and paired interactions among the many thousands of possible combinations. This broad-spectrum data foundation produces results well beyond an IT field of vision, and has enabled the recognition of correlations that had hitherto eluded more narrowly focused research efforts.

SELECTING AN APPROPRIATE PRODUCTIVITY PARADIGM

A Model Describing the Dependent Variable

A key element in describing productivity is to have a measure of economic performance. Commonly used indices of economic performance such as return on investment (ROI), return on shareholders' equity (ROE), or return on assets (ROA) share two main shortcomings. A focus on invested capital makes these partial productivity ratios rather ill suited to measuring how structure and management affect business performance. Furthermore, these ratios are strongly influenced by specific industry characteristics, manifesting themselves predominantly in the operations segment of the business, which makes cross-industry comparison nearly impossible. But working with single-industry databases is generally not feasible, since single industries rarely encompass enough competitors to provide the minimum number of observations (approximately 30) needed for a statistically valid analysis.

For these reasons, the BOP data definitions were expressly structured to make them virtually independent from branch of industry, which subsequently allowed comparison of organizational performances in a wide range of economic activities. This is accomplished by gauging organizational performance as *overhead productivity*, a partial productivity ratio in which full operations costs are deducted from both numerator and denominator. It should be noted that a valid Organizational Performance Index (OPI) calculation, as shown in Figure 3.1, requires the deduction of full costs, that is, including the opportunity cost of capital employed.[4]

This OPI accounting conversion requires operations to be distinguished from overhead:

- Operations tasks involve all aspects of production and delivery of today's products and services in today's market.
- Overhead is the non-operations segment of an organization, where tomorrow's business is developed, i.e. where the focus is on change and where all strategic projects are handled.

During data collection, businesses first identify the various operations and overhead functions in their organization, then likewise reclassify (operations versus overhead) the corresponding headcounts, investments and expenses.

$$
\begin{aligned}
\text{OPI} \;&=\; \frac{\text{overhead output}}{\text{overhead input}} \\[2mm]
&=\; \frac{(\text{value added}) \text{ less } (\text{full operations cost})}{(\text{total costs}) \text{ less } (\text{full operations cost})} \\[2mm]
&=\; \frac{\text{organizational value added}}{\text{full overhead cost}} \\[2mm]
&=\; 1 + \frac{\text{economic profit (before taxes)}}{\text{full overhead cost}}
\end{aligned}
$$

Note: a valid OPI calculation requires the deduction of **full** costs, i.e. including the opportunity cost of capital employed.

Figure 3.1   *The OPI Calculation*

BUILDING THE ORGANIZATIONAL PERFORMANCE MODELS

Following the creation of a statistically reliable BOP database, the (on-going) multiphase screening process could be initiated to determine how each of the tabulated variables, both individually and in various combinations, affected organizational performance. Specifically, this screening process measures the statistical significance of OPI as a function of single, paired, and multiple (> 2) factors.

Surprisingly, it was found that less than one quarter of the single-factor relationships with OPI—as shown through second-order (quadratic) curve fitting—was linear or even quasi-linear, signalling the probability of finding many significant two-factor interactions.

Confirmation was obtained in the second phase of the screening process, with the additional—and even more surprising—finding that many of these statistically significant two-factor interaction effects on OPI were stronger than the component single-factor effects. This key characteristic of organizational performance, on which the academic literature remains virtually silent, illustrates the complex problems encountered in managing business dynamics, and has catalysed the development of BOP's performance contour maps, as displayed in Figure 3.2, to assist managers in navigating such complexities.

Once the statistical importance of the two-factor interactions was demonstrated, a closer look followed at the possible forms that such interactions could take. When x and y interact, the response surface OPI = f (x,y) cannot be a flat plane, by definition. If we use a quadratic equation to represent this surface, the data will appear in one of two possible forms:[5]

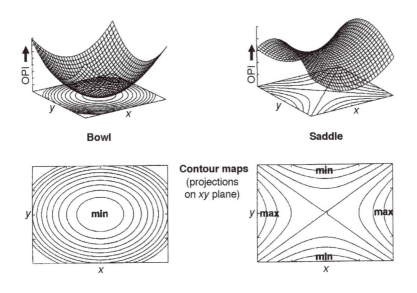

Figure 3.2 *Representing the Model: the Bowl and Saddle*

- a paraboloid (bowl) form, represented by equations such as $OPI = x^2 + y^2$, or
- a minimax (saddle) form, represented by equations such as $OPI = x^2 - y^2$.

These two conceptual possibilities, the bowl and the saddle, are observed repeatedly in the BOP research findings and are compared side by side in Figure 3.2.

However impressive three-dimensional models may be to look at, two-dimensional "contour maps" are preferable to locate a business's current position or to plot a strategic move. Contour maps are projections of the 3-D surface on the horizontal (X–Y) plane. In this chapter the contours are always "iso-OPI lines", that is, lines connecting points with equal economic performance.[6]

It is important to realize that these two forms dictate radically different optimization strategies:[7]

- A bowl model usually has a single set of optimal x and y conditions—within the possible options—which may be approached through continuous (stepwise) change.
- A saddle model generally has two very different sets of optimal x and y combinations (i.e. "max"), resulting in conditional statements such as "if the x value is ... then the optimum y value is ..., but if $x = $ ... then the best $y = $ ...".

Since gradually moving from one optimum ("max") saddle position to the other involves an at best temporary performance deterioration, the recommended strategy is a sudden large "max-to-max" move, in other words a (discontinuous) jump. BOP research shows that the "bowl" model frequently involves investment decisions, while the "saddle" model often represents organizational restructuring.

To summarize: BOP research has found a large (and still growing) number of two-factor interactions that affect organizational performance. These correlations are statistically highly significant, meaning that it is extremely improbable that the observed effects are actually random. However, the *direction* of causality—what is cause and what is effect?—is not provided by the statistics, but must follow from logic.

WHAT IS CUSTOMER SATISFACTION?

BOP's Customer Satisfaction profile quantifies how customers perceive a business's products and services in comparison with all the leading competitors. Key aspects are:

- the opinions of *all* customers in the market are reflected, not just those of the current customers of the unit under study;
- customers evaluate not only the *intrinsic* (or "embedded") characteristics of a product or service, but also the *auxiliary*, delivery-related attributes such as time to completion, staff assistance, convenience of location etc.;
- differences in perception resulting from advertising or corporate reputation are genuine and must be recognized.

Customer satisfaction information should be collected primarily through employees having frequent contact with customers, for example from front office and customer service departments. Ideally, data on customer perceptions should be confirmed periodically through independent market research, using techniques such as conjoint analysis. However, while such research will provide more precise customer satisfaction data, it is not essential for the BOP diagnostics.

The data collection involves three steps:

1. Identify the key concerns (criteria) that affect customer satisfaction.
2. Assign percentage weights to each of the above customer concerns.
3. Rate (on a 1–10 scale) the business under study, as well as its three largest competitors, from the customer's point of view, on all key concerns.

The BOP diagnostics module then calculates (through summation of the weighted ratings over all criteria) the Relative Customer Satisfaction (RCS) scores for each of the (four) major competitors in the market. RCS is a highly actionable variable: through product development, marketing (e.g. advertising) and/or application of IT criteria can be modified, weights can be shifted and (relative) ratings can be altered. RCS also has a strong positive correlation with market share.[8]

DEBUNKING THE IT PRODUCTIVITY PARADOX

As mentioned before in this chapter, the earliest research findings from the database already pointed to what has since been termed a "redistribution mechanism" (van Nievelt, 1984). Nevertheless, both powerful, desktop-resident statistical software (Wilkinson, 1990) and faster microprocessors were needed to investigate this mechanism adequately. Once these tools were in place, however, it became possible actually to recreate—with a microeconomic database—the analysis that had caused macroeconomists to conjure up the productivity paradox. Look at Figure 3.3, based on 300 cases.

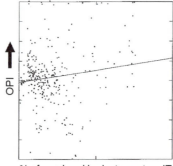

% of overhead budget spent on IT

Figure 3.3   *OPI, Overhead IT Budget and the Productivity Paradox*

Although there *appears* to be a slightly positive effect, the $R^2 = 0.02$ tells us that in fact there is no direct (i.e. linear) correlation between OPI and percentage of overhead budget spent on IT—that is, the relationship is completely random. So far, therefore, BOP appears to confirm that strategic (i.e. overhead-applied) IT does not contribute to economic performance. Put differently: IT might play a labour-saving role in operations, but strategically the technology is no more than a tool that cannot add value *per se*, a finding that is certainly not counter-intuitive.

When we repeat the analysis by fitting a second-order (quadratic) equation to the same 300 data points (Figure 3.4), the R^2 increases from 0.02 to 0.1, still rather a weak correlation. However, the strong curvature of the graph signals that a linear (one-on-one) relationship is definitely inappropriate here, and that we must therefore search for a second, "intervening" variable.

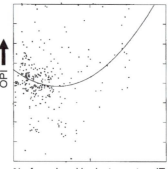

% of overhead budget spent on IT

Figure 3.4   *Reexamining OPI and Overhead IT Expenditure*

A systematic process of elimination eventually proved that customer satisfaction was the key factor, and indeed, on rechecking the correlation with OPI—after adding Customer Satisfaction as a variable interacting with IT—the statistical significance increased to a meaningful level (quadratic regression $R^2 = 0.2$). In contour projection, a stretched-out "bowl" pattern is revealed (see Figure 3.5) once the model is expanded (far) beyond the range of actual observations detailed in Figure 3.6.[9]

The joint effect of customer satisfaction and overhead IT on economic performance can be summarized as follows:

> Applying overhead IT will—by itself—not remedy low customer satisfaction, but IT applications can significantly enhance favourable customer perceptions.

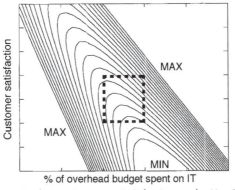

Figure 3.5 *Relative Customer Satisfaction as the Key Factor*

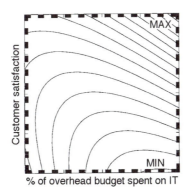

Figure 3.6 *Relative Customer Satisfaction as the Key Factor: Detail*

To understand the strategic consequences of this finding, the contour map of the model OPI = [customer satisfaction]*[overhead IT] is once more reproduced in Figure 3.7, but this time with a heavy line drawn from the lower lefthand corner to the OPI "peak" at the top right. This line can be interpreted in two ways:

1. Reading the map like a mountaineer, it makes good sense initially to follow a contour line (A–B–C), thereby avoiding a steep depression in the terrain (= performance loss) and then (D) to proceed, approximately perpendicular to the contours, along the path of steepest ascent towards the peak. During stage "A", enhanced customer satisfaction derives either from non-IT-based improvements or from commoditized operations systems.[10] "B" and "D" are stages of securing competitive advantages through IT. The most likely interpretation of the "C" segment is a stage of investing in information systems (IS) infrastructure.
2. However, the same (quasi-)diagonal can also be viewed as separating two zones that represent fundamentally different IT investment strategies:
    *   businesses positioned above the line should seek higher performance through additional investments in strategic (overhead-based) information systems;
    *   businesses positioned below the line manifest (potential) misalignment symptoms and should refocus their information systems' development effort towards boosting customer satisfaction.

To initiate the complex process of reprioritizing IS resource allocation, it is useful to perform a process-by-process review of all the business's information systems, focusing on each system's contribution to cus-

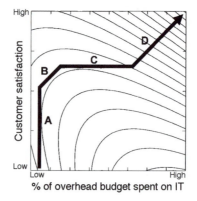

Figure 3.7   *The Redistribution "Zoning Map"*

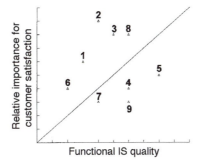

Figure 3.8 *Bank Example: Functional IS Quality Contribution to Customer Satisfaction*

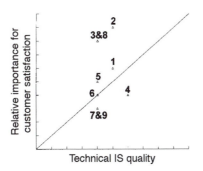

Figure 3.9 *Bank Example: Technical IS Quality Contribution to Customer Satisfaction*

tomer satisfaction and other specified strategic goals.[11] Figures 3.8 and 3.9 demonstrate the results at a bank, when this unit of a financial services corporation reviewed the relative IS contribution towards customer satisfaction for its nine core banking processes.

A perfectly balanced information system would have all nine processes neatly aligned on the 45° diagonal. The farther any point is located above this diagonal, the greater the indicated shortfall in systems support relative to that particular process's importance.

Clearly, processes of marketing (2) and advice and consultancy (3) are prime candidates for a development effort towards enhancing customer satisfaction.

SYSTEMS MUST SUPPORT STRUCTURE

The preceding paragraph focused on the role that applications of overhead IT play in reinforcing a business's *competitive* characteristics, either by exploiting some unique technological advantage or by supporting the existing business's processes, for example by improving its delivery of service. But IT applications play an equally significant role by reinforcing or modifying a business's *structural* characteristics: by improving coordination (e.g. groupware), communication (e.g. e-mail) and integration (e.g. electronic data interchange), as follows:

- Coordination enables many concurrent, often interdisciplinary activities, thereby, for example, reducing the time needed to deliver products to market.
- Communication provides the internal capabilities to produce information and feedback rapidly.
- Integration can link a business electronically with its suppliers and/or customers.

Figures 3.10 to 3.14 illustrate the structural support role of IT applications in overhead. For all five graphs, the x (horizontal) axis represents the same variable, that is, the fraction of the overhead budget spent on IT, while the y (vertical) axis represents a different variable in each exhibit. All five graphs are contour maps (in which the contours again connect points of equal performance) with the saddle pattern. But the orientation of the saddle varies and in Figure 3.11 the saddle point is even "virtual", i.e. outside the range of observed values. The arrows point to max.[6] A brief commentary relates to each figure.

There is in Figure 3.10 a strong interactive correlation between research and development spending for *innovation* and spending on overhead IT. Increased investments in IT can lower R&D expenditures while simultaneously improving economic performance (note: the "virtual" left 20% of the graph was only added to locate the saddle).

In Figure 3.11, *downsizing* also exhibits a saddle pattern, although most of it is virtual. According to this correlation, it is optimal to match

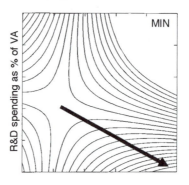

Figure 3.10   *R&D and Overhead IT Spending*

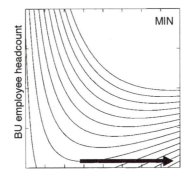

Figure 3.11 *Employee Headcount and Overhead IT Spending*

reductions in headcount with gradual increases in overhead IT—following a contour line preserves performance. The worst combination is simultaneously overstaffing *and* overinvesting in IT.

In Figure 3.12 the third negative correlation shows that the reduction of *organizational complexity*—by eliminating management layers—will only lead to major improvements in organizational performance when the restructuring is accompanied by increased support from information systems.

The positive interaction shown in Figure 3.13 demonstrates that increasing the *organizational quality*—measured as the percentage of knowledge workers in overhead—does not pay beyond a certain level, unless these knowledge workers are also adequately supported by information systems.

In Figure 3.14 overhead *vertical integration* appears to give us a choice: A or B. In fact, these alternatives represent widely different conditions, whereby customer satisfaction (CS) is, once again, the determining

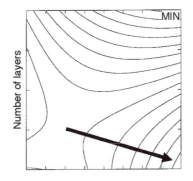

Figure 3.12 *Organizational Complexity and Overhead IT Spending*

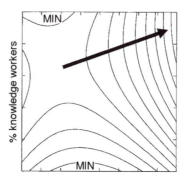

Figure 3.13   *Knowledge Workers and Overhead IT Spending*

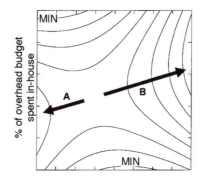

Figure 3.14   *Vertical Integration and Overhead IT Spending*

factor. At low CS, A is optimal: the recommendation is to minimize vertical integration through outsourcing and using centralized corporate functions. But at above average CS select B: now it pays to increase vertical integration (i.e. to enhance core competences), as long as IT support is also provided.

In Summary

Research on the BOP database has uncovered numerous examples of overhead IT—in interactive teamwork with other variables—significantly affecting organizational performance. Although cause and effect can only be inferred, the probability that these correlations would in fact represent random phenomena is extremely small. At the same time, it becomes clear that optimizing a business's organizational structure is an extremely complex process involving the simultaneous adjustment of multiple variables. Information technology plays a key role in that process.

Finally, although the focus of this chapter is on overhead, the BOP database also provides evidence of IT support to operations, for example in controlling working capital requirements. In Figures 3.15 and 3.16 the *x*-axis represents spending on operations IT.

In Figure 3.15, the (negative) correlation of receivables and spending on operations IT shows an "inverted bowl" pattern, i.e. a single set of conditions for optimum economic performance (OPI). IT appears to contribute towards lower capital needs.

In Figure 3.16, the control of inventories (raw materials, work in process and finished goods) exhibits a "double-max" saddle pattern. Our hypothesis is that businesses that can operate with minimal inventories should do so. But if maintaining significant inventories is essential, then operations IS must ensure that the correct inventory is available at the proper time and place.

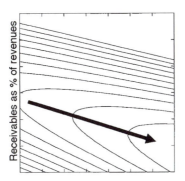

Figure 3.15   *Impact of Operations IT Spending on Capital Needs*

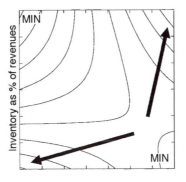

Figure 3.16   *Inventories and Operations IT Spending*

CONCLUSION

This chapter adds to the evidence assembled in the previous two chapters. As also trailed at points in the Introduction to this book, the proposition of the IT productivity paradox—that the application of information technology in business organizations fails to affect productivity—must be rejected as faulty. Statistical analysis of business-unit-level data strongly substantiates a significant and multifaceted effect of IT on productivity.

The evidence incorporated in the BOP database[12] covers a very broad spectrum of business experiences, ranging, for example, from enhancing the effectiveness of a pharmaceutical sales force by equipping them with interactive, laptop-computer-based information systems, to guiding the restructuring of a multinational consumer products company from a country-based to a product-oriented organization.

Additional BOP research (beyond the facts presented with Figure 3.14; see also van Nievelt and Willcocks, 1997) has demonstrated that customer satisfaction is indeed the controlling factor for optimizing an organization. Accordingly, it is clearly inappropriate to impose a uniform ("one-size-fits-all") organization structure on a multibusiness corporation with Relative Customer Satisfaction scores ranging from favourable to unfavourable.

At this point, it may be useful to recall the productivity paradigm in its basic form:

$$\text{productivity} = \frac{\text{output}}{\text{input}}$$

Operational *efficiencies* affect the denominator (input), concentrate on reducing costs and have frequently involved the application of IT in the form of automation. Organizational *effectiveness* involves the creation of value and affects the numerator (output) of the productivity equation.

It appears that by 1996 many businesses had gone about as far as they could in cutting costs or improving efficiency, and that they were now once more switching their strategic focus towards growth (*The Economist*, 1996). However, this was not before they had fundamentally changed their ways of doing business. In other words, strategy may now be shifting away from denominator management and towards numerator management. Since experience has shown that value creation can potentially improve economic performance far more than cost reductions ever could, such a shift would in general be an excellent omen for any economy. Nevertheless, as this chapter has demonstrated, organizational transformation is more like crossing a minefield than a pleasant walk in the country, and requires a highly detailed map.

NOTES

1 The Benchmarking Organizational Performance (BOP)™ research programme, the subject of this chapter, is based exclusively on proprietary, unpublished business-level (i.e. product-line) data.

2 The initial results (van Nievelt, 1984) were analysed with the AQD (Analysis of Quantitative Data) statistical software package. AQD was developed by Robert Schlaifer for student use at Harvard University—at a time when computing meant accessing an expensive, mainframe-based, timesharing system—and was specifically designed to lower costs by minimizing CPU requirements. This was partially accomplished by pre-sorting a data set according to a selected criterion into two or more subsets and analysing each subset separately. AQD results were often presented as a set of bar graphs. Likewise, a three-dimensional response surface was shown as a 3×3 matrix of vertical bars. A major disadvantage of using such a relatively crude tool is that valuable statistical information is discarded in the process. Since 1988, all BOP analyses have been performed with SYSTAT (Wilkinson, 1990).

3 It is curious, nevertheless, that Henderson and Venkatraman emphasize consideration of the competitive market, but nominate customer satisfaction (otherwise undefined by them) as a performance criterion in only one out of the four perspectives in their elaborate alignment model. BOP research findings suggest that they may have underestimated the significance of customer satisfaction as a key determinant of economic success. Inevitably, the question arises as to why academic research so often produces conceptual models, without also providing the evidence that these models do indeed work as advertised.

4 This follows the concepts of *residual income accounting*, originally developed at the General Electric Company in the 1960s, and resurrected in the 1990s as economic value added (Tully, 1993).

5 There is actually a third form (equation $OPI = -x^2 - y^2$) represented by an inverted bowl with a centred maximum.

6 All contour maps in this chapter follow the same convention: the bottom lefthand corner is always the low end of both x and y scales; the contours are "iso-OPI lines", i.e. they connect points with equal organizational economic performances; "max" indicates performance peaks (high OPI) and "min" indicates performance valleys (low OPI). An arrow in the graph indicates the best route to "max".

7 In the real world these models are neither (perfectly) centred, symmetrical nor orthogonal, thus often producing rather distorted contour maps. The location of the actual boundary conditions, relative to the best (max) and worst (min) factor combinations, then determines what strategic options are actually available to management.

8 Relative Customer Satisfaction (RCS) scores should not be confused with the University of Michigan's (unfortunately named) Customer Satisfaction Index (CSI). The latter measures the "gap" between a consumer's baseline of expectations and his or her actual perceptions of quality, i.e. how a product or service compares to an ideal, exclusively from the viewpoint of a current user. CSI leads to results radically different from RCS, e.g. CSI correlates negatively with market share (!) (Griffin and Hauser, 1993; Anderson, Fornell and Lehman, 1993).

9 The Relative Customer Satisfaction scale covers -100 (this business scores below every competitor on all criteria) to $+100$ (this business scores above every competitor on all criteria).

10 Over time, most IT-based capabilities lose their uniqueness and cease to provide a competitive advantage. Keen (1991) calls this "commoditization". It occurs when a particular capability is offered by (almost) all competitors, at which point the application migrates in BOP terminology from strategic (overhead) to commodity (operations). Operations IT applications are unlikely to provide a competitive advantage, but the failure (or absence) of such a commodity system can nevertheless cause significant negative customer perceptions (i.e. dissatisfaction).

11 The author gratefully acknowledges the contributions of H. van Irsel and G.J.P. Swinkels at Amsterdam University in the development of the core process/IS alignment tool. The methodology involves three steps: (1) estimate for each process the relative system importance, e.g. towards enhancing customer satisfaction (y coordinates); (2) determine for each process the relative information systems' functional and technical quality (x coordinates); (3) prepare x–y scatterplots, and focus attention on the points above the ($45°$) diagonal, since these points represent processes inadequately supported relative to the (strategic) importance of the particular process.

12 Note that the BOP methodology can also be used in a "what if" mode, to evaluate proposed IT projects prior to making an actual investment. Market research can test how (potential) customers perceive novel concepts, prototypes of new products, or proposed innovative services. The BOP models translate such customer perceptions into probable economic benefits, giving financial analysts the "hard numbers" required to compare projections of revenues against costs.

REFERENCES

Anderson, E., Fornell, C. and Lehman, D. (1993). Economic Consequences of Providing Quality and Customer Satisfaction. *Marketing Science Institute Report*, Number 93–112, August, 23.

Brynjolfsson, E. (1993). The Productivity Paradox of Information Technology. *Communications of the ACM*, 35, December, 66–77.

Cron, W.L. and Sobol, M.G. (1983). The Relationship between Computerization and Performance: a Strategy for Maximizing the Economic Benefits of Computerization. *Journal of Information Management*, 6, 2, 171–81.

Economist, The (1996). Upsizing. *The Economist*, February 10th, 61.

Griffin, A. and Hauser, J.R. (1993). The Voice of the Customer. *Marketing Science*, 12, Winter, 1–20.

Harris, D. (ed.) (1996). *Organizational Linkages: Understanding the Productivity Paradox*. National Academy Press, Washington DC.

Henderson, J.C. and Venkatraman, N. (1993). Strategic Alignment: Leveraging Information Technology for Transforming Organizations. *IBM Systems Journal*, 32, 1, 4–16.

Keen, P. (1991). *Shaping the Future: Business Design through Information Technology*. Harvard Business Press, Boston, MA.

Nievelt, M.C.A. van (1984). Management Productivity and Information Technology. *Information Strategy: The Executive's Journal*, 1, 1, 9–15.

Nievelt, M.C.A. van and Willcocks, L. (1997). *Benchmarking Organizational and IT Performance.* Oxford Executive Research Briefing No. 6, Templeton College, Oxford.

Tully, S. (1993). The Real Key to Creating Wealth. *Fortune,* September 20th, 38–50.

Wilkinson, L. (1990). *SYSTAT: the System for Statistics.* Evanston, Illinois.

SECTION II

IT Investment Appraisal

4
Information Systems/Technology Evaluation Practices: Evidence from UK Organizations

JOAN A. BALLANTINE, ROBERT D. GALLIERS AND STEPHANIE J. STRAY
Warwick Business School

INTRODUCTION

Globally, computers and telecommunications investments now amount to a half or more of most large firms' annual capital expenditures. According to Willcocks (1996), IT expenditure by business and public-sector organizations in the UK was £33.6 billion in 1995, and expected to rise by 8.2%, 7% and 6.2% in subsequent years, representing an average of over 2% of turnover or, in the public sector, an average of £3546 per employee. Even by the early 1990s, the comparative spend in the USA was larger. For example, Maglitta and Sullivan-Trainor (1991) quote a figure of 2.7% of corporate turnover spent on IS/IT investments, while government statistics suggested that, by 1994, computers and other IT equipment amounted to a half of all business spending on equipment—not including the billions spent on software and programmers each year (Sager and Gleckman, 1994). However, Keen (1991) contends that only 20% of the cost of IT investments is actually visible (see also Davis, 1989), hence actual spending levels are likely to be higher than those reported by organizations.

Coupled with increasing IS/IT spending levels and the global

Beyond the IT Productivity Paradox.
Edited by L. P. Willcocks and S. Lester © 1999 John Wiley & Sons Ltd.

economic and competitive climate which organizations face today, as outlined in the Introduction, there is concern over the measurement of IS effectiveness, cost justification and cost containment. These concerns have been found to rank among the top key IS issues in a number of studies carried out between 1984 and 1997 in the USA, the UK, the Gulf and the Republic of China (see, for example, Dickson and Nechis, 1984; Niederman, Branchaeu and Wetherbe, 1991; Badri, 1992; Clark, 1992; Price Waterhouse, 1994; Galliers, Merali and Spearing, 1994; Kelly *et al.*, 1994; Wang and Turban, 1994; Pollard and Hayne, 1996; Pervan, 1997).

Given the above concerns and rising levels of IS/IT expenditure, this chapter seeks to build on Chapter 2 and provide further insights into the IS/IT evaluation process in organizations in order to understand it more fully. A review of previous empirical work examining the evaluation of IS/IT investments is first presented. The results of a survey carried out in the latter half of 1993, investigating the IS/IT evaluation practices of a sample of the top 1000 UK companies, are then discussed. It is hoped that the findings of the study will add to our existing knowledge of IS/IT evaluation practices.

CONTEXT

The evolutionary use of IS/IT within organizations is well documented and can be seen as moving from one of automating to informating (Zuboff, 1988), and more recently to transformation (see Introduction). In line with this, the role of evaluation has also changed from one of measuring efficiency gains to improvements in effectiveness, to assessing the contribution that IS/IT can make to the way organizations do business (see Chapters 6 and 7 for helpful evaluation frameworks). Thus as the role of IS/IT has changed from one of support to one of strategic importance, the process of evaluation has become an increasingly complex one. Coupled with increasing complexity, Remenyi, Money and Twite (1993) recognize changing attitudes towards investment in IS/IT in the 1990s with even "greater cynicism about IT benefits than ever before" (p. 25). Similar concerns were voiced by Hochstrasser and Griffiths (1991), reporting that IT often fails to deliver acceptable returns (these concerns emanate from a range of studies carried out between 1987 and 1990). For example, their research indicates that only 24% of firms claimed to earn above-average return on capital for investments in IT (see also Farbey, Land and Targett, 1995; Grindley, 1995; Willcocks, 1996).

The IS/IT evaluation issue is clearly an important one given organizations' concerns. Reflecting this, a great deal of research has already been conducted in the IS/IT evaluation area (see for example, Chandler, 1982; Hamilton and Chervancy, 1981; Hawgood and Land, 1988; King and Schrems, 1979; Klein and Beck, 1987; Lucas and Moore, 1976; Parker, Trainor and Benson, 1989; Willcocks, 1994. See also Chapters 7, 11 and 13). However, despite the existence of an extensive literature, the IS community appears to be little clearer as to a solution to the problems of IS/IT evaluation. For example, concerns regarding the difficulty of evaluating the costs and benefits of such investments in a meaningful way have been frequently identified as a major problem for organizations (see, for example, Chapters 5, 6 and 7; Ginzberg, 1979; Willcocks, 1994).

Setting the difficulties of evaluation aside for the moment, why do organizations evaluate IS/IT investments? According to Farbey, Land and Targett (1992, and also Chapter 6), evaluation serves a number of objectives: as a means of justifying IS/IT investments; to enable organizations to decide between competing projects, particularly if capital rationing is an issue; as a control mechanism over expenditure, benefits and the development and implementation of projects; and as a learning device enabling improved evaluation and systems development to take place in the future. Others identify similar reasons that IS/IT investments should be evaluated: to gain information for project planning; to determine the relative merits of alternative projects; to ensure that systems continue to perform well; and to enable decisions concerning expansion, improvement or the postponement of projects to be taken (Angell and Smithson, 1991; Dawes, 1987; Etzerodt and Madsen, 1988; Ginzberg and Zmud, 1988; Grindley, 1995).

PREVIOUS EMPIRICAL STUDIES

The evaluation of capital investments has been widely reported in both the accounting and IS literature. The majority of studies reported in the accounting literature, however, do not generally distinguish between the evaluation practices of IS/IT and other capital investments. Furthermore, many of these studies have tended to concentrate on the financial techniques used to evaluate investments, largely to the exclusion of discussing the problems inherent in the evaluation process itself. For example, past researchers have sought to establish whether a relationship exists between the use of specific techniques and organizational characteristics (such as size), have developed comparisons of national and international practices, and have investigated whether or not the use of specific techniques has changed over time (see, for example, Bower, 1970; Carsberg and Hope, 1976; Gitman and Forrester, 1978;

Kim and Farragher, 1981; Klammer, 1972; Mills, 1988; Moore and Reichert, 1983; Petty, Scott and Bird, 1975; Pike, 1982, 1988; Sangster, 1993; Scapens and Sale, 1981; Schall, Sunden and Geijsbeek, 1978; Sundem and Geijsbeek, 1978; Ward, Taylor and Bond, 1995; Willcocks and Lester, 1996).

On the other hand, the IS literature has tended to report on the evaluation practices of IS/IT investments exclusively. Table 4.1 summarizes the key findings of a number of empirical studies (carried out in the late 1980s and early 1990s), reported in the IS literature, which have addressed the issue of IS/IT evaluation. While some of the studies have concentrated on examining the financial techniques used to evaluate IS/IT investments, the majority have considered many of the wider issues of IS evaluation, including the identification of problem areas.

THE CURRENT RESEARCH

This chapter considers some of the wider issues of IS/IT evaluation alluded to above in order to add to our knowledge of practice. The findings are presented of a study (carried out in the latter half of 1993) which aimed to document the current state of IS/IT evaluation practices within a sample of UK organizations. In particular, the chapter addresses the following issues (additional findings of the study regarding the use of investment criteria and their importance in the evaluation process can be found in Ballantine and Stray, 1998):

1.   How widespread is the practice of IS/IT evaluation within organizations?
2.   Why are IS/IT investments not always evaluated at the feasibility stage?
3.   To which extent do problems arise with the evaluation process?
4.   To what extent does evaluation depend on organizational factors, such as project cost and level of organizational turnover?
5.   Where does responsibility for evaluation exist (corporate or business unit level) and, within that area, who is specifically responsible for evaluating investments?
6.   To what extent does consultation take place with internal stakeholders during the evaluation process, and which stakeholders could usefully have been consulted, but were not?
7.   To what extent do formal procedures of evaluation exist?

In addressing the above issues, the study serves two objectives: first, it enables us to investigate whether evaluation practices have changed from those reported in some earlier studies (see Table 4.1); and secondly, it enables us to obtain a broader picture of a number of important evaluation issues.

RESEARCH METHODOLOGY

A systematic random sample of companies was chosen in late 1993—using the Times Top 1000 companies as the sampling frame—to take part in a survey. The use of a systematic sample ensured that the size distribution of companies in the sample correctly reflected that of the sampling frame. All companies other than public limited companies were deleted from the list of companies before sample selection took place, as it was considered that smaller private companies may not have a separate IS/IT function within their organization, and therefore their participation in the study would not be appropriate.

The selected companies were telephoned before mailing the questionnaire in order to identify the appropriate individual to whom a questionnaire should be sent (Allen, Schewe and Wijk, 1980) and to gain commitment to returning the questionnaire, therefore encouraging a high response rate. This generated 179 firm commitments to participate in the research. Prior to distribution, the questionnaire was subject to a pilot study in which it was sent to individuals (20 in total) who were actively involved in the IS/IT evaluation process within their particular organizations. In addition to written comments received, those involved in the pilot study were contacted by telephone to discuss any problems or ambiguities which they believed were present in the questionnaire. This provided valuable feedback on the design of the questionnaire, which subsequently led to some minor changes before the final questionnaire was distributed. The questionnaire primarily consisted of closed questions. However, where appropriate, a small number of open-ended questions were adopted to address the more difficult aspects of evaluation, for example to enable us to elicit the reasons for adopting a particular practice. Responses to open-ended questions were subsequently manually coded. In order to boost response rates, pre-paid reply envelopes and follow-up telephone calls were used. A total of 98 responses were obtained, giving a response rate of 55%; of these, 97 provided responses suitable for analysis (this compares favourably, for example, with response rates of 39% found by Bacon, 1992 and 13.4% found by Tam, 1992).

The respondents' organizations represent a wide range of industrial sectors, with the largest number of responses from the manufacturing, construction, electronics and engineering, and wholesale/retailing sectors, which accounted for 54% of the total sample. The reported

Table 4.1   Empirical Studies on Feasibility Evaluation

Study	Nature of research	Key issues addressed by study	Key findings
Blackler and Brown (1988)	54 semi-structured interviews with well-infomed "opinion leaders" (including management, trade unions, manufacturers, consultants, academics)	Addresses the adequacy of evaluation research in terms of dealing with prior and post evaluation of new information technologies (CADCAM)	Evaluation research has become distanced from actual evaluation practice. Considerable emphasis was placed on prior justification. Criticism of short-term cost–benefit calculations of evaluation was also identified. Bulk of evaluation is carried out by non-specialized management
Bacon (1992)	Survey of 80 companies (25 American, 23 British, 11 Australian, 21 New Zealand)	The use of financial, management and development decision criteria in selecting information systems/technology investments	Criteria such as the support of explicit business objectives and response to competitive systems are becoming more important in selecting IS/IT investments
Tam (1992)	Survey of 134 senior US IS executives	The use of capital budgeting techniques for evaluating, terminating and auditing information systems investments	Capital budgeting techniques are used in IS development, but have little impact on the evaluation, termination and post audit of IS projects. Problems with estimating costs and returns are identified. A shift in decision authority to corporate level is identified when project costs increase

Farbey, Land and Targett (1992)	16 IT projects which had been implemented or were about to be implemented in UK organizations	Consideration of the investment decision process and evaluation techniques used to justify investments in IT	No consistency to cost justification, very few evaluation techniques were used to justify investment. Just over 50% of organizations had a formal justification procedure
Wilner, Koch and Klammer (1992)	Survey of 100 US organizations	Consideration of the capital investment decision processes used for high-technology projects	Discounted cash flow techniques were mainly used to evaluate high technology investments. However, numerous non-quantitative factors were also included in the analysis process
Willcocks (1992) Willcocks and Lester (1996)	Survey of 50 UK organizations (and follow-up interviews in 32)	Evaluating IT investments at the feasibility stage and at subsequent stages of the development lifecycle	Considerable problems with the evaluation process exist, financial criteria are primarily used during evaluation, evaluation was more widespread during feasibility, users of the system and trade unions were not widely consulted during evaluation

turnover of the respondent organizations (for the period 1992) ranged from a minimum of £9 to a maximum of £10 000 million, with a mean and median of £589 million and £170 million respectively, reflecting, as one would expect, the positively skewed distribution of company size.

In order to validate that our sample was representative of the population used, we compared the sample mean turnover with the mean turnover of all companies in the population (excluding those in our sample). There was found to be no significant difference in the means at the 5% level (no significant difference in medians at the 5% level was also found). Additional tests revealed that the distribution of turnover cannot be regarded as anything other than identical.

In addition to obtaining information regarding the nature and size of respondent organizations, we were interested in obtaining details about the individuals who completed the research instrument. To this end the following were sought: position held, where in the organizational structure they were employed (i.e. corporate level or business unit level) and the number of reporting levels existing between the respondent and the chief executive. The majority of respondents were employed within IS/IT-related positions (see Table 4.2). Only 12% held finance-related positions and these tended to come from the smaller organizations which responded. A total of 57% respondents were employed at corporate level, while 33% were employed at business unit level. The results also show that respondents were employed within reasonably high managerial levels, with 57% within one reporting level, and 86% within two reporting levels, of the chief executive, and just over 10% reporting directly to the chief executive.

While Table 4.2 indicates the wide variety of IS roles performed by the respondents, we do not believe that this has introduced bias into the results, as each of the respondents who took part in the study was actively engaged in the IS/IT evaluation process within their respective

Table 4.2 *Positions Held by Respondents (n = 97)*

Position held	Percentage
IS Director	14%
IS Manager	31%
DP Manager	6%
Computer related	21%
Project Leader	3%
Finance related	12%
Others	12%
Total	100%

organizations (this was confirmed prior to distribution of the question-naire). In addition, since the vast majority of respondents were employed within two reporting levels of the chief executive, we do not believe that this factor has introduced bias into the results. However, we should point out that some bias might arise due to the higher percentage of respondents who were employed at the corporate, as opposed to business unit, level of the organization. Thus the results might tend to be more slightly more representative of a corporate approach to IS/IT evaluation.

RESULTS

Before going on to discuss the detailed results of the study, one should reflect on the economic context within which the study was conducted. During 1993–4, the UK was still in the depths of a recessionary period. Pressures to cut costs led many organizations to focus on the concept of core competencies, which in turn had subsequent implications for outsourcing both IS and non-IS services. Against this bleak background, there was a perception that IT was underperforming (Galliers, 1995), particularly in terms of the extravagant claims made in support of the strategic impact of IS/IT in the 1980s. Thus, while the context within which the study was carried out may limit the extent to which meaningful comparisons can be drawn with earlier (see Table 4.1) and later studies (see Chapter 2), it can, on a more positive note, be used to explain further some of the results found.

In order to address the evaluation issues outlined earlier, the study set out to identify the evaluation practices both for the most recent IS/IT project (defined as an investment which included the costs of, for example, hardware, software, development time, staff time, training) undertaken by the respondents' organizations, and for IS/IT projects in general within those organizations. The reason for asking about both of these was that in some cases we wished to relate responses concerning evaluation to specific aspects of the project (for example, its size) and in other instances we wanted to ascertain what typically went on within organizations. However, it should be noted that asking individuals about the "last time" they did something (i.e. the most recent project) may generate a response of what they typically do (i.e. projects in general—see Belson, 1964; Moser and Kalton, 1971), rather than what they actually did with the specific project in question.

Within the sampled organizations, the IS/IT budget allocation ranged from insignificant to £160 million, with a mean allocation of £7.4 million (median allocation of £1.3 million). Only two of the respondent organizations reported zero budget allocations during the 1992 period, stating that they had no requirement for investment in IS/IT in that particular year. The cost of the most recent IS/IT investment undertaken within the respondent organizations ranged from a minimum of £10 000 to a maximum of £5 million (with a mean and median cost of £404 800 and £150 000 respectively), giving us some idea of the significant size of the projects concerned.

As a percentage of turnover, the mean cost of the most recent IS/IT investment was found to be 0.5% (median 0.1%), while the mean cost as a percentage of the 1992 IS/IT budget allocation was 58% (median of 12.3%). In addition, the IS/IT budget for the sampled organizations was an average of 1% of 1992 turnover (median of 0.7%), which is marginally lower than the levels of spend reported in earlier studies (see for example Willcocks, 1992). In addition, it is perhaps worth noting that just over 40% of the sampled companies had less than 0.5% of their turnover allocated to the IS/IT budget in 1992. The low levels of expenditure found here might well be reflective of the recessionary period (the mid-1990s) during which the study was conducted. However, an alternative explanation is that the reported budget allocations may, as Keen (1991) suggests, include only the more visible costs of IS/IT investments. Additional analysis using analysis of variance indicated no relationship (at the 5% level of significance) between the average size of the IS/IT budget and the industrial sector within which the company was primarily engaged ($p = 0.133$).

DISCUSSION

The Extent of Feasibility Evaluation

Among other things, the study attempted to ascertain whether the most recent IS/IT project and IS/IT projects generally were subject to feasibility evaluation, where evaluation was defined as "the process of establishing by quantitative and/or qualitative means the worth of IS/IT projects to the organization" (Willcocks, 1992) and feasibility was defined as "evaluating the financial and non-financial acceptability of a project against defined organizational requirements, and assessing the priorities between proposed projects". In addition we wanted to determine the extent to which evaluation depended on organizational characteristics such as turnover, size of IS/IT budget and size of project concerned.

Table 4.3 indicates the extent of feasibility evaluation reported. Evaluation was found to be significantly more widespread (at the 1%

Table 4.3 *Extent of Evaluation (n = 97)*

Evaluate?	Most recent project	Projects generally
No	9%	9%
Yes	87%	62%
Don't know	4%	2%
Some projects	N/A	27%
Total	100%	100%

level of significance) for the most recent project than for projects generally. The results also indicate a lower incidence of feasibility evaluation than that indicated by Willcocks (1992), who reported all organizations in his sample (50) evaluating at the feasibility stage. In contrast, Farbey, Land and Targett (1992) (again in the UK) found that only 56% of the (16) projects they investigated were subject to evaluation. However, there appears to be some indication of overreporting of evaluation of the most recent project in our findings. In order for the figure of 87% to be valid, it would require those people evaluating some projects to evaluate 92% of them, so that combined with the 62% who evaluate all projects, we obtain our total of 87% (i.e. 62% + 0.92*27% = 87%). This seems to suggest that the 87% identified here is overstated. However, it may well be the case that, when providing information about the most recent project, individuals are supplying information about the most recent *significant* project, where significance refers to the project's size in either absolute terms or in relation to the IS/IT budget. As we report later, it is the more significant projects that tend to be evaluated. However, an alternative explanation is that feasibility evaluation is now more important to companies than has historically been the case, especially given the concerns over cost justification and containment cited earlier, and therefore that evaluation of the most recent project is more common than is true for projects historically.

The principal reasons given by respondents for not evaluating all projects at the feasibility stage are summarized below, together with the number of organizations which quoted them:

1. Some projects have to be undertaken in order to keep the business moving (n = 8).
2. Evaluation depends on size, value and risk of the project involved (n = 6).
3. Operational urgency does not always permit time. Projects driven by corporate restructuring sometimes allow insufficient time and choice (n = 4).

4. Some projects go straight into functional design, i.e. no feasibility stage (n = 2).
5. Lack of importance of project or enthusiasm to carry out evaluation (n = 2).
6. Evaluation depends on the requirements and general support of key personnel at the time (n = 1).
7. Evaluation depends on how obvious the benefits of the system are (n = 1).
8. There is a lack of organizational structure; i.e. no defined responsibilities (n = 1).

The first two reasons seem to indicate that feasibility evaluation is clearly not relevant for all IS/IT investments. These findings are supported by the Farbey, Land and Targett (1993) research, which identified that the decision to go ahead with a number of projects (44%) was taken at a high level on a "got to do" basis, or that "the organization had a formal justification procedure which was by-passed because the project could not fit into it" (p. 113). However, taking the remaining reasons together (constituting 11% of the sample), a somewhat disturbing picture emerges, in that organizational problems such as a lack of time, management support and organizational structure appear to hinder the evaluation process within organizations.

One might expect that it is the larger IS/IT projects (in absolute terms) that are more likely to be the subject of evaluation. However, analysis (using the Student's t test) indicated that for the most recent project there was no statistically significant difference in the average cost for those that were evaluated and those that were not. Those companies which did evaluate their most recent project had significantly greater (at the 1% level of significance) IS/IT budgets (mean of £8 million) compared to those which did not (mean of £1.1 million). One might expect this to be the case since "large" budgets are much more likely to be the subject of review and scrutiny than "small" budgets. The results also show that those companies which did not evaluate the most recent project tend to be smaller (mean turnover of £274 million) than those which did evaluate (mean turnover of £626 million)—these results are statistically significant (at the 10% level, but not at the 5% level). While the likelihood that an organization would undertake evaluation was not related to the absolute size of the most recent project, companies which evaluated their most recent project had a significantly higher project cost as a percentage of the IS/IT budget allocation for 1992 (an average of 62%) than those which did not evaluate (an average of 29%). Again, we would expect this relationship to hold, since projects consuming large amounts of large budgets are the ones most likely to be scrutinied and reviewed and in this sense it is the significant projects that appear to be the subject of evaluation.

In summary, the findings indicate that feasibility evaluation is relatively widespread within the respondent organizations, particularly for the most recent project undertaken. Evaluation was found to be associated with companies which had higher levels of turnover, and for larger projects, when measured relative to the total IS/IT budget allocation. However, the absolute cost of the IS/IT project did not affect whether or not evaluation was carried out.

Responsibility for Evaluation

The study also identified who was responsible for evaluating the feasibility of IS/IT investments (see Table 4.4). The results show that responsibility rests in roughly equal proportions at both corporate and business unit level, with external sources rarely being responsible for evaluating feasibility. Only a small percentage of organizations (5.2%) generally shared responsibility for evaluation between the corporate and business unit level.

Comparing the most recent project for which responsibility for evaluation lay principally at the corporate level with those where principal responsibility lay at the business level, no significant difference exists (at the 5% level of significance) in the average project cost. This is in contrast to Tam (1992), who found that responsibility for evaluation lay at corporate level when project costs were higher. These contrasting findings might simply reflect differences in the extent to which decision making authority is decentralized. However, since this study did not collect information relevant to this issue, we are unable to corroborate this assumption. No relationship was found between the area of responsibility (corporate or business unit level) and whether or not the project was evaluated, that is, IS/IT projects were no more likely to be

Table 4.4   *Responsibility for Evaluation*

Responsibility area	Most recent project (n = 96)	Projects generally (n = 96)
Corporate level	52%	46%
Business unit level	45%	48%
External source	1%	0%
Corporate and business unit	1%	5%
Corporate and external source	1%	1%
Total	100%	100%

evaluated at corporate, as opposed to business unit level. However, the mean level of turnover is significantly less for those evaluating at the corporate level (£314 million) than at the business unit level (£724 million). This suggests that corporate responsibility for evaluation lies within the smaller companies, possibly because it is more likely that the smaller companies involved in the study do not have a business unit level. It is therefore not surprising to find that the mean IS/IT budget for those evaluating the most recent project at corporate level is (statistically at the 5% level) significantly lower (£3.4 million) than those evaluating at the business unit level (£12.4 million).

Where there was a difference in responsibility level for evaluating the most recent project and projects generally, the following reasons were given by respondents:

1. The nature of the project determines where responsibility for evaluation lies, i.e. if projects are corporate, they are evaluated at the corporate level (n = 9).
2. Responsibility depends on the cost of the project. Those projects exceeding a given expenditure level are normally authorized by the finance director and evaluation will take place at corporate level (n = 3).

Respondents were also asked to indicate which groups, within the level of responsibility identified above, were specifically responsible for evaluating the most recent project (Table 4.5).

As one would expect, the results indicate that the IS/IT department is

Table 4.5   *Responsibility for Evaluating Most Recent Project (n = 96)*

Responsibility—most recent project	Percentage of respondents
Corporate level	
IS/IT department	48%
Finance/Accounting	26%
User departments	17%
Internal Audit department	5%
Business unit level	
IS/IT department	32%
User departments	31%
Finance/Accounting	17%
Internal Audit department	6%
External auditors/accountants	5%
External consultants/bureaux	3%
Others	5%

more likely than any other group to have responsibility for evaluation, at both corporate and business unit level. User departments are much more likely to have responsibility for evaluation if they work at the business unit level of the organization. The finance/accounting function, however, is unlikely to assume responsibility for IS/IT evaluation at either the corporate or business unit level. These results largely support Hochstrasser and Griffiths's (1991) argument that while responsibility for all investments, including IT, has traditionally remained with the finance director, "this tradition is being questioned ... as IT involvement has grown in size and begun to affect a wider range of business functions, it has become increasingly difficult for any single person to fully appreciate the complexity of issues involved" (p. 21). External sources, in the form of auditors, accountants and consultants, were rarely responsible for evaluation of IS/IT projects.

The majority of organizations sampled had more than one group responsible for evaluation at the corporate or business unit level: 40.6% had one group or department responsible, 32.3% had two groups responsible, and 25.1% had three or more groups responsible. The issue of joint responsibility for evaluating IS/IT investments has received surprisingly little attention in the IS literature to date, even by 1998. Of the few authors who address it, Hochstrasser and Griffiths (1991) argue that "split responsibility, if uncontrolled, can lead to confusion of who is responsible for the timeliness and accuracy of data and to the danger that information is not collected and distributed effectively". While their conclusions are discussed in a wider context than the evaluation of individual investment proposals, they obviously have implications germane to the issue here. Furthermore, if problems exist with split responsibility, this study shows that they may be of relevance to over half the respondent organizations.

Although the research presented here did not seek to identify the nature, or existence, of problems associated with joint responsibility, it has identified that this is potentially a widespread issue. The extent to which joint responsibility has implications for organizations in terms of ultimate responsibility and accountability for IS/IT investments, and in terms of how evaluation practices are coordinated across diverse groups and how feedback and control of IS/IT project expenditure are monitored within organizations, are clearly issues which need to be explored further by future research.

Consultation during Evaluation

In carrying out the study, we were also interested in identifying the extent to which consultation with a variety of stakeholders, both internal and external to the respondent organizations, took place when assessing the feasibility of the most recent IS/IT project. In order to ascertain this, respondents were asked to indicate which groups were consulted, in addition to which groups could usefully have been consulted but were not, when assessing the feasibility of the most recent project. The findings suggest widespread consultation with the users of the potential system in particular (85% of companies). These findings are far in excess of figures quoted by others. Willcocks (1992), for example, found that only 36% of the organizations he studied consulted users about evaluation during the feasibility stage of IS/IT project development. A possible reason for the high levels of consultation with users found here might be explained by the nature of the IS/IT projects evaluated. Alternatively, it may be that organizations are over time recognizing the importance of user participation in the IS/IT investment decision-making process, especially given the concerns voiced earlier that such investments often fail to deliver acceptable returns. Unfortunately, this study did not collect data regarding the nature of the most recent IS/IT project or the attitude of organizations towards user participation (this being one of the limitations of the study) which might enable us to substantiate these assertions.

Widespread consultation with the finance/accounting function, particularly at the corporate level of the organization, is also evident. This might be explained as a result of pressures to control costs during the recessionary period in which the study was conducted. Consultation with the corporate strategic planning/logistics group or the human resources/personnel group is comparatively rare. The lack of consultation with corporate strategic planning may indicate inadequate integration of IS/IT projects with strategic planning and the consequent problems associated with evaluating such projects in the context of business objectives (Galliers, 1987; Willcocks, 1994).

Of those organizations which evaluated the most recent project, 6% consulted with one group only, 17% with two groups, 25% with three groups and 25% with four groups. There was no relationship between the number of groups consulted and the size of the IS/IT budget allocation ($r = 0.1016$) or company turnover ($r = 0.1525$). However, as one might anticipate, there was a slight tendency for more departments to be consulted regarding feasibility when the cost of the most recent project was high (significant correlation coefficient of 0.3518 at the 1% level). This is possibly because small projects are less likely to impinge on large numbers of groups than is the case for large projects, or alternatively it may be related to project type.

What is also apparent from the study is that the respondents themselves felt that, in the main, the appropriate groups, both internal and external to the organization, were consulted during evaluation. There was little indication that, even with the benefits of hindsight, they thought that there were additional groups who could usefully have been consulted, but were not. For example, only 10% indicated that they could usefully have consulted external users regarding feasibility (e.g. customers, suppliers), only 6% stated that they could usefully have consulted the strategic planning/logistics group at the corporate management level, and a mere 5% indicated that they could usefully have consulted non-users of the potential system. Whether or not these groups would agree with the present levels of consultation is a separate issue. However, it would appear that *respondents* themselves are generally satisfied with current consultation levels and, as a result, they are unlikely to broaden this process in the future.

Formal Evaluation Procedures

Hirschheim and Smithson in Chapter 13 make the distinction between formal and informal evaluation procedures. The former, they argue, might be considered an objective and rational mechanism which improves communication and learning within organizations; while the latter might be viewed as ill informed, hasty and largely involve subjective judgements. Marsh *et al.* (1988) discuss the role and impact of formal evaluation systems in the context of strategic investment decision making (they do not, however, specifically discuss formal systems in the context of IS/IT investments). A formal process, they argue, provides "a clear paper trail, showing the proposals submitted at each stage, the minutes of committees and meetings, and a record of the point at which capital was officially committed" (p. 13). They go on to present two conflicting views of the usefulness of formal systems of evaluation. The first argues that formal systems are the all-important factor in decision making, while the second argues that they are merely ritual, and therefore of limited use. In the context of their research, Marsh *et al.* (1988) observe that "while the formal systems [used] are ritualistic, they are nevertheless necessary" (p. 28). They also argue that despite being ritualistic, formal procedures do influence reality: "They force the players to be more explicit about their assumptions, both to themselves, and in order to justify them to others" (p. 57). The formal systems "helped to set deadlines, and thereby force the project pace. They facilitated the movement of information up, down and sideways within the organization, generating awareness of, and commitment to, the project. At the same time, they provided a scheduled set of occasions for face-to-face communication across multiple levels of the hierarchy thus giving the chance to debate the specific project" (p. 28).

The present study identified the extent to which formal procedures of evaluation were in place within the respondent organizations, in addition to identifying of what those procedures consisted. Table 4.6 shows that just under half (44%) of the respondent companies have clearly defined procedures for evaluating IS/IT investments. Comparing the extent to which formal procedures of evaluation exist (Table 4.6), together with the extent to which evaluation is carried out by organizations (Table 4.3), it would appear that informal evaluation seems to play an important role in IS/IT investment decision making within the respondent organizations. This pattern is largely confirmed by Farbey, Land and Targett (1992), who report that just over half of the organizations they studied had a formal justification procedure for evaluating IS/IT investments.

Table 4.6 also shows the nature of the formal procedures which organizations have in place to assist in the evaluation process. The "others" group includes the following activities:

- monthly customer progress reviews;
- *ad hoc*, informal meetings and minutes;
- project board meetings;
- formal preparation, demonstration and business presentation;
- detailed technical review of projects.

What does come as something of a surprise is that there is no association between whether or not companies evaluated the most recent project and whether or not they have clearly defined procedures for doing so. Of the 43 companies with clearly defined procedures, 91% (39) evaluated the most recent project, 5% (2) did not evaluate and 5% (2) did not know whether they evaluated or not. This compares with 51 organizations who did not have clearly defined procedures, of which 86% (44) evaluated the most recent project, while 12% (6) did not. The results not only show that evaluation is just as likely to take place

Table 4.6   *Defined Procedures of Evaluation (n = 97)*

	Yes	No	Don't know/missing
Defined procedures?	44%	53%	3%
Financial reviews of cost/savings	94%	5%	1%
Regular meetings	69%	30%	1%
Reporting of costs and performance	56%	43%	1%
Distribution of minutes	49%	51%	1%
Project team workshops	42%	57%	1%
Other activities	9%	90%	1%

whether or not there are formally defined procedures, but that a large percentage of organizations evaluate IS/IT projects despite the lack of clearly defined procedures. However, as one might expect, those companies with clearly defined procedures tended to have (statistically) significantly larger IS/IT budgets than those with no such procedures ($F = 11.973$, $p = 0.001$). The mean budget for those organizations with evaluation procedures was £15.7 million, compared to £0.9 million for those without formal procedures.

These findings suggest a fairly widespread lack of formal procedures, despite the fact that evaluations of IS/IT investments are still undertaken, a finding supported by the survey by Willcocks and Lester (1996). If, as indicated by the findings of Marsh *et al.* (1988), benefits are found to be associated with the use of formal evaluation systems, despite being perceived as ritualistic in some instances, then many organizations evaluating IS/IT investments without the aid of formal systems are likely to be missing out on such benefits. Clearly further research is required to ascertain the extent to which formal procedures facilitate improved evaluation practices within organizations, and whether the lack of procedures found here is a corporate-wide, as opposed to information systems, issue. A further issue for exploration, suggested by Willcocks and Lester (1996), is how far informal evaluation practice has been adopted in order to fill in for recognized limitations in formal evaluation procedures.

Problems with Evaluation

While we did not ascertain the respondents' opinions as to whether or not the existence of formal procedures aided or hindered the evaluation process, we did investigate the problems encountered during the evaluation process. These were classified into three groups: information-requirement problems, knowledge-related problems, and organizational problems. The frequency with which these problems are encountered during the evaluation of IS/IT projects generally is summarized in Table 4.7. It is worth pointing out that no respondent identified the existence of formal procedures as a problem; although, similarly, nor did anyone suggest that a lack of formal procedures was a problem.

The findings indicate that problems were widespread with the evaluation process in the respondent organizations. Only two companies reported no problems occurring during the evaluation of IS/IT projects in general; 60% of respondents indicated problems in two or more of the areas shown in Table 4.7 and 31% indicated problems in three or more areas. A total of 55% of respondents encountered some form of organizational problem, with lack of time being the most frequently

Table 4.7   *Problems Encountered during Evaluation (n = 75)*

Nature of evaluation problems for projects generally	Problem
Information requirements	
Quantifying relevant benefits	81%
Identification of relevant benefits	65%
Quantifying relevant opportunity costs	36%
Identification of relevant opportunity costs	35%
Identification of relevant costs	31%
Quantifying relevant costs	27%
Knowledge related	
Difficulty with interpretation of results	17%
Unfamiliarity with project evaluation techniques	12%
Calculation of discount rate	3%
Organizational problems	
Lack of time	37%
Lack of data/information	19%
Lack of interest	15%
Others	8%

cited. The number of problems encountered was unrelated to the cost of the most recent project and unrelated to either the size of the IS/IT budget allocation or turnover. Consequently, small companies experienced just as many problems as large ones, small projects had just as many problems as large ones, and larger budgets appear to have had no more "headaches" than small budgets. This is not to say that there are not instances when the problems are more difficult to solve, but only that the breadth of problems does not differ.

Information requirements problems—that is, obtaining relevant information for decision-making purposes—are by far the greatest cause of concern for organizations during the evaluation process. In particular, both the identification and quantification of relevant benefits are widespread problems, as is identifying and quantifying costs. Few organizations experience knowledge-related problems, with the exception of difficulties encountered with interpreting the results of evaluation (17.3% of respondents), this perhaps reflecting the backgrounds of the respondents themselves. Organizational problems, such as a lack of time to carry out evaluation, together with a lack of data/information, were also quite widespread among the respondent organizations, confirming some of the earlier comments for not evaluating all IS/IT investments.

These findings serve to confirm the continued existence of a range of problems identified by other studies. Willcocks (1994), for example, identifies a number of problems frequently encountered during evaluation practice: a lack of understanding of the full range of costs associated with IS/IT investments, overstating costs, not fully investigating risk, failure to devote time and effort to evaluate major capital assets, and neglecting intangible benefits. Tam (1992) also identified that estimating returns and costs were significant problems when evaluating IS/IT investments. Given the relatively high percentage of companies here which suffer similar problems to those identified in earlier studies, it would appear that aspects of evaluation still remain particularly problematic for organizations. Worryingly, later survey evidence reported in Chapter 2 suggests that many of these problems were still not being addressed by 1996, despite the rich vein of evidence and the many suggestions for improvement (for examples only see King and McAuley, 1997; Soh and Markus, 1995; Wegen and Hoog, 1996).

In addition, given that the respondents of this study are generally "happy" (or would appear to be so) with present consultation levels, the existence of problems identified here would suggest that they are inherent in the evaluation process itself, and are unlikely, from the viewpoint of the respondents, to be solved by involving additional groups in the evaluation process. Further research is clearly needed to address the main problems experienced here, as they would appear to be no less a problem for organizations than they have been in the past. An associated and further interesting research question is whether such problems are characteristic only of IS/IT investments within organizations.

CONCLUSIONS

The results of this study shed additional light on the IS/IT evaluation practices of UK organizations, in some respects confirming earlier empirical evidence. In addition, however, the findings add to our knowledge by providing a rich picture with respect to a number of evaluation issues. While the results of the study indicated a slight decrease in the level of IS/IT expenditure reported over those of earlier studies, this is in contrast with the findings of the Price Waterhouse Information Technology Review (Price Waterhouse, 1995), which suggests that expenditure on IT had increased over the same period. As suggested earlier, however, this might be explained by the fact that the respondent organizations reported only on the "visible" aspects of IS/IT expenditure. Subsequently, in the 1995–8 period, with or without "visible" expenditure being counted, IT expenditures rose considerably across all the developed economies (Black, 1997; *The Economist*, 1996).

More importantly, the study shows that the majority of respondent organizations evaluate IS/IT investments (this is particularly so for the most recent project), again confirming earlier empirical studies. In addition, evaluation was found to be associated with larger IS/IT budgets, large companies in terms of turnover levels, and larger projects when measured as a percentage of the IS/IT budget. However, the study also highlighted a lack of formal evaluation procedures within organizations. While the existence of procedures was found to be associated with larger IS/IT budgets, a lack of formal procedures did not in any way deter organizations from evaluating the feasibility of investments in IS/IT. Clearly, further research is needed to examine the extent to which formal evaluation procedures benefit the IS/IT decision-making process, or whether they simply retard decision making. Case study research, as in Chapters 2, 6 and 9, would seem to be the most appropriate mechanism for addressing this issue.

Responsibility for evaluating IS/IT investments was shared equally between corporate and business unit levels. Within those levels, the IS/IT department, user departments and the accounting and finance function have a relatively high level of responsibility for evaluation. However, the findings indicate a relatively high percentage of companies assigning joint responsibility for evaluating the same project, which has implications for organizations in terms of coordinating evaluation practices, monitoring, controlling and providing feedback of IS/IT project performance. This is clearly an additional area which future evaluation research needs to address.

Consultation regarding the feasibility of IS/IT projects was found to be widespread with the users of the potential system and the accounting and finance function in particular. This might be explained, as suggested earlier, in relation to the nature of the project concerned, or increasing recognition of the importance of user participation in the decision-making process. The high levels of consultation with the finance/accounting function might be explained as a result of pressures to control costs during the period of the study. In contrast, consultation with the corporate strategic planning group was comparatively limited, which is perhaps reflective of the lack of integration between IS strategy and business strategy. Overall, the findings suggest that current patterns of consultation, from the perspective of the respondents, are unlikely to change in the future.

The study also highlighted the continued existence of a number of problems with the evaluation process, suggesting important avenues for future research. By far the greatest problems encountered during evaluation were the identification and quantification of relevant benefits and costs—a problem likely to be compounded from 1995 on, as the

Introduction to this book establishes. However, problems of an organizational nature were also found, including a lack of time and management support, perhaps reflective of the climate within which evaluation was carried out at the time of the study. A lack of interest in the evaluation process and a lack of data/information were also cited as noteworthy problem areas. In addition, problems of evaluation were found to exist irrespective of IS/IT project size, IS/IT budget allocation or size of organization.

From the above discussion, a number of key research issues emerge. First, more research is needed to examine more fully the problems commonly faced when evaluating IS/IT investments, with a view to proposing measures by which such problems might be resolved, and to ascertaining whether or not these differ in nature to problems encountered when evaluating other capital investments, not just that of an IS/IT nature. In particular, the issues of benefits identification and quantification need to be examined further in the context of the use of evaluation techniques. In addition, the role of formal procedures in the IS/IT evaluation process needs to be more closely examined to identify if their use results in any significant benefits. Additionally, the extent to which problems arise as a result of joint responsibility for evaluation need to be investigated more fully. Finally, the perspectives of a wider range of stakeholders, both internal and external to organizations, are required with respect to ascertaining their satisfaction with current IS/IT evaluation practices, a theme picked up in detail in Chapters 12 and 13.

Evaluation of IS/IT expenditure is a key issue. Senior executives have come to expect value for money from such investments and, given the year-on-year improvements in the cost–performance ratio of IT, expectations are bound to increase, especially while cost containment is high on the management agenda. This research has attempted to provide additional evidence on actual IS/IT evaluation practices. A number of persistent limitations in practice emerge that contribute to the plausibility of the mismeasurement explanation for the so-called IT productivity paradox. Moreover, this chapter supports the arguments advanced in Chapters 2, 6 and 9 for the potential role of evaluation in focusing more advantageously the deployment of IT. Our study shows that, regarding IT evaluation practice at the organizational level, there is very clearly room for improvement.

REFERENCES

Allen, C., Schewe, T.C.D. and Wijk, G. (1980). Foot Technique in the Pre-Call/ Mail Survey Setting. *Journal of Marketing Research*, XVII, 4, 489–502.

Angell, I.O. and Smithson, S. (1991). *Information Systems Management: Opportunities and Risks*. Macmillan, London.

Bacon, J.C. (1992). The Use of Decision Criteria in Selecting Information Systems/Technology Investments. *MIS Quarterly*, 16, 3, 335–53.

Badri, M.A. (1992). Critical Issues in Information Systems Management: an International Perspective. *International Journal of Information Management*, 12, 3, 179–91.

Ballantine, J.A. and Stray, S.J. (1998). Financial Appraisal and the IS/IT Investment Decision-Making Process. *Journal of Information Technology*, 13, 1, 3–14.

Belson, W.A. (1964). Readership in Britain. *Business Review*, 6, 4, 416–20.

Black, G. (1997). The Booming Stats. *Computer Weekly*. October 2nd, 20.

Blackler, F. and Brown, C. (1988). Theory and Practice in Evaluation: the Case of the New Information Technologies. In Bjorn-Anderson, N. and Davis, G.B. (eds) *Information Systems Assessment: Issues and Challenges*. Elsevier, North-Holland, Amsterdam.

Bower, J.L. (1970). *Managing the Resources Allocation Process*. Harvard University Press, Cambridge, MA.

Carsberg, B. and Hope, A. (1976). *Business Investment Decisions under Inflation: Theory and Practice*. Institute of Chartered Accountants in London.

Chandler, J.S. (1982). A Multiple Criteria Approach for Evaluating Information Systems. *MIS Quarterly*, March, 6, 1, 61–75.

Clark, T.D. Jr (1992). Corporate Systems Management: an Overview and Research Perspective. *Communications of the ACM*, 35, 2, 61–75.

Davis, D. (1989). US Giants Run a $50 Billion IS Tab. *Datamation*, November 15, 42–4.

Dawes, G.M. (1987). Information Systems Assessment: Post Implementation Practice. *Journal of Applied Systems Analysis*, 14, 1, 53–62.

Dickson, G.W. and Nechis, M. (1984). Key Information Systems Issues for the 1980's. *MIS Quarterly*, 8, 3, 135–49.

Economist, The (1996). Paradox Lost. *The Economist*, September 28th, 13–16.

Etzerodt, P. and Madsen, K.H. (1988). Information Systems Assessment as a Learning Process. In Bjorn-Anderson, N. and Davis, G.B. (eds) *Information Systems Assessment: Issues and Challenges*. Elsevier, North-Holland, Amsterdam, 333–47.

Farbey, B. Land, F. and Targett, D. (1992). Evaluating Investments in IT. *Journal of Information Technology*, 7, 2, 109–22.

Farbey, B., Land, F. and Targett, D. (1993). *How to Evaluate Your IT Investment: a Study of Methods and Practice*. Butterworth-Heinemann, London.

Farbey, B., Land, F. and Targett, D. (eds) (1995). *Hard Money—Soft Outcomes*. Alfred Waller Limited, Henley.

Galliers, R.D. (1987). Information Systems Planning in the United Kingdom and Australia: a Comparison of Current Practice. In Zorkorczy, P.I. (ed.) *Oxford Surveys in Information Technology*, Oxford University Press, Oxford, 4, 223–55.

Galliers, R.D. (1995). A Manifesto for Information Management Research. *British Journal of Management*, 6, Special Issue 4, S45–S52.

Galliers, R.D., Merali, Y. and Spearing, L. (1994). Coping with Information Technology? How British Executives Perceive the Key Information Systems Management Issues in the mid-1990s. *Journal of Information Technology*, 9, 4, 223–38.

Ginzberg, M.J. (1979). Improving MIS Project Selection. *OMEGA*, 7, 6, 527–37.

Ginzberg, M.J. and Zmud, R.W. (1988). Evolving Criteria for Information Systems Assessment. In Bjorn-Anderson, N. and Davis, G.B. (eds) *Information Systems Assessment: Issues and Challenges*. Elsevier, North-Holland, Amsterdam, 41–52.

Gitman, L. and Forrester, J. (1978). A Survey of Capital Budgeting Techniques Used by Major U.S. Firms. *Financial Management*, Fall, 66–71.

Grindley, K. (1995). *Managing IT at Board Level*, Price Waterhouse, London.

Hamilton, S. and Chervancy, N.L. (1981). Evaluating Information System Effectiveness—Part 1: Comparing Evaluation Approaches. *MIS Quarterly*, September, 5, 3, 55–69.

Hawgood, J. and Land, F. (1988). A Multivalent Approach to Information System Assessment. In Bjorn-Anderson, N. and Davis, G.B. (eds) *Information Systems Assessment: Issues and Challenges*. Elsevier, North-Holland, Amsterdam, 103–20.

Hochstrasser, B. and Griffiths, C. (1991). *Controlling IT Investment Strategy and Management*. Chapman and Hall, London.

Keen, P.G.W. (1991). *Shaping the Future: Business Design through Information Technology*. Harvard Business School Press, Boston, MA.

Kelly, G.G., Watson, R.T., Galliers, R.D. and Brancheau, J.C. (1994). *Key Issues in Information Systems Management: an International Perspective*. Warwick Business School Research Paper No 134, Warwick.

Kim, S.H. and Farragher, E.J. (1981). Current Capital Budgeting Practices. *Management Accounting*, June, 26–9.

King, M. and McAuley, L. (1997). Information Technology Investment Evaluation: Evidence and Interpretation. *Journal of Information Technology*, 12, 2, 131–44.

King, J.L. and Schrems, E.L. (1979). Cost-Benefit Analysis in Information Systems Development and Operation. *Computer Surveys*, 10, 1, 19–34.

Klammer, T. (1972). Financial Evidence of the Adoption of Sophisticated Capital Budgeting Techniques. *Journal of Business*, October, 387–97.

Klein, G. and Beck, P.O. (1987). A Decision Aid for Selecting among Information System Alternatives. *MIS Quarterly*, June, 177–85.

Lucas, H.C. and Moore, J.R. (1976). A Multiple-Criterion Scoring Approach to Information Systems Project Selection. *INFOR*, 14, 1, 1–12.

Maglitta, J. and Sullivan-Trainor, M. (1991). Do the Right Things. *Computerworld: The Premier 100 (supplement)*, 6–13.

Marsh, P., Barwise, P., Thomas, K. and Wensley, R. (1988). *Strategic Investment Decisions in Large Diversified Companies*. Centre for Business Strategy, London Business School, London.

Mills, R.W. (1988). Capital Budgeting Techniques Used in the UK and the USA. *Management Accounting*, 61, 1, 12–26.

Moore, J.S. and Reichert, A.K. (1983). An Analysis of Financial Management Techniques Currently Employed by Large US Corporations. *Journal of Business finance and Accounting*, Winter, 623–45.

Moser, C. and Kalton, G. (1971). *Survey Methods in Social Investigation*, 2nd edn, Heinemann, London.

Niederman, F., Branchaeu, J.C. and Wetherbe, J.C. (1991). Information Systems Management Issues for the 1990's. *MIS Quarterly*, 15, 4, 475–99.

Parker, M.M., Trainor, H.E. and Benson, R.J. (1989). *Information Strategy and Economics*. Prentice-Hall, New York.

Pervan, G. (1997). IS Executives' Views of the Key Issues in Information Management in Australia. *Proceedings of the Fifth European Conference on Informa-*

tion Systems. Cork, Ireland, June.

Petty, J.W., Scott, D.F. and Bird, M.M. (1975). The Capital Expenditure Decision-Making Process of Large Corporations. *The Engineering Economist*, Spring, 159–72.

Pike, R.H. (1982). *Capital Budgeting in the 1980s: a Major Survey of the Investment Practices in Large Companies*. ICMA, London.

Pike, R.H. (1988). An Empirical Study of the Adoption of Sophisticated Capital Budgeting Practices and Decision Making Effectiveness. *Accounting and Business Research*, 18, 72, 341–51.

Pollard, C.E. and Hayne, S.C. (1996). A Comparative Analysis of Information Systems Issues Facing Canadian Business. In Nunamaker, J.F. and Sprague, R.H. (eds) Information Systems-Decision Support and Knowledge-Based Systems, *Proceedings of the 29th Annual Hawaii International Conference on System Sciences*, 2, 68–77.

Price Waterhouse (1994). *Information Technology Review 1993/94*. Price Waterhouse, London.

Price Waterhouse (1995). *Information Technology Review 1994/95*. Price Waterhouse London.

Remenyi, D.S.J., Money, A. and Twite, A. (1993). *A Guide to Measuring and Managing IT Benefits*, 2nd edn, Blackwell, Oxford.

Sager, I. and Gleckman, H. (1994). The Information Revolution. *Business Week*, 13th June, 35–9.

Sangster, A. (1993). Capital Investment Appraisal Techniques: a Survey of Current Usage. *Journal of Business Finance & Accounting*, 20, 3, 307–32.

Scapens, R.W. and Sale, J.R. (1981). Performance Measurement and Formal Capital Expenditure Controls in Divisionalised Companies. *Journal of Business Finance and Accounting*, Autumn, 389–419.

Schall, L., Sunden, G. and Geijsbeek, W. (1978). Survey and Analysis of Capital Budgeting Methods. *Journal of Finance*, 10, 3, 281–92.

Soh, C. and Markus, L. (1995). How IT Creates Business Value: a Process Theory Synthesis. *Proceedings of the International Conference In Information Systems*, Amsterdam, December 10–13th.

Tam, K.Y. (1992). Capital Budgeting in Information Systems Development. *Information and Management*, 23, 4, 345–57.

Wang, P. and Turban, E. (1994). Management Information Systems Issues of the 1990s in the Republic of China: an Industry Analysis. *International Journal of Information Management*, 14, 1, 25–38.

Ward, J., Taylor, P. and Bond, P. (1995). Identification, Realisation and Measurement of IS/IT Benefits: an Empirical Study of Current Practice. In Brown, A. and Remenyi, D. (eds) *The Second European Conference on Information Technology Investment Evaluation Conference Proceedings*, Operational Research Society, London.

Wegen, van B. and Hoog, de R. (1996). Measuring the Economic Value of Information Systems. *Journal of Information Technology*, 11, 3, 247–60.

Willcocks, L. (1992). Evaluating Information Technology Investments: Research Findings and Reappraisal. *Journal of Information Systems*, 2, 3, 243–68.

Willcocks, L. (ed.) (1994). *Information Management: Evaluation of IS Investments*. Chapman and Hall, London.

Willcocks, L. (ed.) (1996). *Investing in Information Systems: Evaluation and Management*. Chapman and Hall, London.

Willcocks, L. and Lester, S. (1996). The Evaluation and Management of IS

Investments: from Feasibility to Routine Operations. In Willcocks, L. (ed.) (1996). *Investing in Information Systems: Evaluation and Management*. Chapman and Hall, London.

Wilner, N., Koch, B. and Klammer, T. (1992). Justification of High Technology Capital Investment: An Empirical Study. *The Engineering Economist*, 37, 4, 341–53.

Zuboff, I. (1988). *The Age of the Smart Machine*. Heinemann, London.

5
Evaluation of Information Technology Investments: Business as Usual?

PHILIP L. POWELL
Goldsmiths College, University of London

Now I saw, though too late, the folly of beginning work before we count the cost and before we judge rightly of our own strength to go through with it. (Robinson Crusoe, Daniel Defoe)

INTRODUCTION

The plethora of texts and papers throughout the 1990s on evaluating investment in information systems and information technology (IS/IT) is testament to the continuing interest of practitioners and academics in the issue. As the Introduction to this book makes clear, there is no doubt that evaluating or justifying investment in IS/IT is problematic. Many sources suggest that IS/IT investment is different from other investment decisions because the costs and benefits are harder to identify and quantify and the intangible factors are likely to be significant (Strassmann, 1997; Willcocks, 1996). Case studies back this up (see, for example, Chapters 2 and 9). There are many currently available methodologies which attempt to address the problem, but none has found universal favour and most are variations on standard investment appraisal techniques discussed in the previous chapter (but see also Chapters 6 and 7, and Section IV). This chapter updates and extends

Beyond the IT Productivity Paradox.
Edited by L. P. Willcocks and S. Lester © 1999 John Wiley & Sons Ltd.

earlier work undertaken in this area by Powell (1992) and examines whether solutions are any nearer.

The chapter reviews existing methodologies while identifying the *raison d'être* for the evolution of new methods into an already crowded field. It then considers if the notion that IS/IT investment is different from other investment decisions really is justified, or if it is just a much-repeated myth. Tentative ways forward from this impasse are then considered. Through case studies we then revisit the issue, trailed in the Introduction, as to whether the coming of the World Wide Web and the Internet means that, as far as evaluation is concerned, it cannot be "business as usual". The chapter concludes by looking at the political, organizational and competitive aspects of IS/IT investment, addressing the question of why firms or individuals may not wish to engage in the formal evaluation of such projects.

Perhaps one of the most difficult initial problems in investigating this area is to provide a working definition of IS/IT. Eaton, Smithers and Curran (1988) quote the classic Department of Trade and Industry definition of information technology (IT) as: "the acquisition, processing, storage and dissemination of vocal, pictorial, textual and numeric information by a microelectronics-based combination of computing and telecommunications". For information systems (IS) we use the definition detailed in Chapter 2: they are organizational applications, increasingly IT based, that deliver on the information needs of an organization's stakeholders. This does provide a flavour of the all-encompassing nature of IT/IS, but, remembering that often between 28 and 40% of IT/IS expenditure is outside the formal IT budget (Willcocks, 1996), there is no doubt that what does and does not constitute IS/IT is often in the eye of the beholder (or the budget holder) and this problem may colour particularly some of the empirical work in this field.

WHY INVEST?

Organizations invest heavily in IS/IT. Weill and Olson (1989) quote a figure of 2% of revenue as the mean level of expenditure in 1983. Willcocks (1992) puts it at 3% for the UK. Weill and Olson argue that such estimates are likely to be understatements due to the decentralized nature of organizations and the purchasing of end-user equipment from revenue rather than capital sources. Evidence for this is that up to 40% of hardware spending is on personal computing items, likely not to be recorded as a capital expenditure (Plunket, 1990). It is clear that large amounts of discretionary expenditure are allocated to IS/IT; much of this, it will be argued, without formal evaluation. Senior executives continue to increase their IT investment. Several reports suggest that by 1998 it accounts for more than 50% of corporations' annual capital investment in the developed economies, and will average 5% of revenues by 2010 (e.g. International Data Corporation, 1995; Keen, 1991; Graeser, Willcocks and Pisanias, 1998).

There must be sound business motives for this investment. Earl (1987) suggests four reasons for using IS/IT as a strategic resource: to gain competitive advantage; to improve productivity and performance; to enable new ways of managing and organizing; and to develop new business (see also Chapter 2 for a listing of reasons for IT investment). Each of these has some economic underpinning. That is, the organization is investing in IS/IT in order to increase its net worth. Overlaying this may be the actions of subgroups of the organization trying to acquire non-monetary gains for themselves, but even here there is still a need for a set of metrics with which to evaluate the investment. If this is the case, the lack of usable and used techniques seems anomalous. Coombs, Saviotti and Walsh (1987), looking at the economics of technical change, comment: "the trend then, can be seen as an attempt by firms partly to internalise and control the potential benefits of technological advances, rather than being a victim of them". This desire for control or self-direction presents an overarching view of why organizations might wish to invest in new technology. An alternative perspective by Ward looks at the types of application: *substitutive* investments to gain efficiency, *complementary investments* to increase effectiveness and achieve innovations (Ward and Griffith, 1996).

The purposes of evaluation are manifold (Farbey, Land and Targett, 1992; see also Chapter 6). It can be as part of the justification process, as an allocation or comparison mechanism, for purposes of control and to provide feedback or learning for the organization. As will be demonstrated, there is scant evidence for this final "learning" purpose, but a little more for the others (see also Chapter 4).

PROBLEMS OF IS/IT APPRAISAL

There is no shortage of researchers who have tackled the problematic task of computer system investment appraisal. Most are of one opinion: that the costs and benefits associated with such systems are difficult to quantify. An early paper by McRea (1970) continues to summarize concisely the mood of IS/IT evaluators: "the computer is a difficult investment to evaluate because the income from the computer is not as clearly defined as it is with other investments". Others concur and, while acknowledging the problems of defining costs associated with information technology, suggest that defining or quantifying benefits is of greater difficulty (see Chapter 7 for supporting evidence).

In fact, there are probably very few business investments which are possible to evaluate easily. The well-known, but possibly not well-used, methodologies for project/investment appraisal rely on assumptions about a number of possibly interrelated factors. Beyond the simple methodologies lie the areas of risk assessment and sensitivity analysis, but there is a need to distinguish between the existence of these methodologies and their practical application. As Willcocks and Margetts (1994) argue, and as Ropponen found (Chapter 8), it may be that suitable techniques exist but, nevertheless, are not widely applied.

Current evaluation techniques are largely an outgrowth of traditional cost–benefit methodologies or are the application of standard accounting techniques to the problem. Zakierski (1987) is useful in dividing the methods into objective and subjective techniques. Objective measures—generally older—seek to quantify system inputs and outputs in order to attach values to the items. Subjective methods (usually qualitative) acknowledge the frailty of the values so computed and rely instead on the attitudes and opinions of users and system builders (see also Chapters 12 and 13 for a critique of evaluation approaches). Certain of the suggested models combine the two approaches. However, these seem to be of the form: "if you can't justify your system objectively, then use subjective techniques". The underlying premise is that the system is worthwhile, it is just difficult to show that this is so. Let us look at these methods in more detail (see also Chapter 6).

Objective Methods

Quantitative techniques (Table 5.1) endeavour to categorize the costs associated with a system or proposed system. These costs may relate to the functions of the system, to those involved in the system or to the lifecycle of the system. It is hoped that by careful cost categorization all sources of cost can be identified, and hopefully quantified, in a reasonably robust manner. A similar set of activities is advocated for the attribution of values to benefits.

An example of such a technique is SESAME, developed by IBM (Lincoln, 1986). This method attempts to identify all significant relevant costs and the corresponding system benefits by asking users how they would manage without the system. To do this the author claims that questionnaires "based on a proven standard" are employed. Despite this "proven standard", it is interesting to note that IBM has other methodologies that claim to do the same task. The results that Lincoln

Table 5.1 Objective Evaluation Methods (from Powell, 1992)

Objective evaluation method	Main reference(s)	1	2	3	4	5	6	7	8
Cost-benefit analysis	Lay (1985)	*					*	*	
MIS utilization technique	Martin and Trumbley (1996)					*	*		
Value analysis	Keen and Scott-Morton (1978)	*			*		*		*
Application benchmark technique	Joslin (1965)					*			*
Multiple criteria approach	Chandler (1982)				*			*	*
Simulation technique	Kanter (1970)					*	*		*
DSS evaluation technique	Keen and Scott Morton (1978)							*	*
1. Decision outputs		*					*		
2. Changes in the decision process							*		
3. Changes in manager's concepts							*		
Decision analysis	Schell (1986)	*		*	*	*	*	*	*
Systems measurement	Sprague and Carlson (1982)		*			*	*	*	*

describes indicate that two-thirds of all applications break even in less than one year and 80% had positive returns on investment. Evans (1989), reporting on a Nolan Norton study, states that returns of 10% can be generated from investment in the "personal computing phase" of information systems, 200–500% in the "connected work group phase" and 1000% in the final "business transformation phase". If such startling results are accurate, then two plausible hypotheses follow. Either no type of analysis needs to be undertaken, since any investment in information technology is almost bound to be worthwhile; why expend effort proving what you already know? Alternatively, the subjective methods are a waste of time, since one can easily point to objective, quantifiable benefits to justify IS/IT investment. All that is required is for firms that need to evaluate expenditure in this field to use a SESAME-type technique. Unless, that is, there are organizational and political motives for engaging in subjective analysis in order, perhaps, to show the widespread impact of IS/IT and secure even greater funding.

Williams and Scott (1965) provide a dated, though still interesting, set of case studies on investment appraisal which serves as a counter example to the above. Two of these, dealing with computer installation, point to the wide discrepencies between *ex ante* and *ex post* savings that failed to materialize. In one case returns were negative compared to a predicted 7–12%, and in the other, an actual return of 10% was achieved while forecasts were of 24–44%. Willcocks (1994) reports cases where the full costs of IT projects fail to be identified. In one manufacturing case, on-going human and organizational costs of a three-year project were over three times other costs, but only 20% of the human/organizational costs were included in the original feasibility evaluation.

However, even if one blindly accepts that investment in IS/IT is beneficial, there is a further rationale for sensible assessment. Overly (1973) identifies it thus: "technology based programmes often result in benefits and costs which were not identified or acknowledged in the planning and resource allocation process, and, as a result, there are beneficiaries who do not pay for their gains and benefactors who must pay costs they do not incur through their own actions". Thus, if the organization operates in any sort of decentralized or devolved budgetary mode, there is a need for some mechanism to identify and allocate costs and benefits. One part of the organization should not be forced to incur higher costs due to an inefficient system installed elsewhere. Similarly, unless computing costs are met centrally, a department should be able to recover some element of the benefit it provides to others by using IS/IT. In the 1980s there were documented moves towards a charging system for computer use being employed by organizations (see for instance Ernest-Jones, 1989), and many organizations continue to operate such systems. The aim is to highlight expenditures and to enhance the department's awareness of the costs of IS/IT. This may cause the end-user departments to consider whether they get value for money, but it sidesteps the issue of how such investment is actually evaluated. The other major step in this direction is outsourcing, in which the whole IS/IT function is handed over to a third party (Lacity, Willcocks and Feeny, 1997). But even here the decision to outsource and the distribution of the costs of outsourcing among departments need some basis of discrimination (see Chapters 2 and 10).

As mentioned, the objective methods predate the subjective. This is probably a reflection of the change in the types of tasks tackled by computer systems. Early systems largely replaced clerical tasks where differential costs and benefits were easier to identify. The movement of computing systems to addressing more decision-oriented tasks necessitated a widening of the scope of costs and benefits. With greater impact on less quantifiable activities, such as "better" decision taking, came the realization that the accuracy or indeed traceability of quantified costs and benefits was increasingly dubious (Strassmann, 1990). Hence the movement to "soft" or subjective analysis. However, even the need to carry out that analysis in-depth has been open to challenge. Goodwin (1989), describing the development of LEO, the first ever office computer, comments: "it was evident that LEO was not merely a tool which would enable clerical work to be performed more economically but . . . a tool which . . . could help management at all levels to control the business more efficiently". Yet the Kobler Report suggests: "companies are moving towards long term effectiveness even though such IT investments were harder to justify quantitatively". Meanwhile, Feeny (1997) has argued for a holistic, business-led approach to IT investment: "Only the adoption of new business ideas can lead to business benefits. If there is no new business idea associated with IT investment, the most that can be expected is that some existing business idea will operate a little more efficiently as old existing technology is replaced by new."

Subjective Methods

Subjective methods first arose in the late 1970s. These methods were propounded as team-building ones. The notion was to get the computer system out of the data-processing domain and into that of the manager or user, hence giving users a sense of participation, ownership and commitment (see Table 5.2).

In some sense, most of the subjective methods are merely spurious, pseudo-quantitative ones. They still try to quantify in order to

Table 5.2   *Subjective Evaluation Methods. (from Powell, 1992)*

Subjective evaluation method	Main reference(s)	1	2	3	4	5	6	7	8
User attitude survey	Hamilton and Chervany (1981)		*		*		*		
User utility function assessment technique	Ahituv (1980); Keeney and Raiffa (1976)		*		*		*	*	
Systems analysis	Senn (1978); McLean and Reisling (1977)		*		*	*			
Potential problem analysis	Chapple (1976)		*	*	*		*		
Event logging	Senn (1978); McLean and Reisling (1977)				*	*			
Aggregate scoring technique	Kepner and Tregoe		*		*		*		
Delphi evidence	Senn (1978); North and Pyke (1969)			*	*	*	*		
Anecdotal evidence	Gibson (1975)	*		*	*		*	*	

KEY
1   Results presented in financial terms
2   Extensive use of questionnaires in procedure
3   Probabilities incorporated into the analysis
4   Large, varied range of personnel involved
5   Can be used *ex ante*
6   Can be used *ex post*
7   Can be used continuously
8   Measures operational performance parameters

differentiate between systems, but the quantification is of feelings, attitudes and perceptions. There is, however, less emphasis on trying to convert these abstract values into a common monetary denominator. Schneiderjans and Fowler (1989) also point to the use of subjective judgement as to what objective factors are desirable, and this clouds the issue even further.

By their very nature, subjective evaluation techniques may only be used *ex post*. The decision to invest, using such methods, can only therefore be taken on the basis of the performance characteristics of similar systems. Although the same could be said of some of the quantitative techniques, their nature does allow cross-sectional system comparison to be undertaken more fruitfully in new proposals. Despite the tendency for hard analysis to drive out soft (Ijiri, 1975) in a reverse application of Gresham's law, subjective methodologies seem to be in the ascendency. Recent research—in Europe at least—concentrates increasingly on soft analysis, to some extent blinding the practitioner to the worth of quantitative techniques. The possible ways forward for objective methodologies are considered later.

THE ROLE OF FORMAL ANALYSIS

Is the evaluation of IS/IT investment dissimilar to the assessment of other investments that the organization may wish to undertake? There seems to be a widespread acceptance, in the literature and in practice, that IS/IT investment is different, because IS/IT *is* different. This does not appear to be a tested hypothesis, and there is mixed evidence from both case studies and econometric work (see for example Farbey, Land and Targett, 1992; Hitt and Brynjolfsson, 1996). The problems inherent in many types of investment consideration are often similar and in such cases the solutions, if solutions there are, may be the same.

Part of the argument that IS/IT is different stems from the standpoint of early researchers. These writers were essentially technologists. They did not possess investment appraisal skills. Later, when the field was encroached by business-related researchers who often had little technical background, the myth had already been established and was not disproved. These researchers took as their starting point the problems of intangible items and their measurement and proceeded to suggest methods of attaching values to intangible benefits and costs. In 1973 Overly commented that "current technological assessment programmes are limited in their ability to account for all benefits and costs as they are too technology-oriented".

Marsden and Pingry (1988) point to the conflict between user satisfaction and company profitability. System designers are entreated to enhance system usage and ease implementation by involving the user. The aim of this is to achieve the Holy Grail of user satisfaction. Yet a satisfied user is not necessarily a productive or profitable user. Satisfaction probably implies "satisficing", which is presumably suboptimal for the organization as a whole. However, optimization requires a metric for the measurement of success. There is a sense, nevertheless, in which IS/IT evaluators have deliberately misconstrued the role of formal analysis in project appraisal. Quantitative techniques are postulated as rigid strictures, the end result of which is an accept/reject decision. There is no role for expertise or managerial application in this case. As Gunton (1988) puts it: "the problem is not that end-user system projects cannot be justified but that they cannot be justified in terms which accountants and many senior managers are prepared to accept at the present time". He goes on to argue that normal measurement techniques do not work and that one should abandon financial analysis and use "gut feelings". Thus, while one could argue that the ascendency of accountants to senior management positions should point to an increased use of formal methods, it is not demonstrably clear that this is the case. Arguably, those lower in the organization may prefer to use subjective methods, or no method at all, in order to obtain project acceptance because they perceive quantitative methods as not successful (Powell, 1993).

As long ago as the 1960s, Williams (1967) was pointing to the same accountants' malaise in other types of investment appraisal: "many scientists have alleged that one important reason why we are often slow into new fields is that the crucial investment decisions are made by bankers and accountants who have a strong aversion to risk and are unable to comprehend the impact of the scientific revolution". The OECD (1972) joined this attack on the accountant's role in the context of a handbook for project evaluation in developing countries: "some costs are of course easy to calculate, but others entail estimates that shock the accountant with his excessive and often unrealistic desire for precision, or the technical expert who is too aware of the wide range of possibilities to give even an approximate answer".

This is a mis-specification of the place of formal methods in evaluation. Leaving aside the need for expert input in the quantification of inputs and outputs, as well as the need for reflection in deciding the very nature and scope of those costs and benefits, there have rarely been advocates of project appraisal performed along the rigid, dichotomized lines thus described. Awad (1988), for instance, writes: "cost/benefit analysis is a tool for evaluating systems, not a substitute for users' final judgement. Like any tool it has its drawbacks;" and earlier: "analysis of the costs and benefits of alternative systems guides the final solution". It might be argued that we are here presenting a softened tone because IS/IT is involved. Yet one can go back to early accounting writers who state, while considering in general terms investment appraisal or capital budgeting, that accounting figures are only the *starting* point for analysis. Thus Anthony and Welsch (1974) wrote: "few, if any, business problems can be solved solely by the collection and analysis of figures". Merrit and Sykes (1973) concurred: "For this analysis to be justified despite uncertainty and imperfect estimates, it is merely necessary that the extra effort involved should yield a worthwhile improvement in the quality of decision making." In the same vein, Batty (1978) argued that: "intuition and judgment cannot be replaced by the collection of facts, but there is no doubt that the decision making mechanism is likely to be strengthened materially by the systematic collection and analysis of relevant data". Likewise, Harvey (1986) argued for a "second entrepreneurial test" to be applied to any computer purchase after having weighed up the proposal "by traditional means".

EVALUATION IN OTHER DISCIPLINES

The idea that the measurement of costs and benefits is problematic has surfaced in fields other than IS/IT. Indeed, there is a whole literature on the cost–benefit analysis of economic and social investments. Here, values are attached to all identified consequences, both favourable and unfavourable, of a particular project.

A traditional area where cost–benefit analysis is common is that of engineering and, within this, civil engineering. The use of economic evaluation has long been recognized. For instance, Rose (1976) is typical: "it is inconceivable that large capital expenditures could be made without an accompanying economic evaluation" and later: "any decision regarding the expenditure of capital therefore should be preceeded by economic evaluation. However, this is never the whole story and 'non-economic' factors should also be taken into account before the decision is made." Antill (1973) concurs with the initial thrust stating that estimation of construction costs is "undoubtedly one of the most important aspects of civil engineering". Riggs (1977) adds that: "revenue is somewhat harder to estimate than costs for many industrial projects", indicating that in the calculation of benefits, rather than costs, IS/IT and engineering suffer the same type of problems. Benefits are recognized to be of various types and "qualitative in nature—more convenience, better living conditions, more leisure time—it is possible to attempt to express their benefits in money terms ... [but] such calculations are full of uncertainty" (Rose, 1976). Thompson (1981) adds weight to Gunton's comments (see above). He writes that cost estimations "are all predictions ... and we do not expect them to be accurate in the accounting sense". Rose, while acknowledging that "cost estimation can be a serious source of error" feels that "it is surprising how much can be expressed quantitatively given a little thought and imagination". Antill agrees: "it is surely somewhat remarkable that an estimator can produce construction works costs with an average accuracy as good as $+/- 10\%$".

The methods propounded by these writers essentially fall into three categories. First, those based on an "exponential or factorial" analysis of similar projects scaled up or down as necessary. Second, the use of unit rates. Databases of costs per identifiable unit exist for most civil engineering tasks. These costs, massaged to take account of atypical circumstances, are multiplied by the units to give a total project cost. The third method is termed operational estimating. This seems to be a catch-all method used in unique projects where costs are estimated for the constituent operations and activities and aggregated. None of these methods is startling or novel, the only difference between this field and the IS/IT one being the existence of a large databank of historical information which is readily available in published form. Writers in the engineering field talk of the accuracy of preliminary estimates of the order of $+/- 15$–20% (Antill, 1973) and $+/- 5\%$ for final estimates (Rose, 1976). Such accuracy, if achieved in the IS/IT area, would be astounding. However, in a computer corollary, Smith (1988) noted three methods of project costing. These relate first to the quantity of code or object instructions, second to the use of past project data and third to an estimation model attributed to Putnam (1980). Boehm (1981) claims that 80% of the time such models can estimate software cost within 20% (see also Charette, 1996); however, the strength of these models is their objectivity and the weakness their subjectivity.

Moving out of the pure engineering field, cost–benefit analysis has been used for a range of social projects. Attempts have been made to measure the returns on investment in schooling (Hansen, 1963), in medical research (Weisbrod, 1971), in advertising and in training. Similarly, analysis has been undertaken in evaluating employment schemes, mental health programmes and disease-control attempts. Although difficulties existed, estimated rates of return of 11–12% were generated for polio research and 10.4–15.3% for different levels of education. The authors of these studies freely admit the large error levels, yet feel, on balance, that the estimates are sufficiently accurate to be useful. In comparison with these fields, IS/IT is a far better bounded domain with less sensitive cost and benefit estimates.

Interesting empirical work in the research and development (R&D) field is reported by Parker (1978). The expected probability of technical success of projects was greater than 80% in 75% of cases reviewed by Mansfield *et al.* (1971). However, actual success rates were 44%. Cost deviations were 20% under budget for half of the projects while, surprisingly, only 15% exceeded budget forecasts by more than 20%. In the same field, Twiss (1986) provides five methods of setting research budgets: costing of an agreed programme, comparison with other firms, as a percentage of turnover or of profit, and finally as an incremental deviation from previous budgets.

Despite the paucity of empirical research showing the magnitude of returns, companies do invest heavily in IS/IT. Not only do they invest, but there is a feeling, often unquantified, that investment is worthwhile. However, one manager quoted in Ernest-Jones (1989) asserts: "I know how much I spend [on IS/IT] and how much payback I get." Yet the only item measured by this evaluator was staff reductions. Perhaps this organization had not yet progressed to supporting intangible areas of activity or, conversely, it felt that in 1989 IS/IT could still be justified on the basis of staff savings alone.

POSSIBLE SOLUTIONS

A way forward would be to accept that IS/IT investment is not different, that standard techniques are applicable, or at least as applicable to IS/IT as to any other type of project. A second would be to acknowledge that IS/IT is very different and unquantifiable. A further way forward would be to develop another method.

The existence of many techniques suggests that the field is already a little crowded and that a "new" method would be likely to add little. As suggested in Chapter 2, getting organizations to apply and stick with techniques, rather than their existence, may be the more critical issue. This has not staunched the flow of ever more involved techniques (see for example Hares and Royle, 1994; van Wegen and de Hoog, 1996; Whiting, Davies and Knul, 1993), which are typically combinations of standard investment appraisal and decision and risk analysis techniques. A further attempt might be to investigate how currently available techniques could be employed and possibly amended to overcome some of the difficulties raised here. Within, or perhaps in parallel to, this is a need formally to identify disbenefits of particular courses of action. A need also exists to look at alternative future scenarios.

A final alternative might be to attempt to establish global multipliers for IS/IT investment. Although crude, such a measure might guide investment strategies in some ordinal sense. That is, there might be a lifecycle of IS/IT development with expected higher returns being given by investment in transactions-processing systems before decision support, before networks. Some empirical and theoretical support for this type of lifecycle exists (Price, 1989). No attempts seem to have been made to develop optimization models along the R&D lines. Parker discusses a number of these which essentially relate optimal R&D expenditure to the price elasticity of the product and to market share. The same author also reports that profit-maximization models are fairly good at explaining budget allocations in this discipline. Again, evidence for this in the IS/IT area is lacking.

USE OF EVALUATION TECHNIQUES IN PRACTICE

Despite the existence of, albeit partial, methodologies for IS/IT evaluation, there is some evidence of lack of use of formal techniques (see also Chapters 4 and 6). Galliers (1991) highlighted the prime barrier to strategic information systems planning as measuring the benefits, yet found that this was attempted in 16% of cases, and formally in only 9%. Similarly, Sheppard (1990) found little evidence of formal evaluation in her case studies. Likewise, Farbey, Land and Targett in Chapter 6 discovered few companies that had *ex ante* evaluations or a strategy on which to base such evaluation. Organizations or groups within organizations do not wish to evaluate IS/IT, at least *ex ante*. Evidence of budgets being set on some sort of competitive parity is available (see for instance Weill and Olson, 1989; Willcocks, 1996). As one example, industry-wide norms may be established through an informal or more formal information exchange, for example in the USA with the annual *Datamation* (1991) survey. This can be likened to one of the methods by which firms establish advertising budgets. Kotler (1995) points to stable advertising budgets, as percentages of sales, in the cosmetics, confectionery and soap industries. Kay (cited in Coombs, Saviotti and Walsh, 1987) also observed stability in R&D budgets, rationalizing this as a managerial preference for stability at the time.

A number of plausible reasons for the lack of use of formal evaluation methods can be identified. The first is quite simple: are most projects evaluated formally? The existence of robust, reliable tools for project evaluation does not imply their use. Where they are used, it may be in an *ex post* justification mode rather than in a proactive one.

There is a substantial body of evidence to suggest that formal evaluation methods have been, and are, widely used in practice. Gurnani

(1984) surveyed the empirical literature on capital budgeting methods. There appeared to be a steady growth in the use of sophisticated techniques. The use of discounting among surveyed organizations grew from 10% in 1959 to 60% in 1975 and 86% a year later (more recent surveys confirm this level: (Pike, 1983 and Ho and Pike, 1992, 1996). Greater use is found in larger corporations, chemical and petroleum companies, utilities and capital-intensive industries. However, from these studies it seems that organizations using such techniques do not apply them universally. Some applied the techniques only to large projects, while others categorized projects and applied different criteria and tests to each category. Categories included research and development, expansion, replacement and mandatory projects. Computer purchase was not explicitly identified. Nearly all (97%) of companies reported approving economically infeasible investments. Non-quantifiable factors are felt to be of extreme importance: 77% of one sample by Petty "acknowledged that, though quantitative factors are dominant ... qualitative factors do influence the final decision". Often these non-quantifiable factors were identified as future possible benefits which might accrue in later years but were currently unassessable. Hence the use of relatively sophisticated techniques is apparent, as is a recognition of where they are inappropriate, but what is not established is if IS/IT considerations do or should fall into the latter category. As early as 1965, Williams and Scott found that their computer-acquisition case studies all involved quantitative evaluation. This was not the case in other investment decisions.

These findings are mirrored in the R&D literature. Parker (1978) found a positive correlation between use of quantitative techniques and firm size. He also quotes Mansfield on the value placed on quantitative appraisals by laboratory directors: "A proper attitude is one of scepticism, biased towards an appreciation that quantitative techniques are no more than an aid." However: "only 10–20% of lab directors regarded such estimates as poor or untrustworthy". Perhaps, then, what is needed is cost–benefit analyses of doing cost–benefit analyses. Limited evidence of the benefits derived from undertaking such analysis is available in such areas as US Defense programmes (Williams, 1967), yet such studies are still not widespread and, as Freeman and Hobbs (1991) suggest, such calculations are information costly. Sheppard (1990) offers a case in which there was "obviously a need for email" but it was felt that it was too expensive to prove that this was so. Of course, this may just reflect a healthy scepticism that evaluation and performance are not necessarily positively correlated (Haka, Gordon and Pinches, 1985), though the process of evaluation can often be more useful than the outcome (Willcocks, 1996).

IT EVALUATION: NOT BUSINESS AS USUAL

As the Introduction to this book makes clear, the sorts of difficulties and issues in IT evaluation detailed in this chapter have been compounded from 1994/5 onwards as we entered a network-based era. The period finds organizations simultaneously making investments in technologies from at least three different eras, to which different underlying economics may well apply. While standard evaluation procedures discussed in this chapter for both IT and non-IT investments may still be relevant, it nevertheless becomes crucial to understand the specifics of the risks, cost structures, benefits and timescales that apply when network-based IT investments are under consideration. The following three network-based cases, compiled from secondary sources (see Willcocks, Graeser and Lester, 1998), are designed to illustrate some of the possibilities and how for IT evaluation practices, in several ways at least, it may not be "business as usual".

CASE 1—FRUIT OF THE LOOM (FOTL): MASTERING THE DISTRIBUTION CHANNEL

By 1996 this company was a major US manufacturer of clothing. For its underwear business it dealt directly with large retailers such as Wal-Mart. For its Activewear products it maintained a network of 50 distributors via catalogues, telephone and fax. Distributors would then fulfil orders for small businesses. Neither customers nor distributors for FOTL products could find out easily whether items were part of the distributor warehouse inventory and, if so, how fast they could be shipped. Customers could readily turn to alternative suppliers in the event of difficulties.

By early 1996 the company already employed a Vendor Management Inventory system for data exchange with distributors, and also processed over 30 000 EDI transactions daily. However, it took an outside digital commerce firm, Snickelways Interactive, to persuade FOTL into a pilot project to use the Internet and the Web to tie together the distributor network and provide information to end-customers about manufacturing and distributor inventories. The system would also enable customers to search alternative warehouses and check the status of their orders, and would suggest alternatives for out-of-stock items.

The pilot system was developed with a single distributor who wanted to reduce costs by replacing order-taking staff and facilities with an automated catalogue. The supplier was reluctant to allow customers to have direct access to the firm's databases via the Internet. Instead, periodically, a relevant file of information was transferred to the Web-based catalogue. The system was developed in 12 weeks at a cost of over $500 000. The initial assessment called for the distributor to reach break-even on the development after six months, with 5% of its business from Web-based ordering after a year. In practice, the latter figure was achieved after three months, and the company has continued to save $10 per transaction.

The emerging issue was how to put 30 or more distributors on the Web more inexpensively. Systems development mainly involved employing new software to support greater scalability and transaction processing. This took FOTL and three suppliers of Web hardware and software three months. A uniform design for establishing a Web site was produced which also allowed each distributor opportunities for customization. Eventually each participating distributor had a Web server and an Oracle database stored on a common OneServer site. Total integration had to be compromised because each distributor had its own inventory and order-handling systems. In the new project, Activewear Online, FOTL underwrote the cost of installation and maintenance of the Web server, while distributors updated their catalogues and paid for the communication links to the servers.

By 1997 each distributor had an on-line catalogue that graphically presented customers with a series of clothing categories. Each category led to more detailed pages produced from current product information, and that also contained ordering instructions. Customers could review their orders, check status and change orders at any time. The system contained the facility to check for alternative sources of supply and also substitute products. Customers needed an account name and password before they could order. Payment was by the normal billing process because there seemed no real advantages, but plenty of risks, in exchanging funds on-line at this stage. Bulletin boards and chatrooms were also included as part of each Web site. By 1998 they were being used for information exchange by customers, for example printing ideas, and for advertising for equipment and new workers.

FOTL underwrote more than $4 million in project costs. However, from the beginning its board did not attempt any detailed return on investment analysis, feeling that this sponsorship generated benefits, like customer loyalty and "mindshare", that could not be expressed financially, though they would have long-term financial impacts (see Introduction). Essentially, FOTL achieved greater electronic information exchange between a majority of its distributors, improved FOTL–distributor–customer relationships, but in a way that focused on FOTL and its products. The Web sites also achieved advantages over competitors, which needed to make matching responses. Interestingly, where FOTL products were not available, the Web sites could suggest competitors' products, but more often FOTL's products were suggested. Using the Web sites FOTL achieved lower costs and more timely information for its catalogues, but also gave itself the opportunity to gain favour with distributors and customers and influence the channel at the same time. The systems also lends itself to a range of competitive enhancements. Early results showed significant increases in overall market share and in transactions booked through the Web sites.

CASE 2—FIRST VIRTUAL CORPORATION (FVC): IT AS A PRODUCT

The possibilities engendered by networking have attracted many start-up companies. One such is FVC, founded in the USA in October 1993 with seed capital of $2 million. Its focus is multimedia. FVC delivers moving pictures and sound across computer networks. It specializes in asynchronous transfer mode technology (ATM) that can manage the massive volumes of data needed to deliver moving images to a personal computer screen.

The company has over 40 products, mostly intelligent hardware capable of turning a local area network into a multimedia one. As one example, it can offer high-quality video-conferencing for under $30 000 (1997 prices). It competes against ATM hardware specialists, but its software gives it distinctiveness in the market.

True to its name, FVC focuses under 40 staff on two identified core competencies: developing innnovative engineering, and signing contracts with large marketing partners around the world. Thereafter, manufacturing is done by Tannon, a local Californian specialist that has agreed to cut its prices to FVC by up to 15% every three months. FVC has one finance officer, with bills and financial statements handled by an outside company, while a bank manages cash flow. The company has no personnel, legal or public relations departments and no overseas staff. All staff work in the same office located at a cheap rental site in Santa Clara. In 1997, FVC was selling through Bay Networks, the world's second biggest networking company, and had deals with PictureTel, a video-conferencing technology manufacturer, and with AT&T, the latter an investor but also doing marketing for the company. It also had partners in Japan, Sweden and the UK.

By 1997, FVC's quarterly sales were exceeding $3 million and it was running at an operating profit. Its start-up success depended on outsourcing, the existence of an infrastructure of fast-moving support businesses typical of the Santa Clara area, and the availability of venture capital. In this case a start-up company identified a niche in developing products to enhance the networking capabilities of other organizations. Here the investment is in IT as the product itself, which means that the business case is all important, and in many ways was conventionally arrived at as for other start-ups. But, initially, there was little attempt to invest in the Internet and a Web site for marketing and selling purposes. The difficulties inherent in generating a critical mass and increasing revenues as outlined in the Introduction are eschewed for a "virtual" approach, depending more on powerful business partners for global reach.

CASE 3—OPEN MARKET INC.: TOWARDS AN ELECTRONIC COMMUNITY

With 12 staff this company launched its first products—software for doing business over the Internet—in October 1994. At the time, Open Market claimed to be the only company focused on providing a complete end-to-end solution for electronic commerce. By this date, over 20 000 commercial organizations were registered on the Internet, with WWW traffic increasing at a rate of 10% a week. There seemed to be a clear opportunity for developing secure systems enabling Internet merchants to offer goods for sale, accept and fulfil orders, receive payment and maintain transaction histories. Some would sell goods and services through an electronic "shopping mall". Retail customers would buy subscriptions to a buying service, which would include software for receiving on-line statements. On-line advertising news and other information would also be available to subscribers.

The start-up required $1.8 million funding. Open Market projected its first profits as arriving by the end of 1996, with transaction fees and other revenue streams increasing from under 45% to over 75% of total revenues by the year 2000. The financial investment was justified on the logic of dynamically increasing revenues, low marginal and distribution costs, and the value and flexibility of retained information (see this book's Introduction).

In mid-1994, Open Market set about attracting clients. Potential clients included a law firm; a large New England bank; Time Warner, an industry leader interested in learning about network-based advertising and secure payment and fulfilment services; the Nexis and Lexis on-line news and legal information service; Harcourt Brace, wanting to advertise and distribute books on the the Internet; and Ipswitch Software, wanting to offer regular product upgrades over the Internet at $5, rather than annually at $40 each. Merchants would pay to use Open Market software to develop "store fronts". For some firms these would act as a substitute for direct mail and advertising, with customers telephoning to order products. For other firms the "store front" would link directly to their own order and fulfilment systems, or ones developed for them by Open Market. The company also made available, initially at no charge to merchants, a Commercial Sites Index (CSI) listing all companies doing business on the Internet, and a digital advertising service matching a customer's profile of desired information. Advertising fees supported the service.

It quickly became clear that not only did competitors already provide free Internet browsers, but customers were not sufficiently interested in on-line shopping to pay an upfront fee. Initially, therefore, Open Market decided not to charge buyers for electronic shopping services. The company also offered free buyer registration software (for the commercial logic of this see Introduction and Figure I.3). Various round-the-clock security features were built into buying procedures, with security heightening as the value of a transaction increased.

By late 1994, the number of competitors offering similar services to Open Market was large and increasing. Moreover, it was difficult to predict where new competitors were going to come from, and how the business case and revenue projections would need to change. The company had already revised downwards its initial forecasts of sales transactions on the Internet. Achieving critical mass was going to be more difficult, while standards for Web browsers, secure payment systems, high-speed modems and other required items needed to solidify (see also Introduction). Meanwhile the original plan of making money by charging buyers for a shopping service, and charging merchants a commission for each transaction, would have to be delayed.

By early 1995, the CSI list was growing by more than 20 companies a day. But a number of strategic investment decisions were needed if the profit returns required for late 1996 were to be achieved. The CSI would be offered free. One option was to sell Open Market Storebuilder software through retailers, agents and other licensed channels. At a unit price of $350, this could produce 1300 unit sales in 1995, and possibly 500 000 in the year 2000. A second option was to focus on providing marketing and payment services. Estimated sales here were 400 for 1995 (initial price $1500), rising to 1 million in year 2000. The third option was to sell general-purpose merchant servers through third-party "value-added" resellers. The estimates here for 1995 were 285 unit sales at a price of $3500 each, rising to 500 000 unit sales in the year 2000. Finally, Open Market could focus on large, custom projects to create vertical industry end-to-end solutions for a limited number of clients. There were only six of these in 1995, though each may be sold for $200 000. The year 2000 unit sales potential was estimated at 5000.

Focusing as we are primarily on IT investment appraisal, it becomes clear from the three cases that a network-based era presents large challenges for existing and start-up organizations. In the case of FOTL, the business proposition was all important, and the Web-based benefits were felt to be too intangible, and the knock-on benefits too unpredictable, to be quantified in any meaningful way. For First Virtual, with IT as its product, a way of organizing had to be found to enable a small start-up company to focus its limited resources and finance on its core competencies. For Open Market Inc., business plans and quantified cost–benefit analyses were continually being supplied but also revised, while the dynamics of increasing returns were going to take time to develop, causing the company to reconsider its strategic options. At the same time, there was little certainty about what competitors would be doing over the 1995–2000 period, and prices and unit sales were necessarily speculative. Moreover, as at 1995 it was fairly clear not only that Open Market could not fulfil all of the options under consideration, but that each had different risks and potential payoffs.

MOTIVES FOR NOT EVALUATING PROJECTS

Turning from the problems of measurement in IS/IT evaluation, the view that there are other motives or reasons for not carrying out such assessments needs to be addressed. A number of arguments for this are proffered below. Perhaps one overwhelming reason is that firms do not have clear objectives, and hence have no yardstick against which to measure proposed systems. Williams and Scott (1965) comment that: "for all firms in our case-studies, we did not find definitions of objectives that acted as a clear-cut basis for investment decisions". Nevertheless, most organizational theorists would accept that organizational goals do exist. These may not be stable, consistent nor beneficial to the majority of participants, yet they do seem to influence organizational actions. However, there is often a lack of clarity about the nature and ranking of these objectives, which then translates into an inability to assess how IT investments can be directed and assessed (Willcocks, Feeny and Islei, 1997). Even agreed organizational objectives do not always seem to be translated into information systems strategies (Farbey, Land and Targett, 1992) and, of course, strategy formulation does not necessarily imply strategy implementation (Ward and Griffith, 1996).

IS/IT as Strategic

Computerization is seen in many instances as "strategic": "The role of IT has changed from one of support to one of strategic importance" (Farbey, Land and Targett, 1992). However, strategic can be a defensive avoidance term, possibly a substitute for "subjective" in quantitative terms. Anything labelled as strategic may well bypass the normal review process (Powell, 1993). It seems odd that firms seek to engage in strategic investments, often substantial ones, but, it seems, quite often do not evaluate or quantify costs and benefits in detail. The reasons for this are likely to be competition or perceived competition. Certainly, in the Powell, Connell and Holt (1992) survey of decision support system (DSS) use in accounting, the most frequently cited reasons for DSS purchase were corporate image and the desire not to be seen to be lagging behind the competition.

Sheppard (1990) suggests that the successful use of IT as a strategic weapon requires, *inter alia*, value-added justification, although returns are primarily measured by staff reductions, gaining a competitive edge and/or by "act of faith". Twiss (1986) dismisses the act of faith argument, arguing that "no company is going to invest heavily in technology solely as an act of faith in the hope that by backing the right people 'something will turn up'". Interestingly, he suggests that R&D investment is a strategic decision but one which is routinely evaluated. Feeny (1997) and Strassman (1990), however, argue against specific, detailed justification of computer purchases in "strategic" cases; rather, justification is via links to new business propositions and strategic goals.

In other instances, the use of shared facilities forces computerization. In the banking community, for example, many of the payments made are by electronic transfer. It is necessary to have the requisite systems in order merely to participate in the current processes. Obligation implies a need to justify rather than to evaluate. Hence such justification is going to be of a "satisficing" rather than optimizing nature, since the aim is to achieve better than a hurdle of some sort, set by the organization. Such hurdles may not be quantified but subsumed into wider, organization-based evaluation. That is, only if the return from the company as a whole is poor are individual elements, such as the computer system, subject to scrutiny. It is not clear if these hurdles are even set *ex ante*. The effect of setting hurdles *ex post* must be one of inducing cognitive dissonance into the evaluation process. Yet hurdle figures set beforehand may also be lacking since, unless a realistic view of system objectives is available, the targets are likely to be set in nebulous terms.

The "strategic" and "obligatory" arguments for investment in an activity without formal analysis being invoked are ones which Cook and Rizzuto (1989) found empirically supported in the R&D field. In a survey of capital budgeting practices for research and development, they found that for basic research only 23.1% of their sample used formal analysis. This figure rises to 76.5% at the development stage. The rationale put forward is that investment in R&D is strategic, and hence obligatory, if the firm is to remain competitive. The expectation here would be that firms would differentiate between investments needed to maintain the industry status quo and those that contribute to increased profitability. However, as early as 1975, Durand argued that informatics should no longer be supported at any cost, but be asked to account for itself. Most investment in IS/IT is, however, not of the research type. Despite the high failure rates, most projects are not especially innovatory.

Strategic justification is usually defended on the grounds of conformity to organizational objectives, but Wassenaar (1988) points to the difficulty of establishing links between intangible benefits and corporate objectives. Mitchell (1990) sees the organizational strategic objective as comprising three elements: knowledge building, strategic positioning and business investment. Certainly, the last of these, business investment, needs to be formally evaluated and a similar case could be made for the other two.

The Do Nothing Option

As Strassmann (1997) argues, in some sense computer system evaluation must be related to what would occur if firms do not computerize. The forces for computerization are such that this alternative is not often considered, except in so far as to be used as a benchmark for computer manufacturers to push dubious system feasibility studies. Turban (1988) adds the further problem, not apparent in some other fields, of partial implementation of computer projects, while Keen (1981, 1991) points to the evolutionary nature of most DSS and other systems.

Costs Do not Dominate

There are also scenarios in which cost may not matter, or may not be a dominant motivator. This is illustrated by two quite different scenarios, first where computerization costs are such a small percentage of total costs. For instance, in the London financial market post "Big Bang", the cost of a dealer's workstation, while high, is small in comparison to the costs of the dealer using it and to the returns available from successful trading. The second situation is the one of R&D

mentioned above. Here funds may be committed without an explicit requirement for return on the investment. There may also be a psychological sense in which more attention is paid to small amounts of investment than to large ones. The "pennies" are more closely guarded and monitored than the "pounds". Indeed, the dominant motivators for IT investments are, according to Sheppard (1990), that the old system is difficult to maintain, the desire to replace old systems with new technology and to exploit an opportunity to expand services. None of these is explicitly cost based. Similarly, Twiss (1986) has seen one of the motivations for R&D expenditure as the "foot in the door" concept; that is, invest to avoid sudden technological surprises.

Hochstrasser (1994) suggests both that indirect costs of IS/IT systems may be four times the direct costs and that cost underestimates of 50% are not unusual. Clearly, organizations that measure only direct costs, or alternatively believe that their estimates are going to be negligible, are more likely to feel that costs do not matter.

Government Actions

Paradoxically, government intervention in new technology may inhibit rigorous evaluation. MITI sponsorship of the Fifth Generation project in Japan, the UK Alvey experience and the European Esprit project all involved governments supporting team-developed IS/IT applications. A number of these were pre-competitive, taking the form of "clubs". The investment, often government matched, for each member of the club was small and therefore easily written off. Little emphasis was placed on economic evaluation as a criterion for success, hence little has been learned in this area to be carried over to other projects. It must be pointed out that government sponsorship of technological advances is not new. There is a history of government intervention going back to the industrial revolution, but this intervention tends to be technologically, not techniques, led.

Poor Specification

Mis-specification of the requirements of computer systems is widely apparent. Clients, whether internal users or external customers, are regularly described as not knowing their requirements fully, or frequently changing those requirements. This induces a tools-led or analyst-led scenario. Ironically, this may increase the pressure on the need for regular changes in specifications. The analogy here is with the defence industry. The developer is frequently working with poor or variable specifications, sometimes at the leading edge of technology.

The technical problems of such operations are likely to be greater than those found in other more stable environments. Coupled with this is the problem of evaluating the likely benefits of a poorly or mis-specified system.

It should be borne in mind that the problems of building a new and probably unique civil engineering undertaking are no less problematic. Nevertheless, it could be argued that, with software development, one is less aware of where one is in terms of the extent to which a project is complete, at any given time. For instance, the amount of effort expended on the user interface in expert system construction has been documented (see for instance Bobrow and Stefik, 1985) at almost 50% of the total system (in terms of coding). This was an unexpectedly high and unforeseen level, and presumably not allowed for in the system specification. Such issues have led Feeny, Earl and Edwards (1997) to urge a different mode of organization and the adoption, for innovatory IT, of a *user* rather than a *specialist* focus in systems development and delivery.

Trade-offs

There is no doubt that there are trade-offs among the cost/time/performance metrics of project appraisal and analysis. If too much pressure is applied to any one of these, then the others will be affected. If costs are too tightly controlled, performance may suffer; rapid production can only be achieved at the expense of cost overruns or performance reductions. Maintaining the right balance may be more important than the individual level of any single item.

Cost Overruns

The computer industry is notorious for its cost overruns. A trawl through computer industry journals will yield numerous cases of cost overruns. So too, however, would a similar fishing trip in an engineering counterpart. It is a standard ploy of contractors to oversell their projects. Thompson (1981), writing from an engineering standpoint, comments that: "in many cases particularly when the sponsors of the project are politically motivated, there is a tendency not to disclose or consider all the risks and to sanction an optimistic estimate of costs in the knowledge that once the project is under way it will rarely be stopped" (see also Chapters 12 and 13). Freeman, writing in 1982 on cost estimation in research proposals, concurred: "the context of estimation will always be one of political advocacy and clash of interest groups, whatever the possibility for sober calculation". Page and

Hooper (1987) offer an information systems view: "Actually one of the most common deficiencies is not the determination of a poor cost figure but rather the complete omission of important costs." Counteracting this deficiency, meanwhile, is another from the same source: "It is common to have unanticipated benefits which are more important than the actually anticipated benefits" (see also Willcocks, 1994). The cost overruns are most noticeable in large projects. Smaller projects may have in relative percentage terms very large cost overruns, but the tendency may be only to focus on the absolute amount of such costs. Also, the options element in investment in IS/IT is large, possibly larger, than that associated with other projects.

Perceived Failure

The past problems of highly publicised computing projects (for instance, in the UK, London Stock Exchange, London Ambulance Service, Wessex Health Authority) may engender a feeling of operating within a world of perceived failure. Such a culture may not be conducive to *ex ante* evaluation in any rigorous sense. The fact that organizations continue to invest, despite this failure, is at odds with most views on the matter. Williams and Scott (1965) point to R&D projects often being judged, not on current quantitative evaluations, but on the track record of the manager concerned. Coulson-Thomas (1991) describes how the cynicism resulting from the earlier generations of technology which did not deliver the hoped-for benefits has given way to a realization that it is the use of technology, not the technology itself, which is of prime importance. However, it might be increasingly beneficial, rather than viewing IS/IT as a means for achieving a competitive edge through better implementation, to see it also to some extent as a form of non-price competition. That is, IS/IT is also a corporate image maker and as such cannot be evaluated in the same way as other projects. This may be at least one of the considerations behind rising organizational investments in the Internet in the 1996–8 period (see Introduction for figures).

Barriers to Entry

There is evidence that IS/IT is a significant barrier to entry to new competitors in certain fields. The high fixed costs and reluctance of customers to duplicate existing facilities have proved a barrier to new entrants in such fields as airline reservation systems, the hospital supply industry and cable television. IS/IT can also be used to create an illusion of entry barriers: witness the number of mergers and acquisitions that have been abandoned due to the incompatibility of the data-processing systems of both parties. The UK building society industry, where 1997 IT spending was 20% of operating costs, has seen a number of such incidents, with system incompatibility cited as a major reason for failure.

Critical Success Factors

Harvey (1986) offered four reasons that computer purchases were not paying off, and these reasons would still seem to have some force in the late 1990s. The first is the mesmerizing effect where benefits are taken for granted. The second is a blinding of the purchaser by science. Third is an underestimation of the human factors involved, and fourth is a lack of purpose in the purchase decision. A further, seemingly ignored, point which may engender caution in any who seek to evaluate IS/IT is that of the critical success factors which have been identified for information systems (for an overview see Willcocks, Feeny and Islei, 1997). One of the main factors to emerge is that of top management support. If IS/IT success is dependent on such factors, then a view of the high level of such support must be taken *ex ante* by the evaluator. This may prove highly problematic and politically unacceptable. Other factors identified by Keen (1991) and Keen and Scott Morton (1978) include early commitment by the user and conscious staff involvement. All these may be difficult to take a view on before the investment takes place. Interestingly, most of the critical success factors identified in IT studies surface in other research on R&D success. Thus Parker (1978) found top management support to be the most important item, followed by such factors as clear identification of need, good cooperation and availability of resources.

CONCLUSIONS

The rapid pace of change in IS/IT technology poses serious starting problems for any large investment. Any long-term, fixed project is almost obsolete before it has started and is certainly passé by the time it is fully installed. This does not, however, negate the need to evaluate projects. It is clear that the justification of IS/IT is difficult, yet techniques are available which give broad indications of success and failure. These standard techniques do not appear to be widely used, even though they have been employed in other fields and are recognized as useful. If IS/IT is to emerge as a beneficial corporate tool, the decision to invest needs to be examined as rigorously as with any other large investment. But then, as Williams pointed out a quarter of a century ago, "the important thing in business is not to make good forecasts but to make them come true".

REFERENCES

Ahituv, N. (1980). A Systematic Approach toward Assessing the Value of an Information System. *MIS Quarterly*, 4, 1, 61–75

Anthony, R.N. and Welsch, G.L. (1974). *Fundamentals of Management Accounting.* Richard D. Irwin, Homewood, Illinois.

Antill, J.M. (1973). *Civil Engineering Management.* Angus and Robertson, Sydney.

Awad, E.M. (1988). *Management Information Systems: Concepts, Structure and Applications.* Benjamin Cummings, California.

Batty, J. (1978). *Advanced Cost Accounting.* MacDonald and Evans, Plymouth.

Binning, K. (1986). Cited in Twiss, B. *Managing Tehnological Innovation.* Longman, Harlow.

Bobrow, D. and Stefik, M. (1985). Presentation at the *IEEE Conference on Expert Systems*, London, Easter.

Boehm, B. (1981). *Software Engineering Economics.* Prentice-Hall, New Jersey.

Chandler, J.S. (1982). A Multiple Criteria Approach for Evaluating Information Systems. *MIS Quarterly*, 6, 1, 61–75.

Charette, R. (1996). The Mechanics of Managing IT Risk. *Journal of Information Technology*, 11, 4, 373–8.

Cook, T.J. and Rizzuto, R.J. (1989). Capital Budgeting Practices for R & D: a Survey and Analysis of *Business Week*'s R & D Scoreboard. *Engineering Economist*, 34, 4, 23–32, Summer.

Coombs, R., Saviotti, P. and Walsh, V. (1987). *Economics and Technical Change.* Macmillan, London.

Coulson-Thomas, C. (1991). Directors and IT, and IT Directors. *European Journal Information Systems*, 1, 1, 45–53.

Datamation (1991). The Datamation 100. *Datamation*, 37, 12, 6–90.

Durand, R. (1975). Cost Analysis of DP Centres. In Frielink, A. (ed.) *Economics of Informatics.* North-Holland, Amsterdam, 100–12.

Earl, M.J. (1987). Information Systems Strategy Formation. In Boland, R.J. and Hirschheim, R.A. (eds) *Critical Issues in Information Systems Research.* John Wiley, Chichester.

Eaton, J., Smithers, J. and Curran, S. (1988). *This Is IT.* Philip Allan, Oxford.

Ernest-Jones, T. (1989). Does Your System Give Value for Money? *Computer Weekly*, February 15th, 6.

Evans, R. (1989). Why Productivity in the Office Is Slowing Down. *Computer World*, October 20th, 8.

Farbey, B., Land, F. and Targett, D. (1992). Evaluating Investments in IT. *Journal of Information Technology*, 7, 2, 109–22.

Feeny, D. (1997). Information Management—Lasting Ideas within Turbulent Technology. In Willcocks, L., Feeny, D. and Islei, G. (eds) *Managing IT as a Strategic Resource.* McGraw-Hill, Maidenhead.

Feeny, D., Earl, M. and Edwards, B. (1997). Information Systems Organization—the Role of Users and Specialists. In Willcocks, L., Feeny, D. and Islei, G. (eds) *Managing IT as a Strategic Resource.* McGraw-Hill, Maidenhead.

Freeman, M. and Hobbs, G. (1991). Costly Information, Informed Investors and the Use of Sophisticated Capital Budgeting Techniques. *Proceedings of AAANZ 1991*, 68–74.

Galliers, R. (1991). Strategic IS Planning: Myths, Reality and Guidelines for Successful Implementation. *European Journal of Information Systems*, 1, 1, 55–64.

Gibson, C.F. (1975). A Methodology for Implementation Research. In Shultz, R.L. and Selvin, D.P. (eds) *Implementing Operations Research/Management Science, Part II*. Elsevier, Amsterdam, 53–73.

Goodwin, C. (1989). In Simmons, J., Leo and the Managers, *Computing*, April, 17.

Gordon, L. (1989). Benefit-Cost Analysis and Resource Allocation of Decisions. *Accounting, Organizations and Society*, 14, 4, 247–58.

Graeser, V., Willcocks, L. and Pisanias, N. (1998). Developing the IT Scorecard: a Study of Evaluation Practices and Integrated Performance Measurement. Business Intelligence, London.

Gunton, T. (1988). *End User Focus*. Prentice Hall, New York.

Gurnani, C. (1984). Capital Budgeting: Theory and Practice. *The Engineering Economist*, 30, Fall, 19–46.

Haka, S., Gordon, L. and Pinches, C. (1985). Sophisticated Capital Budgeting Selection Techniques and Firm Performance. *Accounting Review*, 60, 6, 651–69.

Hamilton, S. and Chervany, N.L. (1981). Evaluating Information System Effectiveness—Part 1: Comparing Evaluation Approaches. *MIS Quarterly*, 5, 3, 55–69.

Hansen, W.L. (1963). Total and Private Rates of Return to Investment in Schooling. *Journal of Political Economy*, 10, 3, 23–38.

Hares, J. and Royle, D. (1994). *Measuring the Value of Information Technology*. John Wiley, Chichester.

Harvey, D. (1986). *The Electronic Office in the Smaller Business*. Wildwood House, Aldershot.

Hitt, L. and Brynjolfsson, E. (1996). Productivity, Business Profitability and Consumer Surplus: Three Different Measures of Information Technology Value. *MIS Quarterly*, June, 121–42.

Ho, S. and Pike, R. (1992). Adoption of Probablistic Risk Analysis in Capital Budgeting and Corporate Investment. *Journal of Business Finance and Accounting*, 19, 3, 387–405.

Ho, S. and Pike, R. (1996). Computer Decision Support for Capital Budgeting: Some Empirical Findings of Practice. *Journal of Information Technology*, 11, 2, 119–28.

Hochstrasser, B. (1994). Evaluating IT Investments—Matching Techniques to Projects. In Willcocks, L. (ed.) *Information Management: Evaluation of IS Investments*. Chapman and Hall, London.

Ijiri, Y. (1975). *Theory of Accounting Measurement*. Studies in Accounting Research No. 10, American Accounting Association, New York.

International Data Corporation (1995). *Executive Insights: a Monthly Commentary on the Future of the IT Industry: Predictions 1996*. IDC, New York.

Joslin, E.O. (1965). Application Benchmarks: the Key to Meaningful Computer Evaluations. *Association for Computing Machinery, Proceedings of the National Conference*, 20, 27–37.

Kanter, K. (1970). *Management Guide to Computer System Selection and Use*. Prentice-Hall, London.

Keen, P.G.W. (1981). Value Analysis: Justifying Decision Support Systems. *MIS*

180   *Philip L. Powell*

Quarterly, 5, 1, 21–38, March.

Keen, P. (1991). *Shaping the Future: Business Design through Information Technology.* Harvard Business School Press, Boston, MA.

Keen, P.G.W. and Scott-Morton, M.S. (1978). *Decision Support Systems, an Organizational Perspective.* Addison Wesley, Reading, MA.

Keeney, R.L. and Raiffa, H. (1976). *Decisions with Multiple Objectives: Preferences and Value Tradeoffs.* John Wiley, New York.

Kotler, P. (1995). *Marketing Management*, Prentice-Hall, New Jersey.

Lacity, M., Willcocks, L. and Feeny, D. (1997). The Value of Selective IT Sourcing. In Willcocks, L., Feeny, D. and Islei, G. (eds). *Managing IT as a Strategic Resource.* McGraw-Hill, Maidenhead.

Lay, P.M.Q. (1985). Beware of the Cost/Benefit Model for IS Project Evaluations. *Journal of Systems Management*, 36, 1, 30–35.

Lincoln, T. (1986). Do Computer Systems Really Pay Off? *Information and Management*, 11, 1, 42–56, August.

Martin, M.P. and Trumbley, J.E. (1986). Measuring Performance of Automated Systems. *Journal of Systems Management*, 37, 2, 7–17.

Mclean, E.R. and Reisling, T.F. (1977). M A P P: a Decision Support System for Financial Planning. *Data Base*, 3, 3, 9–14.

McRea, T.W. (1970). The Evaluation of Investment in Computers, *Abacus*, 6, 2, 20–32.

Mansfield, E., Rapoport, J., Schnee, J., Wagner, S. and Hamburger, M. (1971). *Research and Innovation in the Modern Corporation.* Norton, London.

Marsden, J. and Pingry, M. (1988). End User-IS Designer Interaction. *Information and Management*, 14, 2, 42–56.

Merrit, A.J. and Sykes, A. (1973). *The Financing and Analysis of Capital Projects*, Longman, London.

Mitchell, G. (1990). Alternative Frameworks for Technology Evaluation. *European Journal of Operational Research*, 47, 2, 153–61.

North, H.Q. and Pyke, D.L. (1969). "Probes" of the Technological Future. *Harvard Business Review*, 47, 3, 68–82.

OECD (1972). *Manual of Industrial Project Analysis in Developing Countries.* OECD, Paris.

Overly, D. (1973). In Cetron, M.J. and Bartocha, B. (eds) *Technology Assessment in a Dynamic Environment.* Gordon and Breach, New York.

Page, J. and Hooper, P. (1987). *Accounting and Information Systems.* Prentice-Hall International, Englewood Cliffs, NJ.

Parker, J.E.S. (1978). *The Economics of Innovation.* Longman, London.

Pike, R. (1983). The Capital Budgeting Behaviour and Corporate Characteristics of Capital Constrained Firms. *Journal of Business Finance and Accounting*, 10, 6, 663–71.

Plunket, S. (1990). Making Computers Pay. *Today's Computers*, 3–5, March.

Powell, P.L. (1992). Information Technology Evaluation: Is It Different? *Journal of the Operational Research Society*, 43, 1, 29–42.

Powell, P.L. (1993). Causality in the Alignment of Information Technology and Business Strategy. *Journal of Strategic Information Systems*, 2, 4, 320–34.

Powell, P.L., Connell, N.A.D. and Holt, J. (1992). An Investigation into the Practical Uses of Decision Support and Expert Systems in the USA. In O'Leary, D. and Watkins, P. (eds) *Expert Systems in Finance.* Elsevier, Amsterdam.

Price, C. (1989). In Ernest-Jones T., *Computer Weekly*, February.

Putnam, L.N. (1980). *Software Cost Estimating and Life Cycle Control.* IEEE Computer Society Press, London.

Riggs, J.L. (1977). *Engineering Economics.* McGraw-Hill, New York.

Rose, L.M. (1976). *Engineering Investment Decisions: Planning Under Uncertainty.* North Holland, Amsterdam.

Schell, G.P. (1986). Establishing the Value of Information Systems. *Interfaces*, 16, 3, 82–9.

Schneiderjans, M. and Fowler, K. (1989). Strategic Acquisition Management: a Multi-Objective Synergistic Approach. *Journal of the Operational Research Society*, 40, 5, 333–45.

Senn, J.A. (1978). *Information Systems in Management.* Wadworth Publishing, New York.

Sheppard, J. (1990). The Strategic Management of IT Investment Decisions: a Research. *British Journal of Management.* 1, 2, 171–81.

Smith, K. (1988). *Corporate Accounting Systems: a Software Engineering Approach.* Addison-Wesley, Wokingham.

Sprague, R.H. and Carlson, E.D. (1982). *Building Effective Decision Support Systems.* Prentice-Hall, Englewood Cliffs, NJ.

Strassmann, P. (1990). *The Business Value of Computers.* Information Economics Press, New Canaan.

Strassmann, P. (1997). *The Squandered Computer.* Information Economics Press, New Canaan.

Thompson, P. (1981). *Organization and Economics of Construction.* McGraw-Hill, Maidenhead.

Turban, E. (1988). *Decision Support and Expert Systems: Managerial Perspectives.* Macmillan, New York.

Twiss, B. (1986). *Managing Technological Innovation.* Longman, Harlow.

Ward, J. and Griffith, P. (1996). *Strategic Planning for Information Systems.* John Wiley, Chichester.

Wassenaar, A. (1988). Information Management in an Industrial Environment—an Education Perspective. In Boddy, D., Mccalman, J. and Buchanan, D. (eds) *The New Management Challenge: Information Systems for Improved Performance.* Croom Helm, London, 49–57.

Wegen, B. van and Hoog, R. de (1996). Measuring the Economic Value of Information Systems. *Journal of Information Technology*, 11, 3, 247–60.

Weill, P. and Olson, M. (1989). Managing Investment in IS/IT. *MIS Quarterly*, 13, 1, March.

Weisbrod, B.A. (1971). Costs and Benefits of Medical Research. *Journal of Political Economy*, 25, 3, 38–9, May.

Whiting, F., Davies, J. and Knul, M. (1993). Investment Appraisal for IT Systems. *B.T. Technology Journal*, 11, 2, 193–211.

Willcocks, L. (1992). Evaluating Information Technology Investments: Research Findings and Reappraisal. *Journal of Information Systems*, 10, 2, 243–68.

Willcocks, L. (ed.) (1994). *Information Management: Evaluation of IS Investments.* Chapman and Hall, London.

Willcocks, L. (ed.) (1996). *Investing in Information Systems: Evaluation and Management.* Chapman and Hall, London.

Willcocks, L., Feeny, D. and Islei, G. (eds) (1997). *Managing IT as a Strategic Resource.* McGraw-Hill, Maidenhead.

Willcocks, L., Graeser, V. and Lester, S. (1998). Cybernomics and IT Productivity: not Business as Usual? *European Management Journal*, 16, 3, 272–83, June.

Willcocks, L. and Margetts, H. (1994). Risk and Information Systems: Developing the Analysis. In Willcocks, L. (ed.) *Information Management: Evaluation of IS Investments*. Chapman and Hall, London.

Williams, B.R. (1967). *Technology, Investment and Growth*. Chapman and Hall, London.

Williams, B.R. and Scott, W.P. (1965). *Investment Proposals and Decisions*. George Allen and Unwin, London.

Zakierski, P. (1987). *A Review of New Technology Investment Techniques*. Unpublished MSc Dissertation, University of Southampton, Southampton.

6
Evaluating Investments in IT: Findings and a Framework

BARBARA FARBEY, FRANK LAND AND
DAVID TARGETT

London School of Economics, University of London and
Imperial College, London

INTRODUCTION

Does investment in information technology give value for money? The question has generated concern and been the subject of considerable debate. As the first three chapters of this book make clear, at the level of organization and industry there is evidence that IT does not provide any overall productivity benefits (Loveman, 1994; Landauer, 1995; Strassmann, 1997). Other reports, however, debate these findings (Brynjolfsson, 1993; McKeen, Smith and Parent, 1997) and suggest a number of reasons for purely statistical findings potentially being misleading—poor data, inadequate analysis, timing effects, aggregation effects and so on (see Chapters 1 and 2).

At the level of the project, the evaluation of the costs and benefits of particular IT investments has been a major concern for organizations and their senior managers since at least the late 1980s. Many report that they are uncertain how to measure the impact of new IT investments (Price Waterhouse, 1995; Willcocks, 1996; see also Chapter 4). The importance of this issue stems from the increasing role of IT in organizations and its high and increasing cost as a proportion of revenue. In many industries, IT is now the largest single item of capital expenditure.

Beyond the IT Productivity Paradox.
Edited by L. P. Willcocks and S. Lester © 1999 John Wiley & Sons Ltd.

Evaluations are needed at several stages in the development and management of an IT project. *Ex ante*, organizations wish to decide whether to go ahead with a project. How does this project compare with other IT projects? How does it compare with non-IT projects? Does its internal rate of return exceed the organization's hurdle rate? *Ex post*, organizations wish to know whether a project has been successful. Has it delivered the promised benefits? Have there been unexpected benefits? Is the organization's large and increasing IT expenditure proving worthwhile?

Return on investment (ROI) techniques might seem the obvious choice for such a task, since they are in widespread use for other types of capital expenditure, apparently successfully. However, ROI is not often used for IT, primarily because it is unable to capture many of the qualitative and intangible benefits that IT brings (Farbey, Land and Targett, 1992). Non-IT capital investments also have such benefits and the debate over IT investments may be highlighting a more general problem. Why should IT be in this spotlight if other investments are not? We would have to speculate (see also Chapter 5). Many IT investments are large; many are critical to success; they possibly carry more intangible benefits; strategic IT investments are relatively new and organizations have not learned how to deal with them as they have, say, strategic marketing investments. However, the issue of intangible benefits should not be an insuperable problem, since numerous evaluation techniques are available as alternatives to ROI, many specifically developed to deal with intangibility.

This chapter describes some research into the way organizations take IT investment decisions and goes on to suggest how to improve evaluation practice by matching an IT investment with an appropriate evaluation technique. The first section discusses what organizations mean by evaluation and what their requirements are. The next summarizes a number of currently available evaluation techniques, together with a review of the circumstances in which they can most appropriately be applied. Then the research results are presented, before the final sections speculate on how an IT project might be matched with a suitable evaluation technique.

WHAT ORGANIZATIONS REQUIRE OF AN EVALUATION TECHNIQUE

An organization may want to evaluate (or assess, or cost justify, or appraise) an IT project at any of several stages in its development and implementation. Complementary to Chapter 2, we suggest that the main stages are when:

1. Strategy is being developed. An IT strategy should be being developed alongside the business strategy, and the role of IT will have to be assessed in general terms before either strategy can be finalized. The outcome may be a portfolio of projects, some concerned with specific IT projects and others with the required IT infrastructure. However, it should be noted that the notion of a "strategic" IT investment is being questioned. For example, Peppard (1996) argues that IT planning is only strategic in the sense of decisions to invest in IT infrastructure.
2. A specific project has been defined. This may be an application or a decision to install IT infrastructure. At this stage, the project has usually to be cost justified in the context of other capital investments.
3. The project is in the developmental stage. Checks must be made to ensure that internal and external changes have not affected the feasibility of the project.
4. The project has reached the point of "sign off". Responsibility is being transferred from the IT department to the user department. The users have to sign that the system does what is required.
5. The project has just been implemented. The system is checked to ensure that it is working as planned and is beginning to deliver the anticipated benefits.
6. The project has been in operation for some time. Evaluation at this stage monitors the project's impact, compares actual costs and benefits with planned costs and benefits, identifies unexpected benefits and costs, and records lessons for the future.
7. The project is nearing the end of its life and the feasibility of replacement options is being investigated.

Kumar (1990) has suggested that organizations are not clear about the different purposes of evaluation and may confuse these stages. In particular, what is seen as an evaluation by an IT manager, and even by senior general management, may not be so. It may merely be the "sign off" or closure of the project (see also Norris, 1996).

WHAT EVALUATION TECHNIQUES ARE AVAILABLE?

The different stages at which evaluation is needed indicate the range of requirements that evaluation techniques have to meet. The literature confirms that there are a multiplicity of evaluation methods or approaches available, each with its own characteristics and focus. The methods differ in the level of detail, the management process involved, the level and function of the people involved and the characteristics of the data required. Only two of the techniques, return on investment and cost–benefit analysis, are at all common in formal evaluation exercises. Below we provide an outline of some of the methods referred to in the literature, starting with the most specific and then broadening.

Return-On-Investment (ROI) approaches (Radcliffe, 1982) include a number of formal investment appraisal techniques. A simple example is the payback method, which calculates the time taken before the investment is recouped. But perhaps the best known of the ROI methods are those which are based on evaluating the current value of estimated future cash flows, on the assumption that future benefits are subject to some discount factor. The most widely used method is probably internal rate of return (IRR), which sums up the entire project in one measure: the internal rate of return. This can be compared with a hurdle rate of return, set by the financial management of the organization, to decide whether the project should go ahead.

ROI methods tend to be used by organizations with tight financial disciplines. The techniques are formal, and the calculations are usually carried out by financial or accounting staff on the basis of inputs from the project staff. Although IRR appears to cope with the problem of risk by the means of setting an appropriate hurdle rate, in practice the methods are not good at dealing with projects which have large elements of uncertainty in their projections. Nor are they good at dealing with projects with uncertain lifetimes, a frequent difficulty with IT projects. The main strength of the method is that it permits decision makers to compare the estimated returns on alternative investments, for example permitting a decision to hold cash at the bank rather than to invest in some internal project. The weakness is that some good investment possibilities are withheld because the benefits are difficult to assess in attributable cash-flow terms. Historically, some of the IT projects which have provided the best returns in terms of competitive advantage would not have satisfied the prevailing ROI criteria.

Cost–benefit analysis (CBA) (King and Schrems, 1978) is an approach that attempts to find (or compute) a money value for each element contributing to the cost and benefit of a development project. The approach originated as an attempt to deal with the problem that some elements regarded as benefits or costs have no obvious market value or price. The classic example is: what value is attached to a system which could result in the saving of one extra life?

In CBA, elements which have no obvious market value or price will be assigned a money value based on some notion of valuation. The resulting cost–benefit values can be projected in the form of notional cash flows on a year-by-year basis and the projected outcomes for alternative schemes or designs fed into a decision model based on one of the standard ROI methods. The main weakness of classic cost-benefit analysis (Stern, 1976) is the artificial nature of some of the surrogate measures. In practice, the recommendations coming from cost–benefit analysis are often overturned by decision makers who cannot accept the values selected by the analysts. The approach is used in circumstances where ROI methods are generally appropriate but where there are costs and benefits that are difficult to quantify.

Multi-objective, multi-criteria methods (MOMC) (Vaid-Raizda, 1983; Chandler 1982) are an alternative to cost-benefit-analysis which start from the assumption that there are measures of utility other than money value. Decision makers can appraise the relative value of different desired outcomes in terms of their preferences: they have the capability of ranking goals by applying a preference weight to each goal. The approach recognizes that in any organization different stakeholders may have very different ideas on the value that the various elements of a project will deliver. The approach permits an exploration of these different viewpoints and exposes potential conflict at the decision making, rather than at the post-implementation, stage of a project.

The MOMC approach can be assisted by one of a number of computer-based decision support systems that help the decision-making group to do the calculations and carry out sensitivity and robustness tests.

The approach is best used where there are a number of possible objectives to serve a number of different units or persons in the organization. It is of particular value at the stage at which strategy is being decided. It is also useful where there are a number of design alternatives and there is difficulty in choosing between them because they do not all provide the same outcome.

Boundary values (Martin, 1989) provide a crude check on the comparative spend on IT systems. They are based on ratios of total IT expenditure against other known aggregate values. A typical ratio would be total IT expenditure against total revenue, or against operating expenses. Other ratios used include IT costs per employee, and net benefits attributable to IT systems against IT expenditure.

The ratios can be used in two ways: first, they can be used as a rough guide to what level of IT expenditure to plan for in the enterprise. If the average expenditure ratio in the rest of the industry sector is significantly higher, it suggests that planned increases in IT expenditure are justified. If they are lower, it suggests that expenditure increases should be reviewed and possibly curtailed. Alternatively, they can be used as a check on the efficiency of the IT group in the enterprise. A higher than average expenditure ratio suggests inefficient use of IT resources as against the industry sector. A low ratio could suggest efficient use, in particular if the enterprise is seen to be successful and competitive.

Boundary values are concerned with aggregate statistics. Their use has nothing to contribute to the evaluation of individual applications, or even to the decisions to be made on the installation of IT infrastructure, though if ratios are confined to expenditure on infrastructure they can be helpful in providing useful comparisons with other enterprises in the same industry sector.

Return on management (ROM) (Strassman, 1985; 1990; 1997) is the value attributable to an information system as an incremental change to an already established level of management productivity. The method is to express the outcome of the introduction of a new system as the change to the value added by management stemming from the introduction of a new system. ROM is defined as the residual value after deducting from total revenue the cost and value added by each resource, including capital, but excluding management and the cost of management. The return on the new system is the difference between the ROM computed before the introduction of the new system and the ROM computed after the system has been implemented. The values computed are money values derived from the standard accounting and non-financial data held by an organization.

At the strategy formulation phase, changes in ROM must be based on an estimate of revenue after the change is implemented and estimates of changes to resource costs and contributions. The difficulty of making such estimates suggests that the ROM method of evaluation is better suited to *ex post* evaluation of information systems projects. However, given a large database of such *ex post* computations, it is possible to classify projects in order to associate type of application with ROM and thus help in defining *ex ante* which type of application appears to have the best chance of achieving a high ROM.

Information economics (Parker, Benson and Trainor, 1987) seeks to be comprehensive—to be the one and only method needed to deal with the IT evaluation jungle. In practice, the method is a variant on cost–benefit analysis, tailored to cope with the particular uncertainties and intangibles found in IS projects. It retains ROI calculations for those benefits and costs which can be directly ascertained through a conventional cost–benefit process, but for the decision process puts forward a more complex report based on a ranking and scoring technique for intangibles and risks. The ROI outcome is itself given a score, enabling executives to provide a relative evaluation of tangibles against intangibles. In other words, it seeks to identify, measure and rank the economic impact of all relevant changes on organizational performance thought to be brought about by the introduction of new systems.

Information economics extends normal cost–benefit analysis by three processes. The first is value linking, which looks for the consequential impact of a primary change spreading through different functions. The second process is value acceleration, which attempts to define the value of future systems which are dependent on the introduction of the system in question. Hence the value of a primary system is seen to be enhanced if it is also seen as the platform on which later systems can be built. The third process is job enrichment, which provides an evaluation of the additional value to the organization of the enhanced skills and understanding which its staff may gain from the use of IT.

Information economics therefore attempts to bridge the quantitative/ qualitative divide and has the capability to recognize "costs" such as strategic and technological uncertainty and organizational risk. However, it is time consuming to carry out and requires substantial expertise and resources. It may be unnecessarily complex for well-defined transaction-processing systems with clear costs and benefits. A critique of information economics is supplied by Strassmann (1990) and Willcocks (1994).

Critical success factors (Rockart, 1979) are a well-known strategic approach to evaluating information systems. Executives express their opinions as to which factors are critical to the success of the business. They then rank them according to their significance and go on to examine the role that IT in general, or a specific system, can play in supporting the executive in dealing with the critical issues. The importance of the method is that it provides a focus on those issues which the respondents regard as important—the ones they will back if it comes to a choice of issues which have to be dealt with.

Value analysis (Melone and Wharton, 1984) attempts to evaluate a wide range of benefits, including intangible benefits. The method is based on the notion that it is more important to concentrate on value (added) than on cost saved. It begins with the observation that most successful innovations are based on enhancing value rather than saving costs. To get at value the intangibles must be assessed. Value analysis may use an iterative approach, such as the Delphi method, to provide answers. A further step might be to build a prototype of the system in order to gain more experience of the way in which decision makers might use the system.

Where the proposed system is expected to deliver a variety of benefits, for example where it is expected to help managers to make better purchasing decisions and improve their job satisfaction, the value analysis method groups the benefits into homogenous categories using statistical techniques such as cluster analysis. Having summarized the benefits in their separate categories, a value has to be determined for the benefit. Since the benefits are expressed in a variety of forms, some linguistic, some numeric, a common measure has to be found. Like MOMC, value analysis permits the calculation of utility scores by attaching utility weights to each category of benefit.

Value analysis permits the decision maker to test the sensitivity of the solution to different interpretations and valuations. It is a sophisticated and costly technique, much of whose value stems from the insights gained from the exploratory nature of the process.

The use of *experimental methods* is a recent development in the context of project evaluation. Until recently, the precise impact of introducing new systems *ex ante* could only be estimated, because the investment in developing a system to the stage of obtaining actual impacts was very high. Today a range of software development tools and simulation methods make it possible to develop a prototype or model of the new system rapidly and cheaply. This enables the designer to test and modify the system and its impacts experimentally before decisions on introducing a fully engineered version have to be taken.

There are three main categories of experimental method:

1. *Prototyping* (Alavi, 1984) involves the rapid development of a proto-type form of the system, typically using a fourth-generation language. The prototype is tested and evaluated and if necessary modified and tested again. Typically, after a few iterations users and developers can agree on the shape of the final system and have a clearer picture of the likely benefits that the final system will deliver. At the same time there will be far greater confidence in the projected cost profile of the new system. Prototyping is best used where the impact of the proposed system is highly uncertain, and that usually involves systems which affect the behaviour of the users, such as decision support systems. But it is also relevant for any innovative system which cannot rely on evidence from previous experience. *Adaptive* methods are a variant on prototyping, used when a prototype system is impossible or infeasible to build. The complete system is built in the full knowledge that it must be adapted as it is implemented and its impact becomes understood.

2. *Simulation* (Hertz, 1990) probably has the longest history. It involves building a model of the proposed system and using that as the basis for experiments. The relevance of simulation to IT projects is that sensitivity analysis is particularly useful where assumptions and projections are more than usually uncertain. For example, a

simulation of the cash flows associated with an IT project can be used to test the robustness of the quantification of benefits: does the IRR look quite so good if the manpower reduction is not achieved as planned? A simulation can also test the outcome when the impact of knock-on effects between one cost or benefit and another is varied. If it is possible to formulate the problem in an appropriate form, simulation can be used at a number of stages in an IT project: strategy formulation, detailed design and post-implementation.

3. *Gameplaying* (Hirschheim, 1985) can be used to assess the outcome of a revised way of doing certain tasks. For example, a mail order company was considering the introduction of office systems to support its agent-relation activities. The sponsors of the scheme had clear ideas of the benefits that could be achieved. Management needed more evidence. Rather than building a prototype, consultants suggested that managers and staff should role play each others' jobs first, on the assumption that the existing system was in force, and then assuming that the new office system had been introduced. The outcome was a much clearer appreciation by management and staff of what the new system could accomplish and, equally importantly, what it would not be able to do.

Finally, there are other methods of evaluation which are not often considered in the context of IS evaluation (see also Chapters 12 and 13). As illustrations, we can consider four such methods (the first three are reported in House (1983) in the context of general evaluation).

Art criticism relies on expert knowledge. In the context of IS, the nearest equivalent method to art criticism is probably business judgement. It is an estimate of the worth of the system based not only on explicit, articulated formal knowledge, but also on tacit knowledge acquired through experience.

Accreditation too relies on knowledge, knowledge of how, in general, these things are done. In this it is similar to boundary values. All that these methods (art criticism and accreditation) are in effect saying is that there is no help to be had, either from trying to reach common objectives, or from experimenting to discover how the proposed system will affect the organization. All that is left is to take a broad view using common sense and business judgement.

Adversarial methods means those that rely on the formal presentation of arguments by two sides, as in a court of law. We would guess them to be most valuable in clarifying objectives, rather than providing evidence for cause and effect.

Analogy is a method of evaluation based on case-based reasoning (Allen, 1994; Mukhopadhyay, Vicinanza and Prictula, 1992). A suitable analogy is chosen for the project in question, which is then evaluated by comparison against previous experience with the analogy.

The availability of so many evaluation techniques prompts the question: "What techniques are used in practice?" Building on the findings in Chapters 2 and 4, the next section describes some research that provides an answer.

RESULTS OF THE RESEARCH PROJECT

Our research investigated 16 IT projects, all of which had just been implemented or were about to be implemented. The main focus of the research was to study how the projects had been evaluated. The systems concerned were management related and in the area of office automation. Broadly, 11 of the 16 were specific applications, three were providing infrastructure and two were senior management support systems. The projects were located in a wide range of organizations which are categorized in Table 6.1.

Evidence about each of these systems, from the original conception through to the latest position, was collected from relevant documentation and from interviews with the people involved in the development and running of the systems. In particular, the research sought to interview the "champions", the people who had a major influence in getting the project accepted.

The interviews were structured to ensure that the correct topics were covered. They started with the context of the system: what the company did, whether it had an IT strategy, in which department the system was to be located. This was followed by questions about the motivation which led to the system being proposed, the anticipated benefits, how they were cost justified and the decision-making process. The inter-

Table 6.1 *Organizations Where the Six-teen Projects Were Located*

Business sector	No. of projects
Consultancy	2
Defence	2
Financial services	3
Industrial	2
IT	3
Pharmaceutical	1
Public sector	2
Publishing	1
Total	16

viewees were then asked to describe the system and the implementation process. Next the achieved benefits were discussed, including those which had not been anticipated in the preliminary project study. The final part of the interview was concerned with evaluating the system. How did the achieved benefits compare with those expected? Had a post-implementation evaluation been carried out? Had the system been expanded? What were the future plans for it? A detailed description of the overall findings of the original research appears in Farbey, Land and Targett (1993). Here we summarize the findings and develop an evaluation framework.

As far as evaluation was concerned, *ad hoc procedures* were used in the majority of systems investigated in the research. Even when a formal, prescribed method was used, it was sometimes modified in an *ad hoc* way to suit the exigencies of a particular situation. The *ad hoc* methods used in the cases studied can be classified under the following headings.

1. *Top-down strategic*: senior management believes that IT is fundamental to success.
2. *Top-down by dictat*: corporate headquarters make rules on what divisions can do.
3. *Incremental change*: the next step is determined by technological change or obsolescence.
4. *Competitive imperative*: the organization must use IT to survive.

The tree in Figure 6.1 summarizes the evaluation methods that were used. These findings can usefully be compared with those described in Chapters 2 and 4. The comparison shows little change in actual practice across the 1990s to 1996, except that more recently there have been more determined attempts to move to broader-based IT evaluation systems The next section moves on from what our research showed was being used in the mid-1990s to consider what evaluation techniques could be used. The challenge is to develop techniques sufficiently generic to be applicable to network-based as well as earlier types of investment (see Introduction). The starting point is an examination of the different project and contextual factors which can influence the way in which evaluation is carried out.

TOWARDS AN EVALUATION FRAMEWORK

Factors Affecting Evaluation

Evaluations are required at different stages in the development of an IT project, and for different purposes. But the purpose and timing of the

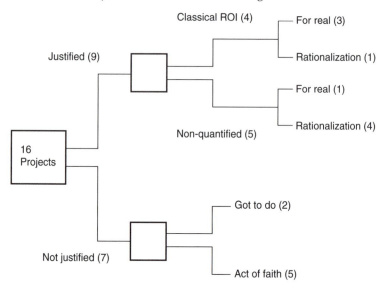

Figure 6.1   *Summary of Evaluation Methods*

evaluation are just two of the factors that can affect the way it is carried out. The range of factors is wide because every IT project, and its organizational context, has characteristics which influence the choice of a suitable evaluation technique. At the same time, every evaluation technique has characteristics which point to the set of circumstances in which it could be applied. A first step in deciding how to evaluate is therefore to understand more about these factors. Our empirical findings suggest that the factors affecting the evaluation of an IT project can be classified into five main groups.

The Role of Evaluation

The role of an evaluation is defined by the time (stage of the project) and level (seniority) at which it is carried out. The point in a project at which a justification or evaluation is carried out has a bearing on the method used. Quite simply, there are different questions to be answered at each of the project stages described at the outset of the chapter.

At the very early stages, the main concerns are broad brush, defining high-level goals, sketching the constraints and often within the province of senior management. Boundary values is a very broad-brush method, not requiring detailed numbers, and indicates roughly the comparative standing of the project or projects. It is therefore worth considering as a candidate method in this situation. For different reasons, multi-objective, multi-criteria (MOMC) methods need to be considered at the very early stages, in order, for example, to gain high-level consensus.

Whereas at earlier stages management is most concerned with defining the scope of the strategy and evaluation methods should help in defining that scope, at later stages the concerns are more detailed, involving exact specifications of what the project is intended to do. At the later stage, the problem is much more one of measurement, of defining the precise impact of the system both in terms of costs to be incurred, developmental as well as operational, and of the benefits which are expected to accrue from the use of the system. Boundary values, for example, are not suitable at more detailed levels of requirements, and specification, whereas cost–benefit analysis might be.

The level of evaluation is more straightforward. At senior levels within the organization the issues are wide, for example defining strategic goals, sketching the constraints. At lower levels the concerns are more detailed, for example the quantification of benefits.

The Decision Environment

The environment in which a decision has to be made may be more or less constrained. IT decisions do not occur in a vacuum, and the choice of a method of justification must, at the very least, match the culture of the organization. The prior history of implementing information systems also has a strong influence. Where there is a proven record of success in the use of IT, management is more likely to accept the estimates of the IT group and to be satisfied with the assurances of "champions". But a history of doubtful applications or failure is likely to make management much tougher about investment decisions, and require a tighter appraisal process.

The evaluation may have to conform to existing procedures, or there may be no established practice. The decision makers may expect only hard, quantified benefits to be considered, or they may wish to deal with soft, qualitative benefits. The cost of the evaluation procedure may also be an issue, as may the availability of staff trained in the use of a method.

In Table 6.2 the characteristics of the environment are shown, broken down into a more detailed set of (sub)characteristics (i.e. of goal, constraint or decision process) and approach. For example, the situation may be goal driven, either in the general sense that all projects must be justified back to an existing "mission", or in the particular sense that the project has to meet pre-specified goals (or both). In the former case a specific project needs to be justified in the context of a broad compari-

Table 6.2   *The Effect of the Environment Dimension*

Characteristic	Sub-characteristic	Approach
Goal driven	Mission related	Broad comparison of all projects
	Detailed/direct	Demonstrate that project meets goals Compare costs
Constraints	Competitive; imposed; legal	Check functionality, compare costs
	Locked into supplier	Check functionality, demonstrate profitability
	Financial hurdles	Show that hurdles are overcome
Decision process	Standard	Follow process
	Ad hoc	Create process
Benefits	Quantitative Qualitative	

son of all projects, in the latter it is necessary first to demonstrate that a project will meet the pre-specified goals and that it compares favourably with others in terms of cost.

The System underlying the IT Investment

This can be described by two variables. The first variable is the nature of the system: whether it is a specific application or provides an infrastructure. The second variable is the relation of the system to the business: whether the system is in a supporting role (e.g. financial, documentation) or core (at the heart of the company's production and delivery chain).

The criteria by which a system should be judged must reflect the nature and the purposes of that system. An evaluation method must therefore include, or provide a means for establishing, these criteria. For example, if a system investment is made for strategic purposes, to increase revenue, then the system must be evaluated using a method which includes increased revenue as a criterion for evaluation. If it does not, or if there is no means of identifying an increase in revenue as attributable to the system, the method is not valid.

The Organization Making the Investment

The competitive position of the organization may also affect evaluation. One factor is the industry situation: whether it is stable or whether there is, or is forecast to be, a lot of change, restructuring, turbulence and high levels of IT development. A stable situation suggests that reliable data may be available and points to a technique which operates on detailed information: return on investment methods, for example. An unstable situation suggests that reliable data may not be available and consequently an exploratory technique such as simulation may be preferable.

The second factor is the leadership role of the organization: whether it aims to pioneer or to follow. In a leadership role, the evaluation is likely to be exploratory and need to give results fast. In a follower role, there will be existing investments by other organizations which will provide a guide to the decision makers. A technique such as boundary values may be used to indicate appropriate levels of expenditure.

Cause-and-Effect Relationships

The degree to which it is possible to predict the impact of the new system is an important factor in determining how to do an evaluation (Kydd, 1989). The impact of the new system may be direct; for example putting in a payroll system will directly reduce the cost of calculating pay and producing payslips. The costs and benefits are likely to be measurable and an accounting-based method can be employed.

But a system designed to provide a manager with "better" information in order to improve decision making depends on the capability of the manager to use the better information to deliver the expected benefit. The impact is indirect and a technique that handles an unknown range of possibly intangible benefits, such as multi-objective, multi-criteria methods, will be more suitable.

The degree of uncertainty is equally important. In a well-defined area the impact of a system may be clear. For example, the analyst may be able to make a precise calculation of the number of staff saved by putting in a computer-based sales order system. But the computation of the likely extra sales generated because of a reduction in stock-outs from a new inventory control system is far less certain. Again, uncertainty will point to a technique which is better at dealing with it, probably one based on exploration as opposed to accounting calculations.

So far, we have described a range of evaluation methods and their characteristics and we have described the factors to do with an IT investment which influence its evaluation. In theory at least, all this information should make it possible to match an IT investment with a suitable evaluation technique, but the process would be both lengthy and imprecise. The purpose in the next section is to find a *systematic* means of performing the matching process.

THE MATCHING PROCESS

The process has three stages:

1. Represent the circumstances of the project as points on a series of 2×2 matrices.
2. Locate each evaluation technique at some point on another 2×2 matrix.
3. Overlay the matrices to match project with technique.

The process will be illustrated by applying it to a fictional "package tour operator": an organization which puts together holiday packages comprising travel and accommodation. It is the intermediary between travel agents and airlines, car hirers, hotel owners and others in the value chain. The project is the installation of a large system which links the tour operator with on one side travel agent's offices located throughout the country, and on the other side airlines, hotels etc. The system means that a customer and his/her travel agent can get immediate information on items such as availability, prices, alternatives, and immediate confirmation.

In this example the evaluation is taking place at an early stage in the development of the project: when the first decision to go ahead is being made, and before the details of the system have been specified.

Stage 1: Representing the Project

The circumstances in which an investment is to be evaluated have the five broad dimensions described previously.

The Role of Evaluation

The role of an evaluation is defined by two subdimensions: the time and level at which it is carried out. This dimension can be represented as a 2×2 matrix (Figure 6.2).

For a particular project, these characteristics can be summarized by placing a cross in the appropriate quadrant. Both vertical and horizontal variables are either/or (rather than, for example, on a scale from 1 to 10) and so the cross is placed in the middle of a quadrant.

For example, in the case of the original justification of the tour operator's system, the evaluation is taking place at the strategic level and at the requirements stage. A cross would be placed in the middle of the bottom right quadrant, as shown.

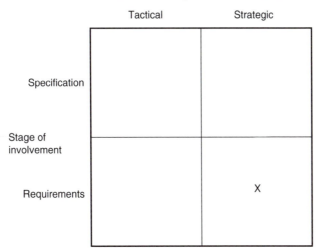

Figure 6.2 *Timing and Level*

The Decision Environment

This dimension has four subdimensions:

1. The decision process: whether it is standard for all projects or *ad hoc*.
2. The type of benefits the project is anticipated to bring: whether they are hard and easily quantifiable or soft and qualitative.
3. The importance of numbers: whether or not an attempt has to be made to attach numbers to all benefits and costs.
4. The cost of the justification technique: whether simple (cheap) methods only can be used or whether sophisticated (expensive) ones are acceptable.

This dimension can be represented by two 2 × 2 matrices (Figures 6.3 and 6.4).

Again, for a particular project this characteristic can be summarized by placing a cross in the appropriate quadrant. However, in this case three of the four subdimensions can be scaled. For example, the importance of numbers can be assessed at some point on a range, perhaps on a 1 to 10 scale. The cross might therefore be placed anywhere in the matrix rather than in the middle of a quadrant. The exception is the decision process: whether it is standard or *ad hoc*. This is a yes/no variable.

For example, in the case of the tour operator's system, the subdimensions might be assessed as below:

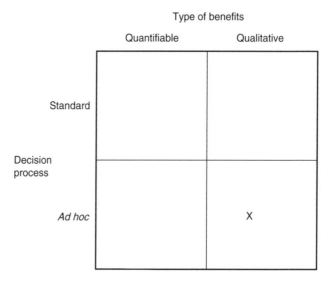

Figure 6.3   *Benefits and Decision Process*

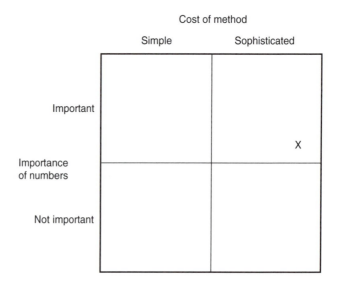

Figure 6.4   *Cost of Method and Importance of Numbers*

1. Decision process: *ad hoc*
2. Type of benefits:

Quantifiable   Qualitative

					×			
1	2	3	4	5	6	7	8	9	10

3. Importance of numbers:

Important   Not important

		×						
1	2	3	4	5	6	7	8	9	10

4. Cost of method:

Simple   Sophisticated

							×	
1	2	3	4	5	6	7	8	9	10

These assessments would result in the crosses being placed as shown in Figures 6.3 and 6.4.

The System Underlying the IT Investment

This can be described along two subdimensions. The first is the purpose of the system. At one extreme it may be a specific application, such as inventory control, and at the other it may provide an infrastructure on which a range of applications could run. The second is the connection between the system and the business: the system may be in a supporting role (e.g. accounting, personnel, documentation) or core (at the heart of the company's value chain). The two subdimensions can be represented by a 2×2 matrix (Figure 6.5).

Both subdimensions can be assessed on a scale. For example, in the case of the tour operator's system, the subdimensions might be assessed as below:

1. Nature of system:

Specific application   Infrastructure

								×
1	2	3	4	5	6	7	8	9	10

2. Relation of project to business:

Support   Core

						×	
1	2	3	4	5	6	7	8	9	10

A cross is then placed on the matrix as shown in Figure 6.5.

The Organization Making the Investment

The competitive position of the organization may also affect evaluation. The first subdimension is the industry situation: stable or turbulent.

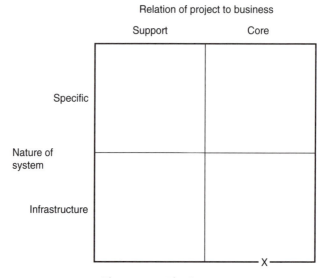

Figure 6.5   *The System*

The second subdimension is the leadership role of the organization within the industry: a pioneer or a follower. Organization characteristics are described by a 2 × 2 matrix (Figure 6.6).

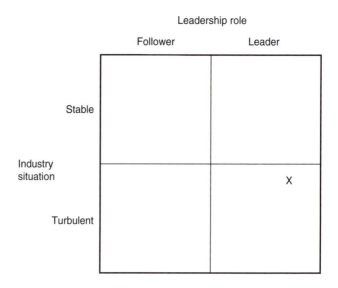

Figure 6.6   *Organizational characteristics*

In the case of the tour operator's system, the subdimensions might be assessed as below:

1. Industry situation:

   Stable   Turbulent

   _____ × _____

    1   2   3   4   5   6 7   8   9   10

2. Leadership role:

   Follower   Leader

   _____ × _____

    1   2   3   4   5   6   7   8 9   10

A cross is then placed on the matrix as shown in Figure 6.6.

Cause-and-Effect Relationships

The impact of the new system may be almost completely predictable or totally uncertain. This dimension can be split into two subdimensions. The first is the directness of the impact. If the impact is direct the system has an immediate first-order effect. The second variable is the uncertainty of the impact. In a well-defined area the impact of a system may be clear. Cause-and-effect relationships can be described by a 2×2 matrix (Figure 6.7).

In the case of the tour operator's system, the subdimensions might be assessed as below:

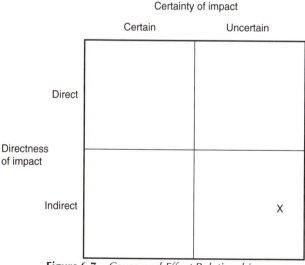

Figure 6.7 *Cause-and-Effect Relationship*

1. Directness of impact: a yes/no situation. In this case the impact is indirect, depending on the usage of the system by travel agents and related travel organizations.
2. Certainty of impact:

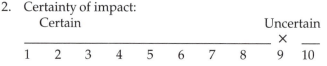

A cross is then placed on the matrix as shown in Figure 6.7.

The six matrices describing the circumstances of the evaluation (Figures 6.2 to 6.7) are then overlaid to provide one overall summary matrix (Figure 6.8).

The horizontal scale of the summary matrix (Figure 6.8) combines the subdimensions shown in Figures 6.2 to 6.7:

1. Level of evaluation.
2. Type of benefits.
3. Sophistication of evaluation methods used.
4. Relationship of project to business.
5. Leadership role of organization.
6. Certainty of impact.

Without suggesting that this is a precise definition, it can be said that the horizontal scale summarizes the *role of IT within the organization: conservative or radical.*

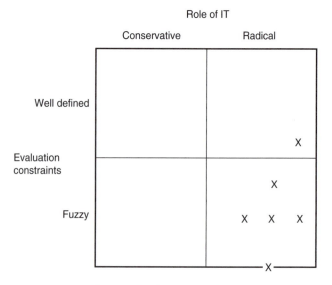

Figure 6.8 *Summary Matrix*

The vertical scale of the summary matrix also combines the sub-dimensions shown in Figures 6.2 to 6.7:

1. Timing of evaluation.
2. Nature of decision process.
3. Importance of numbers.
4. Nature of system.
5. Industry situation.
6. Directness of impact.

Again without attempting a precise definition, the horizontal scale summarizes the *constraints on decision making and evaluation, both inside and outside the organization: well defined or fuzzy.*

Stage 2: Locating the Evaluation Methods

The evaluation methods described earlier also have characteristics which make them most suitable for use in particular sets of circumstances. Comparing the situation dimensions with the characteristics of the evaluation methods suggests that the methods can be allocated to the quadrants of the 2 × 2 matrix as shown in Figure 6.9.

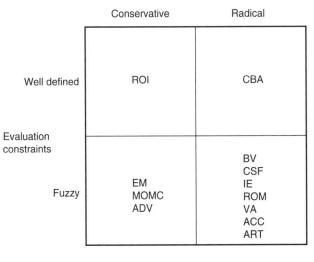

ADV	adversarial	ACC	accreditation	ART	art criticism
BV	boundary values	CBA	cost-benefit analysis	CSF	critical success factors
EM	experimental methods	IE	information economics	MOMC	multi-objective, multi-criteria
ROI	return on investment	ROM	return on management	VA	value analysis

Figure 6.9   *The evaluation methods*

- *Top left quadrant.* Return on investment and payback are located in this quadrant. They are well-established accounting methods and there is long experience of their use when IT is being applied in traditional efficiency-seeking projects in well-defined circumstances.
- *Top right quadrant.* Cost–benefit analysis, like return on investment and payback, is applied in well-defined circumstances. Unlike them, it has the capability to deal with a wide range of benefits. It should be located in the top right quadrant.
- *Bottom left quadrant.* In this quadrant IT is being applied in conservative ways but in a fuzzy decision-making environment. Experimental, MOMC and adversarial methods are exploratory in nature. They can cope with uncertainty in the decision-making process and in particular they have some capacity to bring consensus and commitment to stakeholders.
- *Bottom right quadrant.* This quadrant is probably the most difficult. IT is being applied in radical ways in a fuzzy decision-making environment. Evaluation methods will have dealt with systems which have a wide range of benefits and which are probably large, going right across the organization and outside it. The methods allocated to this quadrant are able to handle large projects with substantial organizational impacts.

Stage 3: Matching

The location of the crosses, whether clustered or dispersed, is used to suggest the range of techniques that might be applied. In some cases all crosses may fall within the same quadrant, giving a strong indication of exactly which techniques might be suitable. In other cases the crosses might be spread around, indicating that the choice is not clear cut and that several techniques could be used.

In the case of the tour operator's system, the crosses lie mainly in the bottom right quadrant indicating that the most suitable techniques are accreditation, art criticism, boundary values, information economics, return on management and value analysis. Return on management would try to capture the wide range of intangible benefits for a system that is at the core of the company's business. In a competitive environment, boundary values would monitor and compare expenditure levels. Information economics would satisfy the need for quantification. Value analysis would analyse the benefits which, at the time the system was being planned, were far from certain. Art criticism and accreditation would bring outside expertise and experience to bear. At the same time, the method indicates that the more straightforward techniques such as ROI might not be appropriate.

A Theoretical Justification for the Matching Process

As described above, the matrices describing project characteristics were derived empirically, abstracting from interviews and the literature. The evaluation methods were assigned to cells according to their dominant features following our definitions of the two axes as:

- "well-defined vs fuzzy" evaluation constraints;
- "conservative vs radical" role of IT.

The method has proved to be effective for the projects we were studying and also for other researchers working independently. However, as presented it lacks theoretical underpinning and is simply a speculation. There is nevertheless a theoretical platform which explains why the method works. The classification, which is due to Hellstern (1986), comes from the "evaluation research" body of work. It is also available in the IS literature in an article by Earl and Hopwood (1987), where it is discussed in terms of strategic decision making. Taking all three classifications together, it becomes clear that they are essentially the same. In particular, the logic which underpins the Hellstern categorization and the language which he uses provide a rationale for our empirically discovered method.

Figures 6.10 and 6.11 show the Hellstern and Earl and Hopwood matrices respectively. The axes are identical and therefore, despite the differences in terminology and context, so are the contents of the individual cells.

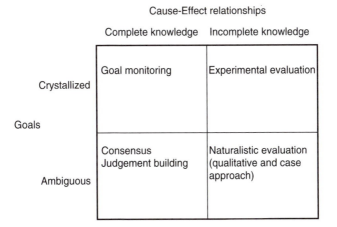

Figure 6.10 *Hellstern's (1986) matrix of evaluation types derived from different knowledge needs in well- and ill-structured problem settings*

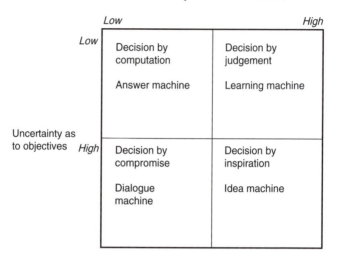

Figure 6.11 *Earl and Hopwood's (1987) matrix of decision types*

Hellstern wrote about the problems of evaluating programmes in the context of public policy. The sorts of programme with which he was concerned were major governmental programmes, such as Head Start in the USA. They were social interventions and, as he writes:

> "technical" program evaluations may be seriously limited as soon as they enter the less well-specified "life" context of a program. Whereas the scien[tific] approach may prove to be successful for well defined problems with clear goals and clear causal relations, most problems do not fall into this category. They are not well-structured and cannot be broken down easily into their components. Most problems for which evaluation research could be useful for policymakers and clients are ill-structured problems, with substantive problems varying from actor to actor and over time; they are dynamic. Such problems are not mechanical and cannot be separated from the context.

This adds a new dimension to the argument which we have been making. We have argued for consideration of different methods principally on the grounds that a variety of methods was necessary to match the variety of situations encountered in evaluating IT. Following Hellstern, it is possible to argue for variety on the grounds that the problems are not only often ill structured, as is suggested in some of our descriptions of situations, but also that the lack of structure itself has two bases: lack of structure with respect to objectives and lack of structure with respect to knowledge of cause and effect.

Expanding the argument, if information systems are complex and pervasive socio-technical systems whose life extends over several months or even years, then investment in IS can be understood as a programme of social action, based on a complex technology and taking place over a substantial period in time. Such investments are in many ways like the programmes of social action which are the subject of evaluation research. In particular, they generally present problems to the evaluator which are poorly structured. The lack of structure has two bases: lack of clear objectives and a lack of knowledge as to the potential impact of the systems and hence a lack of knowledge as to cause and effect. These two "dimensions" are largely orthogonal, in the sense that it is possible to envisage a situation in which the objectives are perfectly clear, but the impact of a new system of achieving them is poorly understood; and, equally, the potential impact of a system may be obvious, but the value of achieving it may not be commonly agreed.

Looking at the axes of matrices we have used to describe the situations as we met them, it can be seen that in most cases the distinction being made follows this same split. The vertical axes (constraints on evaluation) of the individual matrices represent situations where the objectives are not clear, whether the objectives of the system or the objectives of the evaluation. The horizontal axes reflect uncertainty about cause and effect. By definition, conservative action is action undertaken in known circumstances; radical action is not.

What we have done by elaborating the circumstances in which the evaluation might take place and the factors which affect evaluation is to tease out the factors which influence the choice of technique. These form, as it were, a third dimension. By superimposing them, we show where the balance lies across the range of factors. Taking the tour operator example used earlier, this fictional project is basically unstructured but the management, by being willing to consider a sophisticated, possibly costly technique, is signalling a willingness to learn. There is an implicit assumption here, which is that the factors are independent. This would have to be justified in any practical case. If there were significant interdependencies, this would in and of itself add to the loss of focus on objectives.

Looking next at the matrix of methods against which the descriptions are to be matched, and using Hellstern's description of the contexts, we now assert that the critical features of each method are those which determine:

1. How far they contribute to, or are based on, a knowledge of cause and effect; or
2. How far they assume, or contribute to the formation of, clear and agreed objectives.

Taking some examples, ROI methods are most useful in situations which are clear cut on both dimensions and belong to the top left quadrant. Methods which are principally concerned to establish a consensus, MOMC for example, belong in the bottom left quadrant. Experimental methods such as prototyping probably belong here too, since their primary purpose is to establish agreement rather than to provide experimental evidence for anything. On the other hand, certain simulations are used experimentally in the scientific sense of the word, to establish knowledge of cause and effect, and they belong in the top right quadrant. Value analysis involves asking experts, for example the managers for whom the system is being designed, to speculate on their use of the system and to suggest the value of any improved performance which they may achieve. Its primary use is to reduce uncertainty about the impact of the system, i.e. of cause and effect. In so doing it also aims at achieving a consensus, i.e. it aims to reduce both kinds of uncertainty, so that it belongs in the bottom right quadrant. A similar logic would apply to information economics. Critical success factors, by contrast, are primarily about clarification of goals. Although they too reduce uncertainty, they probably belong to the bottom left quadrant.

It is evident that these classifications are not rigid. Most methods will go some way to reducing uncertainty about objectives as well as uncertainty about cause and effect. Perhaps blobs overlapping the cell boundaries would give a truer picture. What we have used to classify the methods is the primary purpose—answering the questions: Does this method pre-suppose well-structured objectives? Does it have as its main purpose the clarification of objectives? Does this method assume that we know how the proposed system will affect the organization and therefore its value? Is its main purpose to illuminate the relationship?

PROBING THE CLASSIFICATION

By way of probing the classification, we can do three things: review our original matrices, try the classification out on some new matrices, and also on new methods.

First, although as we have said the original description largely fits the two dimensions described here, there is, arguably, one exception. On the argument we are making here, the matrix we have labelled "industry situation", and which has a "stable–turbulent" axis set against a "follower–leader" one, ought probably to be reversed. This would place the stable–turbulent axis, which would be more likely to contribute to uncertainty in cause and effect, across the top.

Secondly, some recent research we have carried out (not yet published) suggests a further dimension in the evaluation of projects. Several of the projects we are currently investigating are not standalone projects, but part of a series of interdependent projects. To a greater or lesser extent, these projects stand or fall together and the valuation of the "project in itself" has to come to terms with this phenomenon. We are also meeting situations where there are problems of evaluating "legacy" projects as opposed to "new/radical" ones. Gathering these together in a new matrix, "portfolio position", as shown in Figure 6.12, the legacy–radical axis goes across the top, the independent–interdependent axis down the side, on the argument that it is likely to be easier to crystallize the objective of a single, standalone project than for a multiplicity of interdependent ones.

A key point made above is that the problems associated with IS are often ill structured. In identifying two distinct sources of lack of structure and thus creating four types (cells), Hellstern has also signalled the dominant activity in each cell:

- goal monitoring
- consensus building
- experimental evaluation
- naturalistic evaluation, including qualitative and case approaches (see Figure 6.10 again).

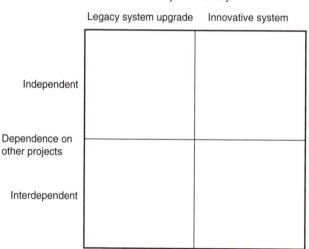

Figure 6.12 *Portfolio Position Matrix*

Earl and Hopwood too see different types of action, including:

- decision by computation
- decision by compromise
- decision by judgement
- decision by inspiration.

As we have said, because the axes are the same, the underlying ideas in each cell must be too, allowing for the difference between evaluation and decision making. In terms of matching a situation to a method, we suggest a combination of the two plus some of our own, as shown in Figure 6.13.

It is this last matrix which we would like to test in our future research and which we hope others will also be interested in testing. Our most recent research suggests that the underlying features may change over time. For example, the environment may change from stable to turbulent during the development period of a project. This perhaps implies a two-stage evaluation. For example, MOMC (to obtain a new consensus in the changed conditions), followed by ROI once the consensus has been reached.

Also, we suspect that different parts of the organization may perceive the project differently. The objectives of the project may, for example, be

		Uncertainty as to cause and effect	
		Conservative	Radical
		Low	*High*
Low	Crystallized	Measure towards goals Decision by computation Answer machine	Experiment Decision by judgement based on experimental evidence Learning machine
High	Fuzzy	Build consensus Decision by compromise Dialogue machine	Use qualitative, interpretive and case study approaches Decision by inspiration Idea machine

Uncertainty as to objectives

Figure 6.13　*Final Matrix: Problem Structure and Methods of Evaluation*

perfectly clear to the sponsoring organization but appear muddled to the developers (see also Chapter 12).

CONCLUSIONS

An organization wishing to sharpen its IT investment decision making must first recognize that there are evaluation techniques other than discounted cash-flow methods such as return on investment. It must then try to determine which technique is most suitable for its IT investment. This chapter has provided the information necessary for the selection of an evaluation method appropriate for the investment being evaluated. Each of the available techniques is applicable to a particular set of circumstances. The task for the organization is to characterize the circumstances in which the IT investment is to be evaluated, using the above five dimensions as a guide, and then to search through the evaluation techniques to find the one which most closely matches the investment.

This chapter goes a stage further. Its purpose has been to propose a *systematic* means for carrying out the matching. The matrix method is a simple, short procedure for achieving a match and encouraging objectivity. Of course, the matching process is by no means precise: in order to make it workable, a trade-off between complexity and practicability had to be made. Nevertheless, the process can promote an awareness of the options available and guide managers' thinking. It is important to pursue the question of matching very carefully, because the process of evaluation can be just as important as the outcome: evaluation creates awareness and understanding of the investment, and this may prevent later implementation problems.

ACKNOWLEDGEMENT

The results reported here have come in part from a research project, The Evaluation of IT Investments, sponsored by the Economic and Social Research Council, UK (R000233758). The authors are grateful to the Council for their support.

REFERENCES

Alavi, M. (1984). An Assessment of the Prototyping Approach to IS Development. *Communications of the ACM*, 27, 6, 556–63.

Allen, B. (1994). Case-based Reasoning: Business Applications. *Communications of the ACM*, 37, 1, 40–42.

Brynjolfsson, E. (1993). The Productivity Paradox of IT. *Communications of the ACM*, 36, 12, 67–77.

Chandler, J. (1982). A Multiple Criteria Approach for Evaluating IS. *MIS Quarterly*, 6, 1, 61–74.

Earl, M. and Hopwood, A. (1987). From Management Information to Information Management. In Somogyi, E. and Galliers, R. (eds) *Towards Strategic Information Systems*. Strategic Information Systems Management series, Abacus Press, Tunbridge Wells, Kent and Cambridge, MA.

Farbey, B., Land, F. and Targett, D. (1992). Evaluating Investments in IT. *Journal of Information Technology*, 7, 2, 109–22.

Farbey, B., Land, F. and Targett D. (1993). *How to Evaluate Your IT Investment*. Butterworth Heinemann, Oxford.

Hellstern, G. (1986). Assessing Evaluation Research. In Kaufmann, F., Majone, G. and Ostrom, V. (eds) *Guidance, Control and Evaluation in the Public Sector*. De Gruyter, Berlin and New York.

Hertz, D. (1990). Risk Analysis in Capital Investment. In Dyson, G. (ed.) *Strategic Planning: Models and Analytical Techniques*. John Wiley, Chichester.

Hirschheim, R. (1985). *Office Automation: a Social and Organizational Perspective*. John Wiley, Chichester.

House, E. (ed.) (1983) *Philosophy of Evaluation*. Sage, San Francisco and London.

King, J. and Schrems, E. (1978). Cost Benefit Analysis in IS Development and Operation. *Computing Surveys*, March, 19–34.

Kumar, K. (1990). Post-Implementation Evaluation of Computer-based Information Systems: Current Practice. *Communications of the ACM*, 33, 2, 203–12.

Kydd, C. (1989). Understanding the Information Content in MIS Management Tools. *MIS Quarterly*, 13, 3, 277–90.

Landauer, T. (1995). *The Trouble with Computers: Usefulness, Usability and Productivity*. MIT Press, Cambridge, MA.

Loveman, G. (1994). An Assessment of the Productivity Impact of Information Technologies. In Allen, T. and Scott Morton, M. (eds) *Information Technology and the Corporation of the 1990s*. Oxford University Press, Oxford.

Martin, R. (1989). *The Utilisation and Efficiency of IS: a Comparative Analysis*. Oxford Institute of Information Management, Templeton College, Oxford.

McKeen, J., Smith, H. and Parent, M. (1997). Assessing the Value Of Information Technology: the Leverage Effect. In Galliers, R., Carlsson, S., Loebbecke, C. *et al.* (eds) *Proceedings of the Fifth European Conference on Information Systems*. Cork, Ireland, June 9–12th.

Melone, N. and Wharton T. (1984). Strategies for MIS Project Selection. *Journal of Systems Management*, 32, 2, 26–37.

Mukhopadhyay, T., Vicinanza, S. and Prictula, M. (1992). Examining the Feasibility of a Case-Based Reasoning Model for Software Effort Estimation. *MIS Quarterly*, 16, 2, 155–71.

Norris, G. (1996). Post-Investment Appraisal. In Willcocks, L. (ed.) *Investing In Information Systems: Evaluation and Management*. Chapman and Hall, London.

Parker, M. and Benson, R. with Trainor, H. (1987). *Information Economics*. Prentice-Hall, Englewood Cliffs, NJ.

Peppard, J. (1996). Is IS Planning Really Strategic? Workshop W1, Requirements Engineering in a Changing World, at the *8th CAiSE Conference*, Heraklion, Crete, May.

Price Waterhouse (1995). *Information Technology Review, Annual Survey*. Price Waterhouse, London.

Radcliffe, R. (1982). *Investment: Concepts, Analysis, Strategy*. Scott Foreman, Glenview, Illinois.

Rockart, J. (1979). Chief Executives Define their own Information Needs. *Harvard Business Review*, 57, 2, 81–93.

Stern, G. (1976). SOSOping or Sophistical Obfuscation of Self-interest and Prejudice. *OR Quarterly*, 27, 4(ii), 915–29.

Strassman, P. (1985). *Information Payoff: The Transformation of Work in the Electronic Age*. The Free Press, New York.

Strassmann, P. (1990). *The Business Value Of Computers*. Information Economics Press, New Canaan, CN.

Strassmann, P. (1997). *The Squandered Computer*. Information Economics Press, New Canaan, CN.

Vaid-Raizda, V. (1983). Incorporation of Intangibles in Computer Selection Decisions. *Journal of Systems Management*, 34, 11, 30–46.

Willcocks, L., (ed.) (1994). *Information Management: Evaluation Of Information Systems Investments*. Chapman and Hall, London.

Willcocks, L. (1996) (ed.). *Investing In Information Systems: Evaluation and Management*. Chapman and Hall, London.

7
Managing Information Technology Resources as a Value Centre: the Leadership Challenge

N. VENKATRAMAN
Boston University School of Management

INTRODUCTION

How best to extract value from information technology resources? This is a major challenge facing both business and IT managers as we enter the twenty-first century. It is particularly challenging as we refocus away from searching for competitive benefits from strategic information systems and striving for benefits beyond process reengineering. At the same time, we are beginning to synthesize key lessons from nearly a decade of IT outsourcing. Astute managers are asking questions also addressed in other parts of this book, such as: How can we move beyond leveraging IT for redesigning current business processes to create new business capabilities? What is the best design for organizing our IT activities as a business driver? How best to exploit the potential benefits of the Internet and the World Wide Web (WWW) for delivering superior value to customers? How to allocate and manage IT investments? How to develop a strategic approach to IT sourcing that balances the risks and benefits of insourcing and outsourcing? (Lacity, Willcocks and Feeny, 1996; Earl, 1996; also Chapter 10). What types of sourcing options should we explore? What truly distinguishes our ability to exploit IT functionality differentially from our competitors?

Beyond the IT Productivity Paradox.
Edited by L. P. Willcocks and S. Lester © 1999 John Wiley & Sons Ltd.

How to achieve and sustain the required strategic alignment between business and IT operations on a continuous basis? What are the driving principles for organizing IT resources in the twenty-first century?

Over the last decade, I have observed, interviewed, participated and analysed how companies respond to such questions and challenges. In this chapter, I synthesize my observations and analyses into a framework for managing IT resources as a *value centre*. I introduce the value centre concept, describe its essential features and highlight its use, in order to reframe the dialogue between business managers and their information systems counterparts on the role of IT in shaping and supporting business strategies. In doing so, I position the value and risks of IT outsourcing as part of a larger challenge of crafting an effective IT strategy.

THE COMPELLING CASE FOR CHANGE

Most managers are painfully aware of the limitations of their legacy technological infrastructure and have plans underway to migrate from their centralized, mainframe technology towards a more decentralized, distributed and multimedia platform (see also Chapter 11). In this arena, the Year 2000 conversion problem seems to be a high priority. Few recognize the potential weaknesses of their legacy administrative architectures. Outmoded IS organizational design and processes, misdirected IS resource-allocation criteria, inappropriate IT planning systems, parochial views on outsourcing and mismatched IT skills with business needs are as critical as obsolete technological platforms. The impact of a legacy technology infrastructure can be benchmarked, quantified and analysed, but the implications of an obsolete administrative logic are less obvious until a critical point is reached—often without any warning signals.

I use three major categories of shifts to develop the compelling case for rethinking the administrative logic for managing IT resources (see Figure 7.1). In the *technical* arena, we see a rapid migration towards a hybrid (centralized and distributed) multimedia platform extended to link the key business processes with suppliers and buyers. At the same time, the fundamental characteristics of the technical infrastructure are shifting from hardware to software standards—an example is Windows-Intel (Wintel) versus network computer (NC). One manager half-jokingly remarked: "We used to define our technical standards in terms of being IBM-compatible; now we refer to it as being Bill Gates-compatible!" More seriously, there is increased reliance on standardizing business processes on software packages such as SAP/R3, Oracle

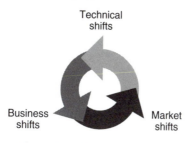

Figure 7.1 *Three Major Shifts*

database or Netscape Navigator—thereby anchoring the infrastructure on software choices. The developments and evolution pertaining to the Internet and intranets also have significant implications for the design and rapid adaptation of the technical infrastructure (see Introduction).

In terms of the *business* shifts, we see renewed expectations of business value from IT investments. Somewhat sobered by the unrealized (and unrealistic) expectations of the 1980s, managers are more cautiously optimistic about the role of IT in driving new business capabilities. In the USA, leading retailers like Wal-Mart, Sears, Gap, Macy's and others are now focusing beyond efficiency benefits in their supply chains towards leveraging their unique knowledge and expertise to fine-tune their marketing strategies. Financial institutions like Citibank, American Express, Baybank, Fidelity Investments and Charles Schwab are evolving from a traditional focus on back-office efficiency to exploring new avenues of service delivery through the Internet. Logistics companies like Federal Express and UPS are leveraging their IT capabilities to derive new sources of revenues and margins. Indeed, in nearly every market, we now observe a range of IT-enabled business capabilities beyond efficiency improvements (Davenport, 1992; Hammer and Champy, 1993; Venkatraman, 1994; Tapscott, 1996).

The final category recognizes the fundamental changes occurring in the external *market* for IT products and services. No longer can leading IT organizations be passive buyers of standard offerings in the market in the wake of the exploding number and type of business arrangements. These include multi-year outsourcing relationships with one primary vendor (Kodak and IBM; Xerox and EDS; General Dynamics and CSC), strategic sourcing involving multiple vendors to simulate competitive pressures and continuous benchmarking (British Petroleum Exploration-BPX and three vendors, Sema Group, SAIC and Syncordia; JP Morgan and the Pinnacle Alliance), joint development (Wal-Mart and Microsoft), cross-equity investments (Swiss Bank and Perot Systems), and joint ventures (Eastman Kodak and IBM joining together to create Technology Services Solutions for multi-vendor PC maintenance and support; CSC and CNA Financial to create an entity to deliver IT services in the life insurance market).

THE CONCEPT OF A VALUE CENTRE

The value centre is an organizing concept that recognizes four interdependent sources of value from IT resources (Figure 7.2). It allows us to differentiate the management approaches needed to realize these distinct sources of value. The cost centre reflects an operational focus that minimizes risks with a predominant focus on operational efficiency. The service centre, while still minimizing risk, aims to create an IT-enabled business capability to support current strategies. The investment centre, on the other hand, has a longer-term focus and aims to create new IT-based business capabilities. Finally, the profit centre is designed to deliver IT services to the external marketplace to realize incremental revenue as well as to gain valuable experience to become a world-class IT organization. Thus, as indicated in Figure 7.2, cost and service centres seek to minimize risk by focusing on current business strategies, while investment and profit centres focus on maximizing

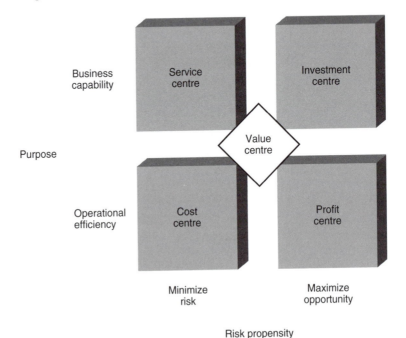

Figure 7.2   *The Concept of a Value Centre*

opportunities from IT resources and shaping future business strategies. Collectively, these four components balance the role of IT in today's operations with the requirements of tomorrow's business context.

Cost Centre

We have historically managed most IS activities as a *cost centre*: we allocated resources on the basis of rigid, quantitative payback criteria (reduction in operating costs or increased margins); we operated the infrastructure such as the data centre and telecommunications network as a utility independent of business strategy; we designed the IS organization as a support unit with a reporting relationship to the finance function; and we assessed IS performance using cost-based indices (see also Chapter 2).

The cost centre is the first building block of the value centre and is valid when the following three conditions hold. One, the value expected from IT resources is *independent* of the firm's business strategy (for example the operational infrastructure involving most data centres, telecommunications network and routine maintenance). Two, the nature of the relationship between input and output is well understood (for example, the impact of increasing the operating budget by a factor of two on output metrics). Three, external comparison standards on relevant performance metrics—like cost per million instructions per second (MIPS), maintenance cost per workstation or training cost per employee on a new operating system—are available and meaningful.

However, we have applied the cost centre logic even when the above three conditions do not hold. In general, companies have been disappointed with their ability to manage the cost centre activities, which have become the cornerstone of IT operations in most organizations. Hence, it is not a major surprise that we have enthusiastically embraced the possibilities of outsourcing. Indeed, most outsourcing discussions and decisions reflect a cost centre perspective. In 1989, Eastman Kodak pioneered the current dominant model of outsourcing when it transferred a significant part of its IT infrastructure and human assets to three different vendors. Subsequently, several major corporations[1] have outsourced at least some parts of their IT operations. In the USA alone more than 60 contracts, each valued at $200 million and more, have been awarded since Kodak's pioneering move.[2]

So, should cost centre activities *always* be outsourced? The answer is clearly no, but every cost centre activity should be evaluated for possible outsourcing using the following two questions. The first question is: *how large is the cost parity gap and what is the impact of this gap on business performance?* Benchmarking the cost levels with key competitors and leading vendors provides a useful external referent. However, care must be taken to ensure that the benchmarking referents are appropriately selected. Often I find that cost centre activities (which do not drive the business strategy of a firm) are compared against seemingly similar activities in other companies—except that those companies might be using the same to differentiate in the marketplace. The ultimate purpose of such a benchmarking exercise is to assess the impact of the cost parity gap on business performance.

The second question is: *is it worthwhile to invest to close the cost parity gap?* This question focuses on the risks and rewards of investing incremental resources to close the projected cost parity gap. Often, looking at cost centre activities in isolation leads to a different decision than from a broader portfolio point of view: can we reassign our internal resources away from the cost centre activities to higher-value activities? When Xerox announced its outsourcing, CIO Pat Wallington said: "We want to focus our internal staff on moving us to the environment that will support us tomorrow." John Cross, the CIO of BPX, said it best: "We have to step out of the kitchen and let someone else do the cooking", implying that IT management should focus on new business capabilities through IT rather than operating and owning the technology (CSC Index Foundation, 1995). So even improvements in the cost centre reflect strategic choices on the part of an organization.

Obviously, decisions on investment levels and sourcing options require a more complete understanding of value from IT resources beyond cost. So, in the paragraphs below, I develop other building blocks of the value centre that complement the better-understood cost centre.

Service Centre

The service centre is the second building block, with a focus on IT-enabled business capabilities that drive current business strategy. These capabilities are not created with a focus on lowest possible cost but as drivers of competitive advantage.

Consider Frito-Lay's business relationship with McCormick & Co. In the early 1990s, Frito-Lay managers could use Lotus Notes® internally, but not with their trading partners, since inter-organizational transactions were based on structured data standards and not Lotus Notes. Frito-Lay's internal IS organization created a specific Notes application to support business exchange with McCormick. This allowed Frito-Lay and McCormick to exchange images and memos in addition to structured data, and McCormick managers could analyse Frito-Lay's inventory information from multiple perspectives. Both achieved lower inventory levels and could place more confidence in the interpretability of data being exchanged. Such a capability could not have been justified under a cost centre logic as it reflects a specific business objective of reduced operating costs through a redefined partnership with a key supplier.

More recently, Lufthansa deployed a new version of its maintenance system that allows its maintenance engineers at geographically dispersed airports to work simultaneously on aircraft malfunctions over ISDN and ATM network links. The multimedia platform allows multiple users jointly to view and edit documents, video and still images, while transmitting video images of faulty aircraft components for problem analyses to specific expert locations. This capability was not driven by cost centre considerations but as a means to minimize downtime and improve its on-time punctuality and reliability. Another example is Bank of America's development of its customer targeting system to allow its sales and service managers to have predictive models on likely customer response behaviour that are better than those of its competitors.

GE Medical Systems has developed a satellite network to provide tips to hospital technicians regarding key parameters of medical imaging. Sears Products Services has equipped its 14 000 service technicians with mobile computing devices to increase customer service dramatically through automation of routine tasks as well as providing a wide range of information (Computerworld, 1995a). In a similar vein, Hale and Dorr—a Boston-based law firm deployed a multi-faceted business platform—home page on the Internet, ISDN links, high-speed servers, voice-recognition systems, laserdisk-driven multimedia presentation devices—to allow its attorneys to access information and leverage their internal expertise base to gain a significant advantage in the courtroom (*Computerworld*, 1995b). Such business capabilities are motivated by the requirements of delivering superior service and could not have been justified on a strict cost centre basis alone.

What differentiates a service centre from a cost centre? One, I do not believe in any *a priori* classification of activities into cost or service centres. Take for instance help desks: they could be treated as a cost centre initiative if the expected benefit was not directly related to business strategy (like responses to queries on company policies or standard software problems) or as a service centre if the expected benefit is directly related to the business strategy (such as the need to tap into the knowledge and expertise base for a consulting or a legal organization). Similarly, the development of a Web site could be treated as a cost centre ("just establishing a presence on the Internet") in one setting, while it is clearly a service centre in settings that view the Web as a platform for delivering superior value to customers ("creating market differentiation through electronic commerce"). For instance, stock-trading companies like Charles Schwab and E-Trade are investing significantly to create web-based service functionality to their customers (see www.schwab.com; www.etrade.com).

Two, we need to focus on the *performance criteria* for allocating resources. A service centre compels the use of specific business unit objectives and not generic indices to allocate key resources as well as assessing the performance. Thus, a help desk is assessed not in terms of operating costs but in terms of the degree of perceived contribution to specific business processes; and Intranet applications are assessed in terms of their business results rather than administrative cost savings. IT-enabled customer service capabilities in companies like Federal Express and American Express are assessed using relevant business indices (end-customer satisfaction, customer loyalty and repeat purchases) rather than cost indices (cost displacement through labour substitution or cost per service call) alone.

A major difference between cost and service centres lies in the degree of service orientation exhibited by the IT organization to understand the role of IT in the business processes. If IT managers proactively bring their skills, knowledge and experience to suggest, demonstrate and create IT-enabled business capabilities (customer service, logistics or new product development), they reflect a service centre orientation. A good example is Astra-Merck, where the "IT people . . . live and work in the process areas that make up [the] business. They are not isolated in a support department" (Yetter, 1995). Similarly, where IT managers are catalysts for redesigning business processes and have performance and compensation stakes in the creation of new business capabilities, they are indeed reflecting a service centre orientation.

Investment Centre

The investment centre is the third component of the value centre. In contrast to the first two, the investment centre has a markedly strategic focus and seeks to maximize business opportunity from IT resources. A forward-looking research and development component is particularly advantageous when the business is undergoing a discontinuous change—and the new business model is likely to be grounded in IT functionality.

Several companies have constituted advanced technology groups charged with the task of scanning, selecting, evaluating and transferring the knowledge about emerging technologies to the business. For instance, the advanced technology group within SmithKline Beecham, a global pharmaceutical company, created a multimedia training system in the early stages of the technology's evolution and achieved demonstrable gains in learning efficiency and job effectiveness. USAA, a leading player in the insurance and financial services market delivering services to military families, has a unit scanning for emerging technologies that could significantly enhance its customer service capability. More recently CIGNA, a leading insurance company, created a 40-person IS R&D organization with a focus on "looking at technologies that are ripe for development" (*Computerworld*, 1995c). Similar units exist in leading companies such as Federal Express, American Express, Wal-Mart, Johnson & Johnson, Citibank, Merck and others.

The management challenge is to ensure that such groups do not become aggressive champions of specific technologies but focus on specific business capabilities that leverage leading-edge technologies. The CEO in a global financial institution charged a joint business–IT team to evaluate options for serving retail customers using a "nontraditional" channel. He did not want the team to be driven by any specific technology such as the Internet but to be focused on delivering enhanced customer value. His challenge was: "Create a new business model even if it destroys our current capabilities. I want us to know very clearly how our business model could be made marginal (or at worst, obsolete) by someone." This team is now in the midst of constructing and assessing a wide range of business models based on alternative scenarios reflecting different technological capabilities.

Another practice within the investment centre is technology licensing—often seen in the form of beta testing of emerging technologies. This is expensive and time consuming, but could provide an edge over competitors if these technologies create new business capabilities. Beta testing of early versions of scanning technologies has helped insurance and credit card companies. Similarly, early experimentation with electronic data interchange helped Wal-Mart to appreciate the potential for enhancing operational efficiency in the supply chain. Now, several companies are experimenting with Sun's Java applets on the Internet. Beta testing of technologies is most useful as a form of advanced intelligence to signal the potential obsolescence of current business capabilities or the creation of new capabilities.

It is possible to go beyond passive participation in beta tests of standard technologies and be an active participant in creating differential capabilities. This requires a much more aggressive investment commitment and involves a range of activities such as technology licensing, joint development and equity investments, as well as joint ventures (see Figure 7.3). During the first half of the 1990s, we have seen several companies entering into technology alliances for creating new differential capabilities. American Express delivers its electronic inter-

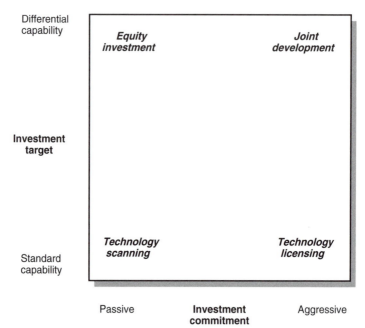

Figure 7.3   *Strategic Options for Managing the Investment Centre*

active services for its members, such as downloading monthly statements into personal finance programs (such as Quicken), through its unique relationship with America Online. Wal-Mart is moving from physical retail stores into online retailing through its special relationship with Microsoft. McGraw-Hill launched its custom publishing initiative, *Primis®*, through alliances involving scanning technology with Kodak and flexible binding capability with RR Donnelley & Sons. Indeed, equity investments and joint development are popular mechanisms to access critical technology functionality.

Some leading companies are beginning to chart their investment centres with an eye towards creating new, future-oriented business capabilities rather than investing in isolated technologies *per se*. Robert Martin, ex-CIO of Wal-Mart and the President and CEO of Wal-Mart International, noted:

> When I'm presented with a proposal to invest in new technology, I look beyond the financial commitment I'm asked to make today and try to understand what my follow-on commitments will be... We have to know how we will get from the investment we make in today's generation of technology to the next generation. (*Harvard Business Review*, 1995a)

Hence, allocation of resources to the investment centre should be based on a multi-stage creation of business capabilities under uncertainty and market shifts rather than a single "go–no go" investment in technology.[3] Thus, the investment centre has a two-pronged role: early identification of the likely obsolescence of the current business model and the proactive creation of the new business platform. Long-term business performance in the fast-changing marketplace is dependent on the successful operations of the investment centre.

The emergence and acceleration of the Web as part of the marketing infrastructure compel every organization to invest in exploring the role of the Web in their business operations. Barnes and Noble reacted to the potential of the Web only after Amazon.com demonstrated a viable business model. Now, we are in the midst of a major duel on the Internet between Amazon.com (www.amazon.com) and Barnes and Noble (www.barnesandnoble.com), with other minor players like Border's Bookstore (www.borders.com) and Microsoft (www.books.com). Similarly, Encyclopaedia Britannica is now in the midst of transforming itself from its traditional paper-and-print business model to compete against a broad array of online content providers on the Internet (www.eb.com). AlliedSignal is creating a very extensive Web site for its parts catalogue as it seeks to establish a leadership position in the automotive after-sales market (www.highperformancedriving.com). As the Web challenges every firm to reassess its business model, investment centre activities (as shown in Figure 7.3) become more important than ever before. The future is not a linear extrapolation of the past and the discontinuities are propelled by information technology.

Profit Centre

The profit centre is the fourth building block of the value centre, with a focus on delivering IT products and services in the external marketplace. Long advocated, previously abandoned and scorned by many when focused only on the financial benefits, its importance can be appreciated when non-financial benefits are also considered. When properly conceived and implemented, this allows an IT organization to have an external focus with opportunities for market-based benchmarking, rapid learning, confidence building as well as incremental revenue and margins.

Over the last five years, several companies such as USX, Humana, Mellon Bank, Sears Roebuck, Kimberly-Clark, Boeing and others have attempted to compete in the IT marketplace with limited success. So why renew the call for a profit centre? The main impetus is the opportunity to pool complementary skills and resources through a wide range of mechanisms to pursue profit centre opportunities (see Figure 7.4).

Central

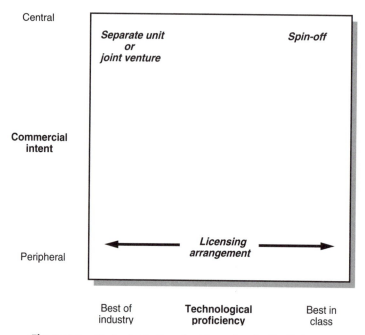

Figure 7.4   *Strategic Options for Managing the Profit Centre*

Consider the case where a company has either best-of-industry or best-of-breed (world class across industry and geographical boundaries) technological proficiency but does not have a major commercial intent to leverage its proficiency. This occurs when a firm realizes its proficiency in areas that are tangential to its primary business purpose; nevertheless, it seeks to realize its full value. In such a setting, it is advantageous to consider licensing its technological proficiency to a commercial entity without distracting the internal IT operations to have an external commercial focus. Wal-Mart's licensing arrangement with IBM to market its best-of-industry supply chain processes is a case in point.

Now, consider a case where a company with best-of-industry proficiency has a commercial intent to leverage its IT proficiency to create new lines of business operations. Then, an attractive option is to go beyond licensing its expertise to create a distinct market-facing unit, either on its own or through alliances. In 1995, Liberty Payment Services was created as a subsidiary of Liberty National Bank and Trust to provide overnight cheque-clearing service for banks. Here, Liberty's cheque-processing capability is combined with the logistics capability of UPS Worldwide Logistics to achieve lower cost and faster speed than offered by the Federal Reserve System. Similarly, Holiday Inn created its hotel reservation business as a separate entity based on its relationship with IBM's ISSC to serve the entire hotel and hospitality marketplace.

Now consider the case of Swiss Bank Corporation (SBC). Its investment banking division, SBC Warburg, has created an entity to market IT products and services to the global financial marketplace as part of a complex cross-equity deal with Perot Systems. SBC has an option of a 24.9% equity stake in Perot Systems, while Perot Systems took a 40% stake in an IT-oriented subsidiary of SBC, Systor AG—which handles the back-office functions.

In November 1996, Computer Sciences Corporation (CSC) and CNA Financial entered into an agreement to create a subsidiary to handle the information processing requirements—in areas such as claims, new policy issuance, accounting and record keeping, tax and related administrative processes. The new entity is expected to function as a subsidiary of CNA delivering services in the marketplace; CSC has no equity stake but has the rights to share in profits based on the entity's performance.

The upper right corner represents a case where a company has best-in-class IT proficiency and has a commercial intent to create new products and services—often unrelated to the company's traditional business intent. Popular examples here include the spin-off of EDS by General Motors and the unleashing of Allegiance Corporation, the distribution and materials management arm of Baxter Healthcare Corporation. In these and related cases, the parents realized that the best-in-class technical proficiencies in their respective units could not be fully nurtured and exploited within the traditional corporate structure. Allegiance Corporation has done well in its first year of operations, with stock price more than doubling. Moreover, *CIO* magazine recognized Baxter/Allegiance's ValueLink system, which enables the company to deliver medical, surgical and laboratory products on a "just-in-time" basis, as "one of the 12 most influential technology applications of the last 10 years". The ValueLink system (Short and Venkatraman, 1992) is the key operational system used in Allegiance's order processing, customer service and electronic data interchange support for stockless distribution programmes.

These cases notwithstanding, whenever I raise the role of the profit centre as a key component of the value centre, I get two objections. The first is that it diffuses the business purpose—especially given the renewed emphasis on core competencies (Quinn, 1992; Hamel and Prahalad, 1994). I have used Figure 7.4 to discuss options for realizing the potential value without necessarily diverting valuable internal resources. Thus, licensing arrangements are more attractive when the commercial intent from organizing IT as a profit centre is peripheral to the business purposes. Delineation of separate units, as in the case of SBC Warburg–Perot Systems, clarifies the specific roles and responsibilities. The second objection pertains to the difficulty of ensuring that key IT competencies (the so-called crown jewels) are not inadvertently given away to competitors in the open market. We overcome this valid objection through a judicious delineation of those few IT-enabled business capabilities that truly provide unique value in the marketplace from those that are at best a competitive necessity. A disciplined view about the scope and relative emphasis of the profit centre within the overall value centre is an absolute necessity.

Ultimately, the profit centre is not attractive when viewed only as a source of incremental revenue. The president of a major chemicals distribution company remarked: "The sales from the profit centre is a round-off error on my sales numbers. I don't want to be bothered by it." He is right. It is important to view profit in broader terms, such as the valuable experience and market knowledge gained by the IT managers. In the case of Barclays Bank in the UK, the IT organization's track record in competing successfully in the external market played a significant part in enhancing its internal standing with the business managers. CEOs are more favourably disposed to the profit centre in the value centre equation when including the spillover non-financial benefits than otherwise.

Table 7.1 summarizes the four components of the value centre along a set of key characteristics. It highlights that the value from each component is distinct, requiring different management approaches.

REALIZING VALUE: REFRAMING THE CEO–CIO DIALOGUE

Take a moment to profile your current positions on the role of information technology using the chart in Table 7.2. Then, profile your desired positions. The chances are that your desired profile is noticeably to the right of the current profile. The implication is clear: you cannot afford to manage IT resources from a cost centre perspective. The value expected is far different from the traditional efficiency enhancements and you need to manage IT operations from a value centre perspective. I have found this to be the case in many organizations that are in the midst of reorienting their business strategies and realigning their business and IT strategies. This is becoming more so as the Web emerges as a key component of the business infrastructure and intellectual assets (as

Table 7.1 A Summary of the Four Components of the Value Centre

Characteristics	Cost centre	Service centre	Investment centre	Profit centre
Objectives	Deliver IT products and services at the lowest cost levels relative to an external referent	Deliver IT-enabled business capabilities to support current business strategy	Proactively create IT-enabled business capabilities that shape new business strategies	Deliver IT products and services in the external market to realize marketplace knowledge, credibility and additional profits
Key capabilities	Managing scale and scope for operational efficiency	Understanding technology's role in the business strategy	Identifying and nurturing a portfolio of technology-enabled new business capabilities	Ability to compete successfully against best-in-class vendors
Performance metrics (illustrative)	Cost/MIPS	Client satisfaction Internal service guarantee levels	Investment payoff reflected in business capability creation	Realized profit levels Market experience and credibility
Role of external alliances and partners	Relationships with best-in-class outsourcers to improve cost levels	Alliances for key capabilities such as help desk, customer service and market intelligence	Support for technology scanning, technology licensing, joint R&D, beta tests and joint ventures	Partnering to combine complementary skills to serve the IT marketplace

Table 7.2   Profiling the Role of Information Technology in Business Operations

We deploy information technology to overcome weaknesses in our current operations	←————→	We view information technology as a fundamental driver of future business capabilities
Information technology is seen as an expense to be managed	←————→	Information technology is seen as an a resource to be leveraged
Our business value is driven by leveraging physical assets	←————→	Our business value is created by leveraging intellectual assets
Our business model is relatively unaffected by the Web and electronic commerce	←————→	The Web and electronic commerce are key discontinuities in our business model
We view IT outsourcing as a threat to our operations	←————→	Our sourcing strategy balances insourcing with outsourcing
We use one rigid criterion for assessing value from IT	←————→	We adopt multiple criteria for measuring IT value
Our IT operations reflect a captive, internal monopoly	←————→	Our IT operations act as a solutions integrator to business requirements

opposed to physical assets) drive competitive advantage and value creation. The characteristics on the left reflect the traditional cost centre logic, while those on the right reflect the emerging value centre perspective. The following questions reframe the discussion agenda between business and IT managers using the value centre concept and are useful in transforming the IT operations.

The *Raison d'Être*: Create Business Capabilities or Rectify Operational Weaknesses?

The first question focuses on the fundamental business purpose of the IT organization: is the focus primarily on deploying IT capabilities to rectify weaknesses in the current operations, or is it on creating future business capabilities?

As part of MIT's Management in the 1990s research program (Scott Morton, 1991), I developed a model of IT's role in business operations (Venkatraman, 1994). Using the same model, we can now compare and contrast two different purposes of IT operations: *rectification of past weaknesses* and *creation of future capabilities*. The former focuses on overcoming weaknesses inherent in the traditional business model through the use of IT (see Figure 7.5). The latter seeks to define the future operating state (in terms of business scope and pattern of alliances and relationships, including outsourcing) before developing the overall logic for process redesign and the purpose of IT operations.

Companies have devoted far more attention to deploying IT for the rectification of past weaknesses rather than for the creation of future capabilities. Thus, cost and service centres have been the dominant focus of management. If future operations are merely a linear extrapolation of the past, then overcoming the deficiencies in the current design could create a foundation for the future. On the other hand, if information revolution destroys traditional sources of advantage while creating new sources of advantage, we need to go beyond rectifying current weaknesses. This requires a value centre profile that goes beyond cost and service centres and includes the investment centre—especially for leveraging newly emerging functionality.

So both business and IT managers need jointly to articulate the *raison d'être* for the IT operations. Some leading companies have realized the advantages of recognizing the broader view of value from IT resources and are articulating their IT mission accordingly. Hallmark Cards is in the midst of developing its strategy for the emerging multimedia marketplace—which could render obsolete its traditional products and associated business model of printing and distributing greeting cards. So it is selectively exploring a range of activities within the investment centre while it manages its traditional supply chain requirements through a mix of cost and service centres. Similarly, as Encyclopedia Britannica shifts its strategy away from selling bound volumes through door-to-door sales towards electronic on-line access and related services, its value centre profile should emphasize the investment centre more than ever before. Levi Strauss is offering customized jeans (Levi's Personal Pair); Boeing innovated in the design and manufacture of its 777 model. Federal Express is now attempting to create a niche in on-line services through its integrated electronic commerce and catalog services in its new initiative *Virtual Order*TM.

What is the new leadership requirement? The answer is articulating the role of information technology in business operations, in terms of the relative emphasis to the different components of the value centre. If the role of IT is simply to rectify current weaknesses, you can organize it with more emphasis on cost and service centres. On the other hand, if the role of IT is to create new business models as well as

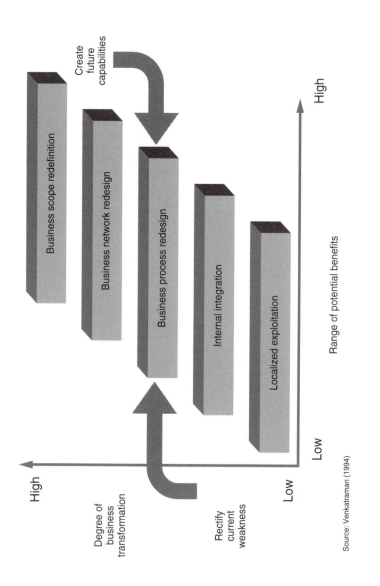

Figure 7.5 *Balancing Future Requirements with Current Realities*

Source: Venkatraman (1994)

change the business scope, a more balanced profile reflecting the four components is required.

Allocating Resources: One Rigid Yardstick or Multiple Distinct Criteria?

The funding level and the criteria used to decide it are key issues pertaining to the second theme. A thorny question for both business and IT managers is: "How much should we spend (or invest) in IT to support our value centre profile?" We see contentious discussions around questions such as: are we spending enough? Are we best leveraging the IT resources that produce business value? How well are we balancing today's needs with tomorrow's requirements?

Unfortunately, in attempting to answer such questions, most companies seem to look outward (seeking to imitate best practices) rather than focus inward (better understanding of the role of IT in its business operations). Benchmarking allows one to take comfort in the fact that the level of *input* (for example the IT budget) or *output* (for example the cost per workstation) is approximately on a par with a referent peer group. Such general benchmarking fails to recognize the differences in the value centre profiles across the companies within the benchmarking pool. Indeed, finalizing the funding level for the value centre based on general benchmarks that do not recognize the differences in value centre profiles is dysfunctional, limiting and misleading (see also Chapters 2 and 3).

Wal-Mart did not decide its level of IT investment on the basis of benchmarking the IT spending levels of Sears or K-Mart. If it had, Sears and K-Mart would probably still be the leaders. Wal-Mart's retailing strategy was to leverage IT functionality, not only for increasing the efficiency in its supply chain but also for effectively replicating successful experiments across its network of stores on a continuous basis. Its spectacular growth in sales and profits over the last decade is based on its ability to learn rapidly from its numerous ongoing experiments. The store managers are connected through a sophisticated, multimedia knowledge network that allows them to exploit their collective expertise and continually fine-tune their marketing strategies. Their particular choice of how IT could contribute to their business strategy influenced their funding strategy.

Moreover, investments in IT should not be treated in isolation from complementary investments required to create specific IT-enabled business capabilities. As Wayne P. Yetter, the CEO of Astra-Merck, observed:

> We do not consider technology investments in isolation. We look at capabilities, such as developing drugs faster or providing customers with service they can shape themselves; and if technology is necessary to make a capability work, then technology investments are part of the package. (*Harvard Business Review*, 1995b)

Such an approach reflects a fundamental belief that IT is only a piece—albeit an important one—of business capabilities and is consistent with an options view of investments.

The value centre requires the use of differential criteria for allocating IT resources to the different components. Capabilities based on cost centre initiatives are allocated resources based on quantitative, financial payback criteria with appropriate external benchmarks. Those capabilities reflecting the service centre are justified based on a specific business plan using a mix of financial and strategic considerations. Business managers quantify and justify the link between IT-enabled business capabilities and marketplace performance to their appropriate business review boards and not to technical committees.

The investment centre requires a longer-term strategic focus on new business capabilities rooted in a wide array of technological developments. The creation of new capabilities might involve a variety of initiatives, such as selective participation in beta tests of emerging applications, pre-emptive licensing of high-potential developments, joint development with vendors, minority equity investment in start-up ventures and potential acquisitions of companies with key complementary capabilities. The selection of particular mechanisms for the investment centre is based on strategic considerations and should be supported by appropriate resource-allocation criteria. Funding for the profit centre is based on sound business cases like any other new business launch, with the caveat of also recognizing possible non-financial benefits.

Acquiring Capabilities: Outsourcing as Taboo or a Strategic Sourcing Network?

Outsourcing is no longer a taboo topic among senior managers, including IT professionals. Now it is not a question of whether to outsource but what to outsource, as companies redirect valuable internal skills and capabilities to high-value-added areas (Quinn, 1992). The ten-year $3.2 billion outsourcing relationship between Xerox and EDS is structured such that while EDS manages the operational components of the IT infrastructure, Xerox will concentrate on new application developments on the new platform. In the words of Pat Wallington: "I view outsourcing as a part of the transformation strategy." Similarly, Henry

Pfendt, former director of information technology management at Kodak, noted in conversation with the author in 1992 that: "through outsourcing, it is possible to transform the IT operations from a service deliverer to a broker and facilitator of needed services for business managers".

Thus, the third topic is the development of a sourcing strategy to support the value centre profile (see also Lacity, Willcocks and Feeny, 1996). No one company could—or indeed should—source the entire set of capabilities for its value centre internally. The sourcing strategy is to balance the required skills and competencies from internal and external sources. Outsourcers are able to bring their expertise to improve cost levels of data centre operations, systems maintenance and the telecommunications network, as well as enhance help desk services and system upgrades. This frees up valuable internal resources for higher-value-added activities. Recently, Owens-Corning contracted with Hewlett-Packard to manage its legacy systems such that it could concentrate its internal efforts on rapidly implementing its chosen SAP R/3 enterprise software and create a new operating platform for growth.

In one insurance company, a balanced approach to sourcing paved the way for a recognition that its skills best matched the cost and service centres, while there was a gap in terms of the investment centre. Instead of expanding its internal skill set (which would have required significant additional resources to match the required quality), it identified a series of strategic relationships with a set of vendors to support the investment centre requirements. In contrast, a global financial services company aggressively examined the feasibility of outsourcing cost and service centres while migrating and transforming its internal operations to support the investment centre and even parts of the service centre—where external sourcing might not have yielded maximum benefits. Similarly, Xerox outsourced its IT requirements in the cost and service centres to EDS, while forming a different set of relationships with Oracle and others to create new business capabilities reflecting the investment and profit centres.

More recently, JP Morgan has announced that it has developed a consortium, Pinnacle Alliance, using CSC as the primary partner and a set of associated players—AT&T Solutions, Andersen Consulting and Bell Atlantic—to manage its data centres, voice and data and software services. Peter Miller, the co-head of Corporate Technology at JP Morgan, remarked: "Technology is moving very rapidly and the constant challenge to get technological skills up to speed is one that any single company will have a difficult time achieving" (Morgan, 1996). At the same time, the internal resources will be directed at the development of complex computer programs needed for securities trading and other leading-edge financial services.

Profiling the value centre in terms of the relative emphasis on the four components of value allows us systematically to evaluate the difference between sourcing options. There is a widespread feeling among IT managers that IT outsourcing will seriously diminish the scope and power of the IT unit relative to other units. This is true if the overall value expected from IT resources is predominantly cost related and independent of business strategy. It is clearly not the case in the emerging information-age economy. So the question is not one of insourcing versus outsourcing but of carefully balancing different sourcing options.

The Xerox–EDS relationship is indeed a portfolio of multiple independent agreements reflecting the different sources of value. The Xerox–Oracle alliance is focused on the investment and profit centres. SBC Warburg has two different relationships with Perot systems—a 25-year, $250 million annual contract for the data centre operations, reflecting cost and service centres, and a cross-equity agreement for the investment and profit centres. On the other hand, JP Morgan decided that its internal skills should be directed at investment centre activities and outsourced its cost and service centres to the Pinnacle Alliance. By sourcing cost and service centre activities through the Pinnacle Alliance, it has been able to concentrate its internal resources on creating distinctive capabilities to outperform its rivals in the financial services marketplace.

In putting such principles into practice, I have found the clarity in the delineation of decision rights among key decision makers is the most important requirement. This involves the specification of who has what areas of responsibility in making decisions about IT, and under what conditions. For instance, when Xerox entered into its multi-year agreement with EDS in 1995, it retained all key decisions pertaining to "information management functions that focus on strategy, architecture and applications" (quoted in *Computerworld*, 1994), while outsourcing operational decisions to EDS. In contrast, Philips Electronics retained operational decision rights over its IT infrastructure while transferring decision rights pertaining to application development to an external entity.

What is often overlooked is that an organization's willingness to reallocate decision rights to an external vendor is a key consideration in vendor selection. For instance, as shown in Figure 7.6, if the vendor is positioned in the upper left quadrant, it typically exercises greater decision rights than if the vendor is positioned in the lower left. Thus, selecting the vendors to be invited as possible sourcing partners should first be guided by an organization's willingness to redistribute key decisions.

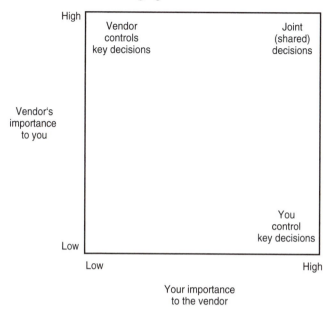

Figure 7.6 *Decision Rights and Vendor Selection*

Clarity of decision rights is particularly central, as the new form for the IT organization is more likely to resemble a network of multiple relationships rather than the traditional command-and-control hierarchy. In some areas, it makes sense to assign joint decision responsibilities, while in other cases, it is more prudent to specify sole responsibilities. Joint, shared decision responsibilities—while appealing—often require more time commitment from managers and should be reserved only for those specific areas where multiple viewpoints are to be reflected.

Thus, the CIO is expected to grow and change from an owner and controller of predominantly internal IT assets to orchestrating a strategic sourcing network of relationships to deliver the required support to the business managers. Orchestrating is a different leadership skill than command and control; unfortunately, the traditional control model is woefully outmoded for the new economy.

Assessment Approach: Single or Multi-faceted Criteria?

Assessing value from IT resource deployment is the fourth, perhaps the most contentious, theme. We have abandoned the search for one universal measure of business performance valid under all conditions (such as market share, return on investment, assets or equity) and recognized the need for a multidimensional set (see also Chapters 2 and 6). This includes quantitative (e.g. return on equity) and qualitative (e.g. corporate reputation, quality) indices; internal (business growth rate) and external (e.g. growth rate relative to market) measures; as well as accounting (e.g. cash flow and liquidity) and financial market (e.g. market value added, MVA) measures. Indeed, the use of a balanced performance measurement that is tied to strategic thrusts is gaining popularity (Kaplan and Norton, 1996). Unfortunately, we are still preoccupied with the search for a unidimensional measure of IT value. This is due to the historic emphasis on the cost centre and the predisposition to deploy IT resources to enhance operational efficiency. Despite obvious limitations, we have not seriously moved away from the use of a single dominant cost-oriented metric of IT value (see also Chapter 4). Indeed, productivity enhancement through IT is still the holy mantra within the IS professional community.

As shown in Figure 7.7, a value centre is predicated on the need for multiple, distinctive metrics for the four components. The cost centre is assessed using cost metrics such as efficiency enhancements or labour substitution and might be anchored with appropriate external benchmarks (best-in-industry levels and best-of-breed levels—typically found in other industries or among leading outsourcing providers). A service centre is assessed through business indices specified by the business managers and, where feasible, compared with a set of peer groups in other industries. An investment centre is assessed through a mix of strategic and quantitative indices reflecting the creation of new business functionality, and a profit centre is assessed in terms of target profit indices and qualitative learning and confidence-building opportunities. In these two centres, given their strategic emphasis, we can selectively use external benchmarking referents to gain possible insights into how these sources of value can be significantly enhanced.

Ultimately, the set of performance criteria is to be directly related to the value centre profile that is developed as the first item on the discussion agenda. Otherwise, we have failed to achieve internal consistency between strategy and performance assessment.

Organizational Logic: Internal Captive Monopoly or a Solutions Integrator?

The final theme relates to the logic of the IT organization. When invoking the value centre concept to designing the IT organization, several questions emerge: who has overall responsibility for the value centre?

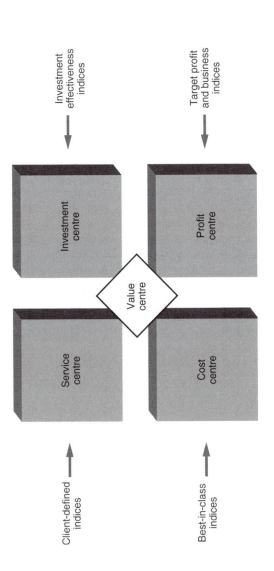

Investment effectiveness indices

Target profit and business indices

Investment centre

Profit centre

Value centre

Service centre

Cost centre

Client-defined indices

Best-in-class indices

Figure 7.7 *Assessing the Value Centre Using Multiple Indices*

Should all the four components of the value centre be under the CIO? Who is responsible for the integrity of the IT architecture? What are the working organizational relationships among the different components of the value centre? Obviously, it is impossible to deal with the full set of organizational design questions in sufficient detail here. I offer some initial ideas for designing the IT organization as *a solutions integrator*. At a minimum, we clearly need to shift away from the historical dominant view of an internal captive supplier.

The organizing logic of a solutions integrator works best when supported by the following five guiding principles. First, we recognize the ownership of IT as a strategic resource by business managers—who have the primary responsibility for specifying the role of IT as part of overall business capabilities (see also Willcocks, Feeny and Islei, 1997). Secondly, we assign an overall custodian of IT architecture—viewed as the underlying engine for the overall business processes. Under conditions of multisourcing from a wide range of providers, it is important to specify who has the supreme authority to resolve conflicts involving specific application and the overall architecture. The IT organization as the custodian works well when it is seen not as a technology czar but as a valued business partner: Johnson & Johnson has assigned overall enterprise-wide responsibility to the Corporate Office of Information Technology. Where a corporate IT office does not have the required credibility, a joint decision-making body composed of business and IT managers—charged to act in the best interests of the organization—is a good alternative.

The third principle is that the IT organization is a solutions integrator and is distinguished from system integrators and system builders— implying a specific emphasis on integrating the various components to deliver business solutions. Ownership of assets and technical focus are not as necessary as the IT organization's ability to source the various pieces (technology as well as complementary drivers) to deliver business solutions. The fourth principle is that business managers will seek the IT organization as their primary source for IT solutions. They, however, have the right to source directly from an external entity when they believe that they are not receiving the required solution from their primary source. The fifth principle pertains to the design and deployment of processes to align business and IT plans on a continuous basis, such that wherever possible sourcing from external providers is done on a coordinated basis across different business units.

The right organizational climate is when IT managers are able to move away from having a captive demand for their technical services towards earning their right to contribute to business capabilities. Over time, the solution integrator receives a revenue stream commensurate with the value added to the business. This will indeed be a far cry from the detached, technically focused cost centre operations with penalty clauses attached to service-level agreements.

CONCLUSIONS

We are at a critical stage in the management of IT resources. As businesses develop their strategies in the information economy, there is more emphasis on technology-enabled capabilities—not only for operational efficiencies but also for strategic effectiveness. This requires a different approach to managing IT resources that goes well beyond outsourcing. In this chapter, I set out to develop a framework for decomposing the key components of value from IT resources. My recommendation is that every organization should focus on these four possible sources of value from IT resources. Their relative importance is clearly dependent on the specific business context. Indeed, the relative mix among these four components reflects the strategic role for IT within a particular business and will undoubtedly change over time. The implementation challenges then focus on ascertaining how best to source the required capabilities, as well as designing and managing a set of processes with business and IT managers to realize business advantage. Successful companies will leverage their IT resources much beyond efficiency enhancements through a cost centre and realize a broader range of business benefits through a value centre.

NOTES

1 Leading companies include McDonnell Douglas, Continental Bank, British Petroleum, Philips Electronics, Inland Revenue in the UK, Xerox, Blue Cross/Blue Shield of Massachusetts, National Car Rental, JP Morgan, Salomon Brothers, Campbell Soup, Swiss Bank and DuPont.
2 Kodak's move indeed elevated IT outsourcing as an acceptable administrative practice. For a technical discussion on the diffusion of this phenomenon within the USA, see Loh and Venkatraman (1992). For a discussion on the state of IT outsourcing, see *Information Week* (1995) and Willcocks and Lacity (1997).
3 Some research is underway at Boston University Systems Research Center by Professor Nalin Kulatilaka and his colleagues on applying the options thinking to IT investments. This approach provides valuable insights into the investment management process under conditions of uncertainty. See especially Amram and Kulatilaka (1998).

REFERENCES

Amram, M. and Kulatilaka, N. (1998). *Real Options: Managing Strategic Investments in an Uncertain World.* Harvard Business School Press, Boston, MA.

Computerworld (1994). March 28.

Computerworld (1995a). Sears Hit the Road with Wireless Devices. *Computerworld*, May 29, 6.

Computerworld (1995b). Law Firm Thrives on Bleeding Edge. *Computerworld*, September 25, 73.

Computerworld (1995c). CIGNA Creates Top Technology Post. *Computerworld*, July 10, 20.

CSC Index Foundation (1995). *New Perspectives on IT Outsourcing.* Report 105, December, 10.

Davenport, T. (1992). *Process Innovation.* Harvard Business School Press, Boston, MA.

Earl, M. (1996). The Risks of Outsourcing IT. *Sloan Management Review*, Spring, 26–32.

Hamel, G. and Prahalad, C.K. (1994). *Competing for the Future.* Harvard Business School Press, Boston, MA.

Hammer, M. and Champy, J. (1993). *Reengineering the Corporation.* Harper Business, New York.

Harvard Business Review (1995a). September–October, 162.

Harvard Business Review, (1995b). September–October, 160–69.

Information Week (1995). Outsourcing Megadeals. *Information Week*, November 6, 10.

Kaplan, R. and Norton, D. (1996). Using the Balanced Scorecard as a Strategic Management System. *Harvard Business Review*, January–February, 53–68.

Lacity, M., Willcocks, L. and Feeny, D. (1996). The Value of Selective IT Sourcing. *Sloan Management Review*, Spring, 13–25.

Loh, L. and Venkatraman, N. (1992). Diffusion of Information Technology Outsourcing: Influence Sources and the Kodak Effect. *Information Systems Research*, 3, 4, 334–58, December.

Morgan, J.P. (1996). Allies with Four Firms, *Boston Globe*, May 14, 55.

Quinn, J. (1992). *Intelligent Enterprise*, Free Press, New York.

Scott Morton, M. (ed) (1991). *The Corporation of the 1990s.* Oxford University Press, Oxford.

Short, J. and Venkatraman, N. (1992). Beyond Business Process Redesign: Redefining Baxter's Business Network. *Sloan Management Review*, Fall.

Tapscott, D. (1996). *Digital Economy: Promise and Peril in the Age of Networked Intelligence.* McGraw-Hill, New York.

Venkatraman, N. (1994). IT-Enabled Business Transformation: from Automation to Business Scope Redefinition. *Sloan Management Review*, Winter, 73–87.

Willcocks, L., Feeny, D. and Islei, G. (eds) (1997). *Managing IT as a Strategic Resource.* McGraw-Hill, Maidenhead.

Willcocks, L. and Lacity, M. (eds) (1997). *Strategic Sourcing of Information Systems.* John Wiley, Chichester.

Yetter, W.P. (1995). The End Of Delegation? Information Technology and The CEO. *Harvard Business Review*, September–October, 160–69.

SECTION III

Development, Sourcing and Infrastructure

8

Risk Assessment and Management Practices in Software Development

JANNE ROPPONEN
Nokia Telecommunications

INTRODUCTION

In this chapter we discuss further dimensions of how a sense of an IT productivity paradox can arise in organizations. It focuses on risks and their assessment in software development projects. Chapter 9 will also examine this subject, together with a detailed set of project management and IT evaluation issues provided by a single case study.

The literature on software development from the 1970s (Brooks, 1974), the 1980s (Lyytinen, 1987; Lyytinen and Hirschheim, 1987), and the 1990s (Barki, Rivard and Talbot, 1993; Lauer, 1996) is replete with statements suggesting that it costs too much, is usually late and comes incomplete. Software development suffers chronically from cost overruns, project delays, unmet user needs and unused systems. This also continues despite huge advances in development techniques, tools and software technologies. Since the early 1980s (Boehm, 1989; McFarlan, 1982) these difficulties have been addressed more vigorously through software risk management.

Software risk management can be defined as an attempt to formalize risk-oriented correlates of development success into a readily applicable set of principles and practices (Boehm, 1991). It embraces

Beyond the IT Productivity Paradox.
Edited by L. P. Willcocks and S. Lester © 1999 John Wiley & Sons Ltd.

techniques and guidelines to identify, analyse and tackle software risk items. A risk item denotes a particular aspect or property of a development task, process or environment which, if ignored, will increase the likelihood of a project failure, e.g. threats to successful software operation, major sources of software rework, implementation difficulty or delay (Lyytinen, Mathiassen and Ropponen, 1996b pp. 5–6). Overall, software risk management has raised considerable hopes for improving system development (Alter and Ginzberg, 1978; Boehm, 1989, 1991; Boehm and Ross, 1989; Charette, 1989, 1996; Mathiassen, Seewaldt and Stage, 1995).

Even though guidelines suggested by proponents of software risk management have increasingly been followed, the knowledge of software risk management practices has been sparse and anecdotal. The goal of this chapter is to improve the knowledge in this area by investigating how software risk management is currently practised. The investigation benefits from Boehm's (1989, 1991) studies on software risk items and risk management methods. Answers are sought to the following two questions: 1) which software risks are common in systems development and do they vary from one context to another; 2) how widely various risk management methods are used, how they are used, and what experiences have been garnered from their use.

The chapter is organized as follows. The first section discusses related research and explains the research problem and method of inquiry applied. The second section reports findings concerning the most critical software risks and provides insight into their contextual nature. The chapter then describes the practices considered in order to manage software risks, and users' perceptions of their usefulness. The final section summarizes the investigation by drawing conclusions on software risk management practice and how the software project risk dimensions of the IT "productivity paradox" can be reduced.

RESEARCH SETTING

Earlier Studies and Research Problem

Software risk management has not been intensively researched in the information system (IS) field despite the widespread nature of IS failure (Lyytinen, 1987; Lyytinen and Hirschheim, 1987; Willcocks, 1996; Graeser, Willcocks and Pisanias, 1998). A useful collection of recent papers appears in Griffiths and Newman (1996). A majority of studies have dealt with normative techniques of effective risk management (Boehm, 1989, 1991; Charette, 1989; McFarlan, 1982). There is not, however, much information available about the extent to which they are followed. Some empirical studies classify and rank software risk items (Barki, Rivard and Talbot, 1993; Boehm, 1989). These studies are useful in obtaining reliable figures of software risks and measuring them along various dimensions. More empirical studies are, however, needed in order to understand what risks are most critical and how they vary.

Some studies discuss cases in which risk management principles were (not) followed and try to learn from their (non) use. These studies have been either single site case studies (Boehm and Ross, 1989; Neo and Kwong, 1994; Markus and Keil, 1994) or multiple site case studies (Willcocks and Margetts, 1994). From these studies it is difficult to deduce to what extent the risk management deliberations were purposefully crafted. A few published studies have gone further and sought to establish systematic impact models of risk management (Lyytinen, Mathiassen and Ropponen, 1996; Ropponen, 1993; Ropponen and Lyytinen, 1997). They have all come to a conclusion that risk management efforts may reduce the exposure to software risks, increase software quality and improve the quality of the systems development process (Boehm, 1989; Charette, 1989; Mathiassen, Seewaldt and Stage, 1995; van Genuchten, 1991; van Swede and van Vliet, 1994). Some studies have focused on specific aspects of the development process such as project delays (van Genuchten, 1991), or dealt only indirectly with risk management issues (van Swede and van Vliet, 1994). Overall, the use of risk management methods has remained unsubstantiated, and more research is needed to gain understanding of the state of the art.

New empirical findings concerning software risks and risk management will be reported in this chapter. More specifically, the present study explores the following issues:

1. What are the critical software risk items and do they vary from one context to another?
2. To what extent are risk management techniques actively pursued, and what risk management principles and methods, if any, are used?

The following paragraphs will introduce the different aspects that were measured in order to address the above questions.

Software Risk Item Ranking

A risk item denotes a particular aspect or property of a development task, process or environment which, if ignored, will increase the likelihood of a project failure (Lyytinen, Mathiassen and Ropponen, 1998). In practice such aspects are numerous; therefore identifying and managing software risk items is a complex task. For example, an ESPRIT study (Laitinen, 1991) observed 42 significant items, 57 considerable and 57 insignificant risk items. In a similar manner, Barki, Rivard and Talbot (1993) identified 144 specific risk items in their literature survey. For ranking purposes these lists are too extensive and unsystematic. Moreover, for practising project managers they are too long and unstructured. Instead, a ranking of top risk items would provide a useful tool to orchestrate effective risk management plans and to concentrate on the most essential risks (Boehm, 1991). Therefore software risk item ranking was measured to determine the relative order of common risk items.

The present study utilizes Boehm's (1989) list of top ten risk items as a basis for ranking risk items (see Appendix 8.1). This list was chosen because it has been compiled by exploring a large number of software projects and their most common risk items. Moreover, it is quite extensive in terms of possible sources of risks (Lyytinen, Mathiassen and Ropponen, 1998) and reflects faithfully a project manager's perspective on software risks. Boehm's list is also the most widely known in practice, and has been applied with some success as a management tool to orchestrate risk management plans (Boehm and Ross, 1989). Results of ranking the risk items (Boehm, 1989) are also available, which allows for cross-comparison. Therefore, despite its limitations,[1] it sufficiently reflects the focus of our study.

Risk Management Methods and their Use

One goal in this study is to learn to what extent risk management methods are followed. The methods embrace techniques and guidelines which help to identify, analyse and tackle software risk items. In investigating the use of risk management methods, Boehm's (1989) classification was utilised.[2] The reader will notice by reading Appendix 8.1 that questions were paraphrased in a manner where a respondent does not know that (s)he is being asked about the use of a *risk* management method. This was done purposefully, because many project managers do not necessarily know the technical terms of "risk identification, risk assessment" (Boehm, 1989).

In addition, respondents' experiences and attitudes towards risk management in general were investigated. They were asked how long and extensively risk management methods had been used, whether the use was voluntary, and what were the experiences of using the methods. The resources allocated for managing risks were also probed by assuming that an allocation of sufficient resources is a reasonable indicator of management commitment.

Research Method and Data

Based on the research problem, a survey instrument[3] was developed to examine the questions clarified earlier. This research method was found appropriate, because the goal was to explore the general status of risk management practices in software development. Major parts of the questionnaire concerning ranking and criticality of top software risk items and risk management practices are summarized in Appendix 8.1. The research data concerning the top software risks and risk management practices was mainly analysed using descriptive statistics (mean values and frequencies). In addition, a t-test was utilized to make inferences about differences between average risk rankings. Appendix 8.2 explains the steps taken to assess the validity and reliability of the research data instrument and sampling bias.

The earlier literature suggests that project managers' responsibilities include risk management tasks such as keeping the project on time and within budget (Boehm, 1989). Therefore, the questionnaire was mailed to 248 randomly selected members of the Finnish Information Processing Association (1991) whose affiliation was project manager or the like. The final sample consisted of 83 project managers (response rate = 33.5%). Overall, the response rate was satisfactory and above average (see for example Igbaria, Greenhaus and Parasuraman, 1991).

Both in-house IS departments and software houses of varying sizes were included in the sample. The respondents in the sample reported experiences of nearly 1100 software projects. MIS applications covered nearly 76% of all projects included in the sample. By US and UK standards the majority of the development projects were small. The largest reported project was 672 person-months. The average size of the last completed project was 15.24 person-months (std = 11.14, N = 75).

SOFTWARE RISK ITEMS—THE CONTEXT OF RISK MANAGEMENT

Software Risk Ranking

Experiences from software projects were explored to clarify the problems situation and nature of software risk management in a concrete manner. In the following we report our findings from the most critical and highly ranked items.[4] Table 8.1 summarizes our data in comparison with Boehm's data (for details see Appendix 8.3). Numbers in bold

Table 8.1   *Ranking of Software Risk Items*

Risk item ranking	Average ranking	Boehm's ranking
1. Continuing stream of requirement changes	2.32	**6**
2. Unrealistic budgets and schedules	2.63	2
3. Developing wrong software functions	5.22	3
4. Gold plating	5.63	**5**
5. Real-time performance shortfalls	6.12	**9**
6. Wrong user interface	6.19	**4**
7. Personnel shortfalls	6.30	**1**
8. Shortfalls in externally furnished components	6.50	**7**
9. Shortfalls in externally performed tasks	6.66	**8**
10. Straining computer science capabilities	6.79	10

depict where Boehm's ranking differs from ours.

As can be seen in the table, the two most critical risk items are: 1) continuing stream of requirement changes, and 2) unrealistic schedules and budgets.[5] This result did not come as a surprise. In fact, it is in line with accepted wisdom in the field and signals the overall difficulty of getting the requirements right—a problem that has been observed since the mid-1970s to be the key problem in software development (Davis, 1982). Several empirical studies also lend support to this finding. For example, Curtis, Krasner and Iscoe's (1988) observed in an extensive field study that managing requirement changes was the most critical software problem. Lyytinen (1988) found that analysts saw the continuing problems in requirements capture to be the most important reason for development failure (see also Griffiths and Newman, 1996).

Unrealistic budgets and schedules are related to requirements changes, because a stream of continuous changes makes it difficult to estimate the cost and time to develop the system. Together they indicate the difficulty in managing the inherent uncertainty of the development task (Lyytinen, Mathiassen and Ropponen, 1996). Another reason for unrealistic schedules is the difficulty in estimating reliably the development effort and its cost. The third comes from the organizational pressures and incentives to deliver the system as fast as possible. All three often amount to the formation of optimistic and unreliable schedules and budgets which later on are transformed into software delays and late deliveries (van Genuchten, 1991; van Swede and van Vliet, 1994). The highly significant difference (t-test, p = 0.0001) of the average rankings from the rest of risk items displays the prominent place of these two risk items in software development.

Contextuality of Software Risks

The research data also allows cross-comparison of software risks in US software development and that of Finland. Overall, project managers in the Finnish sample ranked risk items differently from those in Boehm's study.[6] Most of these differences relate to variation in project environments and management structures in the two contexts studied. Altogether seven risk item rankings differ from Boehm's original rankings. Two of them are ranked remarkably differently: personnel and real-time performance shortfalls. The higher ranking of real-time performance shortfalls is probably caused mostly by the differences the hardware costs and by the specific nature of large projects studied by Boehm. The second difference—in which personnel shortfalls and the continuing stream of requirements have swapped places—is more interesting. Our ranking gives personnel shortfalls a remarkably lower rate (seventh) with significantly lower criticality (6.30). The difference can be explained by the sampling bias, i.e. there are remarkable differences in the environments and size of projects examined in the two studies. Consequently, the higher ranking of the personnel shortfalls in Boehm's study indicates that in large US software projects[7] the supply and demand forces of the skilled workforce are different.

Another point worth considering is why requirement changes have received a much higher ranking in our data set. Such a rating signals that project managers in the Finnish sample were less interested in and capable of managing requirements changes. This is true for a number of reasons which relate to the size and nature of the projects. When projects become smaller, developers are likely to work more "at arm's length" from their clientele. This will lead to more frequent requirements changes as a result of more intensive learning and wide experimentation. Boehm's studies, in contrast, focused on large (military) projects that followed a formal process model and used widely contracted external software development. This kind of institutional arrangement, with rigid incentive schemes and associated penalty fees, constrains the willingness to accept changes in requirements after the initial requirements freeze, and leads to the lower rank of this risk item in the US data. Note, however, that this does not necessarily lead to better system success when measured by overall stakeholder satisfaction (van Swede and van Vliet, 1994). Differences from the US context can also be detected in a more recent version of Boehm's ranking (1995b).[8] It seems obvious that software development risks differ according to variation in environmental contexts—both across and also within cultural contexts[9]—even though some risks seem to pertain more generally.

RISK MANAGEMENT PRACTICES AND THE USE OF METHODS

Use of Risk Management Methods and Understanding the Risk Concept

The respondents were asked whether they utilized any risk management methods. We found that a large majority of project managers (62 observations = 75%) did not follow any detailed risk management approach. When they were asked which of the risk management methods they used, another picture emerged. As Table 8.2 shows, for example, 75% of the respondents used checklists, 93% decision driver analysis, 51% cost models, 67% network analysis, and 30% quality factor analysis. Hence quite a large number of the respondents were engaged in some type of risk management activity.

Yet a striking difference in frequency can be observed with the use of risk management methods to identify risks (16 out of 83 = 19.3%) and to assess the effectiveness of risk-resolution plans (14 out of 83 = 16.9%). Here, the number of method users is lower than the number of respondents who admitted to using some risk management methods.[10] But these two method classes form the core of Boehm's risk management approach, as they require understanding of the formal software risk concept. Consequently, a majority of project managers comprehend only vaguely the software risk concept and its managerial implications.[11] This finding is also supported by the observation that nearly

Table 8.2 *Use of Risk Management Methods N = 83*

Method	No info (%)	Not used (%)	Used seldom (%)	Used often (%)
Checklists	5	21	42	33
Decision driver analysis	1	6	27	66
Assumption analysis	5	24	42	29
Decomposition analysis	2	8	24	65
Cost models	8	41	27	24
Network analysis	10	34	29	28
Decision analysis, decision trees	18	59	20	4
Quality factor analysis	12	58	17	13
Risk exposure	34	47	15	5
Risk leverage	36	47	12	5
Prototypes, analytical modelling	1	17	37	45
Less ambitious objectives	2	12	42	43
Risk transfer	4	17	67	12
Average	10	30	30	29

one third of the respondents had no information on risk exposure and leverage, whereas for other methods the percentage of respondents having no information is lower. Hence Boehm's (1989) claim rings true when he says that many project managers do not have a real understanding of the terms "risk identification" and "risk assessment".

Methods, broadly understood, are frequently used to help execute parts of a risk management plan. Most of them are useful when a project's key risks are already known, though some also help to identify risks. Such methods include decision driver analysis (analysis of key decisions), decomposition analysis, prototypes, and accepting less ambitious objectives. One reason for their widespread use is that their use is quite often dictated in one way or another by the organization's preferred methodology.

Perceptions of Risk Management Usefulness

Project managers committed to risk management methods had garnered varying levels of experience of using them. The majority (15 out of 21 = 75%) had employed the methods for three or more years. They did not see any reason to give up the method used, which is often the case with traditional system development methods (Smolander, Tahvanainen and Lyytinen, 1990). Not surprisingly, most project managers reported good or relatively positive experiences: they saw that projects using risk management methods fared better. They did considerably better in two cases (11%), somewhat better in thirteen cases (72%), and only in three cases (17%) was no difference reported. Moreover, the benefits were achieved with a reasonable cost. Nine respondents (45%) reported that risk management consumed less than 2% of the project's total time, and ten cases (50%) consumed 2–8% of the project time.

Overall project managers saw risk management methods as having a positive impact both on the development process and its outcomes. In particular, they argued that the use of risk management methods provided a more consistent view of the development situation, led to better use of available information, helped to identify project assumptions, improved credibility of plans, and created proactive management and contingency planning. These experiences coincide well with Charette's (1989) findings (see also Lauer, 1996; Charette, 1996). The main concern was the demand on resources. Many argued that the time and effort put into risk management exercises was demanding (in particular with small projects). The situation resembles buying an insurance policy— we think it costs too much until the risks are realized.

CONCLUSIONS

This chapter has sought answers to two main questions concerning the problem environment and practices of software risk management. In this section the findings are summarized and their implications for project management are discussed.

What are the most critical software risk items and do they vary from one context to another?

The ranking of the risk items showed significant agreement among project managers. Therefore, checklists form a reasonable tool to orchestrate risk management tactics and should be adopted widely as a standard project-planning tool. In this sense, the findings support claims made in earlier studies. However, in addition significant differences between the Finnish and US data were observed, both in the overall ranking and in ranking specific risk items. This suggests that practitioners should be careful when applying risk item rankings and checklists in their own environments. Instead, they should try to develop an understanding of their typical risk profiles and checklists, as neither Boehm's ranking nor any other checklist will be universally applicable. In contrast, some risk items—for example the continuing stream of requirements changes and unrealistic schedules and budgets—seem to be more general, and could be used as a "fixed" part of any risk item list. The prominent place obtained by these risk items also highlights the necessity to invest in the quality of requirements specifications, creating shared understanding on system requirements, and exercising strict change control. This is especially true in complex and uncertain situations.

To what extent is risk management actively pursued, what risk management principles and methods, if any, are used, and how commonly are they used?

The exploration demonstrates that the spread of risk management deliberations is relatively thin. Only 25% of project managers actively applied risk management methods. Yet a considerably larger number were engaged in activities (such as requirements scrubbing, prototyping etc.) which can reduce project risk levels. The main reason for the low usage is the astonishingly meagre understanding of the concept of risk, much of which is supported by the studies in Griffiths and Newman (1996). Most managers seem to be managing projects based on their past experience, following "gut feeling" and hoping for good luck. Therefore most managers would seem hardly ever to establish a conscious and systematic risk plan. The minority who used risk management tactics had positive experiences, and had continued their use. This finding suggests that considerable progress in this area can be achieved just by investing in project managers' training and by instituting measures that require managers to carry out risk analysis, for example by conducting obligatory project risk reviews.

This study has examined the general state of software risks and risk management practices. It helps to identify the most critical risks and to suggest improvements in how these risks can be managed. If there is an IT "productivity paradox", then failures in identifying and managing risks in software projects may well be contributory factors to disappointed expectations of the IT payoff. As such, improved risk assessment and management as discussed in this chapter would also seem to provide some obvious paths towards resolving some of these issues.

At the same time, the results here should be interpreted with caution due to the limitations in our study. Some other software risk items may have been ignored, because Boehm's top ten list has been derived with a project management focus and it lacks an integrating conceptual foundation (Lyytinen, Mathiassen and Ropponen, 1998). Moreover, some sampling bias may be embedded, as the project managers investigated come from one small country, though the sample was quite representative in terms of industries covered and types of systems developed. Finally, the study shares the limitations of all survey studies—it reports findings from a single period (Haga and Zviran, 1994). The results of this study can be extended in future research: 1) by introducing more systematic and coherent classification of risk items and their sources, 2) by analysing data from multiple project periods, and 3) by analysing software risk management in several contexts.

ACKNOWLEDGEMENTS

I am grateful to Professor Kalle Lyytinen for constructive and supportive guidance in completing this chapter, and to Lars Mathiassen, Esko Leskinen and Roy Schmidt for comments and constructive criticism.

NOTES

1 For example, there is some lack of rigour in deriving the list. Boehm only mentions that the list is "based on a survey of several experienced project managers" (Boehm, 1991, p. 35). The list was derived from interview data

and an available project database (Boehm, 1995a). Yet the ranking procedure is not systematic. The limitations also include that it only covers a software production-oriented part of software development and ignores, some say, implementation and political risks that were emphasized by some project managers participating in our interviews (see also Schmidt *et al.*, 1998). Therefore the ranking of Boehm's top ten risk items should not be understood as a complete ranking of all potential risk items, but of those that Boehm found in his studies. There may also exist a possible bias in the selection of risk items due to the emphasis on large software projects.

2 Altogether 14 questions from this list were derived. These were selected to cover essential methods in Boehm's list.

3 The author is indebted to several experienced project managers who helped to design and validate the instrument.

4 In addition, nine project managers were interviewed and part of the interview covered the ranking of the risk items. The interviews resulted in nearly the same ranking, the order of which was: unrealistic schedules and budgets, requirements changes, gold plating, personnel shortfalls, external components, external tasks, real-time shortfalls, straining the boundaries of computer science and wrong functions. The only major difference is with the ordering of wrong functions. The similarity between the two results demonstrates that the scores obtained are valid and do not vary considerably due to differences in the research instrument.

5 Kendall's coefficient for concordance (W) was computed for the ranking to measure the level of agreement between rankings (Siegel and Castellan, 1988). This measure expresses the degree of association between k-sets of rankings ($k = 71$) and can thus be used to study inter-test reliability. In other words, the coefficient W is an index of the divergence of the actual agreement from the perfect agreement. Obtained statistic value $W = 0.5685$ (average $aver_s = 0.5623$) was statistically very significant when tested using the Chi square test (chi square $= 282.53$, $df = 8$, $p < 0.01$). Thus, the obtained ranking reflects a very significant consensus among respondents.

6 The statistical significance of ranking differences between Boehm's and our list was tested by computing Kendall's rank-order correlation coefficient (T) for the pair of rankings (Siegel and Castellan, 1988). This coefficient is well suited to analysing agreement among subjects. The obtained statistical value for the rank-order coefficient T was 0.40, which demonstrates a significant difference among the rankings at the level of $p = 0.078$ ($N = 10$, $T = 0.4$). This test was utilized because sufficient information for goodness-of-fit tests (Chi square, Kolmogorov-Smirnov) is not available from Boehm's studies.

7 One explanation could be that project managers in our study did fare better in personnel management. Couger, Halttunen and Lyytinen's (1991) study on human and social skills of systems analysts and project managers in these two countries does not lend support to this claim. In both countries, project managers were badly skilled in managing people—even more so in the Finnish data.

8 1) Personnel shortfalls, 2) schedules, budgets, process, 3) COTS, external components, 4) requirements mismatch, 5) user interface mismatch, 6) architecture, performance, quality, 7) requirements changes, 8) legacy software, 9) externally performed tasks, 10) straining computer science.

9 A tentative analysis performed for Finnish data supports that risk items also vary according to environmental characteristics to some extent within our

sample. The environmental characteristics that seemed to have a bearing on the risks items are: 1) project length, 2) programming environment, 3) case tool utilization, 4) project manager general education, 5) project management training, 6) use of checklists, 7) status of risk management penetration in organization. In order to demonstrate this, we utilized variance analysis on average risk item rankings with a loose assumption of the normal distribution of the data set. Therefore these results need to be handled with particular care and are here left for further analysis.

10 This suggests that some respondents understood risk management methods more broadly than as just covering methods to assess risk exposure and leverage.

11 Some of the better managers may, however, do this unconsciously, as pointed out in Boehm's interviews (1989).

REFERENCES

Alter, S. and Ginzberg M. (1978). Managing Uncertainty in MIS Implementation. *Sloan Management Review*, Fall, 23–31.

Barki, H., Rivard, S. and Talbot, J. (1993). Toward an Assessment of Software Development Risk. *Journal of Management Information Systems*, 10, 2, Fall, 203–25.

Boehm, B.W. (1989). Software Risk Management: Tutorial. *IEEE Computer Society Press*.

Boehm, B.W. (1991). Software Risk Management: Principles and Practices. *IEEE Software*, January, 32–41.

Boehm, B.W. (1995a). *Personal communication*. Helsinki University of Technology, June 20.

Boehm, B.W. (1995b). *Software Risk Management*. Training material, Helsinki University of Technology, June 20.

Boehm, B.W. and Ross, R. (1989). Theory-W Software Project Management: Principles and Examples. *IEEE Transactions on Software Engineering*, 15, 7, 902–16.

Brooks, F. (1974). *The Mythical Man-Month. Essays on Software Engineering*. Addison-Wesley, London.

Charette, R.N. (1989). *Software Engineering Risk Analysis and Management*. Intertext Publications, McGraw-Hill, New York.

Charette, R.N. (1996). The Mechanics of Managing IT Risk. *Journal of Information Technology*, 11, 4, 373–8.

Couger, J.D., Halttunen, V. and Lyytinen, K. (1991). Evaluating the Motivating Environment in Finland Compared to the United States—A Survey. *European Journal of Information Systems*, 1, 2, 107–12.

Cronbach, L.J. (1951). Coefficient Alpha and the Internal Structure of Tests. *Psychometrika*, 16, 3, 297–334.

Curtis, B., Krasner, H. and Iscoe, N. (1988). A Field Study of the Software Design Process of Large Systems. *Communications of the ACM*, 31, 11, 68–87.

Davis, G.B. (1982). Strategies for Information Requirements Determination. *IBM Systems Journal*, 21, 1, 4–30.

Finnish Information Processing Association (1991). Individual Business Members, *Buyer's Guide 1991*. Infoline Oy/Insinöörilehdet Oy, Kustannusosakeyhtiö Otava, Keuruu.

Genuchten, M. van (1991). Why Is Software Late? An Empirical Study of Reasons for Delay in Software Development. *IEEE Transactions on SE*, 17, 6, 582–90.

Graeser, V., Willcocks, L. and Pisanias, N. (1998). *Developing the IT Scorecard: a Study of Evaluation Practices and Integrated Performance Measurement.* Business Intelligence, London.

Griffiths, C. and Newman, M. (eds) (1996). Theme Issue: Information Systems and Risk Management. *Journal of Information Technology*, 11, 4, 275–83.

Haga, W. and Zviran, M. (1994). Information Systems Effectiveness: Research Design for Causal Inference. *Information System Journal*, 4, 2, 141–66.

Igbaria, M., Greenhaus, J.H. and Parasuraman, S. (1991). Career Orientations of MIS Employees: an Empirical Analysis. *MIS Quarterly*, 15, 2, 86–106.

Laitinen, L. (1991). *Ohjelmistoprojektin Riskitekijat Ja Niiden Mittaaminen* (Risk Factors in Software Projects and their Measurement, in Finnish). VTT Technical Research Centre of Finland, Laboratory of Information Processing, October.

Lauer, T. (1996). Software Project Managers' Risk Preferences. *Journal of Information Technology*, 11, 4, 287–96.

Lyytinen, K. (1987). Different Perspectives on Information Systems: Problems and their Solutions. *ACM Computing Surveys*, 19, 1, 5–44.

Lyytinen, K. (1988). Expectation Failure Concept and Systems Analysts' View of Information System Failures: Results of an Exploratory Study. *Information & Management*, 14, 1, 45–56.

Lyytinen, K. and Hirschheim R. (1987). Information Systems Failures—a Survey and Classification of the Empirical Literature. *Oxford Surveys in Information Technology*, Oxford University Press, 4, 257–309.

Lyytinen, K., Mathiassen, L. and Ropponen, J. (1996). A Framework for Software Risk Management. *Journal of Information Technology*, 11, 4, 275–85.

Lyytinen, K., Mathiassen, L. and Ropponen, J. (1998). Attention Shaping and Software Risk—a Categorical Analysis of Four Classical Approaches. *Information Systems Research*, 9, 3.

Markus, L. and Keil, M. (1994). If We Build it, They Will Come: Designing Information Systems that Users Want to Use. *Sloan Management Review*.

Mathiassen, L., Seewaldt, T. and Stage, J. (1995). Prototyping and Specifying: Principles and Practices of a Mixed Approach. *Scandinavian Journal of Information Systems*, 7, 1, 55–72.

McFarlan, W. (1982). Portfolio Approach to Information Systems. *Journal of Systems Management*, January, 12–19.

Neo, B.S. and Kwong, S.L. (1994). Managing Risks in Information Technology Projects: a Case Study of TradeNet. *Journal of Information Technology Management*, May, 183–98.

Nunnally, J.C. (1978). *Psychometric Theory*. McGraw-Hill, New York.

Ropponen, J. (1993). *Risk Management in Information System Development*. Technical Report TR-3, Department of Computer Science and Information Systems, University of Jyväskylä, Finland.

Ropponen, J. and Lyytinen, K. (1997). Can Software Risk Management Improve System Development: an Exploratory Study, *European Journal of Information Systems*, 6, 41–50.

Schmidt, R., Lyytinen, K., Keil, M. and Cule, P. (1998). *Identifying Software Project Risks—an International Delphi Study*. Unpublished working paper,

Hong Kong University of Science and Technology, Hong Kong.

Siegel, S. and Castellan, J.N. (1988). *Nonparametric Statistics for the Behavioral Sciences.* 2nd edn, McGraw-Hill, New York.

Smolander, K., Tahvanainen, V-P. and Lyytinen, K. (1990). How to Combine Tools and Methods in Practice—a Field Study. In Steinholtz, B., Sølvberg, A. and Bergman, L. (eds) *Proceedings of CAiSE'90*, Springer-Verlag, Berlin, 195–214.

Straub, D.W. (1989). Validating Instruments in MIS Research. *MIS Quarterly*, June, 147–65.

Swede, van V. and Vliet, van J. (1994). Consistent Development: Results of a First Empirical Study on the Relation between Project Scenario and Success. In Wijers, G. and Brinkkemper, S. (eds) *Proceedings of the 6th CAiSE Conference*, Springer-Verlag, Berlin, 89–102.

Willcocks, L. (ed.) (1996). *Investing in Information Systems: Evaluation and Management.* Chapman and Hall, London.

Willcocks, L. and Margetts, H. (1994). Risk Assessment and Information Systems. *European Journal of Information Systems*, 3, 2, 127–38.

APPENDIX 8.1: KEY MEASURES IN THE SURVEY QUESTIONNAIRE

Risk Items

In the following we present ten possible sources of problems (risk items) that may occur in projects. Which one of them do you consider to be the most critical ones on the basis of your experience? Write in front of each item a number to order them in a relative ranking from 1 to 10 (1 = most critical risk item).

Ranking	Name of the risk item	Description
	Personnel shortfalls	Lack of qualified personnel and their change
	Developing wrong software functions	Development of software functions that are not needed or are wrongly specified
	Gold plating	Adding unnecessary features ("bells and whistles") to software because of professional interest or pride or users' demands
	Straining computer science capabilities	Inability to implement the system because of lack of technical solutions and computing power
	Real-time performance shortfalls	Poor performance of the resulting system
	Unrealistic schedules and budgets	Development time and budget estimated incorrectly (too low)
	Continuing stream of requirement changes	Uncontrolled and unpredictable change of system functions and features
	Shortfalls in externally furnished components	Poor quality of system components that have been delivered externally
	Developing wrong user interface	Inadequate or difficult user interface
	Shortfalls in externally performed tasks	Poor quality or unpredictable accomplishment of tasks that are performed outside the organization.

Risk Management Methods

In the following we ask questions about methods that deal with managing software risks. Mark one alternative that describes your own use of the method and knowledge of it. (Mark alternative *No info* when you don't know the method; and *Not used* when you know it, but don't use it. Mark either *Seldom* or *Often*, when you use the method based on the frequency of your use.)

Method description	No info	Not used	Seldom	Often
Do you use checklists to identify problems in your project?	1	2	3	4
Do you analyse key decisions, for example hardware decisions, subcontractors, timetables, budgets etc.?	1	2	3	4
Do you analyse design assumptions (for example "The size of the software is not underestimated", "Hardware will be delivered according to the timetable") in order to identify problems?	1	2	3	4
Do you analyse poorly defined parts of a project plan or specifications in order to find problems?	1	2	3	4
Do you use any cost models (a model is used to estimate costs based on e.g. the size of software, experience of personnel, features of hardware etc.) to estimate the cost to develop the software?	1	2	3	4
Do you use network analyses (for example PERT charts) to plan and coordinate a project plan's activities and timetables?	1	2	3	4
Do you use decision trees to estimate the seriousness of problems you have identified (their effects in terms of money, lost opportunity) and what can be done with them?	1	2	3	4
Do you use quality factor analyses (analysis of functionality, validity, maintainability, easiness of use, portability etc.) to identify problematic areas in software?	1	2	3	4
Do you use risk exposure methods (the estimated possibility of some event multiplied by the effects of that event in money or in other units) when prioritizing problems and alternatives?	1	2	3	4
Do you use the ratio of the risk exposure's reduction and its cost to prioritize issues, problems, alternatives?	1	2	3	4
Do you collect information about problematic parts of the system or software being chosen by developing prototypes, using analytical modelling, simulations or surveying properties of function etc.?	1	2	3	4
Do you try to avoid risks by trying to satisfy less ambitious objectives (for example by refusing a complex but efficient and elegant solution)?	1	2	3	4
Do you try to transfer the risks outside the system, for example by changing a check planned to be accomplished by the software to be done by users?	1	2	3	4
Do you use any of these methods repeatedly during the development process to control a project's performance?	1	2	3	4

APPENDIX 8.2: SURVEY INSTRUMENT VALIDATION AND SAMPLING BIAS

Great care was taken to improve the instrument validity. Using Straub's (1989) list of questions, we describe how the instrument was validated.

Content Validity

This question addresses whether instrument measures are drawn from all possible measures of the properties under investigation, i.e. are its questions drawn from a representative universal pool? Because software risk measurement is not a well-understood area, the issue of content validity is a serious one. We took several steps to improve content validity by examining available lists of software risk items and soliciting our questions from a representative sample. Based on their popularity and extensive empirical basis, we decided to apply Boehm's lists as a starting point (see e.g. Lyytinen, Mathiassen and Ropponen, 1998). This was also found to be appropriate because our sample was similar to Boehm's. We also discussed with experienced project managers and other qualified researchers how representative our set of questions was until we deemed it to be sufficient.

Construct Validity

This question addresses whether the measures show stability across methodologies, i.e. whether the data is a reflection of true scores of artefacts of the kind of instrument chosen. We sought to improve construct validity with several measures. First, we gathered the same data using both interviews and the questionnaire and compared the results for possible bias. Secondly we conducted pilot tests which led to modifications in the questionnaire and improved both the content and construct validity. In particular, we tested carefully that all interviewees could understand all items in the questionnaire, so that they could provide an unambiguous answer to each question. To improve this, we added to the questionnaire a list of items that described each technical term used (such as gold plating). During pilot testing, moreover, we asked the respondents to make suggestions to improve the questionnaire, e.g. by removing some items and adding new ones. This step introduced some amendments. We also analysed the possible discrepancies or variations in answers, but found none.

Reliability

This question shows the measures' stability across the units of the observation, i.e. that the same questions are answered exactly or approximately in the same manner. The idea of improving reliability is to decrease the possibility that the measure is due to misunderstanding, error or mistake, but instead reveals the true score. High correlations between alternative measures or large Cronbach alphas are usually signs that measures are reliable (Cronbach, 1951).The reliability of the risk item ranking could not be explicitly measured, as each of the risk items represents a distinct aspect and were ranked in ordinal scale. Instead, we computed reliability scores for the variables measuring the use of risk management methods because these items could be subject to bias. The results in Appendix 8.4 show that the standardized item alpha (0.7157) and the individual item alphas are above or close to the level of 0.70 suggested by Nunnally (1978) as adequate for exploratory research. Hence the reliability of the questionnaire measures can be regarded sufficient. Moreover, the reliability figure (Cronbach alpha 0.79) composed for risk management performance variables (reported elsewhere; see Ropponen and Lyytinen, 1997) in the same questionnaire suggests that sufficiently high reliability applies also for other measures in the research instrument.

Sampling Bias

We also investigated carefully reasons for not responding by calling 24 persons who had not replied. No bias in reasons for not responding was revealed. In fact, more bias would have been generated in our study, as three of the non-respondents did not have any experience in project management. Too little time and the rule of not responding to any surveys accounted for over 50% of the reasons. This suggests that our results in some sense can be biased to convey an overly positive description of the situation.

APPENDIX 8.3: RANKING OF SOFTWARE RISK ITEMS

Risk item ranking	Average ranking	Boehm's ranking	N	Standard Deviation	Median
1. Continuing stream of requirement changes	2.32	**6**	79	2.00	2
2. Unrealistic budgets and schedules	2.63	2	79	2.07	2
3. Developing wrong software functions	5.22	3	72	2.56	5
4. Gold plating	5.63	**5**	72	2.59	5
5. Real time performance shortfalls	6.12	**9**	74	2.37	6
6. Wrong user interface	6.19	**4**	73	2.44	6
7. Personnel shortfalls	6.30	**1**	75	2.46	6
8. Shortfalls in externally furnished components	6.50	**7**	73	2.59	7
9. Shortfalls in externally performed tasks	6.66	**8**	71	2.55	7
10. Straining computer science capabilities	6.79	10	72	2.64	7

APPENDIX 8.4: RELIABILITY SCORES FOR RISK MANAGEMENT METHODS

Standardized item alpha 0.7157.

In order to reveal true reliability scores for the use of risk management methods we used only categories 'not used', 'used seldom' and 'used often' in the computation of Cronbach coefficient alphas. This resulted 42 as the number of used observations used.

Risk management method	Alpha if item deleted
Checklists	0.6568
Decision driver analysis	0.6547
Assumption analysis	0.6701
Decomposition analysis	0.6512
Cost models	0.7085
Network analysis	0.7109
Decision analysis, decision trees	0.6743
Quality factor analysis	0.6708
Risk exposure	0.6755
Risk leverage	0.6780
Prototypes, analytical modelling	0.6653
Less ambitious objectives	0.6874
Risk transfer	0.6988

9
IT Projects and Assessment: Applying Benefits Funding at the California Franchise Tax Board

VALERIE A. GRAESER AND LESLIE P. WILLCOCKS
Oxford Institute of Information Management

INTRODUCTION

As detailed in the Introduction and Section I of this book, there is much debate in the academic and practitioner literature on the existence of an "IT productivity paradox". As we have seen, Brynjolfsson (1993) provided a number of possible explanations for the IT paradox, including measurement errors, timing lags due to learning and adjustment, redistribution and lack of IS/IT productivity at the firm level (see also Chapter 1). In Chapter 2, Willcocks and Lester examined these explanations and arrived at conclusions of their own for a way out of this seeming paradox. Their approach was dependent on introducing assessment systems integrated with business objectives and capable of identifying and supporting improvement areas (see also Chapters 6 and 7). In this chapter, we examine an organization not untypical in that it was confronted with the need for additional IT expenditure in a context of constrained financial resources and concern over past failure of large, risky IT projects—also quantified as a perceived IT productivity paradox. What type of approach can such an organization use to provide IT project funding in the face of a perceived IT productivity paradox, and what are the critical success factors that emerge from the project case histories in such an organization?

Beyond the IT Productivity Paradox.
Edited by L. P. Willcocks and S. Lester © 1999 John Wiley & Sons Ltd.

The organization in question is the California Franchise Tax Board (FTB), hereafter referred to as "the agency". The chapter explains the situation confronting the agency, then examines a generic description of the approach selected by the agency to solve its strategic technology needs. Two projects undertaken using the approach are then reviewed within the framework described. Finally, the agency's solutions are analysed against project results and the IT sourcing and productivity literatures in order to suggest explanations for the relative successes experienced.

The research method used for this case history was a set of qualitative interviews with involved individuals at various levels in both the agency and vendor organizations. More specifically, to obtain a comprehensive perspective of the selected approach and its related context, interviews were conducted with the following individuals:

- G. Alan Hunter, Assistant Executive Officer, Accounts Receivable & Tax Policy Support branch, FTB
- Ralph Shoemaker, Assistant Executive Officer, Technology and Resources branch, FTB
- John Vranna, Accounts Receivable Division Chief, FTB
- Carlos Zamarripa, Director PASS Project, FTB
- Eilene Wilson, Project Analyst, FTB
- John Podlipnik, Vice President, American Management Systems
- Danny Lemon, Project Manager, American Management Systems
- Charlie DeMore, Financial & Contract Analyst, American Management Systems

The interviews were conducted in a semi-structured format, following a general question outline. Interviews were taped, transcribed and reviewed to provide detailed information on the nature of the situation confronting the agency and the steps used to resolve the situation. Additional case-study details were made available by the vendor and agency in the form of presentation materials, contract excerpts and related project and company internal documentation.

CASE STUDY 1993–7: THE FRANCHISE TAX BOARD AND AMERICAN MANAGEMENT SYSTEMS

Pressures for Change

California's Franchise Tax Board (FTB), the state income tax agency, processes over $30 billion in annual tax revenues. At its most simplified level, the agency's mission is to bring in revenue for the state while providing numerous taxpayer services. Table 9.1 provides a high-level picture of both the structure and responsibilities of the agency.

Table 9.1 *The California Franchise Tax Board*

The agency	Business functions	Types of tax returns
• An independent board • 4500 employees • 17 California districts • Multi-state offices in Houston, Chicago, New York, Long Island	• Tax return filing • Revenue/collections processing • Tax policy support • Legislative services • Audits • Administrative services • Technology division	• Personal Income Tax ($22 billion approx. annually) • Banking and Corporation ($5.7 billion approx. annually) • Partnerships

The mass of returns processed and the amount of money involved have dictated a significant level of automation for the agency. However, developments within the tax agency in the early 1990s as well as external factors had begun to erode the agency's ability to manage its business. The agency had identified an increasing "tax gap" between revenues owed to the state and revenues collected. Additionally, the agency's ability to close the tax gap was significantly hindered by deteriorating technology support systems. Technologically, the agency's substantial requirements in automation exceeded—in scope and time frame—the ability of the staff to meet those needs. Project cycles were too long to be manageable, limited technological knowhow within the organization constrained efforts to implement improvements, and automation was fragmented across the agency (Podlipnik, 1996).

As a result of these issues, the agency constructed an organization-wide "strategic systems plan" in 1992. The intention of the plan was to provide a long-term (five- to ten-year horizon) blueprint for the organization's technology needs, including infrastructure and enabling technology investments, as they related to identified business needs, such as improved collections processing and target audit identification. Based on these issues, some degree of IT outsourcing was inherent in the plan (see also Chapter 10).

Although the strategic systems plan predicted that ten years would be required to modernize strategic IT systems (Cohen, 1996ab), the agency was anxious to progress with its plans. Unfortunately, following several recent IT disasters for other California public sector agencies publicized both within the state and nationally there were significant barriers to funding additional large-scale, high-risk IT ventures including unhappiness in the vendor community with the existing process, an aversion to risk on behalf of the overseers, and California's deep recession which placed inordinate demands on general funds. Consequently, the California legislature was sceptical about providing additional funding for IT-based projects for FTB and other California agencies where risk was perceived to be significant. FTB was caught in a seeming IT productivity paradox: given the history of wasted expenditure, why should the legislature commit to providing additional funding for unproven IT projects? Ultimately, it fell upon the agency to identify a convincing approach to funding the critical technology improvements identified in the 1992 plan.

A careful examination of the traditional low-cost procurement process used by the State of California demonstrated that this existing process merely reinforced the problems that the agency was trying to overcome (Betts, 1995; California Franchise Tax Board, 1995). In practice, the limitations were not untypical of other public- and private-sector IT environments (Willcocks, 1994; Willcocks and Griffiths, 1997). Specifically, the procurement process required that the requesting agency develop a stringent set of technical requirements ("Request for Proposal", RFP) which dictated a detailed solution to a particular business issue. The detailed technical nature of the RFP almost automatically classified a project as a "technology" project, without specifying the relationship between the value of the technology and the related business problem. In addition, the overly long RFP cycle combined with the rapid rate of technology advance and related protracted contract negotiation meant that the required technical solution was outdated even before a vendor was selected and design undertaken. Additionally, RFPs were put together by the agency staff. Dealing with business issues was hindered by whatever technological limitations existed within the staff. Ultimately, providing the best solution to the business problem got lost in the details. Whenever an RFP was signed into a contract, the participating vendor focused on providing the explicit technical requirements in the original RFP at low cost, with little or no emphasis placed on reviewing the solution for value and appropriateness to the organization. Clearly, the RFP process would not, in the 1990s environment, convince the legislature to spend money on high-risk "technology" projects.

Developing an Approach: Performance-Based Procurement

The agency wanted to convince the legislature to provide funding for the agency's IT needs. Specifically, any solution to the funding issue needed to address:

1. overly long and unmanageable project cycles;
2. technological limitations within the agency;
3. the legislature's predisposition, in an era of limited funds, to perceive that, in proposed large-scale IT projects, risk was greater than reward; and
4. the focus on low-cost bids vs a focus on effective business solutions.

This section will generically describe the approach pursued by the agency. Afterwards, two projects conducted in the 1993–7 period will be discussed in detail.

FTB was among the California agencies attending a State of California IT Project conference in 1993, also attended by California oversight agencies, other service agencies and private executives. The agencies met to discuss problems with traditional procurement processes and related projects. The participants agreed that 1) small purchases, 2) commodity purchases and 3) large, complex procurements each required distinctive procurement solutions. FTB volunteered to lead a two-year experiment to develop and pilot a procurement solution for large, complex projects based on the already agreed-upon principles of:

- strategic partnering (see also Chapter 7);
- business-driven solutions;
- "best value" evaluation;
- performance-based payments.

In the course of those two years, FTB examined its business needs, conducted market surveys, and invested time in considering methods by which to deal with vendors as partners rather than adversaries. As a result of these exercises agency leadership determined that a "Performance-Based Procurement" (PBP) concept might be the answer to their problem. To use this process, the soliciting agency documented a business problem requiring a well-defined, strategic performance improvement (e.g. order of magnitude improvement in collections, and audit models designed to close the tax gap), then requested the assistance of a vendor not only in providing the technical solution, but first and foremost, assistance in determining a comprehensive business solution. According to this process, interested vendors invested time up front to learn the agency's business in order to craft a solution with assistance and expertise provided by the client. To satisfy the ultimate goal of performance improvement, vendor and client alike had to focus on a value-based solution that made appropriate tradeoffs of risk and reward, rather than focusing merely on low cost. Following Chapter 7, the value centre approach would be moved to "investment" rather than "cost". According to respondents, at that time this approach seemed to have obvious advantages over the former process:

- The agency identified its business problem in detail before a full technical solution had been reached, thus taking advantage of agency business knowledge.
- The vendor and client would work together to identify the "best value" solution (business benefit less cost).
- The client could then select a solution based on "best value" rather than on low cost.

Because this approach seemed to avoid outdated technological solutions engendered by the traditional low-cost procurement process, the agency decided to pursue the PBP process. However, it still required a funding mechanism that reinforced the desired performance improvement goals and, more importantly, convinced the California legislature to provide project approval.

Benefits Funding: a Measurement Mechanism

The underlying mechanism agreed on for effective application of the performance-based procurement process was "benefits funding". In simple terms, benefits funding translates to a vendor willingly taking on the up-front marketing and development costs of a technological solution, then receiving payment from pre-defined benefit streams, identified in the original contract and refined over the course of the project (as opposed to the client paying the vendor out of appropriate funds set aside for the purpose of a project). The approach has similarities with Private Finance Initiatives in the UK public sector, and with performance-based contracts offered by some large IT outsourcing vendors in the mid-1990s. Essentially, the vendor agreed to shoulder a significant amount of the financial risk related to the assumption of a project. Consequently, such funding arrangements focus the client and vendor on the successful delivery of the solution in a timely fashion, the client for the purpose of improving business processes quickly and the vendor in order to get paid.

Because the process represents the need for an effective risk–reward tradeoff, vendors who have concerns about their ability to deliver on time and with those specified performance improvements do not bid. This built-in elimination of "weak" vendors improves the chance of project success. Thus, through reduced financial risk to the state and improved chance of project success, benefits funding seemingly provided the lever required by the agency to induce the California legislature and other related control agencies to approve projects that might otherwise go unfunded.

During the identification of a technological solution to the business problem, agency and vendor would work together to identify the benefits resulting from the implementation of functionality delivered by the project. The benefits identified must be measurable indicators of improved performance. While the most straightforward measures were financial, such as additional revenues to the state or as reduced costs of business, other measures of efficiency and effectiveness gains (such as productivity, cycle time) were also appropriate. Such benefits were refined into "benefit streams" defining the particular source of the benefit as it relates to the project and the algorithm by which it is measured. Over the life of the project, benefits streams would be continually refined, so that on implementation the resulting benefits could be monitored and measured. These measures or benefits were ultimately used to drive not only the measurement process associated with determining the "success" of a project, but also to provide a guidepost for risk–value tradeoff decisions during the course of a project. John Podlipnik, AMS VP, explains:

> When I meet with the customer and there is an issue of scope, we immediately focus on the value of the item in question. If it is highly valuable, the customer and AMS are going to find a way to do it, either by trading off work of less value or by the customer and AMS determining an alternative funding approach.

PBP and benefits funding aimed to align business processes with technology initiatives. Moreover, subsequent measurement of the benefits resulting from process improvements and technological implementations were to be undertaken for the purpose of business management, rather than merely to create an arcane measure of some technological outcome/factor.

It is important to reinforce that performance-based procurement in combination with the benefits funding "measurement" process defines success according to measured results. It would seem that such measured results should be key factors in all projects. In reality, however, many projects fail because of indecisive measurement schemes, usually based on technical outcomes rather than business results (Willcocks and Griffiths, 1997).

Vendor Selection, 1993

Perhaps without fully realizing it, the agency and the State of California had pursued a process that made business needs the driver of IT development and implementation. That direction in and of itself dictated particular requirements for a vendor. At first, the agency believed that the PBP and related benefits funding solutions were a desirable alternative and that several vendors would be interested, but the agency was not sure who to approach, and how to solicit these vendors. Regardless, the agency had a firm belief, as expressed by Alan Hunter, that:

> there was a market ... because the vendor community knew that this was going to be a good way to continue doing business in bad times. It's better to do business on a deferred basis that not do business at all.

In mid-1993, the agency solicited the marketplace to research vendor interest in the PBP/benefits funding process. Six vendors were qualified as appropriate candidates, each being asked to sign a "Quality Partnering Agreement" specifying intentions to undertake with the agency a partnering process based on trust, open communication, and team-work. Only these qualified vendors would be allowed to bid on strategic projects outlined in the agency's strategic systems plan under the auspices of the PBP process.

Next, the agency had to decide how to define individual projects. The performance-based procurement process required that the agency prepare a business problem statement with a defined business scope in the form of a "Solicitation for Conceptual Proposal" (SCP). Strategic technology directions of the agency were outlined but specific technical requirements were not. The SCP was only released to the pool of prequalified vendors. Those who were interested would then review the agency technological situation and business problem in order to define a solution. This period of solution definition required a commitment on behalf of the client to provide "open books" to the vendors describing the state of computing within the organization, future needs and plans, and the business problem at hand. The vendor would take the responsibility for learning the client business, researching an appropriate technical solution, and ultimately presenting a comprehensive solution, which detailed any necessary process reengineering and organizational change, as well as the specific technology solution. The hope was that, with the vendor driving technologically, the client would be free to do what the client does best—analyse the business processes and provide relevant information to the vendors:

> Through the agency–vendor partnership, the combined capabilities of both the public and private sector could be brought to bear to identify the best value solution. (John Podlipnik)

The agency had identified its desire to create long-lasting partnering agreements with vendors in order to provide cohesive business solutions built on a solid infrastructure, known to and understood by the vendor. Yet the agency did not ultimately want to contract out on-going support of delivered products; rather, it envisioned knowledge exchange between the vendor and the agency (Hunter and Podlipnik, 1996).

This definition period comprised a series of face-to-face meetings between the agency and competing vendor partners over a period of two to three months. Prospective vendors provided verbal proposals in exchange for real-time feedback from the agency, ultimately resulting in a set of comprehensive solutions proposed by qualified vendors. Consequently, not only did the agency have on-going access to recommended solutions, it also had a better idea of its ability to work closely with prospective vendors. Ultimately, to select a vendor to undertake the contract process, the agency reviewed the proposed solutions based

on business functionality provided, technological dimensions, perceived partnering ability, and financial benefits/costs to FTB (Darling,
1996a).

The Contract

The contract resulting from a PBP/benefits funding procurement documents anticipated benefit streams, the projected annual amount of
benefit improvement (expressed in dollars) and a proposed formula for
benefit measurement. Such a contract specifies that the vendor would
be paid from the benefit stream improvements identified and related to
the implementation of the business solution. Payment schedules would
be included, as would contingencies for higher or lower than expected
benefits. In any case, as long as the benefits were realized in some
degree, the vendor would be paid up to a contracted cap amount, the
differentiating factor being time. Clearly, there was an incentive for the
vendor was being incented to develop and deliver a solution that
provided planned-for benefits. The agency, on the other hand, was also
induced to provide the most benefit-enhancing solution, since the more
benefits were delivered, the faster the agency could pay the vendor, as
well as accrue financial gains to itself.

Project Organization

Once a PBP/benefits funding contract was signed, a project could begin.
Project roles and organization differed very little from traditional projects; the significant difference was the addition of a "benefits funding"
specialist responsible for determining the benefits to be had from the
business solution and adjusting the benefit measurements as the project
progressed. These roles and the related project structure will be examined in more detail in the next section.

PROJECT EXPERIENCES WITH
PERFORMANCE-BASED PROCUREMENT

The agency pursued the performance-based procurement process for
several projects. Two of those projects will be described here, then sub-
jected to more critical analysis in the analysis and discussion section.

Project 1: Collection Account Processing System (CAPS),
1994–7

In the strategic technology plan, several business problems were identified relating to collections processing and the auditability of pass-

through entities. Collections processing improvement was agreed on as the most critical need and documented in a Solicitation for Conceptual Proposal (SCP) between late 1993 and early 1994. From a field of several preferred vendors, American Management Systems (AMS) was ultimately awarded the contract for the Collection Account Processing System (CAPS) project in March 1994. The contract identified anticipated benefits streams in the form of improved collections of $7.4 million annually, while the vendor payment cap equalled $5.5 million. Once the contract commenced, project members worked together to provide a baseline measure of revenues against which to evaluate resulting benefits. The agency and AMS agreed to specify in the CAPS contract that AMS would only receive payments from incremental state revenue collections resulting from the implementation of the project solution. On the other hand, failure to obtain any identified benefits would result in no payment to AMS; less than anticipated benefits would result in slower payments to AMS, or reduced payment depending on the amount of obtained benefits (internal documentation: contract).

The CAPS project focused on four functions:

1. collector workflow management;
2. definition and validation of collection models;
3. support for external agency collections; and
4. supervisory/management functions within collections processing.

AMS had proposed the use of the proven packaged collections product "Computer Assisted Collections System" for government (CACSPlus) as the foundation software for the project. A client-server architecture that included a graphical user interface would be developed. The final three-tiered architecture ran on an IBM RS/6000 with key components of Unix, Powerbuilder and Sybase. The agency's relatively low technology maturity in light of these products dictated that both client and vendor would spend time working closely together tailoring the software based on user/client needs related to the business problem.

A project team was assembled including 25 AMS analysts, programmers and project managers, as well as 10 FTB systems employees. The project was to be jointly managed by AMS and FTB management. The PBP/benefits funding approach created an environment wherein this team engaged in on-going negotiation rather than a user/IS gap-like arrangement. According to John Vranna, the agency's Accounts Receivable Division Chief and the person given oversight of CAPS project, the project environment provided by PBP/benefits funding encouraged clearer and more focused thinking about the end result:

> Benefits makes you think more clearly, and the staff thinks more clearly, about the rationale as to why we are bringing on these systems in the first place ... moreover ... AMS acts as a nice barometer for us because they don't want to spend money on things they don't think add value since they must front the money and the risk.

The solution was implemented nine months after the project began. Incremental revenues began to roll in almost immediately. Over the course of two years, improved collections translated to an additional $94.8 million for the agency. AMS was paid the full $5.5 million in one payment within three months. After a combined cost of approximately $11.6 million (between AMS's $5.5 million and the agency's costs), the project made $81 million "profit". This initial effort between AMS and the agency formed the basis for a more comprehensive, long-term relationship between the two parties. Contrary to the prevailing notion that vendor/client relationships in traditional RFP-type contracts result in contentious arrangements, the relationship resulting from the PBP/benefits funding CAPS contract was mutually described by both parties as an effective give-and-take relationship based on trust and respect (Walsh-Grisham, 1996). The relationship begun on the CAPS project provided the basis for the second project now described.

Project 2: Pass-Through-Entity Automated Screening and Support System (PASS), 1995–7

The second contract undertaken between the agency and AMS dealt with another major issue identified in the FTB 1992 strategic technology plan: auditing effectiveness and efficiency. PASS developed around the simple business problem that pass-through entities had, for some time, remained fairly inauditable and contributed little in the way of revenue to the agency. Pass-through entities are:

> business entities like partnerships and Subchapter S corporations where the tax liability or (more commonly) the tax benefit is not realized by the PTE itself; instead, the liabilities or benefits are passed through to the individuals, partners, shareholders, partnerships, and so on that own the PTE. (Darling, 1996b)

The PASS project focused on information access related to audit data, the development of a more effective PTE pre-audit process, audit modelling, and an auditor's desktop.

The contract identified four potential benefit streams including (internal documentation, contract):

1. effective assessment of bank and corporation audits with an estimated increase in resulting revenue of $10 million annually;
2. efficient bank and corporation audit process (fewer hours spent) with an estimated increase in related audit revenues of $12 million annually;
3. pass-through audit assessment, with a projected annual benefit of $8 million;
4. pass-through filing enforcement, with a projected annual benefit of $10 million.

The PASS contract, signed in March 1995, specified a fixed price for AMS of $22.2 million with five-year benefits in excess of several hundred million dollars. The PASS contract specifications with regard to anticipated benefit streams were similar to those identified in CAPS. Once the contract commenced, baseline measurements of the benefit streams were established to provide a basis for later measurement. As with CAPS, the contract provided an effective negotiation basis for the project. According to Charlie DeMore, AMS financial analyst, the contract "was written with flexibility" such that "as partners, we [AMS and the agency] can deal quickly and effectively with unforeseen problems before they become overwhelming".

The assembled project team included 35 AMS analysts, programmers and managers, as well as 35 FTB employees, made up of a combination of business analysts and systems staff. Both agency and vendor continued to focus on the desired benefits to tailor the solution. According to Charlie DeMore, in dealing with project issue disagreements, it was "really in both parties' interest for the benefit streams to be both significant and measurable/verifiable".

Within the project staff, a team comprising a vendor financial analyst (Charlie DeMore) and a client financial analyst (Eilene Wilson) took responsibility for more fully developing the benefit stream formulas over the course of the project. Charlie DeMore explained the process:

> Ultimately [benefits] evolved and as they were more carefully scrutinized, concrete measurement algorithms were developed to identify actual incremental revenue. That's where Eilene and I came in, looking at what actually could be reported and extracted and seen with hard numbers that come in on accounting reports that would document the types of benefits that seemed like the project should be able to produce.

Comparison formulae were created and enhanced, resulting in a benefits "cookbook". It is this cookbook that appropriate parties used to review benefit streams at appropriate intervals during and after the project, to identify enhanced revenue streams.

Over the course of the project, AMS and FTB staff worked closely together to develop a comprehensive business solution for the pass-thru auditing identification problem. Although the CAPS project had provided some degree of technological base for the PASS project, the agency users/analysts still depended on AMS staff for IS expertise. Eilene Wilson, FTB financial analyst, explained. "I think we were able to build a system that [FTB or AMS] would not have been able to build individually." In her eyes, AMS provided the resources that "made a difference to the success of the system".

The PASS project was implemented in several stages between mid-1995 and mid-1997. Benefits were measured quarterly and the predictions of $40 million annually in improved revenues to the agency as a result of the project are currently on target. As of March 1998, the project had generated a total of $63.9 million in additional revenues.

Emerging Results

Given the implementation of two projects, the client and the agency agreed on a set of results out of the performance-based procurement/ benefits funding process, represented in Table 9.2 (see above for financial outcomes).

According to respondents, the PBP/benefits funding approach to procurement resolved many of the problems encountered in traditional RFP procurement. The following points offered by respondents provide additional insight to Table 9.2.

Vendor–Client Partnering

Both AMS and agency personnel claim that the relationship resulting from the PBP contract was an enormous change from any they have experienced in traditional RFP procurements. Although relevant literature is sceptical about a client and vendor being able to forge a partnership, in this case both parties willingly describe their relationship as such. In fact, both parties view the completed projects as part of the infrastructure, in terms of both technology and relationship management, for on-going projects (Kory, 1995 and Podlipnik, 1996).

Premium on Delivery of Contracted Services

In traditional RFP-type contracts, the dictated technical solution precludes innovation and tends to result in a user (client)/IS specialist (vendor) gap. Unfortunately, many vendors play the "change order" game as a result; they use the strict technical specifications in the contract to defend their work, then attempt to charge the client for everything that does not fit within that confined scope. In the words of Alan Hunter, under "the old model, once you signed a contract everything else from there on was preparation for arbitration". In performance-based procurement, on the other hand, time comes at a premium: the vendor must be extremely confident of its ability to deliver quickly in order to get paid, and the client desires a quick solution in order to obtain the necessary business process improvements.

Scope control

Based on the mutual desire to design and implement a "valuable" solution, the scope of the technological solution remains controlled.

Lifecycle Definition of Benefits and On-going Measurement

Benefit streams are identified as part of the initial vendor–client relationship, while vendors are identifying potential technical and business process solutions to the proposed business problem. These benefit streams are refined over the course of the project by analysts from both parties specifically tasked with managing the benefits. Moreover, the benefits measurement approach provides a basis for and reinforcement of a continuous improvement programme for the client (Podlipnik and Shoemaker, 1995).

Alignment with Business Strategy

In this particular case, the agency outlined a broad-reaching technology plan that identified the high-level business problems in the organization prior to ever attempting to solve those problems with technology. Carlos Zamarippa elaborates:

> Business does not stay static and neither does technology ... so if you are going to use technology to change the way people do business, then you need some kind of model to give you the flexibility to match dynamic business problems with dynamic technology solutions.

Moreover, the benefit streams or measures developed for each project are business performance improvements, not merely measurements of technology implementation.

Flexible Contract (not Tied to Exacting Technical Specifications that Become Outdated over Course of Project)

Charlie DeMore explains that he frequently reviews "the contract to find areas of potential risk as far as delivery or as far as items that are

Table 9.2   *Emerging Results from PBP/Benefits Funding Process*

Traditonal RFP problem addressed	Action	Comment
1) Restrictive, detailed technical solution that hampers quality solution.	Engaging in on-going problem solution identification aimed at creating "valuable" business-driven solution.	The contract flexibility and the alignment with business strategy create an environment of mutually beneficial discussion and decision making.
2) User-IT specialist gap and adversarial client/vendor relationship in RFP environment.	Vendor–client partnering.	According to John Podlipnik, the basis of the relationship is an economic one: "funding [provided up front by the vendor] is a great catalyst for forming that partnership". The vendor realizes that it must deliver value to get paid. The client, on the other hand, has a huge investment in solving its business problem. Additionally, the client invests a great deal of resources to create a solution. Both parties have a fairly balanced risk–reward relationship. In short, both parties have strong incentives to partner.
3) Protracted contract disputes and bickering over RFP contract details.	Placing a premium on contracted services.	Podlipnik believes that "the fact that it's benefit funded creates a focus on [the project] on the part of a lot of people that keeps it on track". Additionally, any late delivery is far more costly than in the RFP approach.
4) Bickering over RFP contract details.	Controlling project scope.	Because of the mutually-beneficial decision-making environment, both parties are very critical of any "feature" that does not add directly to the "best value" of the technical solution.

5) Discontinuous project measurement in RFP approach.	Defining lifecycle benefits and ongoing measurement thereof.	The refined benefit streams resulting from the PBP process provide a set of measurements that encompass the life of the project. Additionally, the client is left with a measurement and management approach that enables the implementation of an on-going, continuous programme.
6) Technology-driven nature of RFP solution.	Aligning IT strategy with business strategy.	Because the PBP process starts with the search for a solution to a stated business problem rather than the dictation of a specific technical solution, the ultimate use of technology to solve the business problem is readily aligned with the business strategy.
7) Inflexible RFP contract.	Creating a flexible contract.	The contract resulting from the PBP process did not contain a highly specific technical solution; rather, it contained an agreed solution to a business problem with the flexibility to adopt the solution to changing circumstances.
8) Restricted technical solution in RFP.	Introducing innovation.	According to Podlipnik; ''you are balancing leading edge with risk . . . you are leveraging the investments the vendor community has made in leading-edge resources so you can come up with novel solutions built from scratch rather than suboptimal solutions that deliver suboptimal value''.
9) Low-cost RFP solutions that do not provide competitive advantage.	Creating competitive advantage for the customer.	The PBP/benefits funding process allows the vendor to pursue ''competitive'' projects (vs low-cost ones); consequently, the client can take advantage of the competitiveness introduced.
10) Outdated, restricted solutions in RFP process that do not align with strategy.	Achieving strategic goals.	The vendor community is induced to identify the best value solution that aligns with the strategic goals of the client.

not very explicit in terms of requirement, and trying to proactively deal with these issues before they become issues".

In summary, the PBP/benefits-funding approach has been seen to have the following benefits.

1. *Allows innovation:* Because AMS specifically, and a vendor in general in a PBP process, shoulders the burden of development up front and provides a basis for knowledge transfer to the client organization, innovation is more readily fostered in such an environment than in the traditional RFP solution. Podlipnik notes that the "private sector is making significant investments in acquiring leading-edge resources in staff and product. And PBP takes advantage of these investments by allowing innovative solutions to be bid." Additionally, Shoemaker explains "that the best projects are more cutting edge projects ... because such a project has a lot of high risk but there's huge rewards sitting out there if it's successful".

2. *It creates competitive advantage for the customer:* As Podlipnik explains, a PBP/benefits funding process allows a vendor to establish competitive advantage against merely a low-cost solution. In parallel, the client customer now has access to a form of competitive advantage not available under an RFP contract. Shoemaker agrees: "With the old model, we were rigid and we were bureaucratic; we have a new model that is competitive."

3. *Achievement of strategic goals:* Alan Hunter and Ralph Shoemaker believed that their strategic systems plan would take ten years to put in place in its entirety. The PBP/benefits funding process has introduced a process that creates a partnering relationship with a vendor and, consequently, the ability to attain strategic goals leveraging the skills of both parties.

ANALYSIS AND DISCUSSION

To provide a background for analysis, we will look at the AMS/FTB partnership in terms of the much-documented IT productivity paradox and against the background of researched IT outsourcing selection criteria.

Assessing the IT Productivity Paradox

The State of California and its previous experiences with a variety of large-scale, high-risk IT projects provides an adequate representation of a seeming IT productivity paradox experienced in the organization: where is all our money going and what are we getting for it? In such an environment, public agencies in the State of California have been faced with the conundrum of requiring technological solutions with a difficult-to-justify price tag. Herein lies the crux of the debate about IT measurement.

The solution that the Franchise Tax Board chose to pursue—performance-based procurement bolstered by benefits funding—removed the critical focus from the technology and refocused on the business problem at hand. In doing so, the agency subsequently did attain the much talked-about IT alignment with business strategy. However, it did not appear to make this alignment the ultimate goal; rather, the agency chose to let the business needs drive the use of technology, whatever that technological solution may be.

In addition, to monitor the effectiveness of the selected business solution, benefit streams were identified and refined over the course of the project to provide the basis for establishing benefits resulting from the implementation of the project(s). This "measurement" process provided the cornerstone of the ability to manage the business solution and technological implementation. In summary, the benefit streams measurement assisted in focusing both parties on the best value solution; only those features that suitably enhanced the resulting benefit streams would be included in the finally implemented solution. It would appear that AMS and FTB successfully utilized what was stipulated in Chapter 2, namely: "an emphasis on a cultural change in evaluation from control through numbers to a focus on quality improvement ... as one of the better routes out of the productivity paradox".

IT Sourcing Criteria: How Does the FTB/AMS Case Fit?

A model for sourcing criteria is shown in Table 9.3, based on Willcocks and Lester (1996) (see also Chapter 2).

Without in-depth analysis, it might appear that, with respect to the outsourcing decision outlined in the table, the Franchise Tax Board should not have contracted with AMS for the CAPS and PASS projects. Closer analysis, however, will reveal that the agency's IT sourcing decisions can be explained in relationship to each of these criteria.

1. *Future business needs:* Given the nature of public-sector organizations and the budgetary unknowns from year to year, many future business needs for an agency like FTB could rarely be classified as "certain". On the other hand, the agency created a technology plan

Table 9.3   *IT Sourcing Criteria*

Criteria	Tend to outsource	Tend not to outsource
Are future business needs ...	certain	uncertain
Is the potential contribution of this IT service/activity to business positioning a ...	commodity	differentiator
Is the impact of this IT service/activity on the business strategy ...	useful	vital
Is the in-house cost for this IT service/activity compared to the marketplace ...	high	low
Is this IT service/activity ...	discrete	integrated
Is the technological maturity of the client organization ...	high	low
Is the IT capability in-house compared to the marketplace ...	low	high

in 1992 to outline a strategic direction for the organization. It would seem that this plan created some sense of certainty of both business and technological direction for the organization, thus justifying an outsourcing decision if based solely on this criteria. In addition, the existence of such a plan helps the vendor to move in the right direction and provide reinforcement for a longer-range plan through appropriate infrastructure/architecture decisions during the course of a contract such as CAPS or PASS.

2.   *Potential contribution of IT service/activity to business positioning:* In the case of the CAPS collection system, the agency is dealing with a commodity-like system—the sourcing decision in favour of AMS appears effective if based solely on this criteria. The PASS system, on the other hand, is more of a differentiator product, providing the agency with a "strategic" advantage in terms of identifying audits; at first glance, perhaps not a good candidate for outsourcing. Regardless of this, given that the agency is a public-sector agency, it must provide "world-class" service from its systems lest its existence as a public agency (supported by tax dollars) be questioned. As we have seen in the performance-based procurement used by the agency in both these instances, however, the agency and AMS have a "50–50" relationship in the development process *and* the systems will ultimately be operated by agency staff. Consequently, the partnering aspect of the AMS/FTB relationship rationalizes the outsourcing decision in spite of at least one seeming "differenti-

ator" application. However, the IT sourcing criteria would suggest considerable risks inherent in outsourcing that still need to be mitigated.

3. *Impact of IT service/activity on business strategy:* Both the PASS and the CAPS projects are "vital" to the agency's business strategy and, as such, are seemingly not good candidates for outsourcing. In the case of CAPS, at least, it can be argued that, given its "vital commodity" definition, "best sourcing" is the best option (Lacity, Willcocks and Feeny, 1996). Once again, however, the agency's outsourcing decision placed only the development of these applications in the hands of AMS, not the ongoing operations/ maintenance. And as in the case with potential contribution to business positioning, the integrated nature of the FTB/AMS relationship provides a rationalization for the outsourcing decision.

4. *In-house cost for IT service/activity:* For both CAPS and PASS, the cost of doing the project in-house is prohibitive in terms of time. On this dimension, the decision to outsource makes sense.

5. *Discrete/integrated IT service/activity:* Both CAPS and PASS are part of a larger, integrated set of applications used by the agency, which would be an argument for either not outsourcing at all or for "total" outsourcing (see Chapter 10), including on-going maintenance and operations. The decision to outsource in contradiction to the integrated nature of the products is rationalized by the agency's and AMS's desire for a long-term, strategic "partnership".

6. *Technological maturity of user organization (in an absolute sense, not relative to the market):* The agency admittedly did not have the technological knowhow in-house to carry out the PASS and CAPS projects and, based solely on such an aspect according to the proposed model, perhaps should not have outsourced these two projects. However, Feeny, Earl and Edwards's (1997) model of user (client) and IS specialist (vendor) roles provides a critical insight to the AMS/agency situation. The model suggests that in situations of low technological maturity, a user focus should be adopted, with a multifunctional team of users and IT people driving development in order to build up mutual learning on technical capability and business applicability. In situations of high technological maturity where there are fewer problems and the technology is stable, technical specification and business requirements can be more closely defined, and users can allow IT specialists (either in-house or external vendor) to develop and implement with less user oversight. The PBP process forced the client user and IT staff to be very involved during design in identifying business needs and learning alongside the vendor how to implement these needs technologi-

cally. In fact, business needs were quantified and monitored in these instances by benefit streams.

7. *IT capability in-house compared to marketplace:* The agency's in-house capability is low compared to the marketplace; consequently, on this dimension taken by itself, the decision to outsource makes sense.

Critical Success Factors

In light of the analysis provided, it appears that the two most critical factors determining the success of the AMS/FTB deal were:

1. *The preferred contractor relationship* formed by the agency and AMS (or "partnering" quality): both client and vendor were given an incentive by shared risk and reward to produce results. The two parties both played significant roles in achieving results and had longer-term inducements to make the partnership productive (for comparison see Willcocks and Kern, 1998).

2. The *contract* clearly defined the expected benefits from the project, providing a value-based target for both parties, as well as providing the setting for the two parties actively to engage in problem solving on an as-needed basis. Additionally, in these two contracts, the client and vendor were induced to produce a high-quality, marketable solution because of the strategic importance of the solution to their position in the marketplace, based on the contract specification of a royalty to be paid to the agency in the case of future sales of the product by AMS to other parties (for the criticality of the contract, see also Willcocks, Lacity and Fitzgerald, 1995 and Chapter 10).

Hunter elaborates on the long-term perspective:

> Any given project you were working on with a business partner today ought to be viewed as the least significant project because the next unknown project, potentially much bigger, much more profitable and much more ground-breaking, is the one you are really preparing for.

The following critical success factors formulated in the series of case study interviews all clearly align with either the contract factor, the partnership factor or both, lending additional credence to the significance of these two determinants of success. They also align very closely to critical success factors we have found in other major IT projects (see Lacity, Willcocks and Subramanian, 1996; Willcocks and Griffiths, 1997).

Vendor/Client Relationship (Partnering Quality)

Both parties had a desire to maximize benefits; consequently, the two parties were forced into a position where hard decisions had to be made up front in order to gain benefits. As mentioned earlier, client and vendor operated with a common set of goals in mind, driving the process to an effective discussion of outcomes. Hunter explains that:

> we gave our project managers considerable latitude to make decisions ... we did *not* say "we'll be back in three weeks after the executive committee has reviewed it"; rather, we had the feeling that we were able to make decisions.

Know the Business (Partnering Quality)

In order to develop an effective business solution, the client had to understand its business and the vendor had to be willing to enhance its own business knowledge. Under the PBP/benefits funding approach, the vendor's need to learn the client's business and not just focus on technology was a significant one. A "user focus" approach resulted from these necessary interactions. The vendor also had to understand the availability and practicality of using strategic technology and determine how to apply it intelligently in concert with the business solution to provide the client with needed expertise. Shoemaker contended that:

> The business side of the partnership has to be competent ... if I were a vendor, I wouldn't do business with them [incompetent client] on a performance basis because I would not have the confidence they could uphold their half of the bargain.

Results Must be Quantifiable (Contract Quality)

Benefit streams related to the chosen business solution had to be readily quantifiable so that concrete measurements were available.

Executive Support (Partnering Quality)

So that intentions are understood throughout both the client and vendor organizations, both must have high-level executives committed to the resulting interchange of ideas and focus on best value. As demonstrated earlier based on Podlipnik's quote about issue resolution, conversations at the executive level were value focused rather than merely cost focused.

Commitment from Key Staff (Partnering Quality)

The benefits funding solicitation process requires the active engagement of client staff to sharing business processes with vendors. The vendor also had an incentive to commit significant time and staff resources during the procurement process in order to learn the client business and develop an appropriate business/technical solution.

High-Result, High-Risk Projects (Contract Quality)

In the circumstances of the two projects analysed, given the enabling factors present, PBP/benefits funding emerged as appropriate for high-risk, strategic projects, not least because these types of projects offered measurable, strategic business results that incented salient stakeholders.

Measurement System (Contract Quality)

The benefit streams specified in the contract create a measurement mechanism that pervades the life of the project, providing the basis for negotiation on the solution to be delivered.

CONCLUSIONS

In summary, in Chapter 2 Willcocks and Lester suggested a lifecycle measurement approach combined with an "emphasis on a cultural change in evaluation from 'control through numbers' to a focus on quality improvement" as a way out of the seeming IT productivity paradox experienced by many organizations. The PBP/benefits funding process adopted by FTB and carried out with the vendor AMS provides support for that suggestion. In Chapter 7, Venkatraman provided an analysis of the use of IT resources falling into at least four different value centres. The present chapter shows how one organization attempted to shift its management of IT resources from a cost to an investment centre approach. PBP created a solution-driven approach to resolving a business problem, thus aligning the possible technical solutions with the business strategy. Benefits funding provided the mechanism driving parties in the same direction, the client because of the desire for a comprehensive effective business solution in return for time spent developing a solution, and the vendor in order to obtain payment from resulting benefit streams.

It is important to identify potentially extenuating circumstances that may have affected the PBP/benefits funding process in these particular instances:

- The executive officer of the FTB organization, Jerry Goldberg, is not appointed and has been in office for 15 years. This continuity may have contributed to the success of this approach in a manner not herein examined.
- FTB was driven to pursue an alternative procurement method based on a comprehensive strategic systems plan. Without such a plan, the successful client/vendor relationship between AMS and FTB could have been more limited in scope.
- FTB and AMS successfully pursued a PBP/benefits funding procurement process; their specific approach may not be ready-made for other vendor/client relationships. The process would probably have to be tailored to suit the organization in question.
- FTB is a public-sector agency. Without further research, it would be difficult to predict 1) whether the public sector is most effectively suited to PBP/benefits funding and 2) whether or not PBP/benefits funding would work in the private sector.

Finally, for AMS and FTB, IT measurement is a by-product of the larger-scale management process that dictates how the business solution is solved and, ultimately, how the vendor is paid. Consequently, measurement in this instance is truly measurement for the sake of management and decision making, rather than isolated, unaligned measurement of IT processes.

REFERENCES

Betts, M. (1995). Tax Collectors Going To New-Wave System. *Computerworld*, November 20, 5.

Brynjolfsson, E. (1993). The Productivity Paradox of Information Technology. *Communications of the ACM*, 36, 67–77.

California Franchise Tax Board (1995). *Performance Based Procurement: Another Model for California*. California Franchise Tax Board, Sacramento, California.

Cohen, L. (1996a). Re-engineering Revenue Collection, California Style. *ESPG Research Note*. Gartner Group, New York.

Cohen, L. (1996b). California's Performance-Based Procurement. *ESPG Research Note*. Gartner Group, New York.

Darling, C. (1996a). Need An App Integrator? Build a Relationship! *Datamation*, March 1, 23.

Darling, C. (1996b). A New Procurement Paradigm Builds Revenue. *Datamation*, March 1, 22.

Feeny, D., Earl, M. and Edwards, B. (1997). Information Systems Organization: the Roles of Users and Specialists. In Willcocks, L., Feeny, D. and Islei, G.

(eds) *Managing IT as a Strategic Resource*. McGraw-Hill, Maidenhead.

Glover, M. (1995). New Tool for Tax Collectors: Automated Systems Bringing in Millions. *The Sacramento Bee*, September 29, 5.

Hunter, A. and Podlipnik, J. (1996). *Forming and Managing High Performance Partnerships*. California Competes Institute, California.

Lacity, M., Willcocks, L.P. and Feeny, D. (1996). The Value of Selective IT Sourcing. *Sloan Management Review*, 37, 3, 13–25.

Lacity, M., Willcocks, L.P. and Subramanian, A. (1996). *Implementing a Global Client/Server Application: Plus Ça Change?* OXIIM Research and Discussion Paper 96/5. Templeton College, Oxford Institute of Information Management, Oxford.

Podlipnik, J. (1996). *Internal Document*. American Management Systems, California.

Podlipnik, J. and Shoemaker, R. (1995). *Partnering and Performance Based Procurement*. CFTB, California.

Walsh-Grisham, M. (1996). Business Benefit-Based Procurement: California Leads the Way. *G2 Monthly*, August, 1–6.

Willcocks, L. (1994). Managing Information Systems in UK Public Administration—Trends and Future Prospects. *Public Administration*, 72, 2, 13–32.

Willcocks, L. and Griffiths, C. (1997). Management and Risk in Major IT Projects. In Willcocks, L., Feeny, D. and Islei, G. (eds) *Managing IT as a Strategic Resource*. McGraw-Hill, Maidenhead.

Willcocks, L.P. and Kern, T. (1998). IT Outsourcing as Strategic Partnering: the Case of the UK Inland Revenue. *European Journal of Information Systems*, March, 7, 29–45.

Willcocks, L., Lacity, M. and Fitzgerald, G. (1995). *IT Outsourcing in Europe and the USA: Assessment Issues*. OXIIM Research and Discussion Paper 95/2, Templeton College, Oxford Institute for Information Management, Oxford.

Willcocks, L. and Lester, S. (1996). Beyond the IT Productivity Paradox. *European Management Journal*, 14, 3, 279–90.

10

To Outsource IT or not? Research on Economics and Evaluation Practice

LESLIE P. WILLCOCKS, GUY FITZGERALD AND MARY LACITY

Oxford University, Brunel University and University
of St. Louis

INTRODUCTION

Earlier chapters have touched on IT outsourcing issues (see particularly Chapters 2, 7 and 9). In this chapter we report detailed research into the many assessment issues raised for organizations contemplating information technology (IT) outsourcing. In some quarters in the 1990s, IT outsourcing was presented as a major way out of the many dilemmas packaged into the concept of the IT "productivity paradox". However, our own work suggests that pursuing IT outsourcing can create its own dilemmas and disappointments, and that detailed evaluation and, if the decision is made to outsource, detailed measurement and management are vital elements if a new, perhaps IT "outsourcing paradox" is not to arise (Lacity and Willcocks, 1996; Willcocks and Lacity, 1997).

Our earlier work on strategic sourcing suggested several major business and technical factors that need to be taken into account in any IT sourcing decision-making process (Willcocks and Fitzgerald, 1993; 1994). As outlined in Chapter 2, these developed into: degree of "technology maturity" (Feeny, Earl and Edwards, 1997); degree of business

Beyond the IT Productivity Paradox.
Edited by L. P. Willcocks and S. Lester © 1999 John Wiley & Sons Ltd.

uncertainty; whether IT is a commodity or differentiator, strategic or useful in business terms; the level of in-house capability relative to that available on the external market, and the degree of systems interconnectedness and complexity (see Willcocks, Fitzgerald and Feeny, 1995). However, also of critical concern is the degree to which IT outsourcing can amount to an economically effective decision, assessable and controllable as such both in the lead up to and across the life span of the contract. Indeed, while respondents in the present study pursued a range of objectives through IT outsourcing, their primary focus was most frequently the issue of whether or not outsourcing would achieve cost savings while maintaining or improving service levels. Economic and service issues tended to be perceived as forming the skeleton of any successful outsourcing deal.

There is already much advice, and indeed prior academic research, on the economics of IT outsourcing (see as examples only Aucoin *et al.*, 1991; Buck-Lew, 1992; Due, 1992; Gupta and Gupta, 1992; I/S Analyzer, 1990; Krass, 1990; Radding, 1990). However, as at 1998, with few notable exceptions—such as Bergstrom (1991, 1996), White and James (1996) and Lacity and Hirschheim (1993, 1995)—there is little work on how organizations make detailed comparisons with in-house options. A particularly noticeable gap is the inattention given to what emerges from our research as a significant relationship within IT evaluation practice. More specifically, this is the relationship between the characteristics of prevailing evaluation regimes, and the ease or difficulty experienced in carrying out an economically based IT outsourcing assessment. To add to the picture, despite the fact that, on recent estimates (Currie and Willcocks, 1997) IT outsourcing accounted for 6–7% of UK IT formal budget expenditure, there are virtually no published academic studies on these evaluation themes in the wider US and European, let alone the UK, context. The present chapter aims to address these gaps by drawing on evidence from survey and case study work carried out in 1993–6 into medium and large UK-based organizations that have contemplated or undertaken IT outsourcing. In so doing, it will also show that consideration of IT outsourcing may well prove a catalyst for forcing organizations to enhance their evaluation practices. In so far as improved practice contributes to more effective deployment of IT assets, as we saw in Chapters 8 and 9 for example, this can lead to some resolution of the IT "productivity paradox" as experienced in specific organizations.

The chapter first outlines the research base and methodology. Utilizing the survey and case study findings we then review the different evaluation routes that organizations have been found to be taking towards outsourcing IT. The pre-existing IT evaluation system can be a help or a major hindrance as a basis from which to assess vendor bids. The chapter reviews how organizations have gone about evaluating in-house performance and, from the organizational experiences investigated, derives a sounder platform from which to make any IT outsourcing assessment. The chapter then examines organizational experiences on assessing vendor bids against in-house options. We conclude by providing summary lessons on IT outsourcing economics, based on both our case study work and the research literature. Throughout, IT outsourcing will refer to the commissioning of third-party management of IT assets, people and/or activities to attain the required result. Elsewhere we have distinguished this from "insourcing", where a contract calls for a vendor to provide resources that are then deployed under the buyer's management and control (Lacity, Willcocks and Feeny, 1997).

RESEARCH BASE

The research reported here forms part of a larger study of the outsourcing of IT/IS activities in the UK. The overall research aimed to provide a comprehensive picture of IT sourcing practices, including evaluation practices, decision-making processes and post-decision experiences. The present chapter focuses only on findings on pre-decision evaluation issues. The overall research approach harnessed survey and case study techniques.

The Survey

Mintzberg (1979) suggests that successful research requires both systematic and anecdotal data, i.e. both hard and soft information, the hard to uncover relationships and the soft to help explain such relationships. Sympathetic to this view, our research design began with telephone interviews based on a relatively open-ended set of questions to validate the parameters for the study. A set of frameworks and hypotheses were developed for testing. A detailed postal questionnaire was then prepared. A sample of 1000 medium and large organizations was selected randomly from the contact database of Business Intelligence, a UK-based research organization. The questionnaire was sent to senior managers responsible for IT, and elicited a 16.2% response rate. Full details of the survey methodology and findings are published in Willcocks and Fitzgerald (1994).

A particular set of survey findings pointed to the need for detailed case study investigation into the evaluation practice that led up to IT outsourcing decisions. According to respondents, the major risk that materialized after outsourcing was hidden costs, a finding supported in more recent work (Currie and Willocks, 1997). These arose from failure to identify comprehensively present and future requirements, loose drafting of contracts, lack of awareness of costs of managing the outsourcing arrangement, and vendor opportunism. It became clear that many contracts were based on limited tracking of in-house performance and limitedly informed evaluation of vendor bids. Additionally, the top three "very difficult" problems encountered when trying to make decisions on IT outsourcing were cited as: finding convincing evidence of the value of IT, evaluating the in-house effectiveness of IT, and defining service levels. Organizations that had outsourced were also asked if they could quantify the costs and benefits. Worryingly, 9% could not, while 24% had not tried. An additional strong finding from organizations that had outsourced was the recognition of the importance of defining service levels, evaluating costs and monitoring performance more closely than they were doing (Willcocks and Fitzgerald, 1994). Faced with this survey evidence and corroborative evidence from other research-based studies (see Lacity and Hirschheim, 1993; Willcocks, Lacity and Fitzgerald, 1995), we then needed to acquire a more in-depth understanding in order to discover patterns of assessment leading up to an IT sourcing decision, how organizations evaluated in-house performance, and how vendor bids were assessed.

Multiple Case Studies

In order to develop this detailed understanding of IT sourcing practices, we supported the survey with a multiple case study approach. Here an interpretivist perspective was adopted initially. Assuming as the interpretivist perspective does that the most valid way to understand complex social phenomena is to enter into dialogue with people directly, we aimed to interview different stakeholders within the organizations (Van Maanen, 1979; Walsham, 1995; see also Chapter 12). During the period 1993–5 we interviewed 106 participants at 26 organizations (see Table 10.1). The interviews were then used, together with relevant published and internal documentation—including outsourcing contracts, benchmarking reports and outsourcing bids—to develop case studies of IT outsourcing.

Although we make no claims of a random sample, the choice of the case studies was based on the notion of "theoretical sampling" (Pettigrew, 1990). This is where researchers select cases representing polar extremes that enable comparison across important aspects of the evaluation and decision domain. We sought organizations with a wide variety of sourcing experiences, both in terms of degree of "success" claimed and degree of outsourcing, ranging from "total" outsourcing (80% or more or IT budget outsourced) through selective outsourcing, to total insourcing. With this design we sought to generate insights into best sourcing practices by comparing "successes" and "failures". Respondent organizations were identified from personal contacts, published sources and database listings from several research organizations. As Table 10.1 reveals, the accumulated cases cover a wide spectrum of industries and sectors. Nineteen are characterized as large (as designated by their existence in the Fortune 500 or Financial Times European 1000), while the rest are large public-sector bodies or recently privatised medium-sized organizations.

Data Collection

For each case site we conducted face-to-face interviews where possible, with individuals directly involved in the sourcing decisions on behalf of the organization or outsourcing vendor. Each of these interviews lasted between 45 minutes and two hours. In the case of 21 out of the 106 respondents we conducted telephone interviews of between 20 and 40 minutes in length. Interviewees included senior business and IT managers who sponsored sourcing evaluations, relevant IT and contract staff, outsourcing consultants hired to assist contract negotiations and vendor account managers responsible for the execution of any resulting contract. All participants were assured of anonymity so as to promote open discussions. A full listing of respondents categorized by job appears in Table 10.1.

Interviews followed the same protocol, proceeding from an unstructured to a structured format. In the unstructured portion, participants were asked to tell their sourcing story. They were then asked semi-structured questions designed to solicit information on specific issues absent from their previous recollections. These issues included coverage of the scope of the sourcing decision, sponsors, the sourcing evaluation process, contract negotiations, details of any contract, and contract management. All participants were also asked to assess the decision outcome in terms of their perceptions of "success" or "failure". When participants expressed a viewpoint they were prompted to provide specific supporting evidence in the form of documentation, and in some cases further anecdotal evidence. Participants were also asked specific questions about their organization and IT department. The interview guide is detailed in Appendix 10.1.

Table 10.1   Case Study Profiles

Company, industry, size in terms of revenue* and MIPS	Participants	Sourcing decision(s)¹	Year of decision(s)	Formal RFP	No of bids	Length of contract	Expected cost savings	Cost savings achieved	Initiator of the decision(s)
1. RETAIL 1 UK clothing and housewares retailer* > 150 MIPS	1. Logistics Director 2. Contract Manager 3. Vendor A/C Manager 4. Branch Manager	Total outsourcing	1993	Yes	4	10.5 years	25%	Too early to determine	IT Managers
2. PETRO1 UK oil* > 150 MIPS	5. IT Manager 6. In-house Consultant 7. In-house Consultant 8. Vendor A/C Manager 9. Contract Manager	(a) Selective: diverse services (b) Selective: a/cting services (c) Total outsourcing	(a) 1988–90 (b) 1991 (c) 1993	(a) Yes (b) Yes (c) Yes	(a) 4 (b) 3 (c) 6	(a) 3 years (b) 4 years (c) 5 years	(a) 15–20% (b) 20% (c) 20–25%	(a) Yes (b) Most (c) Less than 20%	(a) IT Managers (b) Senior Managers (c) Senior Managers
3. ELECTRIC European electronics* > 150 MIPS	10. IS Director 11. Vendor IS Manager 12. Senior Manager 13. Marketing Manager	(a) Selective: software development and support (b) Total: telecoms and data centres	(a) 1989 (b) 1991	(a) No (b) No	(a) 1 (b) 1	(a) 5 years (b) Annually renewable	(a & b) No cost savings estimated, desire to create variable IT costs	(a) Some cost savings (b) Some savings achieved	(a) Senior and IT Managers (b) Senior and IT Managers

Organization	Interviewees	Type	Year		Number	Years	%		Decision makers
4. INSURANCE UK insurance* < 50 MIPS	14. IS Director 15. Vendor A/C Manager 16. Senior Manager 17. Consultant	(a) Total Outsourcing (b) Selective: maintenance (c) Total insourcing	(a) 1990 (b) 1991 (c) 1993	(a) No (b) No (c) Yes	(a) 1 (b) 1 (c) 2	(a) 1 year (b) 1 year (c) 1 year	(a) No (b) 25–30% (c) 30%	(a) No (b) Yes (c) Yes	(a) Senior and IT Managers (b) As above (c) As above
5. PSB1 UK Inland Revenue Service (PSB)[2] > 150 MIPS	18. IS Director 19. Line Manager 20. IS Operation Manager 21. Outsourcing Consultant	Total outsourcing	1994	Yes	6	10 years	Some savings envisaged	Too early	Government Ministers and IT Manager
6. UTILITY1 UK water company 20 MIPS	22. Business Manager 23. IS Director 24. Manager Operations 25. Vendor A/C Manager	Selective: customer billing systems	1991	Yes	2	5 years	20%	Yes	IT Manager
7. PETRO2 US petroleum refining* > 150 MIPS	26. Director of IS 27. Controller 28. Manager Network Services 29. Data Centre Manager 30. Supervisor Technical Support 31. Manager Applications	Selective: data centre	1991	Yes	2	5 years	16%	Unable to determine	IT Manager
8. RETAIL2 UK retail and distribution* > 300 MIPS	32. Principal, IT Consultant 33. Group IS Director 34. Vendor A/C Manager 35. Business Manager	(a) Selective: corporate telecom (b) Selective: telecom	(a) 1990 (b) 1992	(a) Yes (b) Yes	(a) 3 (b) 3	(a) 3 years (b) 2.5 years	(a) 20% (b) 30%	(a) Yes (b) Yes	(a) IT Managers (b) IT Managers

Table 10.1   *Continued*

Company, industry, size in terms of revenue* and MIPS	Participants	Sourcing decision(s)¹	Year of decision(s)	Formal RFP	No of bids	Length of contract	Expected cost savings	Cost savings achieved	Initiator of the decision(s)
9. CHEM1 UK chemicals manufacturer* > 150 MIPS	36. Group IT Manager 37. Manager Applications 38. Manager Operations Europe and UK 39. Manager IT Development	(a) Selective: system support (b) Selective: development and support (c) Selective: development and support	(a) 1985 (b) 1991 (c) 1992	(a) Yes (b) Yes (c) Yes	(a) 3 (b) 1 (c) 4	(a) 2 years (b) 2 years (c) 3 years	(a) 40% (b) 30% (c) 20%	(a) 50% over 8 years (b) Some (c) Most	(a) Senior and IT Managers (b) Senior and IT Managers (c) Senior and IT Managers
10. FOOD1 UK food manufacturer* 76 MIPS	40. Manager IT Services 41. MD Group Services 42. Consultant 43. Senior Manager	(a) Total insourcing (b) Selective: factory software development	(a) 1990 (b) 1991	(a) Yes (b) Yes	(a) 2 (b) 3	(a) N/A (b) 2.5 years	(a) 20–30% (b) 25%	(a) Yes (b) No	(a) IT Manager (b) Business and IT Managers
11. GOODS UK consumer product manufacturer* > 150 MIPS	44. Director of IS 45. Manager Operations 46. IS staff member 47. Vendor A/C Manager	(a) Total outsourcing (b) Selective: data centre	(a) 1985 (b) 1988	(a) Yes (b) Yes	(a) 5 (b) 4	(a) 5 years, did not renew (b) 3 years	(a) 15% (b) 20%	(a) No (b) Yes	(a) Senior and IT Managers (b) Business and IT Managers

Organization	Roles	Type	Year				%		Senior Business Manager
12. BANK1 US commercial bank* > 150 MIPS	48. Contract Manager 49. Vendor Consultant 50. Senior Manager 51. Data Centre Manager	Selective: data centres	1992	Yes	5	5 years	25%	Yes	Senior Business Manager
13. BANK2 UK commercial bank* > 150 MIPS	52. MD of IT 53. Manager IT Operations 54. Vendor A/C Manager 55. Senior Manager	(a) Selective (b) Selective: systems support and enhancement	(a) 1991 (b) 1992	(a) Yes (b) Yes	(a) 4 (b) 4	(a) 3 years (b) 2 years	(a) 15–20% (b) 20%	(a) Yes (b) Yes	(a) Business and IT Managers (b) Business and IT Managers
14. GLASS UK glass and plastics manufacturer* 40 MIPS	56. Group IS Director 57. Vendor Account Manager of IS 58. Manager of IS	Selective: data centre and systems development	1992	Yes	5	2 years +, renewed for 3 years	24%	Yes	Senior and IT Managers
15. BREWER UK brewing and distribution* > 300 MIPS	59. Director IS Services 60. Vendor Director 61. Contract Manager 62. Production Manager	Selective: central systems development and support	1993	No	4	5 years	Cost increase over 2 years, break even over 5 years	1st year cost increase	IT Managers
16. RETAIL3 UK clothing and food retailer* 150 MIPS	63. Operating and Services Manager 64. Senior Manager 65. Senior Manager 66. Vendor A/C Manager 67. Manager of IT	(a) Selective: data centre (b) Selective: PC maintenance (c) Selective: mainframe maintenance	(a) 1988 (b) 1988 (c) 1990	(a) Yes (b) Yes (c) Yes	(a) 3 (b) 4 (c) 2	(a) 3 years (b) 3 years (c) 3 years	(a) None (b) 15% (c) 20%	(a) N/A (b) Yes (c) Yes	(a) IT Managers (b) IT Managers (c) IT Managers

Table 10.1   Continued

Company, industry, size in terms of revenue* and MIPS	Participants	Sourcing decision(s)[1]	Year of decision(s)	Formal RFP	No of bids	Length of contract	Expected cost savings	Cost savings achieved	Initiator of the decision(s)
17. FOOD2 UK food manufacturer* < 50 MIPS	68. Manager of IS 69. Management Software Development 70. Systems Manager 71. Vendor A/C Manager	(a) Selective: factory software development (b) Selective: data centre	(a) 1988 (b) 1992	(a) Yes (b) Yes	(a) 4 (b) 5	(a) 2 years (b) 3 years	(a) None (b) 30–33%	(a) No, costs doubled (b) Yes, so far	(a) Senior Manager (b) IT Manager
18. UTILITY2 UK electricity supply* < 100 MIPS	72. Manager of IT Operations 73. Contract Manager 74. Services Manager	Selective: distributed PC networks and UNIX servers	1992	Yes	6	2 years	30%	Yes, as of 1994	Divisional Manager
19. PSB2 UK public health authority member < 100 MIPS	75. Director of IS 76. IS staff member 77. IS staff member 78. Contract Manager 79. Regional Manager	Selective: data centre and software packages	1991	Yes	4	5 years	20–25%	Yes	IT Manager

Organization	Interviewees	Outsourcing arrangement (date)	(Q1)	(Q2)	Contract length	%	Outcome	Managers
20. PSB3 UK county council < 50 MIPS	80. Manager of IS 81. Department Manager 82. Vendor Consultant 83. Outsourcing Consultant 84. Contract Manager	(a) Selective: data centre and telecom (a) 1991 (b) Selective: office systems support (b) 1992	(a) Yes (b) Yes	(a) 6 (b) 1	(a) 5 years (b) 4 years	(a) 20% (b) 17%	(a) Yes, 20–22% (b) yes	(a&b) IT, Finance and Business Service Managers
21. PSB4 UK broadcasting corporation* < 100 MIPS	85. Director of IS 86. Contract Manager 87. Production Manager	(a) Insourcing (a) 1988 (b) Selective: data centre (b) 1992	(a) No (b) Yes	(a) 1 (b) 5	(a) N/A (b) 7 years	(a) 25% (b) 35%	(a) Yes (b) Yes	(a) Senior and IT Managers (b) IT Manager
22. AVIATION UK aviation authority* < 100 MIPS	88. Manager, Internal IS Consulting Group 89. Contract Manager 90. Vendor Consultant 91. Vendor Manager	(a) Selective: payroll and financial systems (a) 1988 (b) Selective: PCs and networks (b) 1989 (c) Selective: financial packages (c) 1990	(a) No (b) Yes (c) No	(a) 2 (b) 3 (c) 1	(a) 5 years (b) 4 years (c) 5 years	(a) 15% (b) Some (c) Some	(a) None (b) Minimal (c) Minimal	(a) Senior Manager (b) IT Manager (c) IT Manager
23. PSB5 UK Post Office > 200 MIPS	92. IT Director 93. IT Manager 94. Senior Manager	Total insourcing 1994	N/A	N/A	Revisit decision on a regular basis	Drive to contain costs	Cost savings achieved	IT Director and Senior Managers
24. UTILITY3 UK water company < 100 MIPS	95. Director of IS 96. Vendor Representative 97. Contract Manager 98. Senior Manager	Selective: data centre 1994	Yes	3	3 years	15–20%	Too early to determine	Senior Managers

Table 10.1 *Continued*

Company, industry, size in terms of revenue* and MIPS	Participants	Sourcing decision(s)[1]	Year of decision(s)	Formal RFP	No of bids	Length of contract	Expected cost savings	Cost savings achieved	Initiator of the decision(s)
25. MANUF1 UK defence manufacturer* > 200 MIPS	99. Contract Manager 100. Vendor Consultant 101. Senior Manager 102. User Manager	Total outsourcing	1994	Yes	3	10 years	15–20%	Too early to determine	Board Managers
26. UTILITY4 UK electricity company < 150 MIPS	103. IT Director 104. User Manager 105. Contract Manager 106.En Vendor Representative	Total outsourcing	1992	Yes	3	12 years	20–30%	Some cost savings	Senior Managers

Notes: [1] Some companies evaluated outsourcing on multiple occasions

[2] PSB = Public Sector Body

* = US *Fortune 500* or *Financial Times* European 1000

Data Analysis

The interviews were tape-recorded and transcribed into 630 pages, single spaced. Although we had collected numerous stories of success and failures, we needed to produce a higher level of abstraction and interpretation. To accomplish the research objective, we applied the precepts of intentional analysis to the transcripts. Intentional analysis prescribes four steps for interpreting transcribed interviews from an interpretivist perspective (Sanders, 1982). In the first step, the researcher describes the "facts" of the phenomenon, with "facts" here understood as socially agreed realities agreed on by all participants. In step two, researchers determine the way in which participants ascribe meaning to reality by how participants perceive cause and effect. In step three, researchers identify themes across the interviews. In step four, we switch attention from assessing participants' viewpoints to assessing our own views as to how the accumulated evidence can be interpreted, and whether specific patterns, themes and principles emerge from the rich data of the case studies. This latter set of interpretations makes up the bulk of this chapter. While the validity of intentional analysis defies quantification, we have included excerpts from the transcribed interviews to help readers judge for themselves the validity of our analysis (Astley, 1985; Lincoln and Gubba, 1985).

We developed one further tool to help in judgements on standards of evaluation practice in sourcing decisions. By the end of 1995 the research base comprised 45 sourcing decisions. Of these, 9 were total outsourcing and 4 total insourcing, while 32 were selective outsourcing decisions (see Table 10.1). Benchmarks for "success" and "failure" were established. While each case was different, it was possible to assess performance against espoused objectives, degree of cost savings (over 85% of respondent organizations had cost savings as one of their major objectives) and degree of satisfaction with contract performance. Details of cost savings achieved are shown in Table 10.1. Using these criteria, we found selective sourcing "successful" in 21 out of 32 cases, total insourcing in 4 out of 5, and total outsourcing in 1 out of 9. Three selective outsourcing cases and four total outsourcing cases fell into a "too early to tell/unable to determine financial outcome" category. These detailed results enabled us to compare and arrive at some judgements on respondents' evaluation practices.

We now proceed to provide an analysis and assessment of the evaluation practice emerging from the case studies. In places we support the data with evidence from our survey work. We focus entirely on evaluation practice up to and including assessing the vendor bid. In order to facilitate discussion, the 26 organizations will be referred to by their

names wherever possible or, where anonymity was requested, by pseu-
donyms based on their industry type—CHEM1, FOOD1, ELECTRIC
etc. The five UK public-sector bodies will be referred to as PSB1, PSB2
etc., as necessary. Further relevant details of each organization and its
sourcing decision(s) can be found in Table 10.1.

The analysis that follows is organized into four main sections. First,
we found that pre-existing patterns of assessment greatly influenced
the degree of difficulty and the degree of success subsequently experienced in any outsourcing arrangement. Secondly, our data enabled us
to produce further detail on not only how organizations have sought to
prepare themselves better for making sourcing decisions, but also on
the types of difficulties they experienced. Thirdly, we provide a rich
picture in the form of a detailed case study of how two specific evaluations of vendors' bids were carried out. Finally, based on reviewing
the accumulated evidence, we arrive at some summary lessons on the
economics of vendor bids.

PATTERNS OF ASSESSMENT

Several dominant patterns of performance measurement before outsourcing were found in the respondent organizations. The pre-existing
pattern of in-house IT evaluation had a big part to play in the effort and
approach required in assessing a vendor bid. Although outside the
scope of this chapter, it was also found to influence greatly the success
of subsequent assessments of vendor performance.

"Traditionalists"

These organizations tended to focus their IT evaluation around the
feasibility, development and routine operations stages of IT investment. For feasibility they tended to use predominantly finance-based
cost–benefit criteria. For IT development the major criterion used can be
summarized as "within time and budget to acceptable technical quality". For routine operations the technical efficiency of IT performance,
plus some end-user service measures, were dominant. Examples of
organizations include UTILITY1, RETAIL2, FOOD2, GOODS and PSB3.
In practice, 27 of the 45 sourcing decisions we analysed were made
against a backdrop of "traditionalist" evaluation practices. It should be
noted that such evaluation practices were also well represented in the
surveys discussed already in Chapters 2 and 4. When outsourcing IT,
such organizations tended to pursue one of two paths:

1. *"All Change"*: The first path was to spend a long period—some-

times six to nine months—thrashing out the detailed parameters of service required from a vendor. The extent of effort expended on this depended on the size and criticality of the contract. In some instances the vendor was closely involved in this process before contracts were signed. Two examples were MANUF1 and PSB1, not least because they were embarking on long-term total outsourcing contracts.

2. *"Minor adjustments"*: The second path was to establish a general rule that service would not deteriorate from what it was before, adopt many of the measures previously used in-house and some additional ones where it was felt appropriate. Organizations taking this path sometimes resolved to develop further service measures during the course of the contract, as need arises.

While "all change" would seem better practice, the pre-existing evaluation culture in "traditionalist" organizations sometimes pushed them into the "minor adjustment" approach. From our evidence, the result is usually unanticipated costs for services not specified well enough in the contract, and conflicts with the vendor over quality of performance. An obvious example here is GOODS in its first outsourcing deal. Developing measures during the course of the contract also emerged as a poor choice of action in these circumstances, as emerged for example in AVIATION's first outsourcing experience. The exception, illustrated by GLASS's favourable outsourcing experience, was where a strong client–vendor partnership relationship had been developed.

"Service to the Business"

These organizations, before outsourcing, had moved the evaluation focus from IT efficiency to incorporate degrees of service performance to the user and degrees of business contribution. These objectives were sought through chargeback systems, IT as a profit centre and/or the introduction of service-level agreements with or without penalty clauses. These organizations found it less difficult to make the transfer to having to evaluate the performance of a vendor. Examples include BANK2, RETAIL3, UTILITY3, PSB5. However, many were less advanced down the road to becoming "service to the business" providers than the adoption of appropriate-sounding evaluation systems would suggest. Generally, most organizations were somewhere along the way to refining their in-house performance measures. The transfer to evaluating a vendor's performance invariably still needed a lot of work on developing assessment measures and procedures.

Those operating chargeback systems before and after outsourcing found that, after outsourcing, reallocating costs became a perennial issue in relations with end-users. Organizations also found it useful to revisit any pre-existing service-level agreements, and often saw outsourcing as an opportunity to improve on performance assessment through SLAs. Based on their experiences, most respondents agreed that in-house performance measures were best not taken over as they stood; outsourcing was a new development and its consequences and how vendor performance could be controlled needed to be thought through. The more successful organizations spent a lengthy period— typically four to six months—measuring everything (the "baseline" period) and then created measures for assessing vendor performance from the resulting information. There were usually additional measures to those used before, and on some measures improvements on previous in-house performance were felt to be required. This was the case, for example, with GOODS and FOOD2 in each case in the build-up to the company's second outsourcing arrangement. These findings were supported in our later case study work (Currie and Willcocks, 1997).

"Trading Agencies"

Here organizations moved the IT function to the status of a trading agency able to market its services internally and on the external marketplace. In these arrangements the business divisions frequently also had the right to buy IT services both internally or externally, though the internal IT provider was regarded as "preferred supplier". In some examples the in-house IT department was made a part-owned separate company. Some organizations operating in this way tended to see the trading agency as preferred supplier, although this was not always the case. While they were getting the bulk of their IT needs from the in-house supplier, the latter's business was also mainly comprised of work from the host company. One reason was the difficulty of competing in the market against more established vendors. In the examples of such "trading agencies", determined efforts had been made to set up a more commercially based relationship, with performance on IT and costs made more transparent, with service-level agreements operating, and with much clearer "pay-for-performance" type measures in place. The existence and assessment of such a trading agency were also found to assist the process of assessing bids from alternative vendors. The experience gained and lessons learned also helped in setting up performance measures where an aspect of IT was outsourced to a new vendor. However, "preferred supplier" status tended to protect a trading agency against such incursions, except in the public sector and in examples where semi-independent business divisions in a conglomerate would seek an alternative source for a specific set of IT activities. One example among respondent organizations was ELECTRIC. CHEM1 had moved down this route to some degree, while PSB5 and BANK2 were looking to shift further in this direction at time of interview. The survey uncovered five companies whose IT departments were considered trading agencies in the sense described above.

From this review there would seem to be several evaluation routes taken to outsourcing. Organizations jumping straight from a pre-existing "traditionalist" approach to evaluation found the most difficulty in assessing vendor bids, drawing up contracts and assessing subsequent vendor performance. Other organizations moved further in the direction of an internal "service to business" type evaluation, but still found a number of problem areas when carrying out an in-house versus out-of-house assessment, and when setting up performance measures for an outsourced aspect of IT. "Trading agencies" offered the most clear comparisons between bids by the in-house team and those by external vendors. The experience of setting up a trading agency could also feed into developing measures to assess performance of an alternative vendor. The problem here is that organizations moving from a "traditionalist" position on IT evaluation straight into a "trading agency" one experience increased difficulties at that point (see Figure 10.1). These may well not be resolved where the organization then decides to outsource some or all of its IT.

The move from a "traditionalist", through a "service to business" to a "trading agency" set-up and their associated evaluation systems suggests a maturing of the ability to assess in-house IT costs and performance against a vendor bid, as well as an improvement in the ability to generate performance measures subsequent to outsourcing. Certainly, 14 organizations we investigated tended to be in the second category as a prelude to outsourcing. There would seem to be a conscious process at work, first to make in-house IT performance based more on service to the user and to the business; secondly to enable in-house IT performance to be compared more easily against external comparisons, including outsourcing vendor bids. If our respondents' experiences are not untypical, there will be always problems to manage wherever organizations start from prior to outsourcing. However, having in-house IT in category 2 or 3 (see Figure 10.1) would seem to better facilitate assessment of a vendor bid, and also ease the transition to outsourcing.

Having presented the general picture we now look in detail at how the respondent organizations prepared themselves for assessing an outsourcing case.

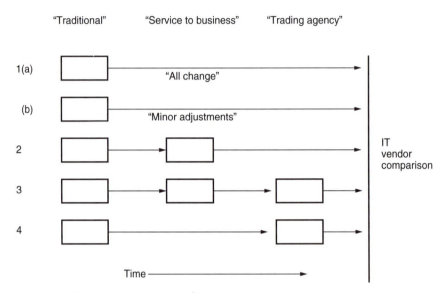

Figure 10.1   *Patterns of Assessment in 26 Organizations*

EVALUATING IN-HOUSE PERFORMANCE

As discussed above, it was all too frequently the case that an organization's IT evaluation practice was not supportive of an immediate assessment of whether some or any degree of IT outsourcing was a good idea. Using examples, this section looks at how respondent organizations attempted to prepare themselves for making better informed sourcing decisions. A number of significant concerns emerged from the case studies, namely evaluating total IT contribution, identifying full costs, benchmarking and external comparisons, the role of charging systems, and the adoption of service-levels agreements by the in-house operation.

Evaluating the Total IT Contribution

As Chapters 2, 5, 6, 7 and 8 underline, organizations tend to have many limitations, and experience a number of difficulties, in their IT evaluation practice. Very few organizations operate an integrated evaluating system covering strategic, business, end-user and technical performance across systems lifetime (Willcocks, 1994, 1996; Willcocks and Lester, 1996). This does not put them in a good position for assessing the viability of outsourcing.

A particular issue emerging from the case studies was ensuring that vendor performance was judged on something more than restricted technical and service-delivery criteria. Vendor performance, we would suggest, needs to be located in a larger evaluation system that assesses the strategic and business contribution of IT, and is able to monitor the technical and business value of specific systems. Why is this important? There are two *a priori* reasons. First, if an organization, before outsourcing, is not in a position to assess the total net business contribution of IT, it may well outsource IT assets and activities that have, in their current state, no real part to play in the IT portfolio. Outsourcing them to reduce their costs is a poor substitute for enhancing their capability or perhaps dropping them altogether. Secondly, after outsourcing, if evaluation is restricted to vendor performance on cost and service targets, the organization may become blinded to situations where what has been outsourced no longer really serves a relevant business purpose.

PETRO1 (BP Exploration) revealed better practice on these issues. The company outsourced its accounting services, including computer systems and 250 staff, to Arthur Andersen in 1991 in a four year, £55 million contract. By 1993 it had also contracted out major IT operations to three vendors in a five-year deal worth £35 million annually:

> We have a whole series of performance criteria for our organization which is based around the balanced scorecard type of approach [see below]. Essentially that has got some infrastructure and applications measures, but it also has measures on business contribution. It is all of one piece in the sense that outsourced infrastructure and applications, and the value added by partners, sits alongside key business performance measures. There are overall measures and a lot of detailed measures that sit underneath. (Contract manager)

INSURANCE also appreciated the need for an evaluation system for total IT contribution. A subsidiary of a major UK-based insurance company, the company was established in 1990 to sell health insurance. Right from the beginning administration, agency and claims systems were contracted out to EDS. The view was taken that, once enough experience had been gained, IT would eventually be brought back in-house. A critical success factor for the business is the performance of computer systems, especially as claims costs represent 80% of the premium income of the company. Such costs need to be controlled by making sure that a valid claimant is paid quickly and others are not:

> We have something like 200 employees now working in our operations area, administration, claims, agency and ourselves [IT], who have no clerical

processes without the computer system. What they did was to buy a clerical system and build the clerical processes around them. It is a critical system in terms that it's available at 8 am and stays up to 10 pm and responds within a normal timeframe, being three seconds for each transaction. It's critical because you have 200 people's productivity affected directly by it. Those statistics on that criticality are something I display to them on a regular basis, for example how many times the print was late, on-line systems performance ... the measurements we have in place are all designed around the company's critical success factors and key performance indicators. (IS Director)

In this case IT was considered vital to successful operations. Management was very alive to the evaluation issues that this posed for the company. More often respondent organizations had indifferent evaluation systems but the threat of outsourcing acted as a major catalyst for improvements. There are many possible approaches to evaluating total IT contribution. Two complementary approaches utilized in several respondent organizations were the balanced scorecard approach described by Kaplan and Norton (1992) and the development of a performance metrics hierarchy of the sort described by Peters (1996) and Norris (1996) (see also Chapter 2).

Full Costs and Charging Systems

Identifying the full in-house costs of IT in potential outsourcing situations is important for several reasons. It may well lead to an improvement in in-house assessment procedures. It can help to identify where costs are too high and where internal action needs to be taken to reduce costs. At BANK1, a US commercial bank, for example, the costs of data centres were driven down through consolidation and careful monitoring over several years before outsourcing was considered. The less economic alternative to such action is to let vendors "pick the low fruit", i.e. reduce those costs themselves and take them as profit. Identifying full costs also enables a more informed assessment of a vendor's bid. Organizations we have researched that are now experienced in outsourcing all stress the importance to them of identifying and monitoring full costs. An example is BANK2:

Part of our job here is to look at cost of ownership and there are a whole range of factors that come into cost of ownership. Certainly when you are looking at developing, supporting and enhancing existing software, the main cost is your staff. You have also got the premises costs and all the things that go with that like catering and the other things you need to provide. You've got system time costs. There is a whole list of things and it's a question of sitting down and understanding them. We do all that, find out what the current costs are because clearly, if we are outsourcing it, we've got to have something to measure the cost of the outsource tender against. (Manager of IT Operations)

Not identifying full costs can also cause problems once an outsourcing contract is signed. A vendor may well discover that profit margins are slimmer than anticipated. This could affect the vendor–client relationship and also levels of service. This occurred for example in the cases of GOODS, AVIATION, and to some degree MANUF1. Alternatively the company may have left a range of costs/activities out of the contract. If the vendor is then required to cover those costs/activities, this may result in additional charges. This occurred for example in GOODS, RETAIL2 and INSURANCE.

On the other hand identifying full costs does permit a number of questions to be posed about vendor bids. Thus BANK1 and RETAIL3 could ask: if a vendor can offer 30% or more cost savings on current operations, does this indicate large-scale in-house inefficiencies that need to be looked at? Or does it mean that the vendor may be treating the contract as a loss leader, or perhaps is going to rely on "excess charges" later on in the contract to bolster profit margins? It could emerge, as GOODS and AVIATION discovered, that the lowest bidder may not really be the cheapest at all, let alone the best bid taking into account all factors. Many organizations also reported that the process of outsourcing itself incurred additional, sometimes considerable, costs which are often left out of the reckoning. Typical omissions reported to us were the costs of preparing information for potential suppliers; of evaluating proposals and drawing up contracts (e.g. legal expenses, managerial time); the initial transfer costs; the costs of managing the contract; and the possible costs of termination.

A further learning point related to cost reallocation systems operated before and after outsourcing. Two organizations—GOODS and BANK2—inherited detailed recharging systems and used them in subsequent outsourcing situations. A significant amount of internal user dissatisfaction occurred. Two further organizations with considerable amounts of outsourcing experience took a different route:

> We used to have a detailed charge-out system. When we looked at in 1989 it was to our horror that we discovered when we looked at it globally we were employing about 50 people to do business with ourselves. So we substituted a block fund mechanism whereby as part of our budget setting process at the beginning of the year we agree an allocation of those costs to each of the major sites in the company. It engages the senior level of the business and really has minimum bureaucracy associated with it. We find it much more positive. It's a once a year system... When we outsourced we took over the same mechanism. Their performance targets fit within our costs, which in

> turn are ploughed back through the block fund. It's early days but so far we have had no serious dispute because generally people [the partners] sit down and are fairly open with one another. (IT Manager, PETRO1)

> We do not operate chargeback, it's not as formal as you get so many £s per CPU minute and so many lines printed . . . more a reallocation of total costs on a proportional basis in terms of general usage. (IT Manager, RETAIL3)

At the same time, the introduction of control devices such as charge-back systems and prioritization of user requests may serve to make in-house performance tighter on cost and efficiency. Introducing such devices may be a more economic proposition than having a vendor do it for the client organization in the course of an outsourcing contract.

The case of UTILITY3 offers some insights on these issues. The company is Wessex Water, one of the 10 large, privatized UK water authorities. As at the end of 1995, it was still regulated for price, efficiency and effectiveness by a Director General. In June 1993, one of the things causing company directors at Wessex Water to look at outsourcing functions such as IT was the cost side, one aim being to meet the regulatory requirements to minimize charges to external cus-tomers. By 1993, the annual IT budget was about £17 million. In IT a particular issue was whether just to outsource the mainframe, or to include other aspects, for example a shortage of technical staff could have required user support to be contracted out.

Initially the company wished to identify its true IT costs. This was not necessarily an easy thing to do:

> Although we've got a centralized IT department, there are other people round the organization. We are now set up as business units, so information services have to be competitive to get the internal customers to use our services, and those internal customers have a choice. They can go outside if they wish. They can go and purchase their own equipment, although they can't connect it into the mainframe without our say so. So there are costs that haven't all been pulled together to say this is what IT is costing us, particu-larly on the communications side where we've got a large communications network, part only of which is within the control of the IS department. (Contract Manager, UTILITY3)

There are difficulties where costs are spread around an organization. At UTILITY3 the accounting system was probably too flexible, and not directive enough as to how and where costs should be allocated. At the same time, users did fear a return to the days of a central IT department "dictating the PC on their desk and what systems they have". Effort was needed to demonstrate that the tracking of full IT costs was a necessary prerequisite to saving money for the company.

The approach to outsourcing IT was to try to get the obvious savings done internally first, then see what the vendors could offer:

> The FM companies are going to be making a profit out of us, hopefully as part of the deal they will be offering us some saving. One of the things we want to make sure of before we actually go out to these companies is that we've got as tight a ship as we can so that any easy savings that can be made will be made, then we will go out to the FM companies and say now offer us a deal. There are bound to be things we have missed and they will spot.

The purpose here was to become less of a hostage to fortune to vendors. One major concern was capacity management on the mainframe, in which internal savings were possible before redefining the service levels and costs expected from a vendor. There were also possible in-house savings with the communications network—through reducing management and duplication costs and through further discounts from telecommunications companies.

The company also sought comparisons on IT cost and efficiency, not just with other water companies, but with companies in other sectors, including FM (facilities management) firms. A benchmarking company, a management consultancy and an ex-FM employee were used to carry out external comparisons. Both operations and development had been independently reviewed against external comparisons, by Compass and BIS respectively. The IT department's business users were surveyed to discover service levels. These reviews enabled feedback on such matters as cost/performance, response times and user satisfaction.

An early vendor bid also proved useful for comparison. One significant saving that the vendor identified was in rental and accommodation costs. However, these did not represent real savings, since they were corporate costs and would have to be shared around the other company users of the building. It was also a saving that could well be made in-house as the company was about to review utilization of all its sites for IT and non-IT work. The company also had at this stage in-house IT service-level agreements with internal users. However, these needed to be tightened before they could form a basis for third-party agreements.

> My guess is that "you are too expensive" is a general user feeling, if you go and ask anyone about an in-house IS department. (Contract Manager, UTIL-ITY3)

Clearly, such a feeling needs to be tested. Wessex Water demonstrates the considerable preparations needed to get an in-house IT department ready for evaluation against possible bids for vendors. This involved identifying full costs, improving internal accounting, seeking detailed external comparisons, in-house user reviews of service, and the development and improvement of in-house service-level agreements. A putative vendor bid also helped in the assessment process.

Benchmarking and External Comparisons

A number of respondent organizations, like Wessex Water, testified to the usefulness of benchmarking IT performance against external comparisons. Usually they utilized specialist benchmarking companies to help them in this task. IT benchmarking of this type did not necessarily lead to the conclusion that outsourcing was a better option. FOOD1 is United Biscuits, a £3 billion conglomerate in the snack, frozen and chilled food and confectionery business. According to its Managing Director of Group Services, FOOD1 benchmarked its two central mainframes on Compass. Though only a 76 MIP shop, they were, in terms of data-processing productivity, in the top half dozen of mainframes up to 200 MIPs (million instructions per second), and top of their own MIP range. In fact, FOOD1 operated very efficiently at the limit of the mainframe technology it was using. A vendor would have to use much bigger machines to get similar economies. Therefore, with outsourcing the cost of the service would have had to increase.

At CHEM1, we found a central computing group running a telecommunications network and computer centres for business divisions. The central computing group charged by unit rates per CPU power and matched its prices against external competitors. CHEM1, one of the business divisions of ICI, signed to stay with the in-house service for two years on a budget plus/minus 10% basis. Within CHEM1, one task on the development side was to evaluate internal service against external groups. Benchmarking was inextricably involved with outsourcing possibilities:

> There is pressure from senior management to benchmark outside against inside and encouraging the IT function to say which bits do you think that you really have to do because you have unique skills, and which bits can we actually get a competitive bid for from outside. That's one overall trend. The second is cost reduction ... ways in which we can run lower cost and lower people numbers. (Manager of IT Development)

However, other respondents revealed that external comparisons were not without their problems:

> There is quite a lot of detailed benchmarking that has to go on. The problem is that it is extremely expensive. One of the things we have found that as an

in-house organization we belong to these firms [like Compass] with databases, but by and large the companies on them are other in-house organizations, because the commercial supplier wouldn't give his data away. We need to do more to find other ways of benchmarking against commercial suppliers and really understand how they benchmark, other than just by numbers of bids they win. (IT Director, Post Office)

Moreover:

The major areas benchmarked so far are voice and data networking and mainframe services and development. On the first two the cost structure and grouping of products and services is often very different from a commercial supplier. We tend to bundle more in, including things like help desk, problem management as part of the overall price. The problem is to un-bundle our in-house services to make them look like external ones so we can benchmark properly. (IT Director, PSB5—UK Post Office)

The issue of unbundling in-house services for comparative purposes, the expense of external comparison, and questions about who you are comparing in-house performance against in commercially available databases are in fact commonly perceived problems, not restricted to the Post Office. Respondents indicated that external comparison also became more difficult the further one moved from making comparisons between traditional data centre operations. Thus at the Post Office, the development area was found to be the most difficult to benchmark. As CASE tools and rapid application development were adopted, the traditional methods of measuring function points became less appro-priate.

Service-Level Agreements and the Internal Market

Many respondent organizations already operated service-level agree-ments (SLAs) with their internal customers. This was often part of a broader move to make the IT function more service oriented and open to market comparisons on performance. This was particularly the case in the UK public sector in the 1990s under the UK government's Competitive Tendering and Market Testing initiatives. However, re-spondents regularly indicated that service-level agreements arrived at with internal customers invariably needed tightening up before out-sourcing could be contemplated. Thus at the time of interview PSB1—the UK Inland Revenue—was looking to outsource on long-term con-tracts most of an annual IT budget of about £250 million:

We have around 100 service agreements between ourselves and a variety of customers around the department. They would have to be enhanced over time because they were, if you like, prepared, agreed, signed off, between colleagues wanting to put our arrangements onto a more business-like footing, remembering that IT in the Revenue, like a lot of organizations, is a free good as far as the wider customer is concerned ... in fact all of our evaluation will come under the microscope before we are paying real money externally to a market player. (Geoff Bush, PSB1—Inland Revenue)

The subsequent history of the Inland Revenue–EDS outsourcing contract is analysed in Willcocks and Kern (1997).

PSB5—the UK Post Office—offered useful experience and guidelines on moving the IT department to a more customer-focused, competitive position in an internal market. IT in PSB5 had gone through several stages before being set up in 1990 as a business centre with some 1220 staff. Other internal suppliers were also set up as business centres or profit centres. A federal structure was adopted, with the IT business centre seen as a supplier offering systems integration, facilities management, package tailoring and consultancy. Businesses represented customers responsible for IS strategy, defining user requirements and local systems. A partnership operated between business and IT on infrastructure, standards and strategy. PSB5 formally adopted an internal market strategy. As at 1993, the internal market was worth about £800 million, with the IT internal market some 10% of this. The Post Office's internal IT group had four major customers—Royal Mail, Parcel Force, Counters and Group.

The internal market for IT set up partnerships whereby the internal customers and supplier agreed the service required, performance standards, the measures and the approach to benchmarking. There was established with each of the major customers a separate benchmarked partnership trading agreement. Independent benchmarking was used to review IT performance. If an area emerged where the internal supplier could not meet "best in class" criteria, a joint programme of improvement had to be agreed with the customer. If that failed to achieve required results within an agreed time period, then outsourcing would be considered. Outsourcing could also occur as a way of benchmarking in-house performance against external competition:

> The philosophy is to get it best in class internally first, and then to get a best comparison outside. I think that fits with some of the things other companies have found, that if they haven't sorted out the in-house supplier first, they won't get a good deal when they go outside. We also do increasingly market-related comparisons. But we have had to look at customer-driven metrics as well as commercially comparable criteria. (Group IT Director)

Customer involvement in assessment emerged as critical. Despite the range of evaluation through benchmarking and external comparison, it was found that the IT supplier doing its own reviews often failed to convince customers. Even with external comparison, customers frequently felt that the figures were being fixed. Therefore an annual customer satisfaction survey was introduced. There have been regular customer meetings dealing with benchmarking, pricing and related issues.

A constant issue was this relationship side of the IT service. On an industry average calculated by Research Solutions, the IT function did well on technical delivery but less well on marketing, sales and customer management. Such findings had to be balanced with the likelihood that customers did not want to pay for a lot of those things:

> The trick is to improve account relationships inexpensively. It doesn't mean we don't have to continue to improve, but the problem is as an internal supplier our customers don't want lots of sales and marketing people so we have had to strengthen our account relationships with our customers to get that commercial management in place. (IT Manager)

On assessment, the main challenges in 1993/4 were streamlining 60 IT products/services into six product streams and benchmarking all of them. The internal market helped to improve evaluation procedures, the delivery of IT products and services, and relations between the IT function and the business users. At the same time, the possibility of outsourcing had not been excluded, but a more robust basis from which to assess vendor bids had been established. By 1998 the Post Office had still not outsourced extensively, but had continued to develop its evaluation processes (see Graeser, Willcocks and Pisanias, 1998).

ASSESSING VENDOR BIDS: A CASE IN POINT

Our survey revealed that there can be considerable economic benefits from outsourcing in the right circumstances, with the right vendor, a finding suppported by later survey work (Currie and Willcocks, 1997). However, the process of assessing the vendor bid emerged as problematical. This section draws on the case of PSB4—the British Broadcasting Corporation—in order to take the analysis further. We provide a rich picture of approaches and problems in assessing vendor bids. Addressing the same set of issues, the final section then discusses summary lessons emerging from our case studies compared to work published by others.

Case Background

During the period covered by this case, 1988–94, the British Broadcasting Corporation (BBC) was divided into a number of different directorates, the main ones being radio, television, world service, news and current affairs and regional broadcasting. There was a devolved management structure. IT was devolved to each of these directorates. Throughout the late 1980s, the BBC became increasingly cost conscious and this caused it to review a number of its non-core activities. IT was not regarded as a strategic resource. The IT budget exceeded £10 million a year on 1988 prices. In 1988 the BBC had its first serious examination of outsourcing IT, in respect of the corporate mainframe bureau. The decision then was not to outsource. The outsourcing decision received a second review in late 1991 in different circumstances and the decision then was to outsource the corporate mainframe operations to the vendor CFM.

The First Vendor Proposal

The first IT outsourcing review was initiated by a vendor's letter to the Director General of the BBC claiming to be able to reduce IT running costs by 40%. This referred to the corporate mainframe data centre operations. In a cost-conscious climate this prompted an investigation into in-house performance versus the outsourcing options. The IT staff that would have been affected by any outsourcing then initiated an in-house option. The potential vendor proposed to save the BBC £11 million on IT costs over five years. A number of benefits were proposed. Management involvement could be reduced. Disaster-recovery facilities would be provided, giving a more secure service. The hardware could be sold to the vendor. There would be much less time and expense in auditing and monitoring the cost effectiveness of the service. There would be enhanced career opportunities for staff in a leading systems company together with an immediate headcount reduction for the BBC. However, the cost saving was not so attractive once the underlying assumptions had been exposed:

> We examined these on a more or less point by point basis. The first one was the £11 million saving. This was on a budget estimated by them of £54 million over the five years, all at 1989 prices. It was accredited on a growth rate of 30% per annum. Now our workload has in fact tended to grow at closer to 20%... But even if we assume the workload did grow by 30%, it was certainly not true that costs grow by 30%. This had been in part recognized by the vendor company because they showed only a 5% growth in staff costs and no growth in transport and ancillary costs. In all the rest, including

hardware and software, they predicted the cost increase to be about 30%. That was clearly a nonsense. If we took a more realistic figure, which would have been something under 10% for hardware and software, this was in fact the bulk of the costs. So instead of a saving of £11 million on a budget of £54 million, we calculated we were liable to end up with a saving of just under £4 million on a turnover of £39 million, something in the region of a 10% saving ... I think you have also got to be careful that cost cuts don't affect quality or the level of your service. For example, you can use bigger disk drives, if you put more data on each thimble then you've got more disk contention and that may affect response times. So you've got to watch those sort of things. (Contract Manager, BBC)

The vendor company also proposed to achieve economies of scale by reducing the number of mainframes used from five to two, concentrating on the latest technology and making use of a nodal architecture. However, it was just as easy to do this in-house. In fact, the vendor proposal included selling surplus capacity as bureau time to external companies. While the BBC charter prevented the in-house group from doing this, judicious use of the multi-nodal architecture could in fact trim capability to meet the demand. In this respect, assessment of the vendor proposal actually assisted the BBC in identifying ways forward for the in-house team.

The next significant area of cost saving in the vendor bid was reduced staff costs. There would be some staff savings made because of the reduced number of machines to be operated. However, reducing the machines to two in number would not reduce the staff by 60% because the overall workload would still be the same. The vendor suggested a reduction in staff costs of some 33%. The proposal did not make clear whether this was from reduced staff numbers, a reduction in salary package or both. Each had undesirable implications for any transferred staff, nor would they necessarily be attracted by work for a vendor rather than for an institution like the BBC. Moreover, the staff saving cost of about £400 000 per annum was more than matched by the vendor's annual management fee of over £600 000. Provided that all the other benefits could be achieved in-house, then the cost-saving argument of outsourcing began to look thin.

The vendor additionally argued that costs would be contractually controlled. However, this only applied if there was no workload growth, and/or no change in requirement necessitating additional or replacement kit or software or other services. In fact, the costs were no more controlled than if the work continued to be done in-house. Moreover, the proposal did not specify what would happen if the growth rate actually became negative. There was no indication of a cost reduction to the client.

On reduced management involvement, the BBC analysis actually suggested that more managers would be needed to manage the contract, not less. This was particularly true in regard to the time and expense to audit the cost effectiveness of the service. On disaster-recovery facilities, there were some advantages in the vendor's proposals. However, the vendor would be servicing a number of users, not just the BBC, so it was probably not practical to give the client the whole machine in the event of a disaster.

There was in fact a great deal of scope for improving the in-house arrangements. For example, the offer of release of capital tied up in computing equipment was very attractive to senior BBC management. In the end, however, the BBC achieved the same objective by using a suppliers' change hire scheme and refinancing the existing mainframes. The BBC also questioned whether it actually needed many of the extra "free" services on offer from the vendor. Ultimately it became clear that, considering all factors, the BBC's in-house IT function could more than match the vendor's bid, and the decision was made to stay in-house.

The Second Outsourcing Evaluation

The second assessment, in late 1991, was prompted by a number of considerations. First, the data centre was in a leased building and faced a move due to lease rationalization within the BBC. Secondly, for the first time the data centre was facing a decreasing mainframe workload. There were no expected mainframe developments on the horizon. The move was to Unix and no perceived demand for corporate systems. For example, each of the directorates had its own financial or costing system. The new finance director indicated that he wanted a corporate finance system. The biggest factor was an ever increasing need to reduce the cost base. Against those changing requirements, the outsourcing options and economics looked quite different from the previous occasion.

In fact, the BBC utilized its previous evaluation experience but controlled the process in a more proactive way the second time. The management team invited bids from their hardware supplier, four vendor companies and also considered the economics of an in-house and a joint venture proposal. The in-house bid amounted to costs of £40 million over seven years if nothing was done, reducible to £33 million if certain cost-saving actions were taken. The joint venture looked attractive, but the financial projections were made on assumptions of turnover and growth that could have turned out to be unrealistic. In the event, none of the in-house options came close to matching the CFM bid of around £20 million over seven years to run the mainframe bureau. The deal did not include technical support, which was retained in-house. The economic case for outsourcing was much more clear-cut in this second investigation. After close examination, there was no way that the in-house option could compete with the vendor bid. This was assisted by the fact that the work done on the first evaluation could feed directly into this second assessment.

There were a number of transfer problems in the early days of the contract. Under the contract, users also experienced things taking longer to happen than previously. This was because change control became tighter with a more bureaucratic approach. Costs to users stabilized and could reduce year on year. Additionally, the 1993 climate of strict financial control was causing systems development teams in each directorate to examine the economics of a greater degree of outsourcing. Outsourcing mainframe technical support was also on the agenda.

Summary

In the first case, a production manager summarized the existing in-house mainframe bureau performance as "what we are getting is a standard service at quality prices. But what we want is a quality service at standard prices." The vendor bid acted as a catalyst in pushing the in-house service to consider action it was already contemplating but would have taken longer to get around to doing. In this respect, the threat of outsourcing acted as a catalyst to closer evaluation and identification of improving IT productivity, thus closing the IT "productivity paradox" gap. The evaluation process here also indicates the importance of examining carefully the assumptions underlying a vendor bid. Without that careful analysis based on an understanding of in-house costs, it would have been all too easy to have accepted the vendor bid as offering substantial cost savings.

The second case indicates the value of regularly revisiting outsourcing assessments. Circumstances and technologies change and so can the economics of in-house performance compared to vendor bids. In this case, IT outsourcing when properly evaluated was anticipated to be a more productive option for deploying many of the organization's IT assets.

ASSESSING VENDOR BIDS: SUMMARY ECONOMIC LESSONS

Here we build on the single case analysis in the previous section by codifying the major additional points on the economics of the vendor bid emerging from the 26 case studies. We support the arguments with corroborative evidence drawn from our 1993 and 1997 survey work and other research studies.

The in-house IT function may be able to achieve similar savings to those offered by a vendor

The economies of scale issue for data centres was discussed above. A number of our respondents reported operating at high efficiency in-house at 150–170 MIPs but also at lower ranges. Examples include PSB1, FOOD1 and CHEM1. According to Bergstrom (1991), after 300 MIPs the benefits of transferring to a larger IS shop are negligible. Lacity and Hirschheim (1995) found three companies running 28, 14 and 17 MIP shops respectively. All were more efficient in terms of cost per MIP than large, vendor-run data centres. Improvements in internal efficiency through tighter control, for example through charging systems, can also be achieved, as for example at CHEM1 and FOOD1. Alternatively the vendor will incur these savings, and not necessarily pass them on to the client. Additionally, Real Decisions Corporation has found companies reducing data centre costs by 17–25% a year without outsourcing (Bergstrom, 1996; Currie and Willcocks, 1997).

Some savings may be more real than others

Costs and savings can be manipulated or may be disguised by the way they are accounted for. Outsourcing will move costs from capital to operating budgets; this can offer increased flexibility in spending. Purchased computers are depreciated over several years, while a vendor's monthly charges can be accounted for differently. Comparisons with in-house costs in the baseline period may become less useful as new factors and circumstances arise. Much depends on how in-house costs/savings are projected for comparison purposes. These issues were pointed out by respondents in UTILITY2, GLASS, PETRO2, RETAIL2 and UTILITY4.

In-house IT costs may already be falling

Organizations can achieve savings through consolidating data centres, as occurred at, for example, BANK1, ELECTRIC, FOOD1. This assumes, of course, that the organization has the technical resources and capital to accomplish the task. When organizations consider vendor bids, they also need to take account of improved hardware price/performance through falling market prices. Relative in-house costs may also already be falling due to changes in demand and usage. These points were made to us by respondents from BANK2, PETRO1, RE-TAIL2 and RETAIL3. They also emerge strongly from subsequent case study work in the 1995–7 period (Currie and Willcocks, 1997).

Organizations may compare the costs of all in-house services against what the vendor is selectively bidding for

Both the UTILITY3 and PSB5 cases point to the difficulties in identifying all services provided in-house relative to their costs. In several other cases we found the vendor and contract being quite explicit about the service levels to be provided. However, the client company failed to identify, and so contract for, several services bundled into what was provided by the in-house function. In other cases the contract was vague on these issues, and this sometimes promoted subsequent disputes between client and vendor.

Vendors may not get any better deals on hardware and software

Large companies can often get hardware discounts similar to those received by vendors. Software companies are becoming harder on charging for the transfer of software licensing agreements and outsourcing vendors may no longer be able to spread software licensing fees over multiple customers. Furthermore, in several of our cases, for example BANK1, UTILITY2, PETRO2 and PSB2, contracts stipulated that the costs of transfer of licensing agreements fell on the client company, not the vendor.

Outsourcing can carry hidden costs

Lacity and Hirschheim (1993) report one petroleum company being charged almost $500 000 in "excess fees" the first month into the contract. We found a range of service items being excluded from many outsourcing contracts. Computer workloads can change dramatically and new applications may be required. As many of our respondents testified, if these events occur during the course of the contract, the vendor was in a good position to dictate price. Several organizations, for example BANK1 and RETAILER1, were surprised at the subsequent high costs in transferring software licence agreements. In three cases—AVIATION, GOODS and MANUF1—the outsourcing deal was so favourable to the client organization that the vendors stood to make losses. Not surprisingly, this triggered opportunistic behaviour. As one respondent from AVIATION commented: "I don't blame them; they were very professional. Every time we sneezed it cost us £10 000." There may also be hidden personnel costs. For example, in the 1989 Eastman Kodak deal, 50 Kodak employees were paid a total of $750 000 to move to the vendor Businessland.

Establish if and where the vendor makes a profit

Many respondents in both the case study and survey research pointed out the value of establishing before signing the outsourcing contract whether there will be financial benefit on both sides. When the Chief Information Officer of Avon Products, New York, assessed outsourcing, he used the following financial guideline:

> If the outsourcer could make a 15% profit and I could save 15% of IS expense, then we'd probably get pretty close to a deal. (quoted in Aucoin *et al.*, 1991)

In this case, the decision was against outsourcing. At the same time, of course, few organizations we researched looked at just the economics. Most often, the direct economics of outsourcing was part of a bigger equation being considered. In practice we have found respondents seeking a mix of business, economic, technical and political objectives in their sourcing decisions (Currie and Willcocks, 1997; Willcocks and Fitzgerald, 1994). In some circumstances, for example for BREWER where the aim was to transfer staff to the vendor rather than make them redundant, the economic criteria may well be less demanding. Even so, allowing the vendor reasonable profit can become important. In BANK1 the vendor provided by far the most economic deal of those on offer. However, in the performance of the contract the vendor stuck to the letter of the contract and offered no real improvement on previous service levels. In another deal worth over £7 million a year the vendor was operating on very tight margins:

> I think that within the vendor this deal was struck for strategic reasons. When the senior guy asked his subordinates "Can we make money at £8 million?" and they said no, his response was well you'd better! So with a tight contract they looked for every opportunity to increase their margins and that was not conducive to a happy relationship. (IT Director, GOODS)

The vendor bid can reveal ways of improving in-house performance

A number of organizations were found to have gained from the experience of assessing vendor bids. These included FOOD1, BANK2, INSURANCE, CHEM1 and PSB4. Here, the bids acted as catalysts in pushing in-house services to consider actions they were already contemplating but would have taken longer to get around to doing. Thus in PSB4:

> All the ways that the FM company could reduce costs were open to us, with the possible exception of some of the staffing implications. On the staffing side they could cut costs by changing conditions of service or trying to operate with fewer staff ... however, the staff saving of £400 000 was more than matched by the vendor's annual management fee of £600 000 ... So the decision was made to stay in-house. (Contract Manager)

This type of finding in our research is supported by a study of six US organizations carried out by Lacity and Hirschheim (1995). Having decided to reject vendor bids, these organizations subsequently saw their in-house functions achieve reductions in IT costs of between 25 and 54%.

CONCLUSIONS

In our research we found many organizations at different stages in what is in fact a common approach to evaluating IT outsourcing options. The approach is to pursue in-house improvements first; establish performance benchmarks and identify full costs; again pursue improvements; then make an in-house/outsource comparison. Where a decision to keep IT in-house is made, the loop is repeated and the outsourcing option reassessed at up to two-year intervals. If an outsourcing decision is made, specific measures need to be developed, though existing benchmarks and metrics may well prove helpful. There needs to be regular monitoring and searches for how vendor performance can be improved. Organizations following this route into outsourcing generally reported anticipated or above-anticipated benefits several years into their contracts.

Having said this, we found many examples of organizations with effective cost-saving outsourcing deals. Most of these selectively outsourced on shorter-term contracts. This may well reflect a low-risk approach by organizations relatively inexperienced in outsourcing which identified cost savings as a primary objective. However, several organizations that undertook outsourcing in such circumstances did not produce the cost savings expected, not least because of failures in many of the evaluation areas discussed in this chapter. It is clear, nevertheless, that even in cases where cost savings were not of paramount concern, evaluation practice leading up to an IT outsourcing assessment, together with more informed approaches to assessing vendor bids, had a critical role to play. To be cost effective, outsourcing can never be treated as a move from managing to spending on IT. Even if it were, this would make critical the assessment process leading up to an outsourcing decision. In practice, the pre-outsourcing evaluation arrangements will need to inform contract monitoring and management—yet another reason for understanding more fully, and measuring more closely, the economics of in-house performance and of vendors' bids.

REFERENCES

Astley, W. (1985). Administrative Science as Socially Constructed Truth. *Administrative Science Quarterly*, 30, 4, 497–513.

Aucoin, P., Almy, F., Heise, R., Landry, R. *et al.* (1991*). Internalizing the Vendor's Resources: Outsourcing in the 1990s.* Report No. C-6-1, Chantico Publishing, Boston, MA.

Bergstrom, L. (1991). *The Ins and Outs of Outsourcing.* Real Decisions Corporation, Darien, New York.

Bergstrom, L. (1996). Measuring and Managing Distributed Computing Environments. Paper at the *Developing the New IT Scorecard conference*, 6–7th February, London.

Buck-Lew, M. (1992). To Outsource or not? *International Journal of Information Management*, 12, 1, 3–20.

Currie, W. and Willcocks, L. (1997) *New Strategies in IT Outsourcing: Trends and Global Best Practices.* Business Intelligence, London.

Due, R. (1992). The Real Costs of Outsourcing. *Information Systems Management*, Winter, 78–81.

Feeny, D., Earl, M. and Edwards, B. (1997). IS Organisation: The Role of Users and Specialists. In Willcocks, L., Feeny, D. and Islei, G. (eds) *Managing IT as a Strategic Resource.* McGraw-Hill, Maidenhead.

Gupta, U. and Gupta, A. (1992). Outsourcing the IS Function: Is it Necessary for Your Organization? *Information Systems Management*, Summer, 44–50.

Graeser, V., Willcocks, L. and Pisanias, N. (1998). *Developing the IT Scorecard: Practices and Prognosis.* Business Intelligence, London.

I/S Analyzer (1990). *Taking an Objective Look at Outsourcing.* United Communications, Maryland, September.

Kaplan, R. and Norton, D. (1992). The Balanced Scorecard: Measures that Drive Performance. *Harvard Business Review*, January–February, 71–9.

Krass, P. (1990). The Dollars and Sense of Outsourcing. *Information Week*, February 26th, 26–31.

Lacity, M. and Hirschheim, R. (1993). *Information Systems Outsourcing.* John Wiley, Chichester.

Lacity, M. and Hirschheim, R. (1995*). Beyond the Information Systems Outsourcing Bandwagon.* John Wiley, Chichester.

Lacity, M. and Willcocks, L. (1996*). On Interpreting IT Outsourcing from a Transaction Cost Perspective.* Oxford Institute of Information Management Working Paper 96/2, Templeton College, Oxford.

Lacity, M., Willcocks, L. and Feeny, D. (1997). The Value of Selective IT Sourcing. In Willcocks, L., Feeny, D. and Islei, G. (eds) *Managing IT as a Strategic Resource*. McGraw-Hill, Maidenhead.

Lincoln, Y. and Gubba, E. (1985). *Naturalistic Inquiry*. Sage, Beverly Hills.

Mintzberg, H. (1979). An Emerging Strategy of 'Direct' Research. *Administrative Science Quarterly*, 24, 4, 582–9.

Norris, G. (1996). Post-Investment Appraisal. In Willcocks, L. (ed.) *Investing in Information Systems: Evaluation and Management*. Chapman and Hall, London.

Peters, G. (1996). Beyond Strategy—Benefits Identification and the Management of Specific IT Investments. In Willcocks, L. (ed.) *Investing in Information Systems: Evaluation and Management*. Chapman and Hall, London.

Pettigrew, A. (1990). Longitudinal Field Research on Change: Theory and Practice. *Organization Science*, 1, 3, 267–92.

Radding, A. (1990). The Dollars and Sense of Outsourcing. *Computerworld*, January 8th, 67–72.

Sanders, P. (1982). Phenomenology: a New Way of Viewing Organizational Research. *Academy of Management Review*, 7, 3, 353–60.

Van Maanen, J. (1979). The Fact of Fiction in Organizational Ethnography. *Administrative Science Quarterly*, 24, 4, 539–50.

Walsham, G. (1995). Interpretive Case Studies in IS Research: Nature and Method. *European Journal of Information Systems*, 4, 2, 74–81.

White, R. and James, B. (1996). *The Outsourcing Manual*. Gower, Aldershot.

Willcocks, L. (ed.) (1994). *Information Management: Evaluation of Information Systems Investments*. Chapman and Hall, London.

Willcocks, L. (ed.) (1996). *Investing in Information Systems: Evaluation And Management*. Chapman and Hall, London.

Willcocks, L. and Fitzgerald, G. (1993). Market as Opportunity? Cases in Outsourcing IT and Related Services in the United Kingdom. *Journal of Strategic Information Systems*, 2, 3, 223–42.

Willcocks, L. and Fitzgerald, G. (1994). *A Business Guide to Outsourcing IT: a Study of European Best Practice in the Selection, Management and Use of External IT Services*. Business Intelligence, London.

Willcocks, L., Fitzgerald, G. and Feeny, D. (1995). Outsourcing IT—The Strategic Implications. *Long Range Planning*, 28, 5, 59–70.

Willcocks, L. and Kern, T. (1997). IT Outsourcing as Strategic Partnering: the Case of the Inland Revenue. *Proceedings of the Fifth European Conference on Information Systems*, Cork, Ireland, June.

Willcocks, L. and Lacity, M. (eds) (1997). *Strategic Sourcing of Information Systems*. John Wiley, Chichester.

Willcocks, L., Lacity, M. and Fitzgerald, G. (1995). IT Outsourcing in Europe and the USA: Assessment Issues. *International Journal of Information Management*, 15, 5, 333–51.

Willcocks, L. and Lester, S. (1996). The Evaluation and Management of Information Systems Investments: from Feasibility to Routine Operations. In Willcocks, L. (ed.) *Investing in Information Systems: Evaluation and Management*. Chapman and Hall, London.

APPENDIX 10.1:   INTERVIEW GUIDE

Questions for total insourcing and total outsourcing

1. Please begin by telling me your outsourcing/insourcing story. Why did you initiate an evaluation, what process did you go through, what was the outcome?
2. What functions were considered for outsourcing?
3. What degree of specialized business knowledge is required to perform this function?
4. What degree of specialized technical knowledge is required to perform this function?
5. Do you perceive that this function is generally available on the markets?
6. Did the scope of the decision change over time?
7. Who first proposed the idea of evaluating outsourcing?
8. Did he or she feel strongly either way, or did he or she just want to test the waters?
9. What was our initial reaction? Did your reaction change over time?
10. What organizational members did you perceive as proponents of outsourcing? Opponents?
11. What was senior management's perceptions of the decision? Do they view IT as a strategic asset or a commodity?
12. Who in your company became the most avid champion of outsourcing? Most opposed?
13. What criteria did opponents/proponents think was most important for deciding whether or not to outsource?
14. What information did opponents/proponents gather?
15. How confident are you that cost estimates are reasonable?
16. Did any organizational members bring in outside experts to assist with the outsourcing decision?
17. What recommendations did the outside expert make?
18. Were any other options or compromises explored in addition to outsourcing?
19. Did any vendor submit a bid that was more desirable than your current MIS operations?
20. How did the internal MIS costs compare with vendor bids?
21. Did you believe that you can run an MIS department as eficiently as a vendor? Why or why not?
22. Can an outsourcing vendor reduce costs in any area in which your company could not reduce costs on their own?
23. How do you think the outsourcing vendor will achieve costs savings?
24. What are the contract terms as far as baseline services, service-level requirements, and penalties for non-performance?
25. What would you do if the vendor unexpectedly terminated the relationship?
26. What do you perceive as the strengths and weaknesses of the contract?

27. How many pages is the contract?
28. Did you hire an outsourcing legal expert to represent your interests?
29. Have you ever been charged for services that you assumed were covered in the contract?
30. Have you had any disputes with the vendor? How were they resolved?
31. What advice would you give to a peer who was about to embark on an outsourcing evaluation?
32. Other company data:
    - Organizational chart/number of MIPS/number of MIS employees
    - MIS budget/accounting structure of MIS
    - Measures (benchmarks) used to demonstrate the value of IS to senior management
    - Number of reporting levels of CIO to CEO
    - MIS planning and budget practices
33. Other participant data:
    - Length of service/job title/length of time in current position/age (ranges provided)

Questions for Selective Sourcing

1. Ask respondent's general view on outsourcing IT, what conditions it and how his/her view has been formed. Personal experiences. What is his/her opinion of what has been seen elsewhere, what works, what does not. Risks, problems, what makes for success?
2. History of outsourcing from 1980 to present?
3. What deals were made?
4. How were they managed?
5. What was kept in-house and why?
6. History of IT:
    - Spend (total and % turnover)
    - Number of people and type
    - Structure (centralized, federal, decentralized)
    - Reporting (to board, finance etc.)
    - How has IT been viewed in the organization up to now?
    - Has this view had an effect on outsourcing/insourcing?
7. How would you describe the current strategy for outsourcing?
    - Reasons for outsourcing
    - Who makes outsourcing decisions
    - Process of decision making
8. What IT is now outsourced?
    - Total, number of projects/areas/when outsourced/overall value
    - Problems and areas of risk/perceptions of success and failure
9. Take 4–6 major contracts one by one. Ask respondent to focus on:
    a. Most successful, the history of each and the reasons for success
    b. Most troublesome, the history, stories, people involved, what would they have done in retrospect?

10. Areas to cover;
    - Area/vendor/value/start date/end date/current stage
11. Process of evaluation
    - Origin of idea/in-house metrics/vendors/SLAs/departments involved
12. Contract
    - Type (fully detailed/relational partnership)
    - People/resources transferred to the vendor
    - Penalty clauses/get out and termination/how changing circumstances dealth with
13. Original perceived benefits
    - Economics/organizational/human resource/business/IT
14. Experiences
    - Perceptions of success/failure
    - How measured/problems encountered/vendor performance
    - Will contract be renewed?
15. Issues in managing
    - Negotiation/legal skills/transferring people
    - Other?

Specific Questions for Different Respondents

IT Manager

- What skills are needed to manage the vendor/contract?
- What impact has outsourcing had on the in-house function?
- What impact on in-house structure and staff?
- How did they react, how can it be managed?
- What are your future plans and your attitude towards future outsourcing?
- How/where do you think the vendors make their money?
- Anything you would not outsource?

Senior Manager

- Who leads business/IT objectives?
- Measurement?
- Control of results?
- If you could do it over, what would you do differently?
- Future outsourcing plans?
- How/where do you think the vendors make their money?
- Is there anything you would not outsource?

Vendor

- Problems in getting the contract?
- Issues in the contract?

- What do you expect from the customer?
- How are problems handled?
- Why did they choose you?
- What advice would you give a vendor based on your experience?
- Where do you make your money?

User Manager

- Perceived service levels
- Problems arising in contracts?
- Skills needed for dealing with a vendor?
- Any measurement of results issues?

Final Questions

- Any issues we missed that you would like to bring up?
- Ask for documentation supporting anything during interview.

11
Four Views of IT Infrastructure: Implications for IT Investments

PETER WEILL AND MARIANNE BROADBENT
Melbourne Business School and Gartner Group

INTRODUCTION: THE IMPORTANCE OF IT INFRASTRUCTURE

The role of corporate IS (information systems) groups is changing as responsibility for IT is dispersed throughout the firm. An important (or perhaps the only) role for the corporate IS group in a decentralized or federated environment is to coordinate the IT infrastructure for the business units (Ahituv and Neumann, 1990; Keen, 1991).

IT infrastructure has consistently been a key concern of IS management (Niederman, Brancheau and Wetherbe, 1991; CSC Index, 1994; Broadbent *et al.*, 1995; Brancheau, Janz and Wetherbe 1996) and its significance is now increasingly being recognized by senior management (Davenport and Linder, 1994). IT infrastructure is the largest contributor to long-term strategic business advantage (Keen, 1991) and accounts for about 57% of IT expenditure (Weill and Broadbent, 1998). The capabilities delivered by IT infrastructure underpin new and sustainable competitive strategies (Boynton, Victor and Pine, 1993; McKenney, 1995), the emergence of new organizational forms (Davidow and Malone, 1992; Miller, Clemons and Row, 1993), international business operations (Neo, 1991; Broadbent and Butler, 1997) and facilitate the development of virtual (or electronic) value chains (Rayport and Sviokla, 1995). IT infrastructure can be a significant barrier or enabler in

Beyond the IT Productivity Paradox.
Edited by L. P. Willcocks and S. Lester © 1999 John Wiley & Sons Ltd.

the practical options available for planning and changing business processes (Grover, Teng and Fiedler, 1993; Wastell, White and Kawalek, 1994). The support of enabling technologies and platforms is an important contributor to successful business process change (Furey and Diorio, 1994; Ramcharamdas, 1994; Caron, Jarvenpaa and Stoddard, 1994).

The purpose of this chapter is to examine the role of IT infrastructure as part of the process of managing the portfolio of IT investments (see also Chapters 6 and 7). The concepts fundamental to managing information technology are those of business, not technology: portfolios, business value, investment and aligning resources with strategic goals. The elements of IT infrastructure and the different roles for IT infrastructure in the strategic context of firms are explained using examples of the role of IT infrastructure in four firms.

This chapter draws on our recent industry research into the role and payoff of IT infrastructure investments. This international project, sponsored by the IBM Consulting Group, examined the role and value of IT infrastructure investments in 54 business units in 27 large for-profit sector firms, spanning three industries including process manufacturing, retail and finance. The research helps answer the questions: why do firms invest in IT infrastructure? What are the role and value of IT infrastructure in different firms? The experience of the firms in the study indicates that IT infrastructure is a critical component in the strategic positioning of firms. The productivity of IT, current and future, is under threat and there is little detailed focus on how IT infrastructure investments are evaluated and managed.

STRATEGIC CONTEXT AND IT INVESTMENTS

Firms have portfolios of IT investments, just as investors have portfolios of financial investments. Managers make decisions about their IT portfolio on a cluster of factors, including the capabilities required now and in the future, the role of technology in the industry, the level of investment, the clarity with which technology investments are viewed and the role and history of information technology in the firm.

The objective of investments in information technology is to provide business value in two ways: to implement strategies successfully and to use the technology to enable new strategies. Strategies are derived and emerge from the firm's complex set of business, competitive, organizational and environmental circumstances.

To achieve the delicate balance between articulating strategic objectives and overwhelming managers with demotivating processes, we use three constructs which help to inform the information technology portfolio needs: strategic intent, current strategy and business goals. Together, these three constructs form critical components of a firm's strategic context.

The *strategic intent* of a firm specifies its long-term, stable goals—a worthwhile destination where a firm desires to be. The notion was popularized by Hamel and Prahalad (1989). The destination should require a stretch for the firm. *Current strategy* specifies how the firm will do business today: what is the combination of products and service that will be offered to which customers, via what channels, at what price and quality levels? Current strategies have relatively short lives and many firms have new current strategies every 12 months. *Business goals* flow from strategic intent and current strategies and include quantitative and qualitative business targets with measures to determine progress.

The key question is whether a firm's investment in information technology is in harmony with its strategic objectives (intent, current and business goals), thus providing business value (see Chapters 2 and 7). This state of harmony is referred to as alignment. It is complex, multifaceted and never completed.

Alignment between strategic context and the information technology portfolio requires planned and purposeful management processes, within both business and information technology disciplines. Complete alignment can never be achieved, as the demands of business, competitor activity, management needs and technology choices are constantly changing. Alignment is also made more difficult by the time it takes, often measured in years, for a firm to build or substantially change its information technology portfolio. As a consequence, non-alignment is the natural state of firms.

The key consideration for firms is:

Are we heading in the right direction in terms of aligning the portfolio with business needs and are we better aligned than our competitors?

The IT portfolio of large firms consists of myriad information systems and technologies. Some of this investment is infrastructure, long term and focused on achieving the firm's strategic intent by providing a shared base of IT capability. Other investments are aimed at the more immediate and direct benefits allied to executing current business strategies. All investment in IT is not alike and it is helpful to distinguish between the different management objectives for different parts of the portfolio.

MANAGEMENT OBJECTIVES AND THE IT PORTFOLIO

In our perspective, firms invest in IT to achieve four fundamentally different management objectives: strategic, informational, transactional and infrastructure. These types of IT make up the IT investment pyramid (Weill and Lucas, 1992). Figure 11.1 depicts these different objectives and their relationships.

At the base of the IT investment pyramid is the *IT infrastructure*. This is the base foundation of IT capability, in the form of reliable services shared throughout the firm and coordinated by the information systems group. The IT capability includes both the technical and managerial expertise required to provide reliable services. For example, IT infrastructure services in a firm often include firm-wide communication network services, management and provision of mainframe computing, the firm-wide intranet, the management of shared customer databases, and research and development expertise aimed at identifying the application of emerging technologies to the business. The IT investment which uses and sits on top of the infrastructure consists of the applications which actually perform the business processes.

The next level of the pyramid is the *transactional IT* that processes the basic, repetitive transactions of the firm. These include systems which support order processing, inventory control, receivables, payables and other transactional processing. Transactional systems are developed to cut costs, often by substituting capital for labour or to make it possible to handle high volumes of transactions. Transactional systems build on and depend on the IT infrastructure being in place and reliable.

The apex of the pyramid contains both the informational and strategic uses of IT, which depend on and are supported by the infrastruc-

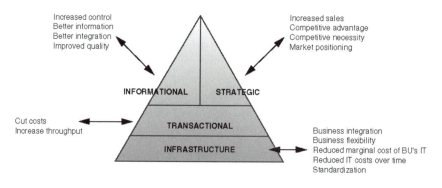

Figure 11.1   *Management Objectives for IT*

ture and the transactional systems. Usually both infrastructure and transactional systems must be in place before informational or strategic systems are feasible.

Informational IT provides the information for managing and controlling the organization. Systems in this category typically support management control, planning, communications and accounting. Data for the informational systems come from summaries of the transactional systems and from data on the industry, competitors and economy external to the firm.

The objective of *strategic IT* investments is quite different. Strategic investments in IT are made to gain competitive advantage or position the firm in the marketplace, most often by increasing market share or sales. Successful strategic IT initiatives usually involve a new use of IT for an industry at a particular point in time (for example, the first finance company to provide online 24-hour, 7-day-a-week loan approvals in car yards using expert systems point-scoring technology).

The nature and extent of IT investment for each of these management objectives is determined by the firm's strategic context, that is, its strategic intent and current business strategies. It is the longer-term component of the strategic context which must drive IT infrastructure investment decisions. IT infrastructure aims to provide the components and services to achieve strategic intent via any number of current business strategies which are consistent with that strategic intent. These current strategies might be, as yet, unspecified.

The strategic intent and current strategy, in combination, drive the other IT investments in the pyramid. Transactional, informational and strategic systems change with changes in current business strategies. For example, a new home loan product in a bank requires a new transactional system. In contrast, the infrastructure services required are relatively stable over time. The new home loan application uses most of the same infrastructure services as the previous application, such as mainframe processing, branch banking PC/LAN network, integrated customer database and security services.

The two firms in Figure 11.2 demonstrate the use of the pyramid to assess the alignment of the IT portfolio with the strategic context. Both are single-business unit firms and have strong alignment of their IT portfolios with business strategy (Weillard and Broadbent, 1998).

The cabinet manufacturer has a strong growth strategy and values flexibility. This is reflected in its IT portfolio which has a flexible and extensive national infrastructure and applications which position the firm in the marketplace. The more extensive and expensive IT infrastructure provides a more flexible base of infrastructure services to enable the quick implementation of new applications. The car rental

Business	Long-term goals	Current strategy	Major IT applications and infrastructure	% of IT investment in pyramid
Car rental	Lowest-cost car rental catering to vacationers in a few busy locations	Providing low rates for pre-loved cars available to hire near airports and cheaper down town hotels. Strong cost-cutting emphasis	Billing Reservations Car tracking Car maintenance General ledger Limited reach and range—minimum infrastructure services	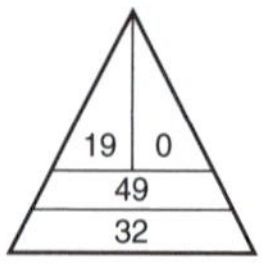 19 | 0 / 49 / 32
Cabinets	Significant growth to product range and geographical coverage, quickly addressing changing customer needs	New range of premium-priced cabinets with solid wood doors in addition to budget range	Instore scanners and systems to enter building plans and determine appropriate sizes, quantities and costs, providing a 3D perspective drawing and confirmed delivery date. Nationwide reach and extensive range of IT infrastructure services.	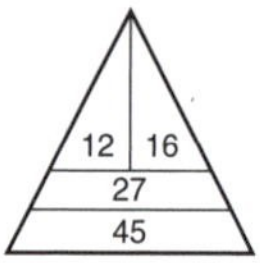 12 | 16 / 27 / 45

Figure 11.2   *Comparing IT Portfolios in two Firms*

firm has a low-cost, no-frills strategy with a limited, inflexible infrastructure which supports applications for processing transactions and providing cost and control information. The family of applications which can be supported by the current IT infrastructure in the car rental firm is significantly narrower than from the cabinet firm.

If either firm had the IT portfolio of the other, a poor alignment between IT and strategy would result.

NATURE OF IT INFRASTRUCTURE

IT infrastructure investments are typically large, long term in nature and underpin the future competitiveness of firms (Keen, 1991). As with public infrastructure investments of roads and bridges, these investments often must be made in anticipation of business developments. The return on infrastructure investments in terms of business results is difficult to track directly as they do not necessarily provide direct business performance benefits (Parker, Benson and Trainor, 1988). The benefits are realized by business systems connected to and enabled by the infrastructure and the rapid implementation of other systems in the pyramid.

The shaded box in Figure 11.3, containing the shared applications,

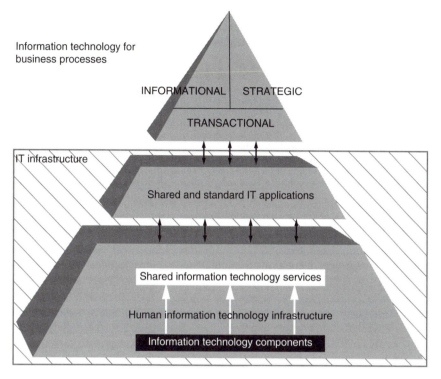

Figure 11.3   *Elements of IT Infrastructure*

shared services and components, make up the firm's IT infrastructure. The objective of the firm's infrastructure is to provide a stable base of reliable services and applications to enable the IT for the business processes to be easily connected and changed. The IT for business processes, however, changes regularly to meet the needs of the current strategy. Often these changes occur on a yearly basis as business processes are changed to serve customers better.

The elements of IT infrastructure depicted in Figure 11.3 were derived from our research and the work of McKay and Brockaway (1989) and Keen (1991). At the base are the IT components (e.g. computers and communication technologies), which are commodities and readily available in the marketplace. The second layer above is a set of shared IT services such as mainframe processing, electronic data interchange (EDI) or a full-service telecommunications network. The IT components are converted into useful IT services by the human IT infrastructure that can be used as building blocks for business systems. The human IT infrastructure of knowledge, skills, architecture and experience binds the IT components into reliable services which form the firm's IT infrastructure.

In our study of 27 firms, 25 distinct firm-wide IT infrastructure services were identified and are presented in Table 11.1. The top five infrastructure services were present in all multibusiness-unit firms with any firm-wide infrastructure. This set of services (Broadbent *et al.*, 1996) is relatively stable over time. Similar services are required from year to year, with gradual improvements over time taking advantage of the new technologies and efficiencies.

The shared IT infrastructure services must be defined and provided in a way that allows them to be used by multiple applications. The

Table 11.1   *Firm-wide IT Infrastructure Services*

5 core IT infrastructure services in firms
1. Management of corporation communication network services
2. Management of group-wide or firm-wide messaging services
3. Recommend standards for at least one component of IT architecture (e.g. hardware, operating systems, data, communications)
4. Security, disaster planning and business recovery services for firm-wide installations and applications
5. Technology advice and support services

20 additional IT infrastructure services
6. Management, maintenance, support of large-scale data-processing facilities (e.g. mainframe operations)
7. Management of group-wide or firm-wide applications and databases
8. Performing IS project management
9. Data management advice and consultancy services
10. Providing IS planning for business units
11. Enforcement of IT architecture and standards
12. Management of business-unit-specific networks (e.g. LANs)
13. Managing and negotiating with suppliers and outsourcers
14. Identification and testing of new technologies for business purposes
15. Development of business-unit-specific applications (usually on a chargeback or contractual basis)
16. Implementation of security, disaster planning and recovery for business units
17. Electronic provision of management information (e.g. EIS)
18. Management of business-unit-specific applications
19. Group-wide or firm-wide data management, including standards
20. Development and management of online and/or EDI linkages to suppliers or customers (e.g. Web page)
21. Development of a common systems development environment
22. Technology education services (e.g. training)
23. Multimedia operations and development (e.g. videoconferencing)
24. Provide firm-wide Internet capability
25. Provide firm-wide electronic support groups

objective is to enable economies, reuse, synergies and flexibility. The nominal owner of these shared services must have firm-wide responsibility (e.g. the CIO). An application such as order processing may use as many as five or six services which must all be in place and accessible. To achieve this level of modularity and integration requires careful specification of the IT architecture (Keen 1995) and particularly the specification of the interfaces to the infrastructure services with which new applications will need to comply.

Shared and standard applications, the centre block in Figure 11.3, form the next part of the IT Infrastructure. In the firms studied we estimate that approximately 5% of the annual IT investment was in shared and standard applications, while 52% (i.e. 57% less 5%) was firm-wide IT infrastructure. Historically these applications have been general management applications such as general ledger, human resources management and budgeting. However, now we are observing a fast-growing trend of strategic positions driving the adoption of shared and standard applications for key processes (e.g. ERP systems).

Unlike IT infrastructure services, the scope of infrastructure applications is for a particular business process. We observed examples where the "notional owner" of the infrastructure applications was a manager of the particular business process (e.g. buying in retailing) or, in some cases, the CIO.

Infrastructures are usually provided at both the corporate and business unit levels. The business unit infrastructure is more tailored to the particular needs of the business unit and connects in a "plug compatible" way to the corporate infrastructure. Some firms have very little corporate IT infrastructure, while others have little or no business unit infrastructure sharing the centrally provided infrastructure services.

The Pacific business of a multinational consumer products firm provides an example of infrastructure that is predominantly corporate. IT infrastructure services of this healthcare company, headquartered in Sydney, include:

- corporate telecommunications network, including EDI linkages to clients;
- large-scale computing services, including a support facility;
- electronic mail facilities for local and off-shore communications;
- corporate shared application systems such as the general ledger, manufacturing systems and the consolidated customer file.

The corporate information services department provides these IT infrastructure services on an AS/400 computer and electronic mail on a Digital VAX computer. These computers are connected via an Ethernet link. Information processing of corporate data is centralized. Business-unit-specific systems, such as sales and retail data, are processed by the corporate information services department but owned by the business units.

The dimensions of the IT infrastructure can be specified in terms of reach and range (Keen, 1991; Keen and Cummins, 1994) provided by a firm's infrastructure. Reach indicates the extent of locations which can be linked. A firm with a limited reach might only be able to link its employees in a single location, while a firm with extensive reach could link customers or suppliers, regardless of their IT base. Range refers to the richness and integration of the services provided and determines the breadth of functionality that can be directly and seamlessly shared across the systems and services. Infrastructure with a limited range provides the ability to send only standard messages. A more extensive range provides the capability to perform multiple transactions which simultaneously updated databases. The combination of the available reach and range is useful in depicting the dimensions of the firm's IT infrastructure in business terms.

A comprehensive IT infrastructure provides flexibility in meeting the incipient trends of the marketplace. For example, Otis Elevators revolutionized the service side of the elevator industry with its highly acclaimed computer-based customer service system, "Otisline" (Otisline, 1990). Otis Elevators was able to produce "Otisline" at least four years faster because of the existence of an IT infrastructure including a flexible database named the Service Management System (SMS). When the database was first installed, "Otisline" had not been conceived. Sufficient flexibility was incorporated into the design to enable the production of "Otisline" in a much shorter time than starting from scratch. Valuing the infrastructure before "Otisline" would have been very difficult. However, the value of the flexibility of the investment is clear in hindsight. The four-year break on the competition was a significant advantage in the marketplace.

Building in flexibility, such as the SMS database at Otis, adds cost and complexity but provides a business option that may be exercised in the future (Kambil, Henderson and Mohsenzadeh, 1993). Otis exercised its option and added the application systems supporting "Otisline", generating significant business benefits to the company.

An IT infrastructure of greater reach and range, beyond what is currently required by the business units, provides flexibility or agility for future needs. The existence of the flexibility allows far more rapid response to an emerging business need. One reason firms invest in infrastructure is to buy flexibility.

Thus, even though investments in IT may be difficult to relate to short-term benefits, the IT infrastructure is a major business resource and perhaps one of the few sources of a long-term competitive advantage (Keen, 1991; McKenney, 1995). Good infrastructure is not a commodity and thus is difficult to duplicate or outsource. The human IT infrastructure of knowledge and skills and the IT management vision provide much of the value added of IT infrastructure.

What firms expect to get from their IT infrastructure investments depends on their view of the role of IT infrastructure. The investment, benefit expectations and value of IT infrastructure are determined to a great extent by the way the firm views IT infrastructure.

FOUR VIEWS OF IT INFRASTRUCTURE

Four different views of IT infrastructure have been observed (Weill, 1993): None, Utility, Dependent and Enabling. These views have now been closely examined in our study of large firms (Weill and Broadbent, 1998).

We have been able to classify the role of IT infrastructure following the collection of extensive quantitative data and on-site interviews with both business and IS executives. Criteria for classifying views of firm-wide IT infrastructure include a combination of:

1. The level of the firm's IT investments relative to competitors.
2. The extent of the firm's investment in IT infrastructure.
3. The firm's approach to justifying investments in IT infrastructure at board level.
4. The reach and range of the firm's IT infrastructure.
5. The extent of the infrastructure services offered on a firm-wide basis.

The different views imply different levels of up-front infrastructure investment, with different approaches to cost justification and different expected benefit profiles. Figure 11.4 depicts the four views of infrastructure and their primary value drivers. We describe each of these views and then present case vignettes which illustrate these views in firms studied.

A None view of infrastructure implies that the firm has no firm-wide IT infrastructure. The firm usually has independent business units with few synergies. This type of firm usually operates with a minimum of mandates from the corporate centre, encouraging each business unit to invest independently in information technology as in other assets. In taking this view, the firm forgoes any potential economies of scale or business synergies from the sharing of IT infrastructure.

An Utility view of infrastructure implies that expenditure on IT

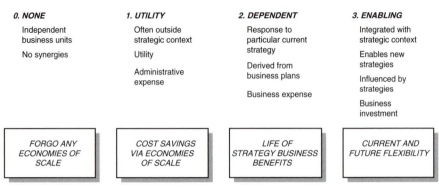

Figure 11.4   *Infrastructure Views and Primary Value Drivers*

infrastructure is seen primarily as a way of saving costs through economies of scale. IT is seen as a utility that provides a necessary and
unavoidable service which incurs administrative expenses. The management thrust is to minimize the expense for a desired level of utility
service.

A Dependent view of infrastructure implies that the infrastructure
investments are primarily in response to specific, known business
strategies. Dependent infrastructure investments are derived from
business plans which specify, or imply, IT needs. Thus planning for
infrastructure is undertaken after current business strategies have been
articulated. For example, a bank might invest heavily by consolidating
previously independent databases into an integrated customer relationship database. This infrastructure investment is dependent on a
current strategy of differentiating customer service through relationship banking.

An Enabling view of infrastructure implies that infrastructure investments relate primarily to long-term requirements for flexibility to
achieve strategic intent. These are often created by expanding the reach
and/or range of Dependent infrastructure beyond the current requirements of the business. The resulting infrastructure enables new, and as
yet unspecified, business strategies to achieve the strategic intent. It
provides future options for implementing strategies. The flexibility of
the infrastructure enables a number of, as yet unspecified, business
strategies to be implemented more rapidly than firms with a Dependent
or Utility view of infrastructure. To take an Enabling view, senior
managers must perceive a flexible infrastructure as an asset of the firm
providing a competitive advantage. This view also implies that the firm
values this flexible asset during the project justification process.

Where greater flexibility and business ''degrees of freedom'' are part of the firm's strategic intent, an Enabling, rather than a Utility, view of infrastructure provides a higher level of alignment between IT and business strategy. Alignment between firm-wide strategic context and an appropriate view of IT infrastructure is achieved through distillation of the implications of strategic intent for long-term IT management decisions on providing information support. Clearly, how IT infrastructure is viewed determines how investments are made, which in turn affects the type and scale of returns from those investments. Let us examine this proposition through four case studies.

CASE VIGNETTES

Summaries of case vignettes illustrate the views of IT infrastructure—None, Utility, Dependent and Enabling—in four firms.

None View of Infrastructure—DiverseCo

DiverseCo manufactures food, household and plastic products and is organized into a divisionalized structure with six divisions. The firm has over 25 000 employees and revenue of over $5 billion.

DiverseCo sees sustainable growth in the late 1990s as dependent on its ability to evolve simultaneously with its diverse markets and even to drive that evolution. Each business is focused on increased speed and accuracy in business processes in serving both trade customers and consumers, and in promoting and defending its brand power. However, the products, customers and brands differ markedly from one division to another.

DiverseCo has a lean corporate office and, as with other functions, responsibility for information systems is dispersed throughout the firm. There is no corporate IS group, the IT portfolios of each division differ significantly and there is no firm-wide IT portfolio. While there is a corporate general ledger, this is maintained by one of the divisions on behalf of the corporate office.

IT infrastructure decisions are made at the divisional level in conjunction with the strategic and operational needs of each division. The firm has no centralized planning process for developing IT infrastructure. Divisions manage their own IT planning, systems development, systems maintenance, security, training and R&D. Approval of IS projects within divisions differs by division. This approach is consistent with the diversified nature of the firm, minimal synergy between products, and a culture where the focus is on brands in divisions rather than corporate branding.

Utility View of Infrastructure—ChemCo

ChemCo is a leading supplier of industrial and specialty chemicals. ChemCo's employees are spread over 80 locations in the Pacific Basin and total sales in the mid-1990s were over $1.5 billion. ChemCo is a divisionalized firm with several business units. Each unit develops and manufactures distinct products and serves largely different markets.

ChemCo aims to be the undisputed supplier of choice for chemicals and related products and services in the market it serves. The company is intent on developing a culture where continuous improvement is sought in all areas to achieve world-class customer service and product quality.

The guiding business principles for the development of IT infrastructure which emerge from ChemCo's strategic context are the provision of IT which:

- reduces costs;
- supports the information-intensive business improvement programme; and
- enables the firm to maintain high standards of customer service and product quality.

There is decentralized responsibility for IS functions in ChemCo. Business units have full autonomy in the way they manage their IT, but are encouraged to seek advice from the corporate IS group and to conform to corporate standards. ChemCo has a corporate-wide architecture policy which includes telecommunications, preferred suppliers, workstation guidelines, electronic mail and general ledger controls. Opportunities exist to move outside these standards with the completion of an exception request which must be justified on business grounds.

The corporate IS group provides communications services (through a communication network) and processing services (mainframe processing) for all ChemCo units. The business units then determine which services they wish to access, usually on a unit charge basis. Use of IT infrastructure services varies considerably among the units. For example, the Advanced Technologies unit controls about 95% of the infrastructure used within that unit and locally supplies processing services using minicomputers. All data for the business unit is stored in this system and only data required for corporate reporting purposes is transferred to the corporate processor. The Chemicals unit, in contrast, has virtually no local infrastructure and relies almost solely on the corporate IS group for the development, management and operation of its business systems. Both business units make extensive use of ChemCo's firm-wide communications network.

Planning for corporate IT infrastructure takes place with input from the IT managers in each of the business units. The IT manager's estimation of future IT needs of the businesses is used to predict corporate infrastructure requirements. Tracking of the usage of infrastructure services is an important component of the IT infrastructure investment decision. In addition, IT infrastructure is primarily viewed as a utility providing the base IS services at minimum cost. The IT requirements are determined in consultation with the business managers to ensure that the strategic needs of the business are being met.

ChemCo has a Utility view of infrastructure, and is heading towards a Dependent view. The decision has recently been taken to reengineer the core business processes and implement a common suite of financial and manufacturing applications across the firm. This level of standardization will lead to a more shared IT infrastructure, including the expertise at implementing the new systems.

The past five years have seen a major push towards decentralization of management and control within ChemCo. IT management has moved from being a centralized function to an activity for which the business units can take total responsibility, if they so choose. However, there has recently been recognition of the need for some form of coordination to maximize resources and reduce duplication. An IT Council has recently been established with a major objective to set standards for further direction and strategy. While this may reduce some of the autonomy enjoyed under the present system, it is designed to introduce a more cohesive approach to IT management across the firm.

Utility view for IT Infrastructure

In ChemCo the IT manager's estimation of future IT trends of the businesses is used to predict corporate IT requirements.
IT Infrastructure services:
- *maintenance and support of the mainframe computing facilities*
- *communication network services*
- *electronic mail facility*
- *consultancy and support services when required*
- *technology education services*

Dependent View of Infrastructure—Petroco

PetroCo is a major manufacturer and marketer of petroleum products to retail and commercial customers. PetroCo has in excess of a 15% share of its local domestic market, revenue over $1.3 billion and employs about 2000 people. PetroCo seeks to "make our customers prefer us to any competing company" and be the most successful downstream oil company in its region as measured by return on assets.

PetroCo's steady financial position has been achieved through a continuing focus on minimizing and reducing costs, operational efficiencies and customer service. In a commoditized industry, it presents a strong corporate image of a quality provider of petroleum products. PetroCo's re-imaging project has contributed to a public perception of the company as a quality brand where the retail outlets provide friendly staff and clean facilities.

The focus for the development of IT infrastructure which flows from PetroCo's strategic context is relationship building with commercial and retail customers and suppliers in a cost-conscious environment. These relationships require the existence of a firm-wide network and IT-literate staff.

PetroCo has decentralized responsibility for IS functions in each of its business units together with a corporate IS group. The past five years have seen increased responsibility for IS planning, development and management at the business unit level, with business units now containing IS staff who report to business unit managers.

PetroCo has constantly reviewed its infrastructure investments at both corporate and business unit levels. Major investments at corporate level have been in the development of communications networks among commercial, retail and manufacturing sites and suppliers. PetroCo supplies extensive communications services through a robust network with an extensive LAN in place at its head office and in capital cities and other major sites. About 2000 PC users have whatever multi-host connectivity is required for their business needs.

Dependent view for IT infrastructure

PetroCo's ISD provides competitive IT services in partnership with clients so that the potential of IT to achieve PetroCo's' business objectives is exploited.

IT infrastructure services:
- *maintenance and support of mainframe computing facilities*
- *communications network services*
- *video conferencing*
- *electronic and voice messaging*
- *data consultancy and support services*
- *business recovery services*
- *client support and technology education services*

Business units have undertaken considerable local infrastructure investments, particularly in the commercial area with new distributorship services. The Retail group is currently making major investments in upgraded retail and EFTPOS (electronic funds transfer at point of sale) systems. Meanwhile, at a corporate level, the firm is closely monitoring the implementation of the international affiliates systems renewal project.

Planning for IT infrastructure in PetroCo is based primarily on current business strategies and is categorized as Dependent. IT infrastructure investments, as with other IT expenditure, must meet a defined business need. They must show clear cost savings and, if part of the customer interface, must demonstrate the delivery of a higher level of customer service.

The cost and quality of IT services are major topics of discussion between business unit managers and senior IT managers. Emphasis on business needs is accompanied by a concern for demonstrating increased operational efficiencies, which usually means providing the service at a lower cost to PetroCo.

PetroCo has extensive reach through its electronic mail system to send standard messages throughout the group internationally. It has developed an inter-company communications infrastructure and connections to third-party networks are in place to facilitate inter-company process simplification. The range of services is being extended by current developments. For example, distributorship systems are extending the range of services to customers and suppliers and some EDI arrangements are operational. EDI is also currently under consideration as part of a redesign of PetroCo's billing process, as are intranets.

The mission and vision of ISD reflect the focus on providing business benefit by exploiting IT for business purposes. The ISD mission is "to provide competitive IT services in partnership with its clients so that the potential of IT to achieve PetroCo's business objectives is exploited". In this context, ISD "is committed to being the quality IT service of choice for PetroCo".

Enabling View of Infrastructure—StoreCo

StoreCo is among the world's top 15 retailers, with revenue in the mid-1990s of over $10 billion. StoreCo's core businesses are department stores, mass-merchandise store chains, supermarkets and specialty retail operations.

StoreCo aims to continue to grow and develop as a predominantly retail-oriented organization which is innovative, competitive and dynamic. It operates as a divisionalized firm with a corporate group and six relatively autonomous business units. The CEO has indicated a strong desire to utilize the synergies in the company.

The guiding principles for StoreCo's investment in IT infrastructure are driven by a strategic intent of strong growth, characterized by innovation and competitiveness. In a retail environment this includes flexibility to accommodate different and changing markets, connectivity throughout the firm and synergy to achieve economies of scale and ensure acceptable levels of profitability. These principles imply the development of a sophisticated communications network and positioning for electronic trading.

StoreCo has decentralized responsibility for IS functions to its business units as well as having a corporate IS group, StoreCo Information Services (SLIS). Corporate-level SLIS exists to ensure current and future business leverage of economies of scale, expertise and scope. SLIS provides the communications backbone services and manages the operation and maintenance of almost all StoreCo's major data-processing services. All large-scale hardware is confined to two sites in one city and these handle the firm's major computing operations. In-store hardware (such as point-of-sale terminals, personal computers), within-store communications and applications development are the responsibility of the business units. The SLIS budget is recouped from payments for services from the business units.

IT usage is integral to all operational aspects of StoreCo's businesses. As a result of firm-wide and business unit planning processes in the late 1980s, a set of key requirements for StoreCo's IT was articulated. These requirements included the need for flexibility to accommodate change, connectivity ("anything to anything"), synergies through economies of scale, growth without corresponding cost growth, reliability, and positioning for new services and technologies.

The firm has a diverse range of hardware architectures. Business groups do not have to limit themselves to the hardware architectures already in place, provided there is a sound business case. StoreCo's communications network is large and sophisticated and is based on a layered approach.

The business units have developed their IT independently from each other but in association with the corporate IS group. Business units have planning cycles which incorporate IT considerations at the highest levels. SLIS has a consultative and advisory role in these processes. In the late 1980s, StoreCo was an early mover into EDI and most business units have now established quick-response implementation groups. SLIS provided the initial focus, expertise, firm-wide strategy and contacts for EDI for the business units.

In the late 1990s StoreCo aims to extract more economies, synergies and flexibility from its IT infrastructure investments. The CEO has stated publicly that a higher degree of sharing of "back-of-store systems" such as ordering, logistics and warehousing will occur. The customer-facing systems will be part of the unique value proposition in each BU (business unit) and the responsibility of the BU management. This initiative will result in significantly more shared IT infrastructure services and more extensive reach and range including Internet shopping.

The objective of StoreCo's Enabling view of IT infrastructure is three-fold:

- To increase business flexibility and agility to enable faster time to market with new initiatives such as new stores or departments within stores.
- To increase synergies across the BUs to enable firm-wide initiatives such as loyalty schemes.
- To reduce costs by removing duplication and achieving economies of scale.

Enabling view of IT infrastructure

Benefits sought relate primarily to the flexibility required to meet future, and as yet unspecified, business needs. Such flexibility is highly valued and is seen to provide a competitive advantage in the retail industry as well as ultimately lowering the cost of doing business. The firm's IT infrastructure reach is extensive and StoreCo's IT infrastructure planning is based largely on future business strategies.

IT infrastructure services include:
- *management, maintenance and support of all large-scale computer hardware*
- *development, management and operation of the firm-wide communications network*
- *monitoring of new technology developments*
- *consultancy and advisory services*

SLIS's vision statement emphasizes the Enabling role of firm-wide IT infrastructure for the StoreCo retail group. SLIS aims to be "a world-class provider of information technology solutions that profitably extends the reach and range of StoreCo retail activities".

There was evidence of both Dependent and Enabling views of local IT infrastructure in the business units and this illustrates the different possible strategies. StoreCo took an Enabling firm-wide view of infrastructure and some BUs took Enabling views, while others took Dependent or Utility views.

DISCUSSION

While DiverseCo has no IT infrastructure, ChemCo, PetroCo and StoreCo share some similarities in their IT management:

- Each firm shared responsibility for IT across the business units and the corporate IS group.
- All firms have business unit IT infrastructures and all but DiverseCo had a firm-wide IT infrastructure.
- In each firm there was a relatively stable set of firm-wide IT infrastructure services. The number and depth of these services increased markedly from a Utility to an Enabling view of infrastructure.
- Each of the firms had IT committees with responsibility for firm-wide IT infrastructure. In the firms with an Enabling or Dependent view, these committees had more senior members, a more strategic view, controlled more funds and had the power to set and implement firm-wide architectures and standards.

Differences between the firms focus on the business use of their IT infrastructure services and the rationale for these in each of the firms:

- There is an increasing percentage of IT expenditure on corporate IT infrastructure from DiverseCo (None), ChemCo (Utility), PetroCo (Dependent) to StoreCo (Enabling).
- To achieve an Enabling view it was necessary to justify IT infrastructure at Board level based on flexibility and responsiveness as well as cost savings.
- A firm-wide communications network becomes increasingly important for firms with a Dependent or Enabling view of IT infrastructure. In firms with an Enabling view, such networks are used extensively for business processes within firms as well as between firms and their customers and suppliers. Currently, firms with a Utility view use the network more for electronic messaging than as part of inter- or intra-organizational systems for business processes.
- StoreCo's corporate IS group, with an Enabling view of infrastructure, played a different role from ChemCo and PetroCo in relation to new technologies. It was more proactive and anticipatory in identifying new technologies which could be utilized for business purposes.
- Business units in StoreCo had higher expectations of access to busi-

ness-relevant IT expertise in their corporate IS group than did those in firms with the Dependent and Utility views.

In these four firms, the view of infrastructure is consistent with the strategic context of each firm:

- DiverseCo has limited synergies among its divisions and their products. No IT infrastructure is consistent with the highly divisionalized nature of the firm, where the locus of responsibility is as close as possible to the specific brand. Lack of IT infrastructure is seen as providing greater freedom to the divisions to develop the specific local infrastructure suited to their business, customers, products and markets.
- The business value that ChemCo sought from its infrastructure investment was primarily to reduce costs, support the business improvement programme, and to maintain quality standards. An emerging focus on customer service, where business processes were more IT dependent, is resulting in a shift towards a Dependent view of infrastructure.
- PetroCo has been making use of its infrastructure to link customers and suppliers to build long-term relationships as part of its current strategy. PetroCo staff make extensive use of IT within the firm for internal communication and for productivity. There is a strong emphasis on a high level of IT-literate staff in PetroCo and the communications network supports this.
- StoreCo values future flexibility, together with economies of scale, scope and expertise. It seeks to be well positioned for new services and technologies.

ChemCo, PetroCo and StoreCo all see IT infrastructure as a major component of their IT portfolio, though their views of infrastructure differ. The four firms have an infrastructure appropriate to their strategic intent and current strategy. A shift in that strategic context, however, might have implications for the level and nature of support which the current IT infrastructure can or should provide.

The four firms discussed in this chapter were chosen as they were typical of the other firms studied with a similar view of infrastructure. The generic characteristics of the four views of IT infrastructure are summarized in Figure 11.5. On average, the None view has the lowest investment in IT relative to competitors, with no firm-wide infrastructure investments and no firm-wide infrastructure services. A Utility view has a low investment in IT relative to competitors and lower than average investment in firm-wide infrastructure as a percentage of total IT investment. The justification of IT infrastructure is based on cost

	CHARACTERISTICS				
VIEW OF INFRASTRUCTURE	Investment in IT relative to competitors	Investment in firm wide infrastructure	Approach to justification	Reach and range	Extent of infrastructure services
NONE	Lowest	None	No attempt	Within business units	None
UTILITY	Low	Lower than average	Cost focus	Within and between BUs for data and simple transactions	Basic
DEPENDENT	Average	Just above average	Balance cost and flexibility	Within and between BUs Some complex transactions Some customers	Basic plus a few services which are strategic
ENABLING	Highest	Well above average	Flexibility focus	Within and between BUs Complex transactions Any customer	Extensive

Figure 11.5   *Characteristics of the Four Views of IT Infrastructure*

savings and economies of scale. The reach and range are limited within and between business units and a basic level of infrastructure services is provided, averaging 13 of the 25 services in Figure 11.4.

A Dependent view of IT infrastructure has an average or just above average investment in IT overall and in firm-wide infrastructure. The approach is based on balancing cost and flexibility. There are usually the basic plus selected strategic infrastructure services, averaging 16 of the 25 services on a firm-wide basis. The reach of the IT infrastructure often extends to some customers, with a range including some complex transactions. An Enabling view has the highest IT investment relative to competitors and investment in infrastructure that is well above average. The focus of justification of IT infrastructure investments is providing current and future flexibility. There is reach with and between business units, often extending to a wide range of customers and supporting complex transactions. Firms with an Enabling view tend to have extensive infrastructure services, averaging 20 of the 25 services.

CONCLUSIONS

IT infrastructure is a critical component of the IT portfolio. It provides the base foundation of IT capability for the development of business applications systems. This IT capability includes both the technical and managerial expertise required to provide reliable services.

Firms take different approaches to information technology infrastructure investments depending on their strategic goals for cost savings via economies of scale, synergies across businesses or longer-term requirements for flexibility. The nature of a firm's information technology portfolio is tailored to firm-specific needs, just as our personal financial portfolio is related to our lifestyle, aspirations and resources. Both types of portfolios require careful thought and planning. The base of a sound information technology portfolio is the infrastructure—the enabling foundation of reliable services.

Each of the four views is driven by different strategic objectives, requires different levels of up-front investment and results in different capabilities with different benefit expectations.

Making infrastructure investment decisions is a major challenge, as they are large, long term and must be put in place before precise business needs are known. Infrastructure investments are significant, accounting for over 57% of the information technology dollars, and have been increasing at the rate of 11% per annum for over five years (1992–7). The purpose of building information technology infrastructures is to enable the sharing of information and expensive resources, the effective execution of business processes and connecting to customers and suppliers as part of the extended enterprise. This sharing can create cross-business-unit or cross-functional integration to benefit from a combination of economies of scale, synergies and flexibility. The combination of objectives is a senior management decision informed by business drivers. Having separate and incompatible infrastructures limits the firm's strategic options and also is an impediment to responding quickly to competitor initiatives.

The benefits that firms derive from their IT infrastructure investments, and the way these investments are justified, are related to the firm's view of the role of infrastructure:

- A None view is driven primarily by a focus on independent business units, lack of synergy and a willingness to forgo economies of scale.
- An Utility view is driven primarily by a concern for cost savings through economies of scale.
- A Dependent view is driven primarily by a concern for business benefits from current strategy.
- An Enabling view is driven primarily by the need for current and future flexibility and agility.

One view of infrastructure is not always superior. The key determining factor is the strategic context of the firm and how it competes in its industry now and in the future. An appropriate view of infrastructure must be taken for the strategic intent. That appropriate view could be any one of None, Utility, Dependent or Enabling.

IT infrastructure investments are large and long-term in nature. They are linked to the ability of firms to achieve their strategic intent and implement their vision. Implementing an appropriate role for IT infrastructure is a major contribution to achieving strategic alignment between the IT portfolio and the business needs.

ACKNOWLEDGEMENTS

The authors would like to acknowledge funding from IBM Consulting Group (International) for this study. Portions of this chapter originally appeared in Weill, Broadbent and St. Clair, 1996.

REFERENCES

Ahituv, N. and Neumann, S. (1990). *Principles of Information Systems Management*. 3rd edn, Wm. C. Brown, New York.

Boynton, A., Victor, B. and Pine, J. (1993). New Competitive Strategies: Challenges to Organisations and Information Technology. *IBM Systems Journal*, 32, 1, 40–64.

Brancheau, J., Janz, B. and Wetherbe, J. (1996) Key Issues in Information Systems Management : 1994–95 SIM Delphi Results. *MIS Quarterly*, 20, 2, 225–42.

Broadbent, M. and Butler, C. (1997). Managing Information Technology Infrastructure Capability for International Business Operations. *Proceedings of the Pacific Asia Conference on Information Systems (PACIS)*, Brisbane, Queensland, 1–5 April, 589–612.

Broadbent, M., Butler, C., Hansell, A. and Dampney, K. (1995). Business Value, Quality and Partnerships: Australasian Information Systems Management Issues. *The Australian Computer Journal*, 27, 1, 17–26.

Broadbent, M., Weill, P., O'Brien, T. and Neo, B. (1996). Firm Context and Patterns of IT Infrastructure Capability. *Proceedings of the 17th International Conference on Information Systems (ICIS)*, Cleveland, Ohio, December, 174–94.

Caron, J., Jarvenpaa, S. and Stoddard, D. (1994). Business Reengineering at CIGNA Corporation: Experiences and Lessons from the First Five Years. *MIS Quarterly*, 18, 3, 233–50.

CSC Index (1994). *Critical Issues of Information Systems Management for 1994*. CSC Index, Boston, MA.

Davenport, R. and Linder, J. (1994). Information Management Infrastructure: the New Competitive Weapon. *Proceedings of the Twenty-Seventh Annual Hawaii International Conference on Systems Science*, IEEE, 885–99.

Davidow, W. and Malone, M. (1992). *The Virtual Corporation*. HarperCollins, New York.

Furey, T. and Diorio, S. (1994). Making Re-engineering Strategic. *Planning Review*, 22, 2, 7–11.

Grover, T., Teng, J. and Fiedler, K. (1993). Information Technology Enabled Business Process Redesign: an Integrated Planning Framework. *OMEGA, International Journal of Management Science*, 2, 14, 433–47.

Hamel, G. and Prahalad, C. (1989). *Strategic Intent*. Harvard Business Review, 67, 3, 63–76.

Kambil, A., Henderson, J.C. and Mohsenzadeh, H. (1993). Strategic Management of Information Technology Investments: an Options Perspective. In Banker, K.D., Kauffman, R.J. and Mahmood, M.A. (eds) *Perspectives on the Strategic and Economic Value of Information Technology*. Idea Group, Middletown, PA.

Keen, P.G.W. (1991). *Shaping the Future: Business Design through Information Technology*. Harvard Business School Press, Boston, MA.

Keen, P.G.W. (1995). *Every Manager's Guide to Information Technology*. 2nd edn, Harvard Business School Press, Boston, MA.

Keen, P.G.W. and Cummins, J. (1994). *Networks in Action: Business Choices and Telecommunications Decisions*. Wadsworth, Belmont, CA.

McKay, D.T. and Brockaway, D.W. (1989). Building IT Infrastructure for the 1990s. *Stage by Stage* (Nolan Norton & Company), 9, 3, 1–11.

McKenney, J. (1995). *Waves of Change: Business Evolution through Information Technology*. Harvard Business School Press, Boston, MA.

Miller, D., Clemons, E. and Row, M. (1993). Information Technology and the Global Virtual Corporation. In Bradley, S., Nolan, R. and Hausman, J. (eds) *Globalization, Technology and Competition: The Fusion of Computers and Telecommunications in the 1990s*. Harvard Business School Press, Boston, MA, 283–308.

Neo, B. (1991). Information Technology and Global Competition: a Framework for Analysis. *Information and Management*, 20, 3, 151–60.

Niederman, F., Brancheau, J.C. and Wetherbe, J.C. (1991) Information Systems Management Issues for the 1990's. *MIS Quarterly*, 15, 4, 475–95.

Otisline (1990). Harvard Business School Case #9-186-304, Harvard Business School, Boston, July.

Parker, M.M. and Benson, R.J. and Trainor, H. (1988). *Information Economics: Linking Business Performance to Information Technology*. Prentice Hall, New Jersey.

Ramcharamdas, E. (1994). Xerox Creates a Continuous Learning Environment for Business Transformation. *Planning Review*, 22, 2, 34–8.

Rayport, J. and Sviokla, J. (1995). Exploiting the Virtual Value Chain. *Harvard Business Review*, 73, 6, 75–85.

Wastell, D., White, P. and Kawalek, P. (1994). A Methodology for Business Process Redesign: Experiences and Issues. *Journal of Strategic Information Systems*, 3, 1, 23–40.

Weill, P. (1993). The Role and Value of Information Technology Infrastructure: Some Empirical Observations. In Banker, R.D., Kauffman, R.J. and Mahmood, M.A. (eds) *Perspectives on the Strategic and Economic Value of Information Technology*, Idea Group, Middleton, PA.

Weill, P. and Broadbent, M. (1998). *Leveraging The New Infrastructure: How Market Leaders Capitalize on IT*. Harvard Business School Press, Boston, MA.

Weill, P. and Lucas, H.C. (1992). *Managing the IT Investment Pyramid for Competitive Advantage*. Working Paper No 11, Graduate School of Management,

University of Melbourne, Carlton, Victoria, Australia.
Weill, P., Broadbent, M. and St. Clair, D. (1996). IT Value and the Role of IT Infrastructure Investments. In Luftman, J.N. (ed.) *Competing in the Information Age: Strategic Alignment in Practice*. Oxford University Press, New York, 361–84.

SECTION IV

Towards Interpretive Approaches

12
Interpretive Evaluation Design for Information Systems

GEOFF WALSHAM
Judge Institute of Management Studies, Cambridge University

INTRODUCTION

As this book has made clear, there is a large and growing literature on the evaluation of computer-based information systems, and many different approaches to the carrying out of evaluation have been proposed (Bjørn-Andersen and Davis, 1988; Strassmann, 1997; Willcocks, 1996; Graeser, Willcocks and Pisanias, 1998). A common theme in this literature is that the evaluation of costs and benefits is difficult. Symons and Walsham (1988) noted that information systems are frequently used to enhance organizational performance without necessarily any reduction in costs, and that they produce benefits that are often intangible, uncertain and extremely hard to quantify in a meaningful way. It is notoriously difficult to obtain accurate estimates in areas such as software development cost (see Chapter 8), and there may be insidious long-term effects associated with the introduction of a new IS, such as the deskilling of work resulting in a decline in job satisfaction and performance. Evaluation of IS thus takes place in conditions of high uncertainty as to the various costs and benefits—precisely why a sense of ''productivity paradox'' arises—and this provides an arena within which different individuals and stakeholder groups can take widely varying positions on the relative merits and demerits of particular information systems.

Beyond the IT Productivity Paradox.
Edited by L. P. Willcocks and S. Lester © 1999 John Wiley & Sons Ltd.

Stone (1991) argued that the different approaches suggested in the literature to address the difficult issues of IS evaluation are not interchangeable, but rather represent fundamentally different ways of understanding. For example, a significant body of the IS evaluation literature deals with static techniques such as cost–benefit analysis, or its variants designed to produce quantitative answers to the evaluation question at a fixed point in time such as the feasibility stage (see Chapters 4 and 6). The focus of this chapter will be very different from this, being concerned with the dynamic process of evaluation at all stages, from the conceptualization of a new information system to its implementation and beyond (see also Chapter 2 for a lifecycle approach). An interpretive approach to evaluation will be discussed, namely one which takes seriously the different interpretations which individuals and groups form and reform over time, and which considers how these changing perceptions influence the progress of the design and implementation of the associated information system.

The rest of the chapter is organized as follows. The first section draws on relevant work from outside the IS literature to define in some detail the nature and purpose of an interpretive approach to evaluation. This is followed by a discussion of interpretive evaluation in the IS literature, including research aimed at establishing the need for such an approach, and some recent work which describes specific attempts to apply interpretive IS evaluation in practice. The penultimate section develops proposals for designing interpretive IS evaluation in the future. Finally, some conclusions are drawn on the current status of interpretive IS evaluation, and its prospects for more extensive use.

NATURE AND PURPOSE OF INTERPRETIVE EVALUATION

The literature discussed in this section describes some interesting work on interpretive approaches to evaluation from outside the IS field. This work provides a theoretical and methodological basis for the subsequent discussion of interpretive evaluation of IS. Two broad streams of work are described below, dealing first with evaluation in the field of education, and secondly with the evaluation of organizational change programmes.

Evaluation in the Field of Education

A major amount of research activity has taken place on evaluation in the education field, and some valuable ideas on interpretive evaluation can be derived from this work. A useful distinction was drawn by Stake (1975, 1983) between a preordinate approach to evaluation and a responsive approach. The former emphasizes the statement of goals, the use of objective tests, and the production of research-type reports; the latter emphasizes the usefulness of the findings of the evaluation research to the people concerned with the programme.

Guba and Lincoln (1981) developed the theme of responsive evaluation as being organized around the concerns and issues stemming from the several audiences that the evaluation will serve, based on their underlying sets of values. A concern is defined as any matter of interest or importance to one or more of the involved parties. An issue is a statement, proposition or focus that allows for the presentation of different points of view. A value is any principle or standard that leads to judgements of either relative or absolute utility, goodness or importance, or that guides choices among alternatives. Values range from the very tangible to the very intangible.

In a later development of this work, Guba and Lincoln (1989) proposed an approach entitled "fourth-generation evaluation", distinguished from previous evaluation generations characterized as measurement oriented, description oriented and judgement oriented. The key dynamic of the new approach is negotiation. This later work is linked explicitly to an interpretive evaluation approach, although it is called a constructivist perspective by Guba and Lincoln. They take the position that evaluation outcomes are not descriptions of the way things really are or really work, but instead represent meaningful constructions that aid individual actors or groups of actors to make sense of the situations in which they find themselves. The approach considers that the constructions through which people make sense of their situations are shaped by the values of the constructors. Power relations are also recognized as important by the view that evaluations can be shaped to enfranchise or disenfranchise stakeholding groups in a variety of ways.

The above descriptions are theoretical in emphasis, but the fourth-generation evaluation approach has an action orientation: defining a course to be followed, stimulating involved stakeholders to follow it, and generating and preserving their commitment to do so. Twelve steps of a methodology are given (Guba and Lincoln, 1989, p. 185) aimed at setting up the evaluation study, developing and enlarging constructions, resolving concerns and issues, negotiating unresolved concerns and issues, and recycling if necessary. The authors state that fourth-generation evaluation is a means to empowerment of stakeholders (p. 227), but they do not say how conflicts should be resolved in cases of fundamental disagreement between actors or interest groups.

They view an interpretive evaluator not as a controller, investigator and discoverer as in the preordinate approach to evaluation, but as a collaborator, learner and teacher, reality shaper and change agent.

Evaluating Organizational Change

A second broad area of evaluation research embraces a wide variety of work undertaken by "professional" evaluators in the field of organizational change, and this work includes a strong interpretive evaluation strand. Legge (1984) summarizes the work of these evaluators as being concerned with issues such as the effectiveness of different project payment systems in enhancing motivation, the relationship between job design and productivity, or the effectiveness of different leadership styles.

Legge notes that the whole process of planned organizational change reflects an evaluatory act, since planning models involve the notion of an assessment, however unsystematic, of some gap between the present and a desired future state. Resistance to change often reflects individuals' or groups' negative evaluations of the likely consequences for them. Legge argues for a form of contingency approach to evaluation research by undertaking a matching process to achieve compatibility between evaluation functions sought and the research design employed. For example, a distinction can be made between formative evaluation, which aims to provide systematic feedback to programme designers and implementers, and summative evaluation, concerned with identifying and assessing the worth of programme outcomes in the light of initially specified success criteria after the implementation of the change programme is completed (this distinction is due to Scriven, 1967). Legge argues that interpretive evaluation designs are best suited to the purpose of formative evaluation.

Legge describes in detail some of the characteristics of interpretive evaluation designs. These include explanation through developing understanding, an emphasis on actions and taken-for-granted meanings, an iterative and emergent process, an emphasis on the richness and meaningfulness of data, and the use of mainly qualitative rather than quantitative methods. In discussing strategies and techniques for interpretive evaluation designs, Legge refers to the earlier work of Guba and Lincoln.

Legge goes beyond the work of Guba and Lincoln in her discussion of the politics and ethics of approaches to evaluation. She notes that the choice of an evaluation design is likely to be constrained by the information that the most powerful participants require and why they require it. She distinguishes between overt functions of evaluation, concerned with the provision of information for decision making, and covert functions, which are understood as those functions of evaluation which one or more stakeholders in the evaluation consider it inappropriate to admit publicly, because they perceive it as in their interests to do so, to the possible detriment of others. These covert functions include rallying support or opposition to a change programme, postponing a decision, evading responsibility, and fulfilling grant requirements. Legge also argues that the meta-function of all evaluations is either to sustain or to question the status quo, and asks whether all evaluation research tend to be conservatively biased towards existing power structures and a gradualist approach to change. Further, she hypothesizes that interpretive evaluation methods may be more open to manipulation by powerful interest groups than traditional positivistic designs, since an admission of multiple realities and values may actually help the powerful to impose their own interpretations. Thus interpretive design may act as a rhetoric for an evaluation ritual, whereby the appearance of democracy and non-elitism serves to disguise the greater room for manoeuvre accorded to the powerful.

INTERPRETIVE EVALUATION AND THE IS LITERATURE

We move now to the specific domain of IS, and consider how the concept of interpretive evaluation has been treated in the IS literature. First, literature which relates to the need for interpretive evaluation of IS is discussed. Secondly, some evidence for the potential value of interpretive evaluation is derived from reports of specific in-depth case studies. Finally, and most directly, two attempts to apply interpretive IS evaluation in practice are presented.

The Need for Interpretive Evaluation of IS

A number of authors have proposed interpretive approaches to IS evaluation and have suggested some of the merits of this perspective. Iivari (1988) considered that the IS design process should be viewed as a process of enquiry into aspects such as the perspectives of interest groups, adaptation strategies and quality criteria, and he argued that this would support an improved process-based approach to IS evaluation. Hirschheim and Smithson in Chapter 13 note that most IS evaluation concentrates on the technical rather than the human or social aspects of computerized systems, and that this can have major negative consequences in terms of the system developed, with respect to individual aspects such as user satisfaction, but also broader organizational consequences in terms of system value. They propose an interpretive approach to evaluation research as a way of gaining a deeper understanding of the nature and process of evaluation itself, including recognition of the informal evaluations carried out by all individuals and social groups who are affected by the computer-based IS. Symons (1991) made a similar point that effective evaluation means understanding and taking seriously the perspectives of individual stakeholders and interest groups. She added that the evaluation process should be regarded as a means to encourage the involvement and commitment of stakeholders.

Although in an early paper Hirschheim and Smithson (1988) were critical of many of the approaches to evaluation based on quantification and largely technical criteria, they noted that the results of formal evaluation studies of this type often have considerable legitimacy. This seeming paradox between a rather circumscribed approach to evaluation and the organizational credibility of its results has been explained by some authors in terms of organizational ritual. Symons and Walsham (1988) suggested that when a formal analysis is carried out, it is more likely to be a symbolic expression of a belief in rational management than a trusted aid to decision making. Floder and Weiner (1983) note a similar point, in the context of the evaluation of major social programmes, that evaluation may be seen as a ritual whose function is to calm the anxieties of the citizenry and to perpetuate an image of governmental rationality, efficacy and accountability. Kumar (1990) described a survey of the actual practice of post-implementation evaluation of computer-based IS in over 90 US companies. He concluded that, where it was conducted, the primary use of post-implementation evaluation was as a disengagement device for the systems development department. Kumar does not use the term ritual, but the post-implementation evaluation processes he described were ritualistic rather than substantive.

Symbolism and ritual in human affairs are very important, not least in business organizations, and ritualistic evaluation exercises should not therefore be condemned out of hand. An interpretive approach to evaluation may give a deeper understanding, but the purposes of ritual are different, aimed at issues such as reassurance and a sense of security. However, two reservations can be made. First, ritualistic evaluation may be a way of supporting powerful interests and a device to suppress the less powerful in organizational terms; no general judgement can be made here, since each case needs to be considered on its own merits, but ritual cannot be divorced from its moral implications.

A second reservation about ritualistic evaluation in the context of IS is that it can be a major hindrance to innovative organizational change. This is well illustrated by the research of Currie (1989) on the justification of computer-aided design (CAD) technology in 20 UK companies. She noted the frustration of engineering managers proposing the introduction of CAD systems, who were forced to "play the game" and engage in "return on investment (ROI) and Discounted Cash Flow (DCF) rituals" (p. 412) based on simple cost-accounting techniques, in order to justify the technology to top management. One way of "getting round the system" was noted as putting additional costs on other budgets. This game playing continued in summative evaluation exercises after the technology was installed, where Currie notes that engineering management continued to manipulate the information to demonstrate to top managers that CAD was achieving the benefits outlined in the proposal documents. The reason for all this deception was that engineering managers perceived the benefits of the CAD technology as rather intangible aspects such as better-quality design linked to long-term organizational goals of quality products and thus an enhanced and competitive position in their markets. Short-term cost savings were not the goal, but these had to be manipulated to produce the right picture for justification purposes. A crucial observation for our purposes here is that "a more qualitative and holistic approach [to investment appraisal for new technology] ... was unacceptable" (p. 416). In other words, interpretive evaluation designs were not politically acceptable.

The above discussion has not attempted to present a case for the elimination of ritualistic evaluation in the context of IS, or to suggest that accounting techniques such as DCF have no place in the evaluation of new technology. The argument is, rather, that there are circumstances where such approaches are highly deficient in generating real understanding of the costs and benefits of a computer-based system and its human and organizational consequences. In such circumstances, it is suggested that interpretive approaches to evaluation have something extra to offer in terms of understanding.

Empirical evidence from IS evaluation practice in the UK provides some support for this view. Willcocks and Lester (1993) gave results from a survey of 50 organizations over the period 1990–92. IS evaluation was carried out mainly at the feasibility stage; there was a fall-off in evaluation at later stages such as development and implementation; and there was little attempt to link evaluation across the lifetime of systems. In addition, there was a highly fragmented approach to learning from evaluation experience for future IS investments. The authors concluded that evaluation practice could be improved, and learning enhanced, if more stakeholder groups participated in the evaluation process and if evaluation were linked across stages and time. Although

Willcocks and Lester do not use the term "interpretive evaluation", the focus of their suggestions on the need for process-based approaches to evaluation and learning is directly linked to the goals of interpretive evaluation design (see also Chapter 2).

In Chapter 6, Farbey, Land and Targett described results from their in-depth interviews with managers in 16 organizations, in which they investigated how these organizations made their decisions to acquire new information systems, what benefits they expected to gain, and the kind of evaluation procedures they used. They found broadly similar empirical results to those of Willcocks and Lester, in that IS evaluation, when it was done at all, was normally carried out at the feasibility stage. However, the authors concluded that multistage evaluation would be valuable, and that an active benefits management policy would enable benefits to be identified and exploited and disbenefits to be controlled (see also Farbey, Targett and Land, 1995). Again, this would point towards process-based interpretive evaluation as one possible approach to achieve these ends.

Evidence from In-Depth Case Studies

A second body of literature which can be cited as evidence for the potential value of interpretive IS evaluation comes from in-depth longitudinal case studies. Symons (1990ab) described a study of this type carried out to investigate the evaluation process which took place during the specification, design and implementation of a material requirements planning system in a manufacturing company. The introduction of the new system was chaotic and this created major problems for the company in terms of its service to customers.

Symons linked this relative failure to aspects of the approach taken to evaluation. Two formal evaluations of the system were carried out prior to its introduction, but both were based largely around technical and economic criteria such as hardware, software and operating costs. The concerns and issues of stakeholder groups such as the sales order processing staff and the warehousemen were not surfaced at all in the formal evaluation, and only started to be considered by management after the initial failure of the system introduction. There is of course no guarantee that an interpretive evaluation approach would have led to a successful system introduction in this case, although it would surely have helped to avoid some of the main failings which arose from an inadequate understanding of work processes and how they needed to change. The case certainly provides a clear example of the severe limitations of formal preordinate evaluation exercises with little involvement of major stakeholder groups.

Walsham (1993) cited the above case in support of the need for an interpretive approach to evaluation, and he also described the evaluation approach taken in two other in-depth case studies. The first of these involved a building society which was very successful in its use of IS for a period of six years under the leadership of a particular chief executive. No formal preordinate approach to IS evaluation was conducted during this period, and the strategic vision for the systems was provided by the chief executive himself. No formal responsive or interpretive evaluation process was carried out either, but it is interesting to note that the chief executive as the key evaluator in this case took account of the concerns and issues of all the major stakeholder groups, through such means as direct personal contact and participative approaches to systems design.

Walsham also described the approach taken to evaluation of information systems in a government agency in a Third World country. The information systems were introduced over a period of more than 10 years, and they were designed to provide increased information for the management and control of development projects in the country. They were largely unsuccessful in achieving this aim, since they did not provide useful support to many of the key stakeholder groups who were supposed to be their users, such as the various central government agencies specializing in particular fields such as health. Formal evaluation of the information systems did take place at a high level, but the approach taken was not responsive to the perceptions and interpretations of many of the stakeholders associated with system use. Again, we cannot be certain of the effect of an interpretive evaluation approach, but it seems likely that it would have supported a more careful analysis of changing user needs leading to potentially more effective information systems.

Interpretive IS Evaluation in Practice

The IS literature discussed so far has made a case for interpretive evaluation based on theoretical grounds, or on a critical analysis of empirical data on existing evaluation practice from surveys or in-depth case studies. Approaches such as these can be valuable in establishing a *prima facie* case, but it can be argued that a rigorous test of the merits of interpretive evaluation can only be carried out by an explicit attempt to conduct such a study in a real situation. Two such attempts are now described.

Serafeimidis and Smithson (1995) argued that an interpretivist framework is needed to understand and study the IS evaluation process, and they described a 12-month project in a UK insurance organization to develop and use a specific evaluation methodology. The focus of this paper is centred more on the use of an interpretive approach as a research tool, rather than on the development of an interpretive evaluation methodology as such. Nevertheless, the methodology that was employed by the insurance company was process based and took account of the shifting interpretations of various stakeholder groups on aspects such as the intangible benefits of the information system. It can thus be considered as a serious practical attempt at interpretive IS evaluation.

Serafeimidis and Smithson argue that the organization learned a lot from the evaluation exercise, but they admit that "the methodology only achieved a relatively limited level of success", and indeed that the methodology in the end fell into disuse. They cite a number of reasons for these problems, including the lack of commitment to the methodology on the part of some senior staff including, crucially, the finance director. In addition, the organizational context shifted considerably over the period of the project, leading for example to a new organizational group made up of business and systems managers charged with evaluating information systems in the context of the overall business. There is no reason that such a group could not have adopted and developed the earlier interpretive evaluation approach, but we are provided with no details of this later stage in the paper.

The results from the above attempt at applying an interpretive approach to IS evaluation must be classed as rather inconclusive, not least because of the lack of detail provided in a necessarily short conference paper. A much more detailed and explicit account of an attempt to apply an interpretive evaluation approach was given by Heiskanen (1994). He described a project, initiated and led by himself in his role as the head of administrative computing, to apply a fourth-generation evaluation approach to a computer-based information system in the University of Helsinki. He detailed how the evaluation process was connected to the design and development process for the IS, how this helped to shape future actions, and how the multiplicity of stakeholder perspectives were brought in to the evaluation approach through four negotiation procedures. These four points for evaluation negotiations were: the subordinate–superior discussions between computing professionals and himself as computing head; annual negotiations between himself and the overall director of the university administration; evaluation seminars involving users and computing professionals; and discussions in the directing group for computing development.

Heiskanen not only provided a detailed and interesting discussion of the practical attempt to apply an interpretive evaluation approach, but also a thoughtful and critical account of the benefits that accrued and the difficulties that were encountered. On the question of benefits, he argued that the case provides a solution to the problem of non-utilization of the results from evaluation exercises. The evaluation was connected to the development work being carried out on the information system in an organic way. Decision makers took part in the evaluation, and the evaluation results were used in shaping future actions in the annual development plans. The concerns of the stakeholder groups were brought into the open to be discussed, and the participants had the opportunity of mutual learning.

With respect to the difficulties and practical constraints which were encountered, Heiskanen cited a range of issues including lack of legitimation for the new approach, an inability to be design specific during evaluation activities, and the relatively open-ended nature of interpretive evaluation where closure is needed at some point. He also described two important problems, which he labelled as political dysfunctionality and human dysfunctionality. The first of these refers to the problem of powerful groups not wishing genuinely to involve the less powerful. The second refers to the subtle point that open-ended evaluation with multiple stakeholder representation can generate an increase in anxieties and fears, since many issues and problems are aired which might normally remain hidden.

DESIGNING INTERPRETIVE IS EVALUATION

This section is aimed at the future design of interpretive IS evaluation. The first two subsections provide a synthesized perspective on the nature of interpretive IS evaluation and the role of an IS evaluator. This is followed by three subsections concerned with specific design tasks for an IS evaluator: considering evaluation purpose and content; understanding evaluation context; and facilitating evaluation process.

The Nature of Interpretive IS Evaluation

IS evaluation involves a socio-political process of enquiry, interpretation and debate. Formal techniques and procedures are often part of the process, but the social context always includes the informal assessments of individuals and stakeholder groups, even if they are excluded from direct involvement in the formal aspects of evaluation. Symons (1990a, p. 189) argues that the discourse of evaluation thus comprises a public rationale undershot by a multiplicity of private rationalities, the formal procedures of evaluation interwoven with informal process.

Interpretive evaluation designs aim to involve a wide variety of stakeholder groups, and their focus is on learning and understanding, and generation of the involvement and commitment which is often lacking if stakeholder groups are not consulted in the evaluation process. This responsive approach is organized around the concerns, issues and values of stakeholders. However, it is important to note that consensus is not always achievable by such approaches, and ways of resolving conflict and arriving at closure involve power relations and necessitate moral choices.

The Role of an IS Evaluator

An IS evaluator can be taken to include any person charged with carrying out a formal evaluation exercise, or a manager conducting a personal evaluation study that has a formal legitimacy due to his or her organizational function. However, in addition to people in formal positions, an IS evaluator can be considered to include anyone concerned with the proposed or actual computer-based IS, who is monitoring actions and consequences and forming their own assessments.

In the case of a preordinate evaluation exercise based largely on technical and economic criteria, the role of an IS evaluator can be taken to include not only quantitative and other assessments, but also a ritual element of demonstrating management competence. In the case of an interpretive evaluation design, the role of an IS evaluator is as a facilitator of the process of enquiry and debate among a wide variety of stakeholder groups. The evaluator in this context can be seen as a learner and teacher, reality shaper and change agent. Ritual may also be present under these circumstances, where involving people represents a symbolic expression of a form of democracy. This can be one reason that interpretive evaluation is sometimes resisted by powerful individuals and groups.

Considering Evaluation Purpose and Content

One specific task in any evaluation exercise is to decide its purpose and content. For interpretive evaluation approaches, the broad purpose is to deepen understanding and to generate motivation and commitment. This goal would normally be stated explicitly, although the form of the exercise will implicitly carry this symbolism of participation in any case. The involvement of a wide range of stakeholder groups is essential to this style of design, and may be one of the practical deterrents for the approach where time or resources for the evaluation are deemed to be in short supply.

The purpose of the evaluation may also be viewed in relation to the different stages in the cycle of development of a computer-based IS. At an early stage, an interpretive evaluation can be considered as a form of feasibility study. During the process of technical implementation, evaluation may be concerned with providing feedback for design modifications. After technical implementation is complete, the purpose of the evaluation may be to decide how well the system achieves various goals with a possible view to further modification, or design of a follow-on system.

Another distinction with respect to evaluation purpose concerns its overt and covert functions. The general philosophy of interpretive evaluation designs would imply being more open concerning motives and possible actions, and thus emphasizing overt rather than covert evaluation functions. Nevertheless, it would be naïve to assume that the covert could or should be eliminated; people will retain covert motives in the most open of interpretive designs, sometimes for reasons of personal self-interest, but also with rather higher motives in some cases. The latter can occur, for example, because it is often unwise to "tell the truth" if this can be hurtful to others; another instance is that radically new ideas may need to be introduced gradually in order not to shock or threaten people.

A related issue to that of the purpose of an IS evaluation is to decide what content or factors should be included in the exercise. In the case of an interpretive evaluation design, factors to consider may be centred around the vocabulary of concerns, issues and values of stakeholder groups. These factors will certainly include technical and economic issues, which it would be foolish in any context to underemphasize, but interpretive approaches also permit much wider perspectives to be explored. Thus the factors considered in an interpretive evaluation design will include human, organizational and political concerns, issues and values in addition to technical and economic criteria.

Understanding Evaluation Context

A second task in an interpretive IS evaluation is for the evaluator to gain a good understanding of the evaluation context. Key elements of this context are the stakeholder assessments, and interpretive designs aim to incorporate more of such assessments than is normal in a typical formal evaluation process. A key rationale for this is that they are present in any case, and if ignored may create a context which leads to the sabotage of later activity on system development and implementation.

Two qualifications are worth making to a view of interpretive evaluation design as incorporating stakeholder assessments. First, it is not possible to do so in any complete way, and informal stakeholder assessments, which change subtly over time, will always shadow and form part of the context of any formal evaluation activity, even if based on an interpretive design (see Chapter 4). Secondly, the view is not being put forward here that all assessments are equally valid. The philosophy of interpretive evaluation design from this author's perspective would see all assessments as worth listening to, but the evaluation process should be an opportunity for learning, and this will and should involve more attitudinal change on the part of some stakeholders.

An understanding of evaluation context applies not just to current perceptions, but also to the history of earlier actions and interpretations. Individuals and groups monitor the intended and unintended consequences from previous stages of an information systems development. These help form the informal stakeholder assessments that are elements of the social context for future evaluations. So the IS evaluator needs to gain an understanding and to facilitate the sharing of experiences from previous evaluation exercises and design stages. This is relatively easy if the IS evaluator has been involved in all stages but, if this is not the case, further effort is required to access these historical elements.

Facilitating Evaluation Process

Having decided the purpose and content of an interpretive IS evaluation, and gained an understanding of evaluation context, an IS evaluator needs to facilitate the dynamics of the evaluation process. A key concept of value here is that of evaluation as learning (see also Chapter 2). An IS evaluator can consciously attempt to create and support a climate within which learning activity should flourish. The ritual significance of participation embodied in the interpretive design itself is one aspect of symbolic action, but this may be viewed as a sham if it is not linked to other activities and stated intentions. Specific action for a given context cannot be prescribed, but certain values can be proposed as likely to provide a supportive environment if explicitly promoted. These include the view that questioning is acceptable, that all assessments are legitimate in the evaluation discourse, that everybody is a learner during the evaluation process, and that moral issues can be debated.

The issue of morality brings us to the important and difficult question of stakeholder conflict. No matter how an interpretive evaluation is carried out, circumstances will arise where differences are irreconcilable, and in these cases decisions are normally reached by the exercise of power to impose. There are no simple prescriptions on the morality of imposed decisions, and each situation must be decided on its own merits. However, it is worth noting that the overriding of stakeholder conflict by dictat or as the "results of the evaluation exercise" can be a hollow victory. The evaluation outcome may provide a facility to enable action in the short term, but in the longer term effective implementation in an organizational sense may not be achieved if norms and values are not shared, and indeed if the imposition of a decision regarding a computer-based IS actually strengthens the opposition of a particular stakeholder group. It seems clear that in most cases consensus is a more desirable state of affairs if it can be achieved, but it may be felt that there is a tradeoff between the time taken to achieve this and the cost of delay. However, more time spent in an interpretive evaluation activity may well repay itself in the longer term.

CONCLUSIONS

The purpose of this chapter has been to put forward a case for the more extensive use of interpretive evaluation design for information systems. Evidence has been drawn from a variety of sources, including the general literature on evaluation, and conceptual and empirical work in the IS field itself. It has been argued that interpretive evaluation can add a missing dimension to more traditional evaluation approaches, such as those based on accounting techniques as described in Chapters 4, 5 and 6, by facilitating learning throughout the lifecycle of an IS design and implementation process. This can help to generate involvement and commitment of the various stakeholder groups who can influence the process. Suggestions were made in the previous section on how an IS evaluator might approach some specific design tasks for an interpretive IS evaluation, although these were rather broad in nature and need further development in practice.

If the case for interpretive IS evaluation is strong, it is reasonable to ask why it is not being used more extensively at the present time. Three broad responses can be made to this question, and a discussion of these responses provides an opportunity to consider future prospects for interpretive IS evaluation. The first response is to argue that there is a relative lack of knowledge of interpretive evaluation in the IS field, and thus what is needed is to introduce these ideas to students and practitioners through the usual media of written and taught material and peer example. If such is the case, then the current chapter can be regarded as a modest contribution to this education process.

A second explanation of relatively low levels of adoption of interpretive approaches to evaluation in the IS field is to point to their weaknesses. These include the fact that the involvement of stakeholder groups in an evaluation process throughout an IS lifecycle is time consuming and thus expensive. However, it can be argued that this short-term cost may significantly increase the chance of long-term success of the information system. A second possible weakness, noted by Heiskanen (1994) in his interesting case study, is that interpretive evaluation may provide a forum in which issues and problems are aired which might normally remain hidden, perhaps leading to an increase in anxiety or fear. There is no simple counter argument to this potential weakness, although sensitive facilitation by an IS evaluator, as discussed in the previous section, should go some way towards addressing this problem.

A third response to the question of why interpretive evaluation is not more widely used is explicitly political in nature. Legge (1984) argued that powerful groups may resist interpretive evaluation because they perceive that it would bring their covert motives to light, or because they believe that it would provide the opportunity for less powerful groups to press their interests. Heiskanen (1994) made a very similar point in his IS case study. Legge also argued that, even where interpretive evaluation is sanctioned, it may take the form of a democracy ritual which actually helps the powerful to impose their interpretations. The view of this author is that the political analyses of Legge and Heiskanen are highly relevant to IS evaluation practice, but that the way in which interpretive IS evaluation meshes with organizational politics is complex, context specific, and not necessarily negative.

Although some counter arguments have been put forward, the above discussion supports the view that interpretive IS evaluation has potential weaknesses. Nevertheless, many of the existing approaches to IS evaluation, such as those based on static accounting techniques, have been increasingly recognized as highly inadequate. Interpretive IS evaluation offers some significant potential advantages, such as continuous learning and stakeholder commitment, and it is thus reasonable to argue that it should be experimented with more widely. However, if this does happen in the future, we will also need careful research on the economic, social and political consequences of its adoption and use.

REFERENCES

Bjorn-Andersen, N. and Davis, G.B. (eds) (1988). *IS Assessment: Issues and Challenges*. North Holland, Amsterdam.

Currie, W.L. (1989). The Art of Justifying New Technology To Top Management. *Omega*, 17, 5, 409–18.

Farbey, B., Targett, D. and Land, F. (1995). Evaluating Business Information Systems: Reflections on an Empirical Study. *Information Systems Journal*, 5, 4, 235–52.

Floder, R.E. and Weiner, S.S. (1983). Rationality to Ritual: the Multiple Roles of Evaluation in Governmental Processes. In Madaus, G.F., Scriven, M. and Stufflebeam, D.L. (eds) *Evaluation Models: Viewpoints on Educational and Human Services Evaluation*. Kluwer-Nijhoff, Boston, MA.

Graeser, V., Willcocks, L. and Pisanias, N. (1998). *Developing the IT Scorecard: a Study of Evaluation Practices and Integrated Performance Measurement*. Business Intelligence, London.

Guba, E.G. and Lincoln, Y.S. (1981). *Effective Evaluation*. Jossey-Bass, San Francisco.

Guba, E.G. and Lincoln, Y.S. (1989). *Fourth Generation Evaluation*. Sage, Newbury Park.

Heiskanen, A. (1994). *Issues and Factors Affecting the Success and Failure of a Student Record System Development Process*. University of Helsinki, Helsinki.

Hirschheim, R. and Smithson, S. (1988). A Critical Analysis of Information Systems Evaluation. In Bjørn-Andersen, N. and Davis, G.B. (eds) *IS Assessment: Issues and Challenges*. North Holland, Amsterdam.

Iivari, J. (1988). Assessing IS Design Methodologies as Methods of IS Assessment. In Bjørn-Andersen, N. and Davis, G.B. (eds) *IS Assessment: Issues and Challenges*. North Holland, Amsterdam.

Kumar, K. (1990). Post Implementation Evaluation of Computer-Based IS: Current Practices. *Communications of the ACM*, 33, 2, 203–12.

Legge, K. (1984). *Evaluating Planned Organizational Change*. Academic Press, London.

Scriven, M. (1967). *The Methodology of Evaluation*. Rand McNally, Chicago.

Serafeimidis, V. and Smithson, S. (1995). The Management of Change for a Rigorous Appraisal of IT Investment: the Case of a UK Insurance Organization. In Doukidis, G., Galliers, R., Jelassi, T. and Krcmar, H. (eds) *Proceedings of the Third European Conference on Information Systems*, Athens, Greece.

Stake, R.E. (ed.) (1975). *Evaluating The Arts In Education: A Responsive Approach*. Merrill, Columbus.

Stake, R.E. (1983). Program Evaluation, Particularly Responsive Evaluation. In Madaus, G.F., Scriven, M. and Stufflebeam, D.L. (eds) *Evaluation Models: Viewpoints on Educational and Human Services Evaluation*. Kluwer-Nijhoff, Boston, MA.

Stone, D.N. (1991). Language, Training and Experience in IS Assessment. *Accounting, Management and Information Technologies*, 1, 1, 91–108.

Strassmann, P. (1997). *The Squandered Computer*. Information Economics Press, New Canaan, CN.

Symons, V.J. (1990a). *Evaluation of Information Systems: Multiple Perspectives*. Unpublished PhD Thesis, University of Cambridge, Cambridge.

Symons, V.J. (1990b). Evaluation of Information Systems: IS Development in the Processing Company. *Journal of Information Technology*, 5, 4, 194–204.

Symons, V.J. (1991). A Review of *Information Systems Evaluation: Content, Context and Process. European Journal of Information Systems*, 1, 3, 205–12.

Symons, V. and Walsham, G. (1988). The Evaluation of Information Systems: a Critique. *Journal of Applied Systems Analysis*, 15, 2, 119–32.

Walsham, G. (1993). *Interpreting Information Systems in Organizations.* John Wiley, Chichester.

Willcocks, L. (ed.) (1996). *Investing in Information Systems: Evaluation and Management.* Chapman and Hall, London.

Willcocks, L. and Lester, S. (1993). How Do Organizations Evaluate and Control Information Systems Investments? Recent UK Survey Evidence. In Avison, D., Kendall, J.E. and DeGross, J.I. (eds) *Human, Organizational, and Social Dimensions of Information Systems Development.* North Holland, Amsterdam.

13
Evaluation of Information Systems: a Critical Assessment

RUDY HIRSCHHEIM AND STEVE SMITHSON
University of Houston and London School of Economics

INTRODUCTION

Although the information systems literature and practitioners appear to be in widespread agreement regarding the need to evaluate the process and product of systems development, the vehicle for undertaking such an evaluation is far from clear. Numerous comments have been offered about what should be done, and there have been various attempts to define how it should be done. Unfortunately, as will be argued in this chapter, much of what has been done under the umbrella of information systems evaluation has been ill conceived. As Chapters 2 and 12 pointed out, the social dimension of evaluation has largely been ignored in the drive to provide a rigorous interpretation and vehicle for evaluation. This, it is argued, is misguided and inevitably leads to an overly rational, simplistic notion of evaluation which is dysfunctional in the long run due to the inherent unintended consequences it invariably brings about.

THE FUNDAMENTAL NATURE OF EVALUATION

Evaluation is endemic to human existence. Whether consciously or not, people evaluate the products and processes of their labour. Food, drink,

Beyond the IT Productivity Paradox.
Edited by L. P. Willcocks and S. Lester © 1999 John Wiley & Sons Ltd.

appearance, social interactions etc. are constantly being evaluated by someone or something (Legge, 1984, p. 3). Evaluation is undertaken as a matter of course in the attempt to gauge how well something meets a particular expectation, objective or need. People, it seems, have an insatiable appetite or curiosity for such things. Consumer products are assessed to see if they meet market demands; academics, as a matter of course, tend to evaluate the intellectual faculties of colleagues through discussions; political ideologies are evaluated on the policies adopted and their expected societal implications; and so forth. Evaluation is apparently an important and intrinsic property of the process of understanding, which in turn is a prerequisite for, or a prelude to, a carefully considered action.

It is only natural, therefore, that people have sought mechanisms to help in the process of evaluation. Various tools, methods and techniques have been developed to aid this process. Criteria such as bouquet and clarity are used to judge the quality of wine; hardware monitors are used in computers to assess their efficiency; econometric models are used to evaluate the state of a nation's economy; formal methods are used to evaluate the correctness of a computer program.

Pressures to improve customer service and quality have led to a growing enthusiasm for total quality management (Garvin, 1988; Grant, Shani and Krishnan, 1994) where the continuous evaluation of quality is an essential part of the approach. Notions of quality are increasingly being applied through formal evaluations in areas which were previously relatively untouched. In the UK in recent years, these include the formal assessment of university research and teaching, secondary (high) schools (based on examination results), hospitals (bed occupancy statistics) and the police service (crime clear-up rates). Often the results are publicised, typically in the form of a "league table", with the implication that they may be taken into consideration in the distribution of resources. These activities are typically associated with specialized quality audit teams, operating according to highly deterministic criteria. This entire evaluation infrastructure represents a considerable expense and commitment from the organizations concerned and has in many cases gained considerable power and legitimacy. In all these cases, while many commentators applaud the publication of the performance of these public-sector institutions, there is genuine concern that complex social functions provided by highly trained experts, like education, health and law and order, are being reduced to simplistic numerical scores that have little real meaning (Power, 1997).

As was noted by Mason and Swanson (1981), underlying these tools and methods is a more basic concept—that of measurement. They called measurement the *sine qua non* of decision. In fact, measurement is the link between evaluation and tools. In order for something to be evaluated it has initially to be measured, which is normally undertaken through the application of tools and techniques. As Strassmann (1985) notes: "You cannot measure what is not defined. You also cannot tell whether you have improved something if you have not measured its performance" (p. 100), a continuous theme in his work (Strassmann, 1990, 1997). Thus, it must first be decided exactly what to measure and why; unfortunately, parts of this simple relationship appear to have been forgotten in the desire to create ever more powerful techniques for evaluation.

This chapter, developing our earlier work (Hirschheim and Smithson, 1988), contends that, at least within the information systems area, in the drive for better tool creation (to improve the process of evaluation) there has been a concentration on the "means" to the detriment of the "ends". That is, the function and substance of evaluation have been given too little attention, while the mechanisms for carrying out evaluation have been given too much attention.

SOCIAL NATURE OF EVALUATION:
FORMAL/INFORMAL ASPECTS

The strong urge to evaluate everything has resulted in the development of many tools and techniques but, particularly in the light of their doubtful effectiveness (discussed in more detail below) and their vulnerability to organizational hijacking by a strong interest group, they are unlikely to satisfy the need to evaluate. Inevitably, as Chapters 4, 5 and 6 made clear, much informal evaluation remains outside of the official evaluation procedures, and there may be considerable tension between formal and informal evaluations. Formal evaluations may appear to be unnecessary, unwieldy and often largely political compared to the apparently effective, non-bureaucratic expressions of what the users really feel, that may be found in informal evaluation. Alternatively, one may take the position that formal evaluations are objective, rational mechanisms aimed at improving the communication and learning within the organization, whereas informal evaluations are ill-informed, hasty and largely subjective judgements.

As Chapters 2 and 12 suggested, formal evaluation studies take place within an organizational environment characterized by much political activity as interest groups jockey for power and status. The results of formal evaluation studies have a considerable legitimacy that can form a sizeable political prize. Where an evaluation team approach is used, comprising members from various organizational groups, the ground is laid for the type of political manoeuvres associated with formal committees. In any case, the questions of who carries out the evaluation, when it is carried out and what criteria are used are important tactical positions to be grabbed en route to the final prize. The political nature of IS development has been emphasized by such writers as Keen (1981), Knights and Murray (1994) and Markus and Bjørn-Andersen (1987) and such a high-profile activity as a formal evaluation study is unlikely to escape political activity.

The urge to evaluate everything, felt by nearly all individuals, results in informal evaluations but these evaluations are unlikely to be performed in isolation. New information systems will be discussed informally by groups who are affected, to varying degrees, by the new system. Particularly where the group has borne the brunt of the impact of the new system in terms of changes to working practice or redundancies, or where the group is near the beginning of the learning curve, experiencing much uncertainty and anxiety, such discussions are unlikely to be either brief or ill informed. The behaviour of work groups has been studied in some detail by organization theorists (see for example Smith, 1973) and much is known, or hypothesized, about the formation of groups, their maintenance, the development of group norms and the sanctions applied to deviants within the group. Where the group feels itself threatened by a new information system, in particular if traditional norms are under pressure, then clearly a great deal of interaction within the group may take place. New group norms may have to be developed or old ones reinforced as the group adjusts to the new situation. Thus the process of informal evaluation may be subject to very considerable social pressures; they differ from those surrounding formal evaluation, being perhaps more subtle and more or less ritualistic, depending on circumstances.

Thus, on the one hand, we have formal evaluation studies which, although technical on the surface, may contain much inter-group political activity underneath and, on the other hand, we have informal evaluations subject to intra-group pressures. Clearly, the common factor is the social nature of evaluation, however it is carried out. In the same way that it is argued that information systems should be regarded more as social systems and less as technical systems (Land and Hirschheim, 1983; Hirschheim, Klein and Newman, 1991), similar reasoning can be applied to the notion of evaluation itself. Furthermore, a parallel may be drawn between formal and informal evaluation and formal and informal information systems (Earl and Hopwood, 1980).

THE INFORMATION SYSTEMS EVALUATION
LITERATURE

People's desire to evaluate everything they come in contact with—particularly those elements which are time consuming to make, expensive to purchase and/or likely to have important consequences—leads to a strongly felt need to assess all forms of technological intervention, for example, computer-based information system (IS) implementation. The literature abounds with examples of IS evaluations; in fact, during the 1980s, there was an entire journal devoted to IS successes and failures: *Systems, Objectives, Solutions.*

Evaluation *per se* can be treated as a very wide area indeed, encompassing many processes that take place during project selection, procurement, system testing prior to implementation, and post-implementation evaluation studies. For reasons of space, and because earlier chapters have dealt with other stages, this chapter concentrates on post-implementation evaluation. Where the term evaluation is unqualified, it should be taken to refer to post-implementation evaluation.

Literature Framework

While earlier classifications of evaluation approaches (for example Sanders, 1984; Srinivasan, 1985) tended to neglect the social nature of information systems and of evaluation, more recent work (for example Farbey, Land and Targett, 1993; Willcocks, 1994, 1996; see also Chapters 6 and 7) has taken a more pragmatic and normative approach in order to select the "right" evaluation tool for the situation. These contingency approaches are discussed further below.

The method of classifying approaches to IS evaluation adopted here recognizes two rudimentary dimensions. The first reflects the (often unspoken) assumptions underlying any particular evaluation approach, and can be thought of as a continuum ranging from the highly objective or rational approaches to evaluation at the one end, to those which regard evaluation as very subjective or political at the other (see also Chapter 5). The second dimension, which is not a continuum, depicts the relationship between IS evaluation approaches and their counterparts in other disciplines. By presenting the IS evaluation literature in this fashion, starting with the most "objective/rational" and moving along the continuum to the more "subjective/political", while paying attention to the origins of the approaches, insight into the nature of evaluation can be gained. This is illustrated in Figure 13.1.

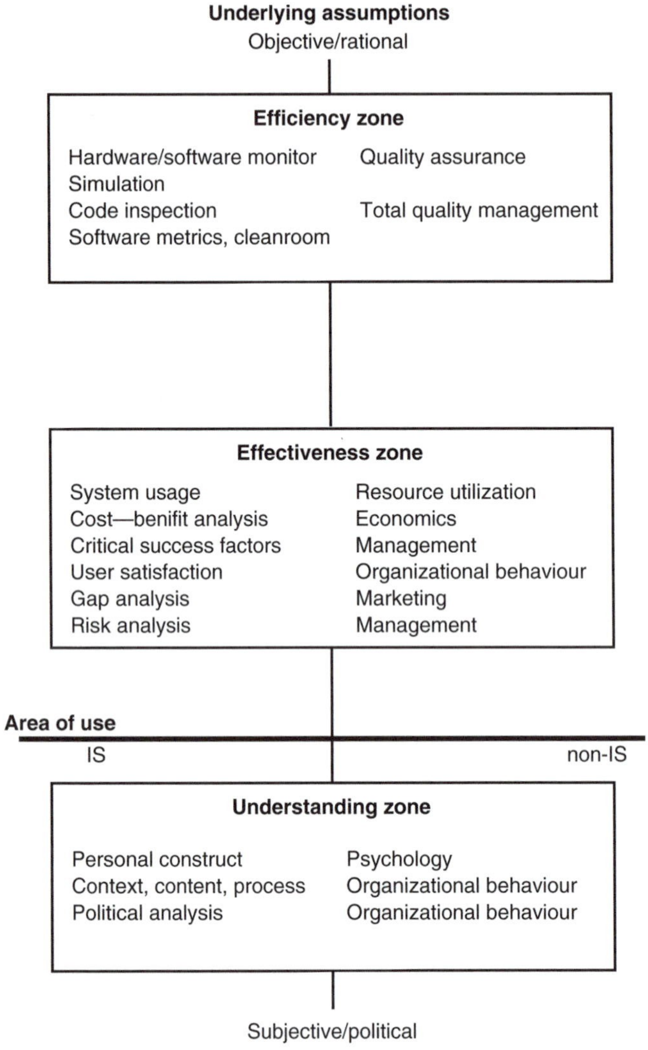

Underlying assumptions
Objective/rational

Efficiency zone	
Hardware/software monitor	Quality assurance
Simulation	
Code inspection	Total quality management
Software metrics, cleanroom	

Effectiveness zone	
System usage	Resource utilization
Cost—benifit analysis	Economics
Critical success factors	Management
User satisfaction	Organizational behaviour
Gap analysis	Marketing
Risk analysis	Management

Area of use

IS   non-IS

Understanding zone	
Personal construct	Psychology
Context, content, process	Organizational behaviour
Political analysis	Organizational behaviour

Subjective/political

Figure 13.1   *Classification of Evaluation Approaches*

Literature Review

Starting at the highly rational/objective end of the continuum, we can identify an area of evaluation literature which might broadly be defined as an "efficiency" zone. Just as the emphasis on quality (including quality management and quality control) came to dominate much of manufacturing industry before being transferred to the services sector, it can also be seen as prevalent within software engineering (for example Gilb, 1988; Zultner, 1993) where the main objective is to make the software as "reliable" as the underlying hardware (Poore, Mills and Mutchler, 1993). Past experience has shown that programming is often a highly unreliable process (see also Chapter 8) such that software developers now make considerable efforts to test program code systematically in order to trace errors and inefficiencies. This may involve the use of rigorous inspection techniques (Knight and Myers, 1993), akin to quality control, using ideas that can be traced back to Fagan (1976). Many IS departments have set up separate quality assurance teams, and there is as a consequence much interest in automated testing tools, statistical process control, software metrics and "cleanroom" techniques (for examples only see Grady, 1993; Mills, Dyer and Linger, 1987; Swanson *et al.*, 1991).

Various quality management standards, both international (e.g. ISO 9000/9001) and national (e.g. BS 5750), have been set up or adapted for software production. Many organizations have expended considerable resources in implementing detailed quality assurance procedures in order to secure accreditation to these standards. However, these techniques, although they may be applied rigorously and systematically, depend for their notion of correctness on matching the systems specifications which are normally regarded as being absolute and non-controversial. Yet these specifications may well be obsolete or misleading due to inadequate requirements analysis or because of changes in the dynamic business and organizational environment.

These approaches are almost solely concerned with efficiency, defined as performing a particular task well in relation to given criteria, compared with effectiveness, which is related to deciding which tasks should be done ("doing things right" vs "doing the right things"— Drucker, 1971). This distinction has been much emphasized by, for example, Grindley, (1995) and Keen and Scott Morton (1978). Moreover, the limits of concentrating on aspects of efficiency (e.g. small savings in a meaningless task) are clear and, in the view of Bjørn-Andersen (1984): "we have overemphasised efficiency at the expense of effectiveness".

Moving along the continuum from the "efficiency" zone at the objective/rational extreme, the first measure of effectiveness would seem to be that of usage or utilization. These measures are widely used in other fields, for example average seat occupancy rate may be used to evaluate the success of an airline service. This idea is based on the notion that the more a system is used the more successful/effective it is. Although much discussed in the 1970s (for example Ein-Dor and Segev, 1978), it has fallen out of favour over the years as being too simplistic. There are problems in determining exactly what constitutes usage, many systems are mandatory anyway (the users have no choice) and this measure ignores the importance or value of the individual task; e.g. the system may be used infrequently but, when it is used, it is crucial (Ginzberg, 1978; Keen, 1975).

Most current approaches in this zone are developments of traditional cost–benefit analysis (King and Schrems, 1978; Powell, 1992a; Sassone, 1988; see also Chapters 4, 5 and 6). Originating in the area of economics (see for example Layard, 1980), this is one of the standard approaches in project selection and procurement as well as in evaluation. Where costs and benefits are easy to identify and quantify, this technique has many advantages in terms of acceptability and comprehensibility.

However, many writers (for example Keen, 1975; Hogue and Watson, 1983) have long argued that in most IS developments the benefits are largely qualitative. The determination of costs may be relatively straightforward, although Strassmann (1985) and Willcocks (1994) criticize the frequent failure in practice to include all the true costs. The calculation of benefits, however, is fraught with difficulties (Land, 1976; Strassmann, 1990). The problem of accounting for qualitative benefits is usually surmounted by attributing to them some quantitative value, treating them as a side issue or ignoring them altogether (Keen, 1975, 1991).

As this book makes clear, the notion of productivity is especially problematical. While the introduction of a new information system would normally be expected to improve the productivity of its users, the research evidence is very mixed. This leads to the "productivity paradox" debate that is central to this book (Hochstrasser and Griffiths, 1991; Roach, 1991; Strassman, 1990; Weill, 1992). It is interesting here that some writers (e.g. Panko, 1991) can still take a relatively optimistic view, while others, such as Sivula (1990) and Strassmann (1997) can see no general improvement in productivity as a result of the introduction of computer-based systems. As Chapters 1, 2, and 3 pointed out, there is also reason to question the statistics used in some studies. At base, this debate founders on the difficulties of conceptualizing productivity in the context of administrative (or clerical or knowledge-based) and managerial work (Boddy and Buchanan, 1984; Loveman, 1994; Schafer, 1988). Improved information, systems may lead to better information which may improve decision making, but this is almost impossible to measure (Farbey, Land and Targett, 1993).

The superficiality of much cost–benefit analysis can be seen in the lack of attention given to the identification and management of benefits (Peters, 1996; Ward, Taylor and Bond, 1995). Many organizations seem just to list the potential benefits in the course of the feasibility study and then promptly forget about them. These authors argue that much greater care should be taken in ensuring that the planned benefits are actually achieved, because without some form of planned, regular evaluation, potential benefits can easily evaporate.

In order to reduce the overall complexity of evaluation, there is a temptation to reduce voluminous cost–benefit analyses to simple single figures. Thus, Strassman's (1990, 1997) "return on management" tries to determine the increase in management productivity (or value added by management) as being a meaningful yet easily calculated statistic. However, this assumes that management is directly responsible for the financial residue remaining, after the cost of labour and capital has been subtracted from the firm's revenue. This is rather dubious, as it takes no account of environmental effects such as changes in fashion or economic climate (for a critique see also Chapter 6). Some organizations evaluate their IS function by comparing particular cost–performance ratios (e.g. IT expenditure against turnover) with industry benchmarks (Bendell, Boulter and Kelly, 1993; Bullard, 1994). However, such comparisons tend to ignore specific contextual information and assume that the ratios are in fact comparable when the underlying calculations may diverge significantly.

An alternative approach to effectiveness which avoids the difficulties inherent in trying to measure costs and benefits precisely is to examine the information system with respect to either the organization's, or the system's, objectives. The notion of critical success factors (Rockart, 1979) is an example of management thinking transferred to IS evaluation. Authors such as Earl (1992) and Willcocks, Feeny and Islei (1997) argue that IS evaluations should focus more on the impact on business and should thus consider business goals and critical success factors, rather than "pure" costs and benefits. Thus it may be more meaningful to evaluate measures such as delivery time, sales targets or time to market for new products. Earl argues that it is much easier to justify IS investments in terms of business plans because senior managers are more likely to understand and accept them and so the particular IT investment can be built into the business strategy.

In their information economics method, Parker, Benson and Trainor (1988) relate IS to specific business goals, as well as attempting to overcome the problems of dealing with intangible benefits and the time value of benefits. However, objectives are often not clear and the objectives of different groups in the organization may conflict. There is a danger that finance-based techniques will favour a short-term view that is incompatible with long-term infrastructure investments. Approaches such as Schafer *et al.*'s (1988) benefit analysis within the Functional Analysis of Office Requirements (FAOR) project view evaluation as a continuous process within organizational change.

Instead of relying on the quasi-objective measures produced by cost–benefit analysis or a comparison with some objectives, one can adopt the position that success is a more subjective notion which is best measured in terms of user satisfaction. Evaluators can take the answers to an appropriate questionnaire and manipulate them according to a weighting scheme to arrive at a numerical value. This approach can be thought to have its roots in social surveys (cf. Bulmer, 1977, particularly in relation to their use by Charles Booth in the late nineteenth century) from a methodological perspective, and in the socio-technical school of organization theory (Mumford and Banks, 1967) in its regard to the satisfaction of the user. However, the measurement of satisfaction is not easy; Ives, Olson and Baroudi (1983) discuss the various measures, concluding in favour of the 39-point questionnaire and weighting scheme from Bailey and Pearson (1983). While the approach has much to commend it, there has been on-going criticism both of the underlying theory that user satisfaction is a good indicator of IS effectiveness (Melone, 1990) and the methodology of measurement (Doll and Torkzadeh, 1988; Galletta and Lederer, 1989) due to the imprecision and unreliability of the measuring tools.

Ginzberg (1981) emphasizes the role of expectations in user satisfaction, both in regard to realistic/unrealistic and positive/negative expectations, finding that unrealistic expectations are often associated with system failures. Other researchers have experimented with service quality gap analysis (e.g. Pitt, Watson and Kaven, 1995), a technique borrowed from marketing (Parasuraman, Zeithini and Berry, 1985) which tries to identify and measure gaps between the expectations of users and developers and the actual performance. Although this technique is useful in identifying large gaps for particular performance criteria (e.g. the users' expected response time compared to their perceptions of the actual response time), these gaps still need to be weighted somehow in order to determine their real significance.

There are considerable risk and uncertainty in information systems development, ranging from the risk that a system may not meet its requirements (which themselves may have changed during the development process) to risks of security breaches and other serious failures (see Chapter 8). This sparked an interest in risk analysis for information systems, with Boehm's (1988) spiral model of software development emphasizing regular risk analysis. There are clearly many different types of risk (Clemons, 1991; Coleman and Jamieson, 1994; Parker, Benson and Trainor, 1988), from high-level commercial risk to lower-level project risks. However, Baskerville (1991) argues, in connection with IS security risks, that much risk analysis lacks formal statistical rigour and its inherent subjectivity makes it wide open to organizational misuse, such that the analysis can be fixed to give the desired result. However, he recognizes its value as a communication technique to increase decision makers' awareness of the existence of particular risks.

The evaluation of an information system has long been recognized as a complex and elusive notion with inherent problems (Blackler and Brown, 1988; Dickson, Weels and Wilkers, 1988; Land, 1976; Willcocks, 1994). In an earlier paper (Hirschheim and Smithson, 1988) we emphasized the subjectivity underlying even the most formal approaches to IS evaluation, such that the subjective judgements of the people concerned in answering the questions of "what", "how" and "when" to evaluate tend to determine the final result of any evaluation study.

The introduction of a new information system is likely to have consequences in economic terms (e.g. costs, output, turnover), organizational terms (e.g. changes in organizational structure or procedures), social terms (e.g. social interaction, quality of working life, organizational culture), and management terms (e.g. information access and decision making). Any of these aspects may improve or deteriorate and it is often problematic to isolate the factors which cause particular costs and benefits, especially when these factors themselves are highly interdependent. In addition, there are often unplanned consequences of introducing a new system and the business application area concerned may be subject to impacts from planned changes or unforeseen events which are at most only indirectly linked to the new system (Schafer *et al.*, 1988). It is thus a huge problem deciding "what" to measure, especially as many of these aspects are highly intangible (Brown, 1994). DeLone and McLean (1992) classify evaluation criteria under six categories: system quality, information quality, use, user satisfaction, individual impact and organizational impact—none of which is free of the measurement problems which have long been recognized as problematic in organizational settings (Mason and Swanson, 1981).

Information systems are social systems that evolve over time and so deciding when to carry out an evaluation is extremely difficult; the learning difficulties of users tend to delay the delivery of benefits (Brynjolfsson, 1993). Willcocks and Lester (1993) highlight the lack of understanding of the human and organizational costs involved, the danger of overstating costs, the neglect of intangible benefits and risks, the use of inappropriate measures, and the problems with traditional finance-based evaluation techniques. Ballantine, Galliers and Stray (1994) emphasize the problem of getting the system requirements right in the first place, as well as the identification and quantification of relevant costs and benefits, together with the time taken in carrying out an effective evaluation study. From their survey, Canevet and Smithson (1994) found organizations experiencing difficulties in getting users to participate, choosing appropriate measures, measurement inaccuracy and the acceptability level of the results.

Most evidence suggests that organizations normally carry out some form of evaluation as part of a feasibility study or investment appraisal, typically using traditional cost–benefit analysis (Ballantine, Galliers and Stray, 1994; Willcocks and Lester, 1993). However, the relative balance between formal, quantitative appraisals and more subjective, qualitative ones is unclear. Currie (1989) found that engineering managers disdained accounting-based techniques as spurious and ritualistic but felt that these techniques had more legitimacy than their own preferred, more qualitative approach (see also Chapter 2). Hochstrasser and Griffiths (1991) found that formal evaluation methods were less likely to be used for information systems that were in any way strategic to an organization. Grindley (1995) found that the vast majority (83%) of cost–benefit analyses used to support IT investment proposals were basically fiction. While Powell (1992b) argues that intangibles are increasingly used to justify a business case for IT investment, Farbey, Land and Targett (1993) found that intangible benefits were not generally acceptable, a view that might need to change if the argument on era shifts presented in the Introduction to this book is accepted.

As Walsham makes clear in the previous chapter, a key problem concerns the often conflicting perceptions of different stakeholder groups such that evaluation may become a highly political activity (Goddard, 1989; Walsham, 1993). For example, Symons (1991) notes that improved access to headquarters information might be seen as a benefit for those working in the field but as an erosion of the power base of managers at headquarters. While the information itself may have highly political implications in some organizational situations (Davenport, Eccles and Prusak, 1992), costs and benefits are also frequently politically charged (Lederer *et al.*, 1990) and may be redistributed through political activity such that they become even more difficult to trace.

Thus, within the effectiveness zone, advances have been made over the past decade but many problems still remain.

Moving along the continuum towards the subjective/political extreme, we emerge from the effectiveness zone into a qualitatively different area, which might be called the understanding zone. By this is meant an understanding (or appreciation) of the functions and nature of evaluation, as well as the limitations and problems inherent in the process of evaluation. Unlike the other two zones, measurement is not attempted, rather the aim is the understanding of evaluation. In our earlier paper, we noted much research activity in the efficiency and effectiveness zones and, as argued above, this seems to have continued over the last 10 years. However, although in 1988 there seemed to be little interest in the understanding zone, this seems to have changed over the last 10 years, at least in parts of academia.

The subjectivity of evaluation suggests that it might be useful to try to understand how individuals assess or judge situations or phenomena. One approach would be to use personal construct theory from the field of psychology (Kelly, 1955). This theory attempts to show how people construct personal mental models of the world. According to Kelly, these personal constructs are bipolar in nature (e.g. "black–white", "kind–cruel"), each having a particular range of application. This theory is clearly relevant in seeking to explain the process of informal evaluation, as users apply their personal constructs to a new information system. A related notion is that of technological frames (Orlikowski and Gash, 1994), where these are a group's shared assumptions, expectations and approach to understanding technology. Although personal construct theory has been used by researchers in man–machine interfaces (Gaines and Shaw, 1980) and information requirements analysis (Grudnitski, 1984), as far as we are aware such theories have not been discussed to any degree within the IS evaluation literature.

Gregory and Jackson (1992) regard evaluation methodologies as goal based (or functionalist), systems resource based (concerned with adaptation to environment), culture based (organizational culture) or multi-actor based (political analysis). They relate this classification to the evaluation team (or "evaluation party") based on the team's approach to organizations (objective or subjective) and their internal "variety" (range of available perspectives—Ashby, 1956). Thus, they argue that a goal-based approach would suit an evaluation team with an objectivist approach and low variety, while a multi-actor approach would work better with an evaluation team characterized by a subjectivist approach and high variety. Although this classification provides insight, in practice much depends on the precise role and political power of the team.

As remarked above, evaluation is a largely social activity, whether formal or informal, and the object being evaluated—an information system—is equally a social entity. The conflicting interests and views of different stakeholders, reflecting the political forces in the organization, pose problems for both the development and evaluation of IS (Carnall, 1982; Land, 1976; Mendelow, 1984). Land proposes that a consensus regarding the objectives and criteria should be arrived at by negotiation between the parties at an early stage of system development.

The use of rational tools is frequently accompanied by highly political behaviour. Boland and Pondy (1983) suggest that there is a rational myth in the foreground and political manoeuvres in the background, while Franz and Robey (1984) found that:

> The rational elements are tools used by participants to gain new ground or to protect ground already won. They also serve as "facades" to mask political motives and legitimise self-interest.

Similarly, Laudon (1985) found that environmental (objective/rational) factors were used during project selection as a legitimizing tool, whereas institutional (political) factors determined the utilization and management of new systems. On a similar theme, Kling and Iacono (1984) noted that: "key actors used the language of efficiency to push the CBIS in a direction that increased their own power and control in the organization".

A particularly useful way of trying to understand the myriad issues involved in an evaluation and its context is in terms of content, context and process (Symons, 1991), based on the contextualism of Pettigrew (1985). Content is concerned with "what" is to be measured and evaluated and involves the selection of relevant criteria and values. This is likely to stretch beyond narrow costs and benefits. Notions of risk and links to the organization's strategy can be considered here. Process involves the "how" of evaluation, i.e. the way it is carried out, when, how often and how the results are to be made available. This is linked to the notion of organizational learning. The context involves the consideration of the questions of "why" the evaluation is to be carried out and "who" is to do it. Considerations of context may involve the external organizational context (e.g. aspects of the business environment) and/or the internal context (e.g. the structure or culture of the organization).

Walsham (1993) uses the content, context, process (CCP) approach in a detailed analysis of three case studies. He concludes that "the process of IS evaluation involves a discourse, often mediated by formal procedures, but in the context of informal stakeholder assessments" (p. 179). He notes that the evaluation process has both overt and covert functions and in some organizations it may be seen as largely a ritual. However, its outcome provides an interpretive scheme, incorporating certain norms and values, although these may not be accepted completely by all the stakeholders concerned. The importance of discourse as part of an evaluation exercise can be linked to the work of Lyytinen, Klein and Hirschheim (1991), who use a social action perspective to derive nine different effectiveness measures for office information systems. They relate four types of social action (instrumental, strategic, communicative and discursive) to three contexts (technology, language and organization) to give a much broader picture of effectiveness than is normally presented.

Willcocks and Margetts (1994) use the CCP approach to propose a framework for examining risk which includes consideration of a project's external business context, internal organizational context, the process by which the project is carried out, the content of the project (e.g. size, complexity) and the project outcomes (e.g. cost, time, impact on the business).

As well as breadth of understanding, the CCP framework also lends itself to the use of rather different tools to those of narrow cost–benefit analysis. These include stakeholder maps (Gilbert *et al.*, 1988) to identify the various stakeholders (e.g. users, developers, senior and middle managers, customers and trade associations) and multi-objective, multi-criteria analysis (see Chapter 6). The latter, together with value analysis, prototyping, simulation and game/role playing, is classed as an exploratory or experimental technique by Farbey, Land and Targett in Chapter 6. Furthermore, Serafeimidis and Smithson (1994) use the CCP framework as a foundation for their conceptual model of evaluation which underpins a discussion of software support for the evaluation process.

With such a wide range of evaluation techniques and approaches available and with practical pressures demanding meaningful evaluations of operational systems, practitioners would clearly gain from advice on which techniques fit particular situations. Thus an important step towards understanding evaluation is the recognition that an organization typically uses a wide range of information systems with different functions and objectives and so different evaluations may be required; i.e. there is no "one best method" suitable for all situations. Thus, an evaluation approach which suits a simple structured payroll system is unlikely to be appropriate for a strategic, high-profile marketing system or a groupware support tool. The literature offers various classification schemas (for example Hochstrasser, 1990; Parker, Benson and Trainor 1988; Ward, 1990), although Willcocks (1994) advises organizations to develop their own classification based on their own goals, objectives and characteristics of their particular industry (see also Chapter 6).

Farbey, Land and Targett (1993) offer a benefits evaluation ladder with eight "rungs" to classify different types of application according to the difficulty of evaluation. Moving up the ladder generally leads to increasing benefits but also increasing risk and uncertainty, as well as increasing complexity in carrying out the evaluation. This ranges from the first rung, mandatory changes, where the function of evaluation is to compare the technical and cost aspects of alternative solutions for a change that has to take place, to the top rung, business transformation, where IT needs to be evaluated as part of an entire major change initiative.

As well as recognizing the need for different evaluation approaches for different types of system, authors such as Farbey, Land and Targett (1993) recognize that evaluation stretches over the entire systems life-cycle. However, its nature changes over the lifecycle such that the early stages (strategy selection, problem identification and feasibility study) are characterized by senior management activities such as defining strategy and high-level goals, identifying constraints, and interpreting costs and benefits. In the later development stages, project managers are concerned with evaluating progress against detailed plans and precise specifications through project control and acceptance testing. After implementation, an evaluation team may identify costs incurred and benefits achieved, and the extent to which these resulted from the IT intervention (on the lifecycle approach see also Chapter 2).

The difficulties in evaluating information systems in both theory and practice should be seen in the light of "evaluation research" (cf. Weiss, 1972). According to Legge (1984), it specifically addresses the difficulties associated with formal evaluation studies (in particular those concerned with social change) within the political environment of an organization. She discusses positivistic and interpretive approaches to evaluation in the light of what she sees as the three crises of evaluation:

1.   utilization (whether the results are used);
2.   verification (the methodological validity);
3.   accreditation (the values underlying the evaluation).

Of these, she regards the third as being the key factor. Kling (1985) attempts to incorporate social values through a "social impact analysis" at various points within the information systems development cycle. He agrees that there are no simple formulae for such evaluation. However, to be meaningful, evaluation must take into account the values intrinsic to the process of evaluation. These often conflict, are unspoken, and are the source of considerable confusion.

The political nature of evaluation has led many writers to conclude that evaluation is meaningless. Beer (1981) suggests that the result of evaluation can often be made to show whatever is desired simply by choosing a technique which supports the underlying value position. According to Suchman (1970), this can be effected through the use of one of two types of evaluation: "eye wash" or "white wash". The former refers to evaluation as a way of justifying or supporting a weak system by choosing to look at only those aspects which show the system in a favourable light. The latter is used to conceal the truth by avoiding any objective appraisal. Similarly, Gowler and Legge (1978) postulate two types of goals associated with an organizational intervention: overt and covert. They state that "real" success is often seen in terms of achieving covert goals. All that is required from the success criteria of the overt goals is that they are sufficiently broad to allow room for politically advantageous interpretation.

Using, in particular, the "underlying assumptions" continuum, we have depicted in Figure 13.1 the different approaches to evaluation. These are represented between the two poles of objective/rational and subjective/political. Clearly, the approaches from the efficiency and effectiveness zones have received the most attention to date and are widely accepted in industry and academia. We see much more research activity than before (Hirschheim and Smithson, 1988) in the understanding zone but, as discussed in the analysis below, the acceptance of such research is not guaranteed.

CRITICAL ANALYSIS OF THE ASSUMPTIONS INHERENT IN INFORMATION SYSTEMS EVALUATION

The above literature review shows that, until quite recently, IS evaluation has largely been based on an objective/rational grounding, but that a relatively small group of researchers are now taking a more subjectivist or political view of IS evaluation. Given that evaluation is by its very nature subjective, then one might expect a major shift towards this direction. However, although the techniques discussed above in the "understanding zone" seem to be well founded academically, there remains a significant reluctance to accept them, both by academics and practitioners (see also Chapter 5). Why is this? Why cling to an approach which is entirely objective and rational? While the objectivist is likely to argue that such approaches are valuable because they bring into the open the criteria used in evaluation, as well as providing a "logical" vehicle for assessing an information system, both logical argument and practical experience raise serious doubts about the validity of an objectivist approach. We believe that this is due to a number of underlying assumptions and beliefs which have gone relatively unchallenged. In particular, the following seem to us to need close scrutiny:

1. that a concentration on the development of tools and techniques is a meaningful basis by which to advance the state of IS evaluation knowledge;

2. that the "scientific" approach is a meaningful basis by which to develop tools and techniques for evaluation;
3. that information systems are themselves inherently objective and rational and thus capable of being evaluated in an objective/rational fashion.

The Concentration on Tools and Techniques

From an examination of the literature, it seems to us that much research on evaluation has largely been misdirected toward tools and techniques for measurement and away from understanding the process of evaluation itself (see also Chapters 2, 6 and 12). It is likely that this is a major reason that there continues to exist so much consternation and confusion over evaluation. Instead of concentrating on developing a rich understanding of the subject of study, academics have sought to apply more formal tools, techniques and methods. This appears to be consistent with society's desire to formalize, quantify and measure the apparent quality of an ever increasing range of activities, services and products. This allows more "scientific" approaches to be applied. Evaluation is hence enhanced because the methods are grounded in science. Unfortunately, in the drive to develop better and better tools and techniques (particularly more formal ones), the basic reason for, and goals of, the research (i.e. understanding the process of evaluation) has been forgotten. The "means" have ostensibly taken over the "ends".

Clearly, there is more to evaluation than simply the application of a particular objective methodology. Evaluation must contain a large measure of subjectivity; it must consider the political and social domain. Rationalizing these processes so that they can be dealt with through the application of some formal and objective tools and techniques must surely be suspect. This is not to suggest that a structured approach to evaluation is not feasible nor desirable, rather that the emphasis of evaluation should be brought back to understanding the subject of enquiry. This is an epistemological issue and leads directly into the second challenged assumption.

The Adoption of the "Scientific" Paradigm for IS Evaluation

The general belief appears to be that by adopting a more scientific approach, better evaluation can be obtained. This seems to continue into the recent focus on approaches such as the "Balanced Scorecard" (Kaplan and Norton, 1992). In fact, it is the belief in a scientific approach which is largely responsible for the IS community's misplaced concentration on the tools and techniques for evaluation rather than the nature of evaluation itself. Fundamentally, it is the uncritical adoption of the so-called scientific method which is at the root of the problems with IS evaluation.

The notion of evaluation is inextricably bound up with the scientific community's strong predilection towards positivism. The adoption of positivism and its associated research methods irrespective of its appropriateness for the subject matter of study has been referred to as "scientism" (Klein and Lyytinen, 1985; McCarthy, 1982). The adoption of this paradigm ostensibly leads to the rejection of subjective data (except for the case of conjecture development) and thus the large-scale dismissal of social criteria in evaluation. The alternative is to "objectivize" the subjective data so that analysis techniques appropriate for objective data can be applied. However, this is likely to be unsound in most cases and lead to questionable conclusions (cf. Legge, 1984).

The fundamental difficulty here is an epistemological and ontological one. Positivism searches for regularities and causal relationships and treats individuals as though they are deterministic, although they "respond to events in predictable and determinate ways" (Morgan and Smircich, 1980, p. 495). While a positivistic approach may be appropriate and acceptable for dealing with a subject of study which does not possess free will, information systems are not of this kind. As information systems are fundamentally human and social entities, positivism is felt to be an inappropriate basis for enquiry and hence evaluation. This theme is well discussed in the social science literature (see Burrell and Morgan, 1979; Garfinkel, 1967; Halfpenny, 1979; Morgan, 1983; Reason and Rowan, 1981; Van Maanen, 1979) and is gaining prominence in the information systems literature (see Mumford *et al.*, 1985; Nissen, Klein and Hirschheim, 1991; also Chapter 12).

The emergence of alternative research approaches based on hermeneutics (Klein and Hirschheim, 1983) and phenomenology (Boland and Day, 1982) was a response to the unease that many individuals conducting research within the domain of information systems feel towards positivistic methods. Walsham (1995 and in Chapter 12) discusses the emergence of interpretivism in IS research, citing the work of Orlikowski (1991, 1992), Suchman (1994) and Zuboff (1988) among others. Hirschheim, Klein and Newman (1991) propose a social action perspective on information systems development, while Robey and Newman (1996) use a social process model clearly based on an interpretivist epistemology. The latter authors make use of Kling's (1980) perspectives in their analysis. Similarly, Hirschheim and Klein (1989) compare four "paradigms" of information systems development.

However, irrespective of its appropriateness, positivism has been the basis of IS evaluation, but not necessarily because it has been successful. Legge (1984), for example, notes its ritualistic value (see also Chapter 12):

> Positivistic [evaluation] designs prosper largely through acting as a rhetoric for an evaluation ritual whereby the lack of rationality of actual decision making and the accountability and responsibility demanded of the idealised decision maker, are reconciled. (p. 112)

Basically, positivism has been adopted because it is widely believed to be the only "right" way to undertake enquiry. Alternative approaches adopting a more interpretive and subjectivist stance are considered "unscientific" and an unacceptable basis for evaluation (see also Power, 1997). This, it is felt, is a mistake, and can only lead to a furthering of quantitative tools and techniques which assume that individuals are deterministic and behave in a rational and objective manner. With such a conception, IS evaluation is likely to continue down the path of irrelevancy.

"Information Systems Are Inherently Objective and Rational"

Traditional IS evaluation approaches have assumed that information systems are objective and rational, and thus capable of being evaluated by the use of objective/rational tools and techniques. The adoption of positivism reflects and cements this belief. It is possible, however, to conceive of two alternative positions about the nature or ontology of information systems, of which the objective/rational is only one. The second is subjective and political. The former ontological position we will refer to as the analytic perspective, the latter as the interpretivist perspective.

The perspectives differ on a number of dimensions. For example, the former sees information systems functions and activities as largely deterministic, rational and overt whereas the latter conceives of them as mostly non-deterministic, political and covert. The analytic perspective metaphorically conceives of the organization as "structure"; the interpretivist sees the organization as an "agent" or "culture". This metaphorical difference (based on Argyris and Schon's (1978) theories of organizational learning) reflects two alternative views of organizations. The "structure" view sees organizations as "an ordered array of role-boxes connected by lines which represent flows of information, work, and authority" (Argyris and Schon, 1978, p. 324). The "agent" or "culture" view notes that organizations are both instruments for achieving social purposes and small, restricted societies where:

people create for themselves shared meanings, symbols, rituals, and cognitive schemas which allow them to create and maintain meaningful interactions among themselves and in relation to the world beyond their small society. (p. 327)

The analytic perspective sees organizational action in terms of manifest behaviour; the interpretivist, in terms of the shared social meaning of the actors. The former is observable and empirical, the latter is symbolic and largely non-empirical. It follows, therefore, that the appropriate measurement instruments and research paradigms must also differ. The analytic perspective adopts formal models using empirical methods as the appropriate measurement instrument, while the interpretivist uses phenomenological study. The former embraces a quantitative research paradigm; the latter, a more qualitative one. This is similar to the Burrell and Morgan (1979) dichotomy of "objectivism" vs "subjectivism". Last, the two perspectives differ in their focus: for the analytic, the focus is on analysis; for the interpretivist, it is understanding. The former seeks to analyse organizational operations and functions by breaking them down into their constituent parts. Knowledge is acquired through the scientific endeavour of reductionism. The latter is less concerned with analysis and more concerned with understanding. Knowledge is available only in the context of understanding the social actions and meanings of the participating actors in a social setting. The focus is on understanding these social actions and meanings. Table 13.1 summarizes the differences of the two ontological positions.

It is our belief that the ontological position adopted in traditional IS evaluation, i.e. the analytic perspective, is misguided and does not reflect the reality of organizational life. Information systems cannot be treated as objective and rational as this is too simplistic a conception. Organizations are complex, social and political entities which defy

Table 13.1 *Comparison of analytic and interpretivist perspectives*

	Analytic	Interpretivist
IS functions	Largely deterministic, rational, overt	Largely non-deterministic, political, covert
Metaphor	Organization as "structure"	Organization as "agent" or "culture"
Action as	Manifest behaviour	Social meaning
Appropriate measurement instrument	Formal models	Phenomenological study
Research paradigm	Quantitative	Qualitative
Focus	Analysis	Understanding

purely objective analysis. As information systems form part of organizational reality (i.e. a *gestalt*), they cannot be viewed in isolation. To
do so simply perpetuates the naïve and technical notion of information
systems and leads to unintended and deleterious consequences (Klein
and Hirschheim, 1983, 1985).

CONCLUSION

The concentration on tools and techniques, the adoption of the values,
beliefs and methods of positivistic science, and the objectivist/rational
conception of organizations and information systems have provided
the foundation and inspiration for traditional IS evaluation. The result
has been a more "technical" interpretation of evaluation: not only in
terms of the mechanisms used, but also the substance being evaluated.
Most IS evaluation has concentrated on the technical rather than the
human or social aspects of the system. Part of the reason for this lies in
the ontological beliefs of the evaluators—that information systems are
fundamentally technical systems (although they may have behavioural
consequences). With such a belief, it is not surprising that only the
technical aspects of IS are evaluated, especially considering the difficulty of evaluating social aspects. Bjørn-Andersen (1984) captures this
succinctly: "we tend to spend more and more time and use even more
refined technological tools for solving the wrong problem more precisely". It may well be that this approach to evaluation underlies much of
the mismeasurement pointed to in earlier chapters as founding the IT
"productivity paradox".

Unfortunately, such technical evaluation, with its omission of the
social domain, is unlikely to produce a true or meaningful evaluative
picture. Moreover, it can have unintended and harmful consequences.
It is, in fact, these unanticipated consequences which are perhaps the
most worrying aspect of current IS evaluation. For example, an IS
which is technically elegant, and evaluated highly because of that, may
have a negative influence on its users' job satisfaction and social environment. The worsening of job satisfaction could lead to high staff
turnover, absenteeism and the like. Systems which score poorly using
technical criteria may be strong on the social side. IS evaluation must
therefore take into account both the technical and social aspects of a
system. In order to incorporate the latter, more problematic aspects into
the evaluation, a deeper understanding of the nature and the process of
evaluation itself is required. Adopting a more interpretivist IS perspective seems to us to be the best vehicle for doing so. It provides a more
fruitful basis for understanding IS and its evaluation.

While progress has been made by some academics in utilizing interpretive approaches, there is little evidence of its acceptance by practitioners. Rather, it seems that organizations have invested heavily in formal approaches and current short-sighted preoccupations with "bottom-line" profitability are likely to reinforce this myopia. While it seems certain that IS evaluation will remain a key issue up to and beyond the millennium, it seems likely that interpretivist approaches face an uphill struggle for acceptance, both within academia and within organizations. It can only be hoped that pioneering researchers continue to experiment with interpretivist approaches and are able to demonstrate their validity to a wider audience.

REFERENCES

Argyris, C. and Schon, D. (1978). *Organizational Learning: a Theory of Action Perspective*. Addison-Wesley, Reading, MA.

Ashby, W.R. (1956). *An Introduction to Cybernetics*. Methuen, London.

Bailey, J. and Pearson, S. (1983). Development of a Tool for Measuring and Analyzing Computer User Satisfaction. *Management Science*, 29, 5, 132–48.

Ballantine, J., Galliers, R. and Stray, S. (1994). Information Systems/Technology Investment Decisions: the Use of Capital Investment Appraisal Techniques in Organizations. In Brown, A. and Remenyi, D. (eds) *Proceedings of First European Conference on Information Technology Investment Evaluation*, Henley on Thames, UK, 13–14 September.

Baskerville, R. (1991). Risk Analysis: an Interpretive Feasibility Tool in Justifying Information Systems Security. *European Journal of Information Systems*, 1, 2, 121–30.

Beer, S. (1981). Questions of Metric. In Mason, R. and Swanson, B. (eds) *Measurement for Management Decision*. Addison-Wesley, Reading, MA.

Bendell, A., Boulter, L. and Kelly, J. (1993). *Benchmarking for Competitive Advantage*. Pitman, London.

Bjørn-Andersen, N. (1984). Challenge to Certainty. In Bemelmans, Th. (ed.) *Beyond Productivity: Information Systems Development for Organizational Effectiveness*. North Holland, Amsterdam.

Blackler, F. and Brown, C. (1988). Theory and Practice in Evaluation: the Case of the New Information Technologies. In Bjørn-Andersen, N. and Davis, G.B. (eds) *Information Systems Assessment: Issues and Challenges*. North Holland, Amsterdam.

Boddy, D. and Buchanan, D.A. (1984). Information Technology and Productivity: Myths and Realities. *Omega*, 12, 3, 233–40.

Boehm, B.W. (1988). A Spiral Model of Software Development and Enhancement. *IEEE Computer*, May, 61–72.

Boland, R. and Day, W. (1982). A Phenomenology of Systems Design. In Ginzberg, M. and Ross, C. (eds) *Proceedings of the Third International Conference on Information Systems*, Ann Arbor, Michigan.

Boland, R. and Pondy, L. (1983). Accounting in Organizations: a Union of Natural and Rational Perspectives. *Accounting, Organizations and Society*, 8.

Brown, A. (1994). Appraising Intangible Benefits from Information Technology

Investment. *Proceedings of the First European Conference on IT Investment Evaluation*, Henley on Thames, UK, 13–14 September.

Brynjolfsson, E. (1993). The Productivity Paradox of Information Technology. *Communications of the ACM*, 36, 12, 67–77.

Bullard, K.M. (1994). The Contribution of Benchmarking to the Problem of Assessing the Value of Information Technology. *First European Conference on IT Investment Evaluation*, Henley on Thames, UK, 13–14 September.

Bulmer, M. (ed.) (1977). *Sociological Research Methods*. Macmillan, Basingstoke.

Burrell, G. and Morgan, C. (1979). *Sociological Paradigms and Organizational Analysis*. Heinemann, London.

Canevet, S. and Smithson, S. (1994). *A Survey of Evaluation Practice in the UK*. Working Paper, Information Systems Department, London School of Economics, London.

Carnall, C. (1982). *The Evaluation of Organizational Change*. Gower, London.

Clemons, E. (1991). Evaluation of Strategic Investments in Information Technology. *Communications of the ACM*, 34, 1, 22–36.

Coleman, T. and Jamieson, M. (1994). Beyond Return on Investment: the Case of the New Information Technologies. In Willcocks, L. (ed.) *Information Management: the Evaluation of Information Systems*. Chapman and Hall, London, 189–205.

Currie, W.L. (1989). The Art of Justifying New Technology to Top Management. *Omega*, 17, 5, 409–18.

Davenport, T.H., Eccles, R.G. and Prusak, L. (1992). Information Politics. *Sloan Management Review*, 34, 1, 53–65.

DeLone, W.H. and McLean, E.R. (1992). Information Systems Success: the Quest for the Dependent Variable. *Information Systems Research*, 3, 1, 60–95.

Dickson, G.W., Weels, C.E. and Wilkers, R.B. (1988). Toward a Derived Set of Measures for Assessing IS Organizations. In Bjorn-Andersen, N. and Davis, G.B. (eds) *Information Systems Assessment: Issues and Challenges*. North Holland, Amsterdam, 129–47.

Doll, W.J. and Torkzadeh, G. (1988). The Measurement of End User Computing Satisfaction. *MIS Quarterly*, 12, 2, 259–73.

Drucker, P. (1971). Entrepreneurship in Business Enterprise. *Journal of Business Policy*, 1.

Earl, M. (1992). Putting IT in its Place: a Polemic for the Nineties. *Journal of Information Technology*, 7, 100–108.

Earl, M. and Hopwood, A. (1980). From Management Information to Information Management. In Lucas, H., Land, F., Lincoln, T. and Supper, T. (eds) *The Information Systems Environment*. North Holland, Amsterdam.

Ein-Dor, P. and Segev, E. (1978). Organizational Context and the Success of Management Information Systems. *Management Science*, 24, 10.

Fagan, M. (1976). Design and Code Inspections to Reduce Errors in Program Development. *IBM Systems Journal*, 15, 3, 182–211.

Farbey, B., Land, F. and Targett, D. (1993). *How to Assess Your IT Investment: a Study of Methods and Practice*. Butterworth Heinemann, Oxford.

Franz, C. and Robey, D. (1984). An Investigation of User-led System Design: Rational and Political Perspectives. *Communications of the ACM*, 27, 12.

Gaines, B. and Shaw, M. (1980). New Directions in the Analysis and Interactive Elicitation of Personal Construct Systems. *International Journal of Man-Machine Studies*, 13, 1, 28–39.

Galletta, D.F. and Lederer, A.L. (1989). Some Cautions on the Measurement of

User Information Satisfaction. *Decision Sciences*, 20, 3, 419–38.

Garfinkel, H. (1967). *Studies in Ethnomethodology*. Prentice Hall, Englewood Cliffs, NJ.

Garvin, D.A. (1988). *Managing Quality*. Free Press, New York.

Gilb, T. (1988). *Principles of Software Engineering Management*. Addison-Wesley, Reading, MA.

Gilbert, D.R., Hartman, E., Mauriel, J.J. and Freeman, R.E. (1988). *A Logic for Strategy*. Ballinger, Cambridge, MA.

Ginzberg, M. (1978). Finding an Adequate Measure of OR/MS Effectiveness. *Interfaces*, 8, 4.

Ginzberg, M. (1981). Early Diagnosis of MIS Implementation Failure: Promising Results and Unanswered Questions. *Management Science*, 27, 4.

Goddard, A. (1989). Are Three 'E's Enough: Assessing Value for Money in the Public Sector. *OR Insight*, 2, 3, 16–19.

Gowler, D. and Legge, K. (1978). The Evaluation of Planned Organizational Change: the Necessary Act of the Possible? *Journal of Enterprise Management*, 1, 20–35.

Grady, R.B. (1993) Practical Results from Measuring Software Quality. *Communications of the ACM*, 36, 11, 62–8.

Grant, R., Shani, R. and Krishnan, R. (1994). TQM's Challenge to Management Theory and Practice. *Sloan Management Review*, Winter, 25–35.

Gregory, A.J. and Jackson, M.C. (1992). Evaluation Methodologies: a System for Use. *Journal of the Operational Research Society*, 43, 1, 19–28.

Grindley, K. (1995). *Managing IT at Board Level: the Hidden Agenda Exposed*. Pitman, London.

Grudnitski, G. (1984). Eliciting Decision-makers' Information Requirements: Application of the REP Test Methodology. *Journal of Management Information Systems*, 1, 1, 24–37.

Halfpenny, P. (1979). The Analysis of Qualitative Data. *Sociological Review*, 27, 4.

Hirschheim, R. and Klein, H. (1989). Four Paradigms of Information Systems Development. *Communications of the ACM*, 32, 10, 1199–216.

Hirschheim, R. and Smithson, S. (1988). A Critical Analysis of Information Systems Evaluation. In Bjørn-Andersen, N. and Davis, G.B. (eds) *Information Systems Assessment: Issues and Challenges*. North Holland, Amsterdam, 17–37.

Hirschheim, R., Klein, H. and Newman, M. (1991). Information Systems Development as Social Action: Theoretical Perspectives and Practice. *Omega*, 19, 587–608.

Hochstrasser, B. (1990). Evaluating IT Investments: Matching Techniques to Projects. *Journal of Information Technology*, 5, 4, 215–21.

Hochstrasser, B. and Griffiths, C. (1991). *Controlling IT Investments: Strategy and Management*. Chapman and Hall, London.

Hogue, J. and Watson, H. (1983). Management's Role in the Approval of Decision Support Systems. *MIS Quarterly*, 7, 2.

Ives, B., Olson, M. and Baroudi, J. (1983). The Measurement of User Information Satisfaction. *Communications of the ACM*, 26, 10.

Kaplan, R. and Norton, D. (1992). The Balanced Scorecard: Measures that Drive Performance. *Harvard Business Review*, January–February, 71–9.

Keen, P. (1975) Computer-based Decision Aids: the Evaluation Problem. *Sloan Management Review*, 16, 3.

Keen, P. (1981) Information Systems and Organizational Change. *Communications of the ACM*, 24, 1.

Keen, P. (1991). *Shaping the Future: Business Design through Information Technology*. Harvard Business Press, Boston, MA.

Keen, P. and Scott Morton, M. (1978). *Decision Support Systems: an Organizational Perspective*. Addison-Wesley, Reading, MA.

Kelly, G. (1955). *The Psychology of Personal Constructs*. Norton, New York.

King, J. and Schrems, E. (1978). Cost-benefit Analysis In IS Development and Operation. *Computing Surveys*, 10, 1.

Klein, H. and Hirschheim, R. (1983). Issues and Approaches to Appraising Technological Change in the Office: a Consequentialist Perspective. *Office: Technology and People*, 2.

Klein, H. and Hirschheim, R. (1985). Fundamental Issues of Decision Support Systems: a Consequentialist Perspective. *Decision Support Systems*, 1, 1.

Klein, H. and Lyytinen, K. (1985). The Poverty of Scientism in Information Systems. In Mumford, E., Hirschheim, R., Fitzgerald, G. and Wood-Harper, T. (eds) *Research Methods in Information Systems*. North Holland, Amsterdam.

Kling, R. (1980). Social Analyses of Computing: Theoretical Perspectives in Recent Empirical Research. *Computing Surveys*, 12, 1.

Kling, R. (1985). Computerization as an Ongoing Social and Political Process. *Proceedings of the Conference on Development and Use of Computer-Based Systems and Tools*, Aarhus, Denmark.

Kling, R. and Iacono, S. (1984). The Control of Information Systems Developments after Implementation. *Communications of the ACM*, 27, 12.

Knight, J.C. and Myers, E.A. (1993). An Improved Inspection Technique. *Communications of the ACM*, 36, 11, 50–61.

Knights, D. and Murray, F. (1994). *Managers Divided*. John Wiley, Chichester.

Land, F. (1976). Evaluation of Systems Goals in Determining a Design Strategy for a Computer-based Information System. *Computer Journal*, 19, 4.

Land, F and Hirschheim, R. (1983). Participative Systems Design: Rationale, Tools and Techniques. *Journal of Applied Systems Analysis*, 10, 91–107.

Laudon, K. (1985). Environmental and Institutional Models of System Development: a National Criminal History System. *Communications of the ACM*, 28, 7.

Layard, R. (ed.) (1980). *Cost-Benefit Analysis*. Penguin, Harmondsworth.

Lederer, A.L., Mirani, R., Neo, B.S., Pollard, C., Prasad, J. and Ramamurthy, K. (1990). Information System Cost Estimating: a Management Perspective. *MIS Quarterly*, 14, 2, 159–76.

Legge, K. (1984). *Evaluating Planned Organizational Change*. Academic Press, London.

Loveman, G. (1994). An Assessment of the Productivity Impact of Information Technologies. In Allen, T.J. and Scott Morton, M.S. (eds) *Information Technology and the Corporation of the 1990s*. Oxford University Press, Oxford.

Lyytinen, K., Klein, H. and Hirschheim, R. (1991). The Effectiveness of Office Information Systems: a Social Action Perspective. *Journal of Information Systems*, 1, 1, 41–60.

Markus, M.L. and Bjorn-Andersen, N. (1987). Power over Users: its Exercise by System Professionals. *Communications of the ACM*, 30, 6, 498–504.

Mason, R. and Swanson, E. (1981). *Measurement for Management Decision*. Addison-Wesley, Reading, MA.

McCarthy, T. (1982). *The Critical Theory of Jurgen Habermas*. MIT Press, Boston, MA.

Melone, N.P. (1990). A Theoretical Assessment of the User Satisfaction Construct in Information Systems Research. *Management Science*, 36, 1, 76–91.

Mendelow, A. (1984). Information Systems for Organizational Effectiveness: the Use of the Stakeholder Approach. In Bemelmans, Th. (ed.) *Beyond Productivity: Information Systems Development for Organizational Effectiveness.* North Holland, Amsterdam.

Mills, H.D., Dyer, M. and Linger, R. (1987). Cleanroom Software Engineering. *IEEE Software,* September, 19–24.

Morgan, G. (ed.) (1983). *Beyond Method.* Sage, London.

Morgan, G. and Smircich, L. (1980). The Case for Qualitative Research. *Academy of Management Review,* 5, 4.

Mumford, E. and Banks, O. (1967). *The Computer and the Clerk.* Routledge and Kegan Paul, London.

Mumford, E., Hirschheim, R., Fitzgerald, G. and Wood-Harper, T. (eds) (1985). *Research Methods in Information Systems.* North Holland, Amsterdam.

Nissen, H-E., Klein, H.K. and Hirschheim, R.A. (eds) (1991). *Information Systems Research: Contemporary Approaches and Emergent Traditions.* North Holland, Amsterdam.

Orlikowski, W.J. (1991). Integrated Information Environment or Matrix of Control? The Contradictory Implications of Information Technology. *Accounting, Management and Information Technologies,* 1, 1, 9–42.

Orlikowski, W.J. (1992). The Duality of Technology: Rethinking the Concept of Technology in Organizations. *Organization Science,* 3, 3, 398–427.

Orlikowski, W.J. and Gash, D.C. (1994). Technological Frames: Making Sense of Information Technology in Organizations. *ACM Transactions on Information Systems,* 12, 2, 174–207.

Panko, R.R. (1991). Is Office Productivity Stagnant? *MIS Quarterly,* 15, 2.

Parasuraman, A., Zeithini, V.A. and Berry, L.L. (1985). A Conceptual Model of Service Quality and its Implications for Future Research. *Journal of Marketing,* Fall, 41–50.

Parker, M.M., Benson, R.J. and Trainor, H.E. (1988). *Information Economics: Linking Business Performance to Information Technology.* Prentice Hall, Englewood Cliffs, NJ.

Peters, G. (1996). Beyond Strategy: Benefits Identification and Management of Specific IT Investments. In Willcocks, L. (ed.) *Investing in Information Systems: Evaluation and Management.* Chapman and Hall, London.

Pettigrew, A.M. (1985). *The Awakening Giant: Continuity and Change in ICI.* Blackwell, Oxford.

Pitt, L.F., Watson, R.T. and Kaven, C.B. (1995). Service Quality: a Measure of Information Systems Effectiveness. *MIS Quarterly,* 19, 2, 173–87.

Poore, H.H., Mills, H.D. and Mutchler, D. (1993). Planning and Certifying Software System Reliability. *IEEE Software,* January, 88–99.

Powell, P. (1992a). Information Technology Evaluation: Is it Different? *Journal of the Operational Research Society,* 43, 1, 29–42 .

Powell, P. (1992b). Information Technology and Business Strategy: a Synthesis of the Case for Reverse Causality. *13th International Conference on Information Systems,* Dallas, Texas, December.

Power, M. (1997). *The Audit Society: Rituals of Verification.* Oxford University Press, Oxford.

Reason, P. and Rowan, J. (eds) (1981). *Human Inquiry: a Sourcebook of New Paradigm Research.* John Wiley, New York.

Roach, S.S. (1991). Services under Siege: the Restructuring Imperative. *Harvard Business Review,* September–October, 82–92.

Robey, D. and Newman, M. (1996). Sequential Patterns in Information Systems Development: an Application of a Social Process Model. *ACM Transactions on Information Systems*, 14, 1, 30–63.

Rockart, J. (1979). Chief Executives Define their own Data Needs. *Harvard Business Review*, March–April, 75–86

Sanders, G. (1984). MIS/DSS Success Measure. *Systems Objectives Solutions*, 4, 1.

Sassone, P. (1988). A Survey of Cost-Benefit Methodologies for Information Systems. *Project Appraisal*, 3, 2, 73–84.

Schafer, G. (1988). Benefit Analysis of Office Systems: Concepts for a Method. In Bjorn-Andersen, N. and Davis, G.B. (eds) *Information Systems Assessment: Issues and Challenges*. North Holland, Amsterdam.

Schafer, G., Hirschheim, R.A., Harper, M., Hansjee, R., Domke, M. and Bjørn-Andersen, N. (1988). *Functional Analysis of Office Requirements: a Multiperspective Approach*. John Wiley, Chichester.

Serafeimidis, V. and Smithson, S. (1994). Evaluation of IS/IT Investments: Understanding and Support. In Brown, A. and Remenyi, D. (eds) *Proceedings of First European Conference on Information Technology Investment Evaluation*, Henley on Thames, UK, 13–14 September.

Sivula, C. (1990). The White-Collar Productivity Push. *Datamation*, 15 January.

Smith, P. (1973). *Groups within Organizations*. John Wiley, Chichester.

Srinivasan, A. (1985). Alternative Measures of System Effectiveness: Associations and Implications. *MIS Quarterly*, 9, 3.

Strassmann, P. (1985). *Information Payoff: the Transformation of Work in the Electronic Age*. Free Press, New York.

Strassman, P. (1990). *The Business Value of Computers*. Information Economics Press, New Caanan, CN.

Strassmann, P. (1997). *The Squandered Computer*. Information Economics Press, New Caanan, CN.

Suchman, C. (1970). Action for What? A Critique of Evaluative Research. In O'Toole, T. (ed.) *The Organization, Management and Tactics of Social Research*. Schenkman, New York.

Suchman, L. (1994). Working Relations of Technology Production and Use. *Computer Supported Cooperative Work*, 2, 21–39.

Swanson, K., McComb, D., Smith, J. and McCubbrey, D. (1991). The Application Software Factory: Applying Total Quality Techniques to Systems Development. *MIS Quarterly*, 15, 4, 567–79.

Symons, V.J. (1991). A Review of Information Systems Evaluation: Content, Context and Process. *European Journal of Information Systems*, 1, 3, 205–12.

Van Maanen, J. (1979). Reclaiming Qualitative Methods for Organizational Research: a Preface. *Administrative Science Quarterly*, 24, 4.

Walsham. G. (1993). *Interpreting Information Systems in Organizations*. John Wiley, Chichester.

Walsham, G. (1995). The Emergence of Interpretivism in IS Research. *Information Systems Research*, 6, 4, 376–94.

Ward, J.M. (1990). A Portfolio Approach into Evaluating Systems Investments and Setting Priorities. *Journal of Information Technology*, 5, 4, 222–31.

Ward, J., Taylor, P. and Bond, P. (1995). Evaluation and Realisation of IS/IT Benefits: an Empirical Study of Current Practice. *European Journal of Information Systems*, 4.

Weill, P. (1992). The Relationship between Investment in Information Technology and Firm Performance: a Study of the Valve Manufacturing Sector.

Information Systems Research, 3, 4, 307–33.

Weiss, C. (1972). *Evaluation Research*. Prentice Hall, Englewood Cliffs, NJ.

Willcocks, L. (1994). Introduction: of Capital Importance. In Willcocks, L. (ed.) *Information Management: the Evaluation of Information Systems Investments*. Chapman and Hall, London, 1–27.

Willcocks, L. (ed.) (1996). *Investing in Information Systems: Evaluation and Management*. Chapman and Hall, London.

Willcocks, L., Feeny, D. and Islei, G. (eds) (1997). *Managing IT as a Strategic Resource*. McGraw-Hill, Maidenhead.

Willcocks, L. and Lester, S. (1993). Evaluating the Feasibility of Information Technology Investment. *Oxford Institute of Information Management, Research and Discussion Paper, RDP93/1*, Templeton College, Oxford.

Willcocks, L. and Margetts, H. (1994). Risk Assessment and Information Systems. *European Journal of Information Systems*, 3, 2, 127–38.

Zuboff, S. (1988). *In the Age of the Smart Machine*. Basic Books, New York.

Zultner, R.A. (1993). TQM for Technical Teams. *Communications of the ACM*, 36, 10, 78–91.

Index